Transnational Feminist Politics, Education, and Social Justice

Also available from Bloomsbury

Educating for Peace and Human Rights: An Introduction, Maria Hantzopoulos and Monisha Bajaj

Education, Equality and Justice in the New Normal: Global Responses to the Pandemic, edited by Inny Accioly and Donaldo Macedo

Education, Individualization and Neoliberalism: Youth in Southern Europe, Valerie Visanich

Feminists Researching Gendered Childhoods: Generative Entanglements, edited by Jayne Osgood and Kerry H. Robinson

Hopeful Pedagogies in Higher Education, edited by Mike Seal

Identities and Education: Comparative Perspectives in Times of Crisis, edited by Stephen Carney and Eleftherios Klerides

International Perspectives on Critical Education, Peter Mayo and Paolo Vittoria

On Critical Pedagogy, Henry A. Giroux

Politics and Pedagogy in the "Post-Truth" Era: Insurgent Philosophy and Praxis, Derek R. Ford

Race, Politics, and Pandemic Pedagogy: Education in a Time of Crisis, Henry A. Giroux

Theorizing Feminist Ethics of Care in Early Childhood Practice: Possibilities and Dangers, edited by Rachel Langford

Transnational Perspectives on Democracy, Citizenship, Human Rights and Peace Education, edited by Mary Drinkwater, Fazal Rizvi and Karen Edge

Transnational Feminist Politics, Education, and Social Justice

Post Democracy and Post Truth

Edited by
Silvia Edling and Sheila L. Macrine

BLOOMSBURY ACADEMIC
LONDON • NEW YORK • OXFORD • NEW DELHI • SYDNEY

BLOOMSBURY ACADEMIC
Bloomsbury Publishing Plc
50 Bedford Square, London, WC1B 3DP, UK
1385 Broadway, New York, NY 10018, USA
29 Earlsfort Terrace, Dublin 2, Ireland

BLOOMSBURY, BLOOMSBURY ACADEMIC and the Diana logo are trademarks of
Bloomsbury Publishing Plc

First published in Great Britain, 2022

Copyright © Silvia Edling, Sheila L. Macrine and Bloomsbury 2022

Silvia Edling, Sheila L. Macrine and Bloomsbury have asserted their right under the
Copyright, Designs and Patents Act, 1988, to be identified as Author of this work.

For legal purposes the Acknowledgments on p. xxv constitute
an extension of this copyright page.

Cover image © Tina Gutierrez / Alamy Stock Photo

All rights reserved. No part of this publication may be reproduced or
transmitted in any form or by any means, electronic or mechanical, including
photocopying, recording, or any information storage or retrieval system,
without prior permission in writing from the publishers.

Bloomsbury Publishing Plc does not have any control over, or responsibility for,
any third-party websites referred to or in this book. All internet addresses given
in this book were correct at the time of going to press. The author and publisher
regret any inconvenience caused if addresses have changed or sites have
ceased to exist, but can accept no responsibility for any such changes.

A catalogue record for this book is available from the British Library.

Library of Congress Cataloging-in-Publication Data
Names: Edling, Silvia, editor. | Macrine, Sheila L., editor.
Title: Transnational feminist politics, education, and social justice : post democracy
and post truth / Edited by Sheila Macrine and Silvia Edling.
Description: London ; New York, NY : Bloomsbury Academic, 2022. |
Includes bibliographical references and index.
Identifiers: LCCN 2021026897 (print) | LCCN 2021026898 (ebook) |
ISBN 9781350174467 (hardcover) | ISBN 9781350174450 (paperback) |
ISBN 9781350174474 (pdf) | ISBN 9781350174481 (epub)
Subjects: LCSH: Transnationalism. | Feminism–International cooperation–Cross-cultural studies. |
Social justice and education–Cross-cultural studies. | Feminism–Political
aspects–Cross-cultural studies. | Women–Violence against–Cross-cultural studies.
Classification: LCC JZ1320 .T727 2022 (print) | LCC JZ1320 (ebook) | DDC 305.8–dc23
LC record available at https://lccn.loc.gov/2021026897
LC ebook record available at https://lccn.loc.gov/2021026898

ISBN:	HB:	978-1-3501-7446-7
	PB:	978-1-3501-7445-0
	ePDF:	978-1-3501-7447-4
	eBook:	978-1-3501-7448-1

Typeset by Integra Software Services Pvt. Ltd.
Printed and bound in Great Britain

To find out more about our authors and books visit www.bloomsbury.com
and sign up for our newsletters.

DEDICATION

This volume is dedicated to the memory of feminist icon, Justice Ruth Bader Ginsburg (1933–2020), premier and resolute champion for justice, women's equity, as well as equal opportunity and justice for all.

Contents

Notes on Contributors — ix
Foreword *Antonia Darder* — xi
Acknowledgments — xxv

Transnational Feminist Politics, Education, and Social Justice
Sheila L. Macrine and Silvia Edling — 1

Part 1   Overviews: Challenges and Possibilities

1 Borders and Bridges *Chandra Talpade Mohanty* — 23
2 The Refugee Crisis Is a Feminist Issue *Sheila L. Macrine and Silvia Edling* — 41
3 How the Neoliberal Ultraconservative Alliance in Brazil Threatens Women's Lives: Learning to Fight and Survive *Inny Accioly* — 59
4 The Antidemocratic Fantasmatic Logic of Right-Wing Populism: Theoretical Reflections *Gundula Ludwig* — 75
5 Technologies of Surveillance: A Transnational Black Feminist Analysis *K. Melchor Quick Hall* — 89
6 Hot Rockin' Vampires on Skateboards *Robin Truth Goodman* — 107

Part 2   Contextualizations: Education and the Teacher Profession

7 Feminism and Anti-feminism in Sweden, in the wake of #MeToo *Sarah Ljungquist* — 123
8 Suppression of Teacher's Voices: Agency and Freedom within Neoliberal Masculinist Performativity *Geraldine Mooney Simmie* — 141
9 Marias, Marielles, Malês: Southern Epistemologies, Resistance and Emancipation *Maria Luiza Süssekind and Ines Barbosa de Oliveira* — 155

10 The Greek Crisis and the Gender Gap: Reinforcing Connections between Education and Women's Empowerment *Maria Nikolakaki*	171
11 The Emergence of the Anti-gender Agenda in Swedish Higher Education *Guadalupe Francia*	185
Conclusion *Silvia Edling and Sheila L. Macrine*	199
Notes	214
References	230
Index	276

Contributors

Inny Accioly is Professor of Education at the Fluminense Federal University, Rio de Janeiro, Brazil. She is co-editor of *Education, Equality and Justice in the New Normal* (Bloomsbury, 2021).

Antonia Darder holds the Leavey Presidential Endowed Chair of Ethics and Moral Leadership at Loyola Marymount University, Los Angeles, USA, and is Distinguished Visiting Professor of Education at the University of Johannesburg, South Africa.

Silvia Edling is a Professor of Curriculum Theory at the University of Gavle, Sweden. She is the co-author of Democracy and Teacher Education (2020), Historical- and Moral Consciousness: Learning Ethics for Democratic Citizenship Education (2022), and co-editor of Professional learning and identities in teaching. International narratives of successful teachers (2021).

Guadalupe Francia is Professor in Education at the University of Gävle, Sweden.

Robin Truth Goodman is Professor of Literature at Florida State University, USA.

K. Melchor Quick Hall is faculty member in the School of Leadership Studies at Fielding Graduate University, USA, and a Visiting Scholar in the Women's Studies Research Center at Brandeis University, USA.

Sarah Ljungquist is Senior Lecturer and Researcher in Gender Studies and Literature at the University of Gävle, Sweden.

Gundula Ludwig is Post-Doctoral Researcher at Bremen University, Germany.

Sheila L. Macrine is Professor of STEM Education and Teacher Development at the University of Massachusetts Dartmouth, USA. She is the author of Critical Pedagogy *Critical Pedagogy in Uncertain Times* (2012), and co-editor of *Revolutionizing Pedagogy* (2010) and *Class in Education* (2010).

Chandra Talpade Mohanty is Distinguished Professor of Women's and Gender Studies, and Dean's Professor of the Humanities. Syracuse University, USA.

Maria Nikolakaki is Associate Professor of Pedagogy and Education at the University of Peloponnese, Greece.

Inês Barbosa de Oliveira is Associate Professor in the Faculty of Education at Estácio de Sá University, Brazil, and Researcher at the State University of Rio de Janeiro, Brazil.

Geraldine Mooney Simmie is Senior Lecturer in Education at the University of Limerick, Ireland.

Maria Luiza Süssekind is Professor at Federal University of Rio de Janeiro, Brazil.

Foreword

Antonia Darder

We are of the generation
of women who ventured
beyond boundaries;
who embraced the body,
who relished passion,
who dreamt of justice.

We are of the generation
of women who rejected
the narrow limits;
who trampled on conformity,
who spit on subjugation,
who dreamt of freedom.

We are of the generation
of women who transgressed
the holy scriptures;
who dared to speak;
who caressed untouchables,
who dreamt of deliverance.

We are of the generation
of women who endured
the punishment;
who wrestled fears,
who defied solitude,
who dreamt of liberation.

I begin with my poem, *We Are*, in that as I read through the courageous and powerful essays in **Transnational Feminist Politics, Education, and Social Justice,** written by women who are public intellectuals—scholars and activists—

from around the world, I was deeply struck by the manner in which they speak remarkably in unison about the struggles of our sisters everywhere. To produce the transnational perspectives offered to readers across these pages, these women have had to wage battle with a recalcitrant patriarchal system of knowledge construction that would gladly silence us all, in order to shroud the psychological, emotional, and spiritual hardships and brutalities that women encounter daily. This continues to be the reality today, despite generations of women from every ethnicity and of every color who have persistently given their lives to this ongoing fight for gendered and racialized equalities worldwide. In a myriad of ways, the beautiful strands of wisdom evoked in this book emanate as much from a multitude of communal struggles on the ground, and from the radical academic confrontations that women within education have been subjected to unmercifully in their arduous transnational quest to construct a theory in the flesh within the conditions of neoliberalism and its looming threat to democracy.

Neoliberalism and the Crisis of Democracy

> The neoliberal ideological project ... reinforces the political culture that emphasizes and promotes individualism, individual responsibility, and choice, without any accompanying discussion about existing inequities in power and economic status or between genders, and how these influence the ability of people to make choices in their lives.
> —Kendra Coulter (2009, p. 28)

At the heart of the neoliberal project has been an unrelenting pursuit to unravel all liberal social contracts formerly embraced by democratic governments regarding the protection of the common public welfare as a human right. Instead, entrepreneurial competition has reigned for more than three decades and former business regulations have been undone, while destruction of the social safety net is nearly complete, targeting every form of public service for privatization, including education, health care, and prisons. In the process, notions of equality and public responsibility have been subsumed by a merciless ethos of rampant greed, wholesale surveillance, and the containment of impoverished populations—a large majority who are women. Even in the midst of the Covid-19 pandemic, the neoliberal agenda has led to the investment of billions of dollars worldwide in private enterprises to perpetuate the surveillance of citizens and control the movement of populations, in the name of controlling the disease.

As neoliberalism continues to assert its debilitating form of economic rationalism, notions of community empowerment and questions of gender equality transnationally have been ignored or deliberately sidelined. Collective social action, similarly, is considered a gross obstacle to the freedom of individuals and their implacable drive to sell and consume. In the process, neoliberal policies have effectively derailed democratic ideals of social and economic justice, as it commodifies and consumes, literally and figuratively, every aspect of public life. Rampant individualism and a bootstrap mentality function as a means to end state regulation, considered to be a major culprit in stifling the free-market's ability to flourish and its capacity to protect private interests. Western rationality that underpins neoliberal sensibilities is marked by principles that privilege individual identity, binaries, atomism, and an artificial separation from nature—of which we are all a part.

Furthermore, alongside the unimpeded competition of neoliberal economic forces, the manipulation of quantifiable data and draconian social policies have indeed intensified poverty and perpetuated gendered and racialized inequalities and exclusions. As such, neoliberal policies and practices grounded upon a narrow economic rationality provide an intellectual anchor from which "mega-rich" conservatives and liberals alike collaborate for control of not only the marketplace, but all public institutions. For example, even in the midst of the coronavirus pandemic, the unrelenting drive to further privatize education has loomed powerfully, as arguments of crisis and urgency have been deployed. In the United States, the advancing three-decades-long momentum to virtualize higher education has reached new heights in the midst of an overzealous demand for online learning to sustain the enterprise of education. Of concern here, of course, is the expanding reliance likely to result from a broadening normalization and extension of disembodied forms of learning, which privilege fractured and fragmented curricular content at the expense of students' relational engagement with the world—an aspect of intellectual formation so essential to the fortitude of democratic life.

Numerous critical scholars have critiqued the impact of neoliberalism to the undoing of democracy. Brown (2015), for example, notes the indefensible connection at work between neoliberalism, conservatism, and the breakdown of democracy, arguing that neoliberalism devalues political liberty, equality, substantive citizenship, and the rule of law, in favor of market-driven governance and institutional policies, on one hand; and the valorization of state power for moralistic ends, on the other. Brown insists that this results in undemocratic institutional forms, despite neoliberal rhetoric of inclusivity, which is indifferent to the veracity of claims or genuine accountability, and to political freedom and equality, defying democratic ideals. So much so that "neoliberal reason has converted the distinctly political character, meaning, and operation of democracy's constituent elements into *economic one's*" (17).

Similarly, Giroux (2011), has argued, "As a theater of cruelty and mode of public pedagogy, economic Darwinism extends its reach throughout the globe, undermining all forms of democratic solidarity and social structures that depend on long term investments and are committed to promoting the public and common good." He borrows the term *economic Darwinism* (drawn from social Darwinism) in order to illustrate the manner in which neoliberal policies within higher education have, overtly and covertly, perpetuated the oppressive ethos of "the survival of the fittest." Accordingly, policies of deregulation, privatization, and lack of concern for the public good have rendered democratic education and social welfare programs, particularly those related to women and the control of our bodies and destinies, endangered species. Meanwhile, values of "unchecked competition, unbridled individualism, and a demoralizing notion of individual responsibility" (Giroux, 2012) are vastly implicated in the current legitimation crisis and moral impoverishment of a national politics steeped in a profit logic that fundamentally undermines our humanity.

Sufficiently able to marginalize and diminish political contestation, the colonizing logic of neoliberalism has become deeply entrenched across institutions worldwide. In its wake, the corruption of democracy perpetuates structures of patriarchy that fuel the repression of gendered and racialized sensibilities in knowledge production that could potentially counter the greed and human disregard of neoliberal reforms. Here, I am reminded of hooks' (2004) cogent warning: "The crisis facing men is not the crisis of masculinity, it is the crisis of patriarchal masculinity. Until we make this distinction clear, men will continue to fear that any critique of patriarchy represents a threat" (p. 32). What she makes clear is that substantive institutional or societal change is impossible without a critique of patriarchy within capitalist relations. As this book repeatedly shows, the phenomenon of racialized and gendered oppression is a massively transnational one, which extends itself across borders and across cultural, social, political, and pedagogical contexts, creating enormous challenges for women as they struggle to navigate and negotiate their everyday lives.

About this, Dalla Costa (2008) argues that neoliberalism has exacerbated the oppression of women, resulting in a crisis of social reproduction that has "led to the disappearance of individual and collective rights achieved through hard struggle in the preceding decades, and to the withdrawal of resources available for the pursuit of a life that would not be 'all work' in a context of increasing precarity and uncertainty" (p. 30). The consequence here is that women transnationally have been forced to bear the burden of neoliberalism and, more recently, the coronavirus pandemic, as they are the ones who are expected to do the extra work necessary to accommodate massive losses associated with the state's withdrawal from social public responsibility for its people, as well as its redirecting of resources and production to preserve the health of national economies and contend with a growing crisis of accumulation. This phenomenon is mirrored publicly, for example, within institutions of higher education, where the physical labor of women is absolutely indispensable to its economic success.

Hence, it should not be surprising that many of the contributors to this volume highlight the ways in which oppression is reinforced by neoliberal policies and practices of accountability, privileging financial exigencies over the well-being of women, as if the concerns of women occur in a vacuum; relying on abstract knowledge by excluding the lived experience of women; upholding instrumentalized curricula that fractures and fragments knowledge; perpetuating accountability schemes that shroud daily injustices on the ground; and reproducing gendered and racialized policies and practices that negatively impact the lives of women in the flesh.

In Search of a Theory in the Flesh

> A theory in the flesh means one where the physical realities of our lives—our skin color, the land or concrete we grew up on, our sexual longings—all fuse to create a politics born of necessity.
>
> —Cherie Moraga and Gloria Anzaldúa (1981, p. 19)

Almost forty years ago, *This Bridge Called My Back,* edited by Moraga and Anzaldúa (1981), struck a direct blow at the racialized patriarchy that subsumed the existence of women of color everywhere—women, who despite their heartfelt efforts to participate within families, communities, and nations, often could not find the spaces to speak a truth indelibly marked upon their bodies. Their work, as the work of the contributors to this volume, was indeed born of necessity, with the intent to break out of the cultural silence and moral vise of sexist, racist, and homophobic interpretations of mainstream society. Toward this end, they wrote boldly about their lived experiences of oppression and its impact upon their minds, hearts and bodies. This unrelenting insistence on speaking to the truths anchored in their existence is what gave rise to a theory in the flesh. So, it is from that particular historical moment in the development of my political consciousness as a colonized Puerto Rican woman, that I now am able to comment on the transnational feminist insights of this volume, which sheds light on the complexities of women's lives under the disembodying triangulation of neoliberalism, conservatism and nationalism around the world today.

The place of women within many societies today is echoed in the words of South African musician, Simphiwe Dana: "We are the cornerstone and builders of our society, yet by and large, we are oppressed." The oppressive conditions faced by women transnationally cannot be understood outside a theory in the flesh, which grapples with the physical realities that shape the conditions of women's lives. Writing about women in capitalist societies, Marx (1848) asserted that the social progress of any society could best be measured by the position that women are afforded within that society. His perspective on the positionality of women within capitalist society was certainly linked to the materiality of women's lives, concerns later taken up by contemporary Marxist scholars. In *Marx, The Body, and Human Nature*, Fox (2015) asserts that the body and broader issues of materiality play a far more significant role in Marx's theory of capital than previously acknowledged. Hence, the place of the body or the flesh is inextricable to comprehending the place of women in the social order.

Marxist feminist engagement with nature and the body directly challenges the dehumanizing belief that "our bodies have only an instrumental role in living a full and truly human life" (Fox, 2015, p. 2). It is precisely this instrumentalizing negation of the body that enables neoliberal debates to contend with women's issues and concerns as if these were largely independent of our bodies or as if there were separate things or objects, disconnected from nature. This tendency toward disembodiment of political questions has supported false notions of neutrality and functions to "invisibilize" key distinctions between the lives of women and men within advanced capitalism. In *Power of Women and the Subversion of Community*, Dalla Costa and James (1975) rightly point to an embedded patriarchal epistemology of the West, ensconced in ideas (even on the left) that remain blind to intersectional questions related to gendered oppression—an oppression reproduced and perpetuated through the materiality of social relations and within daily interactions.

The discussions in this volume focus on gendered oppression overwhelmingly from an intersectional approach, an approach that has been employed often in the critical scholarship of feminist of color. Through the lens of intersectionality, there is a recognition that all aspects of our histories and lived experiences impact how we perceive and make sense of the world. Hence, it is an epistemological shift away from Western notions of absolute objectivity and neutrality, in the process of examining and disentangling social and material oppression. However, as several contributors to this book infer, we cannot lose sight that the phenomenon of intersectionality unfolds within the internationalization of capital and its totalizing impact worldwide. Moreover, what the last four decades have shown us, only too well, is that identity politics or a politics of representation alone, disassociated from anti-capitalist struggle, has failed to alter substantially the gendered and racialized inequalities that persist. Yet, similarly, many feminist scholars of color would argue that without an intersectional engagement with gendered and racialized oppression, our politics, scholarship, and activism can too easily devolve into an economic determinism that fails to account properly for the different ways in which domination and exploitation shape women's lives beyond economic considerations.

Nevertheless, when examining gender disparities from an intersectional approach, we must still confront the 500-year history of capital rule, in which the unpaid labor of women has been fundamental to the systematic exploitation of waged workers and the dirty little secret behind the extractive economy of capitalism (Dalla Costa cited in Federici, 2004). Moreover, Federici (2004) provides an important historical analysis of women's experience, noting that "even when men achieved a certain degree of formal freedom, women were always treated as socially inferior beings and were exploited in ways similar to slavery" (p. 13). Accordingly, men have retained a significant amount of political and economic power over women, which continues to nurture blatant antagonisms based on a gendered division of labor—antagonisms physically enacted and experienced and most deeply marked transnationally, within the unjust labor dynamics of women who are racialized and minoritized within contemporary societies. This phenomenon is broadly reflected in the fractured and contentious gender and racialized politics of the last century, which has failed to overcome the ruthless manner in which working women are oppressed worldwide. Phillips (2015), of the London School of Economics Commission on Gender, Inequality and Power, argues that in confronting gender inequality, progress today remains slow and uncertain despite major changes over the last century.

The fierce persistence of patriarchy as an overriding political and economic ideology of contemporary societies constitutes a major stumbling block to the transnational embodiment of gender and racialized equality. Fittingly, essays in this book boldly argue that the pigheaded political nature of patriarchy must be transformed within both the personal and public spheres. Therefore, if we are to move effectively toward eradicating gender and racialized inequalities, we will need to disrupt and overcome the ideological, institutional, and relational structures of everyday life that proliferate victim blaming attitudes, policies, and practices, which safeguard white male privilege, while holding in contempt the emancipation of women. This demands that we opt for new ways of being and laboring together that stem from a just political-economic stance, an intersectional view of oppression, a forthright engagement with the flesh, and a global commitment to collective human rights.

Often, in speaking of social and material forms of exclusions, particularly with respect to women, there is a tendency to abstract and disembody this phenomenon, in ways that camouflage oppressions and justify the suffering endured by women transnationally. The violation of women's human rights, lack of political representation, structures of political, psychological, and economic violence, and the insidious intersection of poverty, racism, and sexism perpetuate brutalizing indignities that women worldwide must endure daily. Women are subjected to lower pay and poorer conditions of labor, with few or no maternity benefits and generally inadequate childcare. In maquiladoras, the labor of young women is hyper-exploited, while they must contend with precarious conditions that have cost many their lives. Meanwhile, refugee women on the run from such oppressive conditions within their countries of origin are further traumatized by terrifying experiences of forced displacement. The feminization of poverty persists everywhere, with millions of women and their children living in poverty. The repression of reproductive rights, even within the United States, persists, where *Roe v. Wade* has been seriously threatened by the efforts of twenty states to overturn this ruling that has protected the medical rights of women to choose since 1973. The health and mental treatment of women still remains largely informed by a patriarchal lens. Consequently, interventions in domestic violence and rape cases still tend to place the burden of responsibility on women. This problem persists worldwide, where rape and sexual violence against women persist as an everyday occurrence, affecting millions of women and girls over their lifetimes. Other abuses against women include the increasing incarceration of women worldwide. In the United States, for example, between 1980 and 2016, the number of incarcerated women increased by more than 700 percent (Equal Justice Initiative, 2018). Women of color who live in poverty have been subjected to forced sterilization, as well as utilized as subjects for testing of pregnancy prevention methods. The unrelenting exploitation and commodification of women's bodies for profit by corporate media have proven to be a peril to the mental health of women of every age. And, even for women who seem to be more affluent, institutional structures of meritocracy and seniority create major obstacles to leadership opportunities, recognition, and promotion.

As persistent examples of devastating gendered and racialized inequalities, these conditions still remain largely unaltered, given that issues of poverty, racism, and "a woman-focused policy arena does not figure prominently [if at all] in the broader agenda" (Coulter, 2009, p. 39) of neoliberal governments. Moreover, seldom are the in-the-flesh experiences of impoverished and racialized women considered, particularly given their lack of political and economic power within technocratic neoliberal contexts, fueled by pragmatic approaches that easily obfuscate, confuse, bewilder, or flat out negate the suffering of women nationally and transnationally. The great consequence here is that racialized women, as embodied subjects, are considerably more affected by the colonizing conditions of poverty, inadequate health care, poor schooling, unemployment, reduction of wages, incarceration, everyday forms of violence, and diminishing political or human rights.

In considering a theory in the flesh from a feminist transnational perspective, it is impossible to overlook the obstinate link between patriarchy, capitalism, gender oppression, racialization, and the violent colonization of the body. The feminist Latina artist, Ana Alvarez Errecalde notes, "Violence toward women begins with the repression of sexuality, the appropriation of childbirth, the interferences with vital cycles and the creation of manipulative roles. A negated mother will also negate her body and her presence to her children, so they will all ultimately conform, to our unattended, unloved, and unnourished society" (cited in Gore, 2017). To negate the place of the body, then, within the context of any vision of liberation is to negate the unrelenting manner in which our bodies are afflicted and occupied by every form of human oppression (Shapiro, 1998).

Politics of Embodiment

> The body is also directly involved in political field; power relations have an immediate hold upon it; they invest it, mark it, train it, torture it.
> —Michel Foucault (1995, p. 259)

For women, there is no question that we live in a society of the incarcerated body, the schooled body, the enslaved body, the embattled body, the surgically altered body, the starved body, the abused body, the worn and the torn body, the tortured body. Everywhere the scars of our separation with nature and with our bodies are evident, particularly in the lives of working women of color. Moraga (2009) speaks of these scars of separation as internalized stories of the body; "the story of conquest and the story of colonization or the story of indigenous enslavement or the story of all of the forced displacement, all of this, these are things that we carry in our bodies." Given the vital relationship that exists between the flesh and consciousness (Darder, 2015), reengaging politically with our embodied stories is significant to breaking with the tendency of our consciousness to become more and more abstracted, as we become more and more detached from nature. As such, the intersectionality of exclusion, exploitation, and domination cannot be readily examined nor understood if theoretical or practical inquiries are conducted independent of the societal conditions that normalize and perpetuate the violation of women's bodies. Kraidy (2013), moreover, contends,

> Opportunities afforded by using the body as a focal point include a fuller consideration of human agency that eschews technological determinism when studying power and resistance, a historically grounded analytical approach that preempts an uncritical dalliance with presentism, the body being in effect the "oldest medium," and an analytical advantage whereby the body functions as a heuristic eye of the needle through which all empirical materials, and theoretical considerations are filtered, considered and interpreted.
>
> (p. 285)

In considering further the politics of embodiment, we can safely conclude that a veiled function of mainstream education is, indeed, to initiate and incorporate poor, working-class, and racialized women into social and material conditions of labor that normalize their alienation and systematic detachment from the body. This is essential within the context of a capitalist economy, which necessitates mass poverty and the social control of much of the world's population, in its quest to safeguard unjust and unequal political-economic interests—interests predicated on colonizing relations of power that persist worldwide. More to the point, physical control is a hallmark of political repression, given that our bodies are the medium through which we wage political struggle and through which we transform historical conditions as individuals and communal beings (Eagleton, 2003). It is not surprising then that under oppressive regimes of power, women's bodies are left numb, alienated, fragmented, and often defenseless at the mercy of capital. In tandem, the marketplace and the culture industry jointly manufacture and reify false desires and treacherous myths that betray the organic beauty and sensuality of fully embodied women, seducing us to mistakenly believe that self-abnegation and unnecessary consumption constitute the true path to love or happiness. Nothing, of course, could be farther from the truth.

A Feminist Platform for Our Times

> Addressing the economic plight of women may ultimately be the feminist platform that draws a collective response. It may well become the place of collective organizing, the common ground, the issue that unites all women.
> —bell hooks (2000, p. 54)

In myriad ways, the essays in ***Transnational Feminist Politics, Education, and Social Justice*** are vital transnational maps of radical ideas for resistance and survival, written by women from around the world committed to remaking the feminist platform in groundbreaking and deeply inclusive ways. As repeatedly stated, this work seeks to grapple with the powerful relations that perpetuate human oppression and co-opt or appropriate revolutionary perspectives, while leaving untouched the cruel and inhumane epistemological and structural conditions that disempower women daily. Palpable in Macrine and Edling's outstanding volume is the idea that transnational change for enduring forms of gendered and racialized inclusivity will necessitate fundamental shifts in the political dynamics of societies and institutions, that is, shifts in the unjust ideologies, social policies, and political practices that drive exploitative and discriminatory decision-making and organizational relations of power that reproduce the economic plight of women around the globe.

Essential to this stance is both the unveiling and transforming of the fascistic rigidity and authoritarianism of capitalism, ordained by patriarchal and racist ideologies of supremacy, privilege, extraction, and accumulation. Such a platform must also contend with commonsensical allegiances to traditions of racism and gender oppression that blind us from our own complicities in perpetuating double-standards of exclusion and the triple oppression that disfigures the lives of women of color transnationally. This, of course, also necessitates that we, as transnational feminists, shine a radical consciousness upon the theories, stories, and beliefs that define and give meaning to our ideas, decisions, and labor, in order to ensure that our capacity for love and human connection can flourish through our political and pedagogical labor. And, as evidenced by the contributors in this book, none of this can be accomplished in isolation, but rather we are compelled to enter into ongoing relationships with people on the ground.

The chapters in ***Transnational Feminist Politics, Education, and Social Justice*** also illustrate the manner in which two key dimensions of our longstanding commitment to an anti-capitalist and anti-imperialist project support our capacity to become more critically conscious and alert to the underlying forces at work in women's lives. The first is the idea of geographies of gendered and racialized inequalities. This points to examining transnationally the ongoing relationships that exist between the geographical conditions of the environment and the complex interactions at work in the production of gendered and racialized oppression. All societal institutions function to either include or marginalize the needs, issues, and contribution of women. Those committed to women's rights transnationally must then contend with the history and geographic landscapes of women's experiences, from the urban to the rural. As such, our scholarship and activism must forthrightly engage with questions of gender and racism in ways that are rooted in the lived experiences of women. This entails bringing into the scholarly and political mix the complexities of cultural, social, political, and economic factors, along with the recurring personal relationships that unfold at the nexus of power, space, and materiality.

The second, which has been overwhelmingly significant to the feminist scholarship of women of color and the contributors of this volume, is the intersectionality of oppressions. From this perspective, there is an essential recognition that all aspects of our histories and lived experiences impact upon how we perceive and make sense of ourselves, one another, the world. Hence, the intersectionality of oppression points to an indispensable epistemological shift away from Western epistemological traditions that render views from outside of the Eurocentric mainstream to be marginal, irrelevant, or invisible. An underlying issue here is that the phenomenon of intersectional oppression is enacted within the neoliberal context of internationalized capital. Therefore, identity politics or a politics of representation, disassociated from anti-capitalist struggle, has failed to radically alter the social and material inequalities women continue to endure. Yet, similarly, we cannot deny that a purely economic focus has also been fraught with racialized and gendered exclusions, despite espoused commitments to the liberation of all workers. With these contradictions in mind, a move toward a scholarship of intersectionality constitutes an essential feature of a feminist platform fully committed to gender equality, social justice, and economic democracy.

Hence, the contributors of ***Transnational Feminist Politics, Education, and Social Justice*** rightly argue that we must remain ever cognizant that all forms of inequalities and social exclusions are deeply rooted within the interactive dynamics of human oppression. This understanding comprises an essential ethos of a transnational feminist platform in that it emboldens greater collaboration, dialogue, and solidarity with women around the world. True to this ethos, the feminist struggle for women's rights must be a democratically participatory one, which calls for our embodied presence in ongoing community dialogues. This is critical to our emancipatory labor in schools, universities, and communities, if we are to shatter the culture of silence and overcome the common tendency to view issues of oppression one-dimensionally. About this, Audre Lorde (1982) notes, "There is no such thing as a single-issue struggle because we do not live single-issue lives." Her words signal an embodied politics that moves across the complexities and ambiguities of our economic, gendered, racialized, and sexual differences, in humanizing ways, that nurture feminist solidarity and propel us toward a revolutionary transformation of the world—a transformation that does not erase or leave women out of the equation. Moreover, we cannot change institutions or the world, without a willingness to also be transformed by the collective processes of our emancipatory struggles. Critical consciousness within a transnational feminist platform must encompass the passion and courage to open ourselves to the world, so that we may be touched by both the anguish and power of women, in ways that connect and mobilize us to fight in the interest of our collective humanity.

There is no doubt that ***Transnational Feminist Politics, Education, and Social Justice*** is a powerful book for our times, in that it demonstrates the different ways in which a transnational embodied politics, tied to political action through intersectional scholarship and grassroots activism, can foster and safeguard feminist ideals—ideals that include political, economic, and pedagogical values of justice, which protect bodily integrity and autonomy, reproductive rights, freedom from sexual violence, opportunities for full political participation, and equal rights for women across the home, work, and community. At a time when women the world over are standing up to overturn the collective oppressions of centuries, a volume like this, written by women for women who uncompromisingly defend the dignity and right of women to build radical transnational movements, is precisely the feminist platform we need for today.

Here we are reminded again that it is by way of the collective and embodied actions of women and their allies that a new transnational feminist consciousness is born. Through our daily actions with students, colleagues, and comrades, we embrace a new consciousness of gender and racialized equality, as we work to transform the social and material conditions of society that have betrayed our revolutionary dreams. Hence, great moral courage is required to counter the oppressive theories, policies, and practice worldwide, which in many instances even attempt to negate our right to exist.

With a spirited sense of hope and faith in the power and insights of women, *Transnational Feminist Politics, Education, and Social Justice* beautifully argues that the transnational liberation of women can only be accomplished through an embodied politics and a transnational struggle committed to unfettering our bodies, minds, and hearts—embracing unapologetically our liberation as sensual, thinking, knowing, feeling, and loving subjects of history. And all this we do because we believe, at our core, that it is through our committed scholarship and with our boots on the ground that we will ultimately enact a feminist revolution—an embodied, living, and loving revolution, grounded in a politics of self-determination, an inclusive political and economic vision of justice for all, and a shared sense of kinship with all life.

Acknowledgments

We take this opportunity to thank various people for their contributions to this volume. Special thanks to Mark Richardson, Commissioning Editor at Bloomsbury Publishing, Plc. for his prescient belief in this project. Indeed, thanks also goes to the whole publishing team at Bloomsbury Publishing, Plc. We also thank distinguished Professor Antonia Darder for her inspiring and masterful *Foreword* which not only captures the objectives of this book, but also manages to show the urgency of this kind of literature in a world where democracy and human rights are under threat. A special recognition to renowned feminist scholar Professor Chandra Talpade Mohanty whose chapter contributes a master-class on global feminist politics as she unpacks the notion of "Transnational Feminist" theory and politics. Sincere appreciation goes out to all of the contributors to the volume. We cannot thank the emerging Transnational Feminists' community enough for coming together in this interdisciplinary effort to better understand the multiple and layered oppressions of women and LGBTQ persons globally. Also, thanks to the University of Gävle for providing time for Professor Edling to complete this project. And gratitude to the University of Massachusetts-Dartmouth which provided a course-reduction for Professor Macrine to complete this volume.

Transnational Feminist Politics, Education, and Social Justice

Post Democracy and Post Truth

Sheila L. Macrine and Silvia Edling

Introduction

This book looks at how the "triangulation" of neoliberalism, conservatism, and nationalism not only has consolidated power, but has significantly intensified austerity politics, weakened gender and racial equality, hollowed public education, harshened immigration policies, and increased anti-feminism linked to the exclusionary nationalism of emerging right-wing political parties.[1] *Transnational Feminist Politics, Education, and Social Justice: Post Democracy and Post Truth* shows how these political trajectories are profoundly interrelated and come together to form a "triangle" of oppression that informs politics, policies, and actions.[2] Furthermore, the volume considers the move toward a post-democratic society, defined by Crouch as: *"[O]ne that continues to have and to use all the institutions of democracy, but in which they increasingly become a formal shell. The energy and innovative drive pass away from the democratic arena and into small circles of a politico-economic elite."* We also consider the serious consequences for democracy within the current post-truth era and its pernicious polarizations.[3] As a discursive political and economic mechanism, post-truth generates public anxiety, distrust, polarized views, and well- and mis-informed competing convictions, as well as elite attempts to produce and manage these "truth markets" or competitions.[4] Post-truth and its so-called "fake-new" are proliferated through various news outlets, internet, and social media, as well as various think-tanks that confuse, disorient, generate political divides (i.e., "us" vs. "them"), and create knee-jerk responses that lead to the rise in conservatism and the growth in right-wing populism. Some of post-truth's most pernicious polarizing strategies consist of mobilizing voters through divisive, demonizing discourse, by exploiting existing grievances, and opposing political elites then reciprocate with similarly polarizing tactics or fail to develop effective nonpolarizing responses.[5] Written by an international group of women scholars and activists, these essays demonstrate how the increasing entanglements of neoliberalism are shaped by socioeconomic and cultural structures that contribute to gender and racial oppressions, inequities, and threaten emancipatory projects and ambitions.[6]

Drawing attention to both the local and global struggles, this volume reveals a great deal about women's oppressions, human rights, treatment, access to education, and impact in the global world today. We specifically focus on women's oppressions and struggles, and explicate how neoliberal ideological and conservative political projects triangulate, overlap, complement, and at times are contrary to each other (Harmes, 2012a) in their impact on historical, cultural, social, political, economic, and educational contexts. We use the term "triangulation" to help understand, criticize, and hopefully correct how gender operates within the convergences of the above-mentioned political projects. We also utilize it to inform the theoretical triangulation of feminist oppressions which leads to rich examination of the intersections of power, privilege, and oppressions both critical and symbolic (Pitre & Kushner, 2015). Our approaches also utilize "Intersectionality" as a theoretical framework for understanding how aspects of women's social and political identities (gender, race, class, sexuality, ability, ethnicity, etc.) combine to create unique modes of discrimination. Research approaches using triangulation and intersectionality also help to expose the underlying mechanisms that facilitate and create oppressions, as well as help to maintain such inequities. Subsequently, our chapters elucidate beyond the traditional understanding of women's oppression, which tends to exist in isolated and "compartmentalized categories," as well as show how systems such as triangulation and intersectionality can extend knowledge in order to illuminate the potential for change and action within a social justice agenda.[7]

Unfortunately, many of the oppressed become so powerless and silenced that they do not even talk about or name their oppression, according to Paulo Freire who referred to it as a "Culture of Silence."[8] Moreover, the very concept of "oppression" cannot be strictly defined or corralled within one clear boundary with no attribute or set of attributes that all oppressed people have in common.[9] The late feminist intellectual Iris Young described the five "faces" or types of oppression as: violence, exploitation, marginalization, powerlessness, and cultural imperialism. Such individual, institutional, and symbolic oppressions create "interlocking systems of oppression" defined as "intersectionality" by the Black Feminists of the Combahee River Collective.[10]

The ideological impetus and simultaneity of oppressions against women and the powerless generate an illiberal political climate that gives rise to conservatism, authoritarianism, right-wing populism, and nationalism. Our position is that these conditions create and validate the subordination of women through linkages among: cultures of intolerance, the rise of sexual violence, the denouncement of gender-sensitive policy reforms, the lack of personal autonomy, self-ownership, and self-determination over one's own body, the push for ethnic homogeneity, social engineering, with serious threats to democracy. Ironically, the far-right and conservatives also claim "cultural oppression" citing the ever-widening influence of the "liberal elites" in media, academia, or government.[11] Right-wing populists claim that they themselves are political outsiders speaking for a "silent majority" creating the political divides leading to protectionism, fanatical nationalism, and xenophobia. Right-wing populism isn't a monolithic, as it represents different things in different countries. Yet, there are common elements that can include some or all of the following: xenophobic, nationalistic traits, a tendency toward authoritarianism, aggressive leadership, and an anti-elitist message. As a result, and especially during these intolerant times, we need a *broad democracy* (see: Edling & Mooney Simmies, 2020). By broad democracy, we mean, among other things, a democracy that builds a public climate of participation, tolerance, and debate, as well as to hold politicians and government officials permanently accountable. These guaranteed protections of human rights and freedoms are being weakened, and in some cases eliminated.

In response, this book provides a space for an international group of women scholars to analyze the ways that neoliberalism's politics and policies criss-cross with the advancement of conservatism, authoritarianism, and "Far Right" nationalism that negatively impact the lives and survival of women and children. Therefore, we focus on current global and international political changes and their local impacts to highlight the resultant gender inequity, racial inequality, anti-immigration, as well as the neoliberalism of education. Put differently, the chapters explore and frame the intersections of neoliberalism, conservatism, and nationalism, much of which have been analyzed in separate contexts, in other words "compartmentalized."[12] This compartmentalization has limited the critical analyses of their political contexts, impacts, and policies, as well as the resultant exploitation of women's labor in the global economy.[13]

The growing interest in questions of globalization, neoliberalism, and social justice has fueled the emergence and growth of transnational feminism.[14]

More specifically, transnational feminist approaches to the examination of neoliberalism seek to provide frameworks for better understanding gender and racial injustices, as well as the xenophobia associated with neoliberal globalization.[15] Hailing from different countries and contexts, informed by transnational and intersectional feminist politics and theorizing, our authors illustrate the ways in which these entwining systems of oppression have shaped and negatively impacted the lives of women and children, while advocating for emancipatory social movements and actions at the local, national, and transnational levels.[16] In doing so, the chapters engage in critiques of the triangulation, intersections, and coalitions of various neoliberal projects, including the rise of conservatism cherishing exclusionary nationalism and patriarchy, as well as a desire to preserve status quo. The consequences of these ideas tend to impact negatively on those who are involuntarily forced into subordination like women and girls connected to *right*-wing *authoritarianism* (RWA), exclusionary nationalism, and patriarchy.[17]

Neoliberalism, Conservatism, and Nationalism

Over the past forty years, neoliberalism's global hegemony has become so pervasive and insidiously ubiquitous that we scarcely recognize it, yet its anonymity is both a symptom and a cause of its power and domination.[18] Neoliberalism, a social orthodoxy[19] since the 1970s, is grounded in a conception of power as network-like, eclectic, highly diffused, and decentered (Bellamy & Palumbo, 2010). It has played a major role in a remarkable variety of global crises: the financial meltdown of 2007–8; the offshoring concentrations of wealth and power; the slow collapse of public health and education;[20] the erasure of social safety-nets; the oppression of women; resurgent child poverty; the rise of gender violence, racism, and anti-immigration policies; the destruction of unions; the collapse of ecosystems; the privatization of public education; and the rise of Trumpism, authoritarianism, and alt-right mentalities. Largely unregulated, the neoliberal political economy embodies a market-driven mentality by promoting the ideals of free markets and individual choice through entrepreneurship while it maximizes economic efficiency and growth, technological progress, and distributive justice.[21] Equally important, the rapid growth of neoliberalism has created a one-world global economy through the internationalization of goods, capital, and money markets[22] and limits the power of democracies with devastating effects on the world's most vulnerable population—women and children.

In other words, neoliberalism places property and profits beyond the reach of democracy or as Chomsky[23] writes "Profits over People." This market-driven ideology with its individualistic view of "everyone for themselves" is in juxtaposition to democracy's communitarian worldview that stresses the collective.[24] Still, the outward attractiveness of neoliberalism's philosophies of individual freedom, prosperity, patriarchy, and economic growth makes it challenging[25] for the public to realize that neoliberalization is designed to benefit only a very small class of people and nation-states.[26] A worldview such as this makes it easier to justify the thought that some people deserve much more than others. This is advanced by the echo of the neoliberal refrain that "we are all responsible for our own destinies."[27] Rather than the promise of democratic citizenship, neoliberalization's uncritical lessons promote the values of economic dominance, exploitation, enterprise, and entrepreneurship at all costs.[28]

Neoliberalism does its most destructive work through its hegemonic lessons to citizen-subjects and nation-states alike that their place in the new world order is to either to comply and tow-the-line or suffer the consequences of failure and abject poverty, with no one to blame but themselves.[29] As a result, this "neoliberal turn"[30] transforms and acquiesces societies, spaces, subjectivities, and modes of organizing toward "an increasingly broad range of neoliberal policy experiments, institutional innovations and politico-ideological projects."[31] These neoliberal turns are successfully achieved through various pathways (i.e., think-tanks, policy institutes, policy briefs, political agendas, universities, schools, as well as media, post-truth, dis-information, fake news, etc.). Many of these think-tanks are solely dedicated to policy-related expertise, consulting, confusion, and diffusion in order to secure, produce, and channel selected knowledge.[32] For example, conservative think-tanks such as the Brookings Institute, the Heritage Foundation, or the Ludwig von Mises Institute are constantly researching neoliberal "solutions" to a variety of the world's problems, and then arguing, advocating, and lobbying for policy changes at local, state, and federal levels.

The resultant spaces and the possibilities for a broad democracy, itself, as well as democratic aspirations, are under threat in both emerging and established democratic countries/nations. This shift toward democratic decline comes from neoliberal ideology, fundamental religious values, authoritarianism, and radical-right movements that are closely intertwined with conservative aspirations.[33] Tragically, democracy has been so conflated with late-capitalism/neoliberalism that it has slid toward autocracy, all by maintaining the outward appearance of democracy through elections, but without the rights and institutions that are equally important aspects of a functioning democratic system.[34]

On the heels of the neoliberal turn is the "authoritarian" resurrection of conservatism, nationalism, fascism, and extreme right-wing movements that promote social and racial hierarchies by adhering to the procedural aspects of democracy but reject dimensions of democracy that stress social justice and pluralism.[35] At the core of a strong broad democracy as described by Dewey, Benjamin Barber, Chantel Mouffe, Maxine Green, and so on is a value of plurality, as well as equal opportunity that extends majority rule and encompasses a way of life. In other words, democracy is not something a society "gets"; democracy must be fought for each and every day in concrete instances, "even long after democracy is first constituted in a society."[36] According to Mouffe, when absolute basic ethical values of human plurality, civil liberties and rights, as well as participation are not fought for politically democracy ceases to exist.

Extreme right-wing movements are not necessarily on the page as conservatism and nationalism (ideas/ideologies which render the definitions a bit confusing). However, all of these movements are infused by ideas/ideologies and contra ideas/ideologies. For example, the extreme right has four common denominator traits: (1) anti-democracy, (2) nationalism, (3) racism, and (4) the strong state.[37] This new extreme right movements, along with the liberal conservatives, stress small government, free markets, and individual initiative. The rise in antiliberal populist movements of the far right—those that emphasize national sovereignty, are hostile to immigration, and reject constitutional checks on the will of the majority—has been most effective at seizing the open political space.[38] These movements have, in some countries (i.e., Thailand, Hungary, and Brazil), crushed democracy in favor of a type of totalitarianism and neo-fascism through mock elections and/or military coups that in some cases declare martial law, armed soldiers into residential areas, take over radio and TV stations, issue restrictions on the press, tighten some limits on travel, and take certain activists into custody.

Wendy Brown argues that neoliberalism has provoked the rise of an "enraged" form of majority rule, characterized by an "enraged" form of majority rule. This movement is characterized by conservatism, the ruling ideology that many movements (smaller/larger groups) like the far-right groups, Catholic religious policies, other religious fundamentalists and extremists, the noble, and paternalists, tap into. Within conservatism there are dimensions of nationalism that are more or less strongly articulated in various groups. As a result, these movements are freed from any form of civil norms, and fueled by resentment including using markets and morals to erase the very notions of popular sovereignty, the social, and social justice.[39] For example, the push for nationalism aims to create a sense of "we" comprising a homogenous collective that shares language, race, history, culture and political actions, such as the illiberal democracy promoted by Hungary's Prime Minister Viktor Orbán. It is founded on the belief that a strong nation provides a sense of security, belonging. and a home, while demanding loyalty of its citizens while limiting human rights. Nationalism risks becoming dangerous when it starts to exclude the plurality and subsequently oppresses and harms those who are different, as well as obstructs peace among nations.[40]

Nationalism has been represented as "antithetical to neoliberalism" in the International Political Economy (IPE) literature.[41] Yet, scholars now argue that indeed nationalism is compatible with neoliberalism, noting how nationalists employ neoliberal policies for nationalist reasons.[42] What's more, David Harvey has noted that "the neoliberal state needs nationalism of a certain sort to survive" (p. 84). In addition, Hooghe and Marks (as cited in Harmes, 2012) observe that "Neoliberals have skilfully combined economic internationalism and political nationalism in an effort to create national governance and international market competition. They have linked their cause to nationalism to block the development of a Euro-polity capable of regulating the European economy ... Yet, unlike nationalists, neoliberals have goals that stretch beyond defending the sovereignty of national states. They have sought to limit the capacity of any political actor, including national states themselves, to regulate economic activity (1997: 9)." So, neoliberalism, a very complex phenomenon, takes on local characteristics in diverse geopolitical, economic, and cultural settings, while retaining a core commitment in all its manifestations to market fundamentalism.[43] As a result, the spaces and possibilities for democracy and democratic aspirations are under threat in both emerging and established democratic countries/nations by neoliberalism, fundamental religious values, authoritarianism, and radical-right movements that are closely intertwined with conservative values and objectives.[44]

During these social struggles the question of education becomes highly important to shed light on seeing that education always has been a mirror of ruling ideologies.

Education and Schooling

Education and schooling play a vital role in a democracy, and they function as keys for transformation of the world into a fairer, more caring and democratic place.[45] In a democracy, education is based on respect, open and ongoing dialogue, shared power, cooperative decision making in order to shift power structures within the classroom and the greater society in a fluid manner.[46] Yet, there are no *neutral educational* systems,[47] thus any ideological project is a political entity whether visible or veiled.[48] Therefore, it follows that politics are important influences in education as evidence in the historical left-right pendulum swings in educational reforms. For example, those who believe that market-logics are fundamental for good social functioning also have their own educational projects arguing that education should be neutral, yet what they are really arguing for is a version of education in which nobody is accountable.[49]

Education also serves as a "public good" that goes beyond individual self-interest to serve greater public purposes and hope for social reconstruction. It also serves to provide citizens with qualifications necessary to cope with life including work-life. In this sense, education, schooling, and pedagogy are not so much about training, but rather to prepare citizens to critically utilize their reasoning capacities, capable of addressing their relationship with others and with the larger world and *participate* effectively in the governance within a democracy.[50]

Historically, educational reform evidenced in various countries oscillates between broad and narrow ways of understanding both the scope and the function of education as well as teaching as a profession. In a general sense, public education has a number of different purposes, including to provide knowledge, to socialize and promote equal treatment,[51] to stimulate qualification, socialization, and subjectification connected to economic arguments, to prepare the workforce, to economic development and growth,[52] but more to provide students with political literacy as the knowledge and skills needed for citizenship, or cultural literacy more generally, and for the greater good and democracy.[53]

Besides knowledge and thus qualifications, another purpose of education is socialization. Socialization has to do with the process of character formation in relation to cherished values and norms of a social order. Sometimes it is demanded for education to explicitly socialize young people other times the socialization takes a hegemonic form that is hidden.[54] A third purpose of education is to actively promote equal treatment which means stepping in, making changes in order to stimulate conditions for everyone to grow[55] and democratic equality in pursuit of the greater good. This can be compared to subjectification which is about allowing plurality and hence people's differences to enter into the social order in ways that at times allow questioning and change of that order.[56]

At a time of neoliberal reforms, the feminization of teaching, the attack on teachers' unions, the silencing teachers, the scripted curricula, vouchers, charter schools, it is easy to see that education and teaching are at the heart of political controversy around the world. So, as gender shapes the legal and occupational reforms that bind the global-to-the-local movement of reform ideas, gender is also implicated in the new forms and controls over teaching—the labor process—revealed.[57] With the advent of neoliberal educational reforms, it is easy to see that education and teaching are at the heart of political controversy around the world. The authors in the second section of this volume demonstrate how neoliberal school change is about changing the work of teachers. They also show teachers can enact pedagogy in order to become transformative agents of change and stress the importance of teacher agency.

In the next section, we delineate to research approaches with descriptions of Intersectional analyses to explore intersecting patterns between different structures of power and how people are simultaneously positioned—and position themselves—in multiple categories, such as gender, class, and ethnicity.[58] then we delineate Transnational Feminist theory and politics.

Intersectionality

Intersectionality was originally coined by Kimberlé Creshaw in 1989 as a way to demarginalize the intersections of race and sex within a Black Feminist theoretical critiques. Crenshaw argued that Black women are discriminated against in ways that often do not fit neatly within the legal categories of either "racism" *or* "sexism"—but as a combination of both racism *and* sexism. Crenshaw describes intersectionality as a metaphor of automobiles (oppression) entering an intersection at the same time. As feminist theory of intersectionality has evolved, it is now seen as a synthesis of multiple overlapping oppressions and has proven necessary to understanding a wide range of difference and the connections between gender and socio-political categories, such as race, ethnicity, class, sexuality, nationality, (dis)ability, and others.

Patricia Hill Collins uses the concept of intersectionality to analyze how "oppressions [such as 'race and gender' or 'sexuality and nation'] work together in producing injustice." But adds the concept "matrix of dominations" to this formulation adding that: "In contrast, the matrix of dominations refers to how these intersecting oppressions are actually organized. Regardless of the particular intersections involved, structural, disciplinary, hegemonic, and interpersonal domains of power reappear across quite different forms of oppression" (Collins, 2002, p. 18). Therefore, the notion of intersectionality describes, "micro-level processes—namely, how each individual and group occupies a social position within interlocking structures of oppression described by the metaphor of intersectionality. While, intersectionality was originally perceived as a way to explore how experiences of race, gender, and sexuality intersected with other social constructs of difference, including race/ethnicity, class, and age, it is now informed by the idea that gender intersects with other aspects of a person's identity, such as class, race or nationality, unequal transnationalized terrains of gender, race, class, citizenship, disability and sexuality, and the renewed horizons of exclusion and hatred and/or legal violence.[59]

Similarly, in terms of the political economy, Nancy Fraser[60] offers the concept of "boundary struggles" which overlap with and entwine with class struggles in an expanded sense, just as they overlap with and entwine with gender struggles and with struggles over racial oppression and imperial predation (p. 11.). She adds that "boundary struggles" focus on the way in which social conflict centers on and contests capitalism's constitutive institutional separations, then won the group divisions and power asymmetries that correlate with those separations. In other words, Fraser argues that we cannot exclusively view oppression through the lens of class (or, for that should matter, of gender or race) which would miss the underlying structural-institutional features of capitalist societies with which domination is entwined and through which it is organized. But the converse is also true. According to Fraser (2019) to this view, such a struggle exclusively from the boundary vantage is to miss the social fault lines and relations of domination to which those institutional divisions give rise (p. 11).

Transnational Feminism

Transnational feminism identifies as part of the newly energized feminist "resistance." It is concerned with how globalization and capitalism affect people across nations, races, genders, classes, and sexualities. The growing interest in questions of globalization, neoliberalism, and social justice has fueled the emergence and growth of transnational feminist.[61] Accordingly, transnational feminism is seen as both a contemporary feminist paradigm[62] and a corresponding activists' movement.[63] It uses intersectional analysis and democratic practices for devising strategies with other mass movements that can redistribute resources and emancipate women.[64] This powerful combination of using both the transactional feminist theories and activist practices is concerned with how globalization and neoliberalism (late capitalism) impact people across nations, races, genders, classes, and sexualities.[65] This movement critiques the ideologies of traditional white, classist, Western models of feminist practices from an intersectional approach and how these connect with labor, theoretical applications, and analytical practice on a geopolitical scale.[66]

The term "transnational" is reaction and rejects terms like "international" and "global" feminism.[67] This is because transnational feminists believe that the term "international" puts more emphasis on nation-states as distinct entities, and that "global" speaks to liberal feminist theories on "global sisterhood" that ignore Third World women and women of color's perspectives on gender inequality and other problems globalization brings inherently (Mohanty, 2003a; Swarr & Nagar, 2010). As a result, transnational feminists are public intellectuals dedicated to challenging neoliberalism's power, dominance, and oppression against women and children. Finally, transnational feminism political theory refers to both a contemporary feminist paradigm (Grewal & Kaplan, 1994) and a corresponding activist movement (Disch & Hawkesworth, 2016) that is concerned with the influential role played by globalization and neoliberalism in shaping economic, social, and educational programs.

In response, transnational feminists, academics, scholars, and activists are asked to be seen and to see themselves as public intellectuals who provide an indispensable service to the world, and to resist the narrow confines of academic labor by becoming multi-literate in a global democracy in ways that not only allow access to new information and technologies but also enable us to become border-crossers in fighting such oppressions.[68] Critical transnational feminist praxis, therefore, is a call to all public intellectuals to take action and to develop democratic emancipatory projects that challenge neoliberalism's power, dominance, and oppression.[69]

In sum, the purpose of the book is to explore, both broadly and in depth, what the increase of neoliberalism, authoritarianism, fundamental religion, and radical conservatism/nationalism implies for democracy, social justice, and emancipatory dimensions in society and education both internationally and globally.

More specifically, the chapters respond to the following questions:

- How are feminist and gendered values coded in society, in immigration policies, and in educational debates today, and what kind of consequences might they entail?
- How and in what way are democratic, feminist, and emancipatory works in society and educational spaces influenced and affected by current trends?
- What are some critical possibilities for emancipatory and democratic work in society and educational spaces?

We believe that this book provides a much-needed international feminist critique, discourse and presents critical challenges to radical nationalism, conservatism, and authoritarianism which threaten emancipatory projects, as well as seeks to explicate this global moment of neoliberal gendered political projects. A number of the book's chapters provide scholars, researchers, teachers, educational researchers, and others interested in democracy and emancipation viewed through feminist lens to interpret and challenge the neoliberal impact in their international environs. The notion of the interplay between masculinity and femininity within a neoliberal nationalist agenda is particularly highlighted—which gives the book its special characteristics.

Chapter Roadmap

The book is divided into two sections. The first section situates transnational feminist movements, discussing definitions, foundational knowledge, and feminist theory and praxis, and the current context in which the volume is positioned. The second section examines transnational feminist movements at the global, institutional, and "glocal" levels, highlighting the many strategies of transnational feminist engagement through education, knowledge creation, advocacy, networking, and alliance building. Collectively, the book chapters provide rich insights and analyses on how these triangulated tendencies impact women and children in society, immigration policies, as well as schooling and education in various countries around the globe. We argue that the current increased anti-feminism is linked to the exclusionary nationalism and racism of the emerging right-wing populist parties. The concluding chapter synthesizes the strategies proposed by the contributors and editors with an eye toward the future.

- Part 1 of the book provides foundational knowledge using a feminist lens to examine current threats to democracy and how they impact emancipatory work.
- Part 2 of the book looks more specifically at global neoliberalization's impact on education, schooling, and teachers, through reforms such as privatization, recasting teaching and education as scripted and teaching to the test, facilitating different forms of consumer choice, the takeover of schools by corporate management companies, and the infiltration of market-based principles in the public sector.

FOREWORD by Antonia Darder challenges the immorality of inequality. She points to the problems in education that often reflect far greater social problems. She adds that we live in a society that privileges individualism, competition, quantifiable phenomena, and a bootstrap mentality that always seems to lead us back to inequality. Meanwhile, poverty and educational difficulties are blamed on the most vulnerable populations, rather than on policies that privilege the wealthy, bolster a permanent culture of war, destroy the environment, and suck dry the coffers of resources that should be in the service of many, rather than a few.

INTRODUCTION is written by the editors Sheila L. Macrine and Silvia Edling and lays the groundwork for the volume. The chapter begins with an explanation of how neoliberal nationalism, conservatism, and authoritarianism threaten emancipatory projects and ambitions associated with democracy and social justice. It also provides rich insights on how these tendencies impact women in society, schooling and education in various countries globally. We assert that current exclusionary practices of xenophobic nationalism, protectionism, racism, and gender-based biases of emerging right-wing nationalist's parties are linked to increased anti-feminism.[70] The chapters that follow provide the reader with a much-needed transnational feminist critique by offering not only descriptions and critique but also a clarion call to critically challenge radical nationalism, conservatism, and authoritarianism as they threaten emancipatory projects at this particular global moment.

In Chapter 1, ***Borders and Bridges: Securitized Regimes, Racialized Citizenship, and Insurgent Feminist Praxis***, Chandra Talpade Mohanty defines transnational feminist praxis anchored in these very particular intellectual and political genealogies—in studies of race, colonialism, and empire in the Global North and South, in the critiques of feminists of color in the United States, and in studies of decolonization, anti-capitalist critique, and LGBTQ/Queer studies in the North and the South. She writes that this category is anchored in her own location in the Global North, and in the commitment to work systematically, and overtly against racialized, heterosexist, imperial, corporatist projects that characterize North American global adventures. Mohanty argues that her interest lies in the connections between the politics of knowledge, and the spaces, places, and locations that we occupy. Therefore, this chapter is an attempt to think through the political and epistemological struggles that are embedded in radical critical, anti-racist, anti-capitalist feminist praxis at this time.

Sheila L. Macrine and Silvia Edling's Chapter 2 is entitled ***The Refugee Crisis Is a Feminist Issue***. Globally, there are now more refugees and displaced people worldwide than ever before (Edwards, 2016), creating a "refugee/migrant crisis." While this declared global "refugee crisis" has received considerable scholarly attention, yet little of it has focused on the intersecting dynamics of oppression, discrimination, violence, and subjugation of women. The chapter interrogates the inextricable linkages among racial, gendered, sexual, and class oppressions on refugee/migrant women and how they are constructed and contested. This chapter also compares the responses to the refugee crises in the United States and Sweden by using a critical feminist framework to examine intersections of race, class, and gender as additive factors in the oppression of women refugees.

Next, we turn to the Global South and the plight of rural women workers in Brazil in Chapter 3, ***How the Neoliberal Ultraconservative Alliance in Brazil Threatens Women's Lives: Learning to Fight and Survive***, by Inny Accioly. This chapter analyzes the neoliberal links among capitalism, neoliberalism, conservatism, and gender, by connecting the latest stage of neoliberalism—the debt economy—to reproductive rights, health, working conditions, and the education of women. It further explicates how the articulation between neoliberalism and conservatism has impacted educational policies and curricular reforms in basic education in Brazil during 2016/17. Finally, the chapter discusses the historical importance of linking school curriculum and practices in the struggles of the social movements of rural women-workers for the defense of democracy and the human right to life.

In Chapter 4, ***The Antidemocratic Fantasmatic Logic of Right-Wing Populism: Theoretical Reflections***, Gundula Ludwig asserts that "Anti-genderism," homophobic attacks, the dismantling of feminist achievements, and the promotion of a heteronormative gender-order are key elements of the current anti-democratic discourses and politics. She first looks *at* gendered and sexual politics in Germany, and outlines how anti-feminism and the undoing of democracy are intertwined. She argues that gender politics are a crucial terrain for organizing consensus to the dismantling of democracy that brings together right-wing political actors and conservative actors. The second part of the chapter looks into the genesis of the current crisis of democracy. *She argues that the* shifting relations of force are manifested in the rise of right-wing parties and the increas*ed* acceptance of right-wing-positions also among conservative and liberal actors—the anti-democratic elements of liberal democracies culminate in the rise of an authoritarian, masculinist, anti-feminist era.

Technologies of Surveillance: A Transnational Black Feminist Analysis, Chapter 5, written by K. Melchor Quick Hall, focuses on the realities of technologies of surveillance in such a context. She discusses the relationship of

US American (read: white supremacist) nationalism, (neo)conservative politics, and a neoliberal agenda. Importantly, Hall calls attention to the detrimental impacts of liberalism that often allows the growth of (neo)conservative policies, and does not offer any radical (i.e., addressing root cause) solutions. The chapter focuses specifically on the racialized dangers of neoliberal surveillance, before introducing a TBF analysis. Importantly, the chapter speaks to ideas about resistance to these technologies, by engaging the idea of "dark sousveillance" (Browne 2015) before concluding.

In Chapter 6, Robin Truth Goodman's *Hot Rockin' Vampires on Skateboards: Neoliberalism's Feminism* considers how neoliberal ideology appropriates feminism's oppositional rhetorics to gloss neoliberalism as oppositional to imperialism, religious conservatism, and authoritarianism. In other words, Goodman argues that feminism is being used for neoliberalism's purposes in order to make neoliberalism seem as though it is oppositional to the global *Realpolitik* that it practices. The chapter traces a brief history of intersections between neoliberal ideology and popular liberal feminism, and then uses that analysis in a discussion of an Iranian/British/American feminist filmmaker's 2014 debut feature film *A Woman Walks Home Alone at Night*. Using critical theory and postcolonial theory to update the insights of the celebrated psychoanalytic feminist film theory of the late seventies, the chapter criticizes the popular appeal of a type of feminism that celebrates neoliberal market integration as a heroic feminism that will save us from regressive, parochial, patriarchal authoritarianism.

Section 2: Contextualizations: Education and the Teaching Profession

Sarah Ljungquist's Chapter 7, **Feminism and Anti-feminism in Sweden, in the wake of #MeToo**, critically discusses the forces launched by hegemonic masculinity—that is the prevailing view of masculinity according to Rawyen Connell—is threatened by societal changes and democratic achievements for justice, equal and gender equal conditions (Connell 1995). The global campaign #MeToo is an example of a current worldwide revolution. Thanks to women sharing their stories of having been sexually harassed by men, the problem was recognized as a gender power problem, a structural problem. The chapter examines the conflict and tension between the emancipatory forces that want to challenge the prevailing patriarchal order and the populist reactive forces that want to prevail. The main part of the examination takes place in a seminar course on democratic and social justice issues at the teacher education in Sweden.

Geraldine Mooney Simmies from the Republic of Ireland adds Chapter 8 entitled *Suppression of Teacher's Voices: Agency and Freedom within Neoliberal Masculinist Performativity*. This chapter describes teaching in Europe and elsewhere where it is regarded, often with deep suspicion, as a feminized profession, with upwards of 80 percent of the teaching workforce in some EU countries, including Ireland, registered as female. Within a public policy understanding—this is a flawed situation that needs to be overcome in a twenty-first-century knowledge economy. Instead, a new hard-edged evidence-based (clinical) construct of an ideal teacher is presented and subjectified within the neoliberal policies of a Global Education Reform Movement (GERM) for a limited performativity and dominance of the markets (Ball, 2003; Tan 2014; Mooney Simmie & Moles, 2019; Paolantonio, 2019). This chapter describes globally how teacher's agency and autonomy, while couched in discourses of freedom, recognition and choice, are instead triangulated by reductionist forces of neo-liberalism, scientism, and paternalism acting downward for a new pedagogy of teacher ethical suppression. Finally, this chapter illustrates how recent policy reforms in Ireland seek to reposition teachers as a "new professional class" of creative and critical thinkers. This is not for emancipatory purposes and the existential possibilities of an Invisible Pedagogy (Mooney Simmie & Moles, 2019) but rather for regulation of teachers' bodies and souls arcing in the direction of primacy of the markets.

The neoliberal economic debt crisis and austerity are taken up by Maria Nikkola in Chapter 9, entitled *The Greek Crisis and the Gender Gap: Reinforcing Connections between Education and Women's Empowerment*. This crisis has had devastating effects on Greek society politically, financially, and culturally, and has created new forms of gender-based discrimination. Greece has been suffering from a debt crisis since 2009; Nikkola argues that IMF-ECB-EU interventions have not helped but rather have accelerated a neoliberal management. She adds that the consequences of austerity policies and the Eurozone crisis are leading to further shifts in traditional gender roles. The chapter explores both the challenges and possibilities of the current crisis and how education can nurture the empowerment of women.

Marias, Marielles, Malês: Southern Epistemologies, Resistance, and Emancipation, Chapter 10, is written by Maria Luiza Süssekind and Ines Barbosa de Oliveira. This chapter addresses everyday life forms of resistance and emancipation in understanding school's curricula as an ecology of knowledges

(Santos, 2007; Oliveira; Süssekind, 2018). The authors first situate the coup in Brazil and its consequences in the context of a *"Transnational Conservative Tsunami"* pointing out that the struggle for a fair world should not allow itself to be paralyzed. Second, they highlight the forms of resistance from a decolonized theoretical approach aimed at recognizing "invisibilized knowledges," displacing the centrality of the eurocentrism, and deconstructing the proleptical and abyssal modern thinking claiming, at the same time, the empirical consistency to the notions formulated by Santos around the need of learning from the South.

Turning to back to Sweden, Guadalupe Francia wrote **Chapter 11, *The Emergence of the Anti-Gender Agenda in Swedish Higher Education***. She writes that, after decades of progressive reforms in terms of gender and sexual rights, an anti-gender agenda has emerged around the world creating resistance to all kinds of gender equality struggles. With the purpose to develop a deeper understanding of this international anti-gender agenda, this chapter analyses individuals' perceptions of the role of gender studies in Higher Education present in narratives published in internet postings of one social media website with focus on Swedish Higher Education issues.

In the ***Conclusion*, Silvia Edling and Sheila L. Macrine** reflect on and capture some of the major themes threaded throughout the volume that explicate threats to democracy and the oppression of women. Each chapter provides country-based evidence where social justice and democracy are challenged and point to emancipatory efforts suffocated by movements toward conservative right-wing world-views that stress masculine values. This chapter concludes with a look toward emancipation and social justice for victims of gender-based violence and oppression. The concluding section is particularly focusing on the interconnectedness between purpose, practice, and condition.

Finally, the volume is dedicated to understanding the ways that women participate in, become drawn and incorporated into, are affected by and negotiate their encounters with contemporary forms of global economic restructuring commonly referred to as neoliberal globalization.[71] The impetus of this volume came as a result of our various encounters with international women at various conferences. Each of us, from a different part of the world and cultures, realizes that while the individual problems may look different, they still reflect the oppressive nature of the triangulation of neoliberalism, conservatism, and authoritarianism. So, we asked ourselves, how can we create critical responses to current neoliberal and conservative socio-political policies and to build bridges between activism and academia. Subsequently, our authors respond to Niamh Reilly's (2007) call to all feminists to take action and to develop emancipatory political projects that demand critical engagement with international human rights by developing global feminist consciousness and actions that: (1) contests patriarchal, late capitalist, gender and racist power-dynamics in the context of neoliberal globalization; (2) develop cross-boundaries dialogue that recognizes the intersectionality of forms of oppression; (3) promote collaborative transnational feminists' strategizing on concrete issues; and (4) the utilization of global forums as sites of cosmopolitan solidarity and citizen action (p. 180). These authors show how local and global economic restructuring exacerbates women's economic and social vulnerabilities (Gunewardena & Kingsolver, 2007, p. 1) by examining the ways in which these interlocking systems of oppression have shaped and influenced the historical, cultural, social, political, and economic contexts of the lives of women and children, as well as the political, social, and educational movements at the local, national, and transnational levels (Zinn & Dill, 1996). Collins (2002) notes that "the notion of interlocking oppressions refers to the macro-level connections linking systems of oppression such as race, class, and gender ... describing the social structures that create social positions." In challenging diminished powers and compromised democratic agency, Goodman (2010) notes that the waning of power in the public sphere diminishes the influence that citizens can have in deciding on the conditions of life, and therefore minimizes the changes that feminists can envision or enact in the social field to work toward equality, access, deliberation, participation, just distribution, rights, and authority for women.

That said, the chapters respond and contribute to emerging transnational feminists' development of counter-hegemonic actions, processes of grassroots resistance, and transformations while creating an alliance between emancipation and social protection.[72] In sum, our actions in this volume are reflected in Monbiot's[73] quote:

> Without countervailing voices, naming and challenging power, political freedom withers and dies. Without countervailing voices, a better world can never materialise. Without countervailing voices, wells will still be dug and bridges will still be built, but only for the few. Food will still be grown, but it will not reach the mouths of the poor. New medicines will be developed, but they will be inaccessible to many of those in need.
>
> (p. 1)

As we go to publication, we mark the 100th anniversary of Women's Right to Vote in the United States in 2020 and January 1921 in Sweden. The women scholars in this volume urge us to stand in solidarity with all of our sisters to advocate for the rights and protections for women worldwide. We call for action to develop emancipatory projects that challenge rising conservatism and neoliberalism's power, dominance, and oppressions, to defend democracy, democratic public life and the public sphere in these uncertain times. In response, academics, scholars, and activists are asked to be seen and to see themselves as public intellectuals who provide an indispensable service to the world, and to resist the narrow confines of academic labor by becoming multi-literate in a global democracy in ways that enable us to become border-crossers (Giroux, 2006; Macrine, 2016). Reminiscent of incredibly courageous, brave, and forward-thinking women of the early 1900s, we are inspired by the memory and legacy of Justice Ruth Bader Ginsburg, and dedicate this volume to this resolute defender of women's rights and equality, and champion for equal opportunity and justice for all.

Part One

Overviews: Challenges and Possibilities

1

Borders and Bridges

Securitized Regimes, Racialized Citizenship, and Insurgent Feminist Praxis

Chandra Talpade Mohanty

"Voyager, there are no bridges, one builds them as one walks."
Gloria Anzaldua

It is July 2020 and we are in the midst of an unprecedented global health pandemic that has laid all social inequities bare, an ongoing anti-racist revolution in the streets of US cities and around the world proclaiming *Black Lives Matter* following the violent death of George Floyd (and Breonna Taylor, Ahmaud Arbery, Tony McDade, among others), an acute economic crisis and the "failure of the social experiment that is America" as Cornell West named it. So, what does a radical, anti-racist, anti-imperialist feminist struggle entail in these violently racist, misogynist, neoliberal times?[1] What do anti-racist feminist scholars, activists, and cultural workers need to know, analyze, and learn about so we can forge ethical solidarities across material and virtual borders, and build the landscapes of racial and gender justice that we dream about and struggle for? What does it mean to craft insurgent knowledges through our writing, our art, our cultural productions, our activism, and our pedagogies?

In 2020 our understandings of feminism, decolonization, and transnationalism are in flux, contested in social movements, State policy, and social and political theory. In 2020, the transnational necessitates acknowledging explicitly carceral regimes, geopolitical climate destruction, militarized national borders, massive displacement of peoples (war, climate, and economic refugees), proliferation of corporatist, racist, misogynist cultures, lean-in and glass ceiling (liberal) feminisms, decimation of labor movements, and the rise of right-wing, proto-fascist governments around the world (Modi in India, Erdogan in Turkey,

Bolsonaro in Brazil, Trump in the United States). All these phenomena are of course connected to global economic crises (the oil crisis in the 1970s and the stock market crash in 2008 and now 2020), neoliberal governmentalities, global racialities, and mass unemployment, displacement and dispossession of particular groups of people worldwide.

Undergirding all of my scholarly work are my activist commitments to building radical, anti-racist, transnational feminist communities in all of the spaces I have lived in over four plus decades of living in the United States. None of this work would be possible without these dissident communities. And this I think is the key to living an insurgent life as an anti-racist, anti-imperialist feminist in these times. Building and sustaining the "intellectual neighborhoods" (Toni Morrison) and communities of dissent that inspire and can sustain an insurgent feminist life. The very first "intellectual neighborhood" I collaborated in building and which set me on my journey over four decades ago was as a graduate student at University of Illinois, Urbana-Champaign. I co-organized with Ann Russo, the *Common Differences: Third World Women and Feminist Perspectives* conference in 1983—I believe this was the first or one of the first conferences of this scale to bring US women of color and feminists from the "third world" into conversation about the "common differences" in our feminist praxis. It was the beginning of my intellectual journey in the company of feminists of color. Historically, the conference emerged from decades of anti-colonial, anti-capitalist, and national liberation movements that women in the Global South (we called ourselves third world women then) had waged since the 1940s, and the revolutionary freedom and civil rights movements that women of color had waged in Global North. Questions of intersectionality and relationality of structures of power and women's place-based resistance; the complexities of working across race, class, sexuality, and nationality in the context of multiple colonial legacies and imperial adventures of the United States; the centrality of economic issues, poverty, and class in envisioning and enacting gender justice; the significance of identity and community (who are the "we"?); and the theoretical and epistemological contributions of a decolonial feminist engagement were all issues that emerged from this collective space—and that have stayed with me through all the work I have done since then.[2]

I have always believed that the intellectual work we are passionate about is in some way connected to (but not identical with) our own biographies. My experience of a radical community of third world and women of color thinkers at the *Common Differences* conference made it clear that an anti-racist, anti-capitalist, and anti-imperialist feminist community was possible, indeed necessary, in and outside the academy. My definition of transnational feminist praxis is anchored in these very particular intellectual and political genealogies—in studies of race, colonialism, and empire in the Global North and South, in the critiques of feminists of color in the United States, and in studies of decolonization, anti-capitalist critique, and LGBTQ/Queer studies in the North and the South. My use of this category is thus anchored in my own location in the Global North, and in the commitment to work systematically, and overtly against racialized, heterosexist, imperial, corporatist projects that characterize North American global adventures. My interest lies in the connections between the politics of knowledge, and the spaces, places, and locations that we occupy. This essay is an attempt to think through the political and epistemological struggles that are embedded in radical critical, anti-racist, anti-capitalist feminist praxis at this time.[3]

Neoliberal Regimes: Capitalist Dispossession, Securitized States, Imperial Democracies

I began thinking about borders and bridges—specifically about neoliberal/securitized regimes, anti-racist struggles, and anatomies of violence after hearing about the building of a US "mega-security wall" along the South Texas-Mexico border, and the struggles of immigrant activists and the Lipan Apache Women's Defense (LAW Defense) organization to halt this explicitly imperialist partition project. What seemed obvious was the use of unjust, militarized state practices similar to those used in the war zones of Iraq and Afghanistan, using the pretext of the "war on terror" and its earlier iteration, the "war on drugs" to mobilize simultaneous discourses of Islamophobia and nativism. And yet, at that time, a decade ago, the struggles of LAW Defense, even the building of the mega security wall in East Texas were almost completely absent from public discussion, in the media, and in left/feminist circles. Now of course the family separation of migrants has its epicenter in Texas, especially in the Rio Grande Valley. It is home to the largest center for "undocumented migrants and asylum seekers" and the "Casa Padre" shelter for minors which has a capacity to hold 1,400 children. While US imperial projects are not new, the post-9/11 global formation and operation of securitized states, anchored within the rhetoric of protectionism and the war on terror and accompanied by militarized, neoliberal corporate ambitions, is a phenomenon that deserves our ongoing attention.[4]

In this chapter, I examine three neoliberal, securitized regimes and three specific geopolitical sites—the US-Mexico border struggles around immigration, and cross-border indigenous rights in the Lower Rio Grande Valley in Texas; Israel's rule over the occupied Palestinian territories of the West Bank/Gaza; and India's military rule and occupation of the Kashmir Valley (Jammu and Kashmir) as zones of normalized violence. Needless to say, each site is precisely about racialized citizenship projects that are constitutive of each of the three nation-states. At these sites, neoliberal and militarized state and imperial practices are often sustained by development/peace-keeping/humanitarian projects, thus illuminating the old/new contours of securitized states that function as neoliberal, imperial democracies.

Each site encodes genealogies, memories, and traumas of colonial occupation, partition, and violence in the building of the nation—what novelist Bapsi Sidhwa calls the "demand for blood" when the earth is divided. And in each of these geopolitical sites at the territorial borders of the nation, civilians are subjected to militarized violence anchored in the production of reactionary gender identities and dominant and subordinate (often racialized) masculinities. These three sites constitute occupied, disputed territories with violent colonial histories, and together they illustrate a new/old global order of militarized, racist violence engendered by neoliberal economic priorities.

Since the early 1990s, with India's shift to neoliberal economic and political policies, the ties between the United States, Israel, and India have been forged through the vision of the regimes in power at that time: Bush and the neoconservatives, Sharon and Likud, and the BJP/Hindu Right. As Rupal Oza (2007) suggests, since the early 1990s, the geopolitical triad of the United States, Israel, and India share a vision of threat and security based on Islam and Muslims as the common enemy, cemented through close and ongoing economic and military alliances. The same anti-Muslim rhetoric is evident in the current refugee crisis in Europe, where the Hungarian Prime minister Viktor Orban's says, "Muslims must be blocked to keep Europe Christian … Europe and European identity is rooted in Christianity." We witness neo-Nazi attacks on asylum seekers in Germany (remember the majority of the refugees from Syria, Iraq, and Afghanistan are Muslims), and the growth of detention centers, "reception centers," or "camps" in Hungary and Turkey.

And we cannot forget Trump and his deployment of an "us and them" language of a securitized state, talking about refusing Muslims' entry to the United States, and holding the government hostage to the building of a wall at the US-Mexico border. As Naomi Paik (2020) argues, Trump signed three executive orders immediately after taking office in January 2017: the so-called "Muslim ban," an order focused on border security (building the wall), and a third order that bolstered immigration enforcement (giving Immigration and Customs Enforcement a sweeping mandate to remove all "illegal immigrants"). Taken together these executive orders are in fact an explicit legacy of the building of an historical US citizenship project anchored in governance practices of exclusion and exploitation anchored in race, gender, and labor. Since 2015, a new federal government initiative called CVE (Countering Violent Extremism— a pilot project in Los Angeles, Boston, and Minneapolis) has been under way. CVE is described as a program that aims to deter US citizens from joining "violent extremist" groups by bringing community and religious leaders together with law enforcement, health professionals, teachers, and social service employees. In Los Angeles, CVE, in partnership with the American Muslim Women's Empowerment Council (AMWEC), the LAPD, CIA, and FBI are partners in the creation of "patriotic Muslim women" who take on the task of countering violent extremism in their communities—thus producing empowered, loyal, Muslim women citizens. Basarudin and Shaikh (2020) suggest that it is liberal feminist discourses of motherhood and empowerment that are appropriated in the service of national security and "motherwork" deployed so that gender appears and disappears in the war on terror. In moments that the US policies of rendition and/or torture impose violence on their bodies they become invisible, but in moments when there is a productive convergence between the empowered Muslim woman and state policies she becomes hypervisible.[5]

However, while the "us vs. them" ideologies of securitized states justify borders, walls, and regimes of incarceration and more recently, regimes of mass deportation in the name of protection of the homeland, it is the connectivity and commonality of analysis and vision of justice (the bridges) between peoples across borders that feminists and anti-partition activists have in common that inspires my reflections. I argue that we have much to learn from analyzing the resistance politics and collective aspirations of freedom and selfdetermination across these sites and that developing these transnational feminist frameworks is in fact key to envisioning solidarities and building bridges across borders. A comparative analysis of the wars, and walls (symbolic and material) that constitute the securitized regimes, and colonial/imperial ventures of the United States, India, and Israel, reveals the ideological operation of discourses of "democracy" within the overtly militarized, securitized nation-states of India, Israel, and the United States, and suggests that the militarization of cultures is deeply linked to neoliberal capitalist values and the normalization of what Zillah

Eisenstein (2007) and Arundhati Roy (2004) have called "imperial democracy" (Roy, 2004, p. 42; Eisenstein, 2007, p. 17). Needless to say, militarization always involves masculinization and heterosexualization as linked state projects, and neoliberal economic arrangements are predicated on gendered and racialized divisions of labor, and constructions of subjectivities, thus necessitating *feminist* critique.

National security states or neoliberal securitized regimes typically use connected strategies of militarization, criminalization, and incarceration to exercise control over particular populations, thus remaking individual subjectivities and public cultures. Tanya Golash-Boza (2016) adds another layer—she argues that mass incarceration is the other side of the coin of mass deportation, and that mass deportation is a gendered and racialized tool of state repression implemented in a time of crisis. So for instance, while Black men are the largest group incarcerated in the United States, Latino men are the largest group facing mass deportation. This understanding of mass incarceration and State violence is now in the public domain after Ferguson and the Black Lives Matter movement (not to mention George Floyd and call for defunding the police). The now-visible history of mass deportations since Obama (today nearly 90 percent of deportees are Latino and Caribbean men) and its link to the gendered and racialized immigration history in the United States is also no longer obfuscated by state managers. In addition, in terms of the so-called European "refugee crisis," Greece built a barbed wire fence along the Greece-Turkey border in 2013, Hungarian prison inmates worked on preparing materials for 900 military personnel to begin construction of the 109-mile-long razor wire fence along the border with Serbia in order to "protect" Europe from migrants, they are ready to build a fence along the border with Romania, and Austria, Slovakia and the Netherlands all introduced border controls to "manage" the refugee crisis. There are all connected sites of neoliberal citizenship projects that are deeply raced and gendered, anchored in colonial and neocolonial histories and economic priorities.

As feminist philosopher Iris Young (2003) argues, security states mobilize a particular gendered logic of masculinist protection in relation to women and children—a logic that underwrites the appeal to "protection and security" of the nation, and expects obedience and loyalty at home (patriotism). At the same time, the state wages war against internal and external enemies. In the context of the United States, it is this logic that Young claims legitimates authoritarian power in the domestic arena, and justifies aggression outside its borders. Here again the AMWEC and CVE example is instructive. As Basarudin and Shaikh argue: "Partnering with law enforcement in celebrating American multiculturalism and women's empowerment is problematic when nestled firmly within a logic of securitization, surveillance, and vitriolic xenophobia against immigrants and people of color. Mining motherhood for soft counterterrorism becomes a productive convergence between state agencies and AMWEC members" (Basarudin and Shaikh, 2020, p. 127).

Militarized, neoliberal state projects in the United States, Israel, and India create and sustain endless wars, and border zones of violence while normalizing incarceration regimes within their respective domestic landscapes. The United States invests in a fast-growing, privatized prison industrial complex within its own borders, while consolidating post-invasion regimes of torture and collective punishment in Iraq and Afghanistan. Similar questions need to be posed in relation to the "democracies" of Israel and India. In all three geopolitical contexts, the state mobilizes a masculinist securitized ideology based not on defense of the nation but on coercion that requires neither participation nor consent from its citizens (Lutz, 2002). This gendered ideology is anchored in militarized masculinities (or muscular militarism) and in patriarchal ideologies of protection and security that require obedience and consent from citizens.

In the Texas-Mexico borderlands, the West Bank and Gaza, and the Kashmir Valley, dispossession of particular subjects (e.g., women, poor, indigenous, migrant, Muslim) involve the social control and legal dispossession (or social death) through "justified" forms of surveillance and violence at multiple levels. The political economy of securitized states is focused fundamentally on the permanent abandonment of certain "captive populations" (Gordon, 2006) that are marked as threats to the neoliberal order. After all, surveillance and security have always been conjoined techniques of colonial control of so-called "dangerous populations." Here militarized capitalism enshrined within securitized states works in concert with fundamentalist Hindu, Muslim, Zionist, and Christian social movements to produce a surge of reactionary neoliberal gender identities. Kalpana Wilson et al. (2018) suggest that "Within contemporary Hindutva, virulent Islamophobia, caste supremacism, and patriarchal values are intertwined with a commitment to supporting the interests of neoliberal corporate capital through the intensification of gendered processes of exploitation, displacement and dispossession" (Wilson et al., 2018, p. 2). Thus, in this context, Statecraft, economic imperatives, and gendered narratives of patriotism are profoundly intertwined.

Securitized Regimes, and Cultures of Impunity

Speaking of Argentina in the twentieth century, Rita Arditti (1999) refers to the exercise of state violence within a culture of impunity. A culture of impunity occurs when the state operates without fear of punishment, and impunity is normalized as routine procedure across political and legal domains producing a kind of disordered order or state of exception (Agamben, 2005) necessary for the process of domination. This is a form of governmentality where the state regimes of surveillance, criminalization, and the legal suspension of rights in the name of protecting the nation from so-called "insurgents" and "illegals" operate with impunity—disappearing citizens, imprisoning others, and denying basic civil and economic rights to particular marginalized communities. Migrant detainees form one of the fastest-growing prison populations around the Western world. Three countries including the United States and Israel have built 3,500 miles of walls on their borders, and over 40,000 deaths since 2000 are linked to migration. A very brief snapshot of the operation of securitized regimes in each of the three sites follows.

Democracy and Security in Israel and Palestine

In an incisive analysis of gendered violence in occupied Gaza, Hagar Kotef (2010) argues that the framework of democracy in Israel is now the framework of security—a radically inequitable frame where the security of some groups means the insecurity of others, where Israel's security constitutes so-called democracy for Palestinians. The state of Israel bases its democracy entirely on an ethnic, demographic notion of citizenship with the "right of return" for Jews only. Israel is a capitalist, class-divided, securitized state that excludes non-Jews and Arabs from citizenship—non-citizens have very few rights and no claim on the Israeli state (Bannerji et al., 2010). Since 1948, the "partition" of the Palestinian territory has meant the establishment of the state of Israel, and the simultaneous uprooting of and mass dispersal of Palestinians from their homeland. Thus, while 1948 represents the building of a homeland for Israel, it represents "al-Nakba" the "catastrophe" for Palestinians—defeat, displacement, trauma, dispossession, and the beginning of a liberation movement (Greenberg, 2005).

Kotef suggests that the contemporary discourse of terror collapses the distinction between civilians and soldiers in national security states and that "humanitarian" actions thus become accessories to state violence against

Palestinians. She argues that humanitarianism provides, alongside terror, the logic of security (Kotef, 2010, p. 8). It is in fact Israel's closing off of the Gaza strip that has led to a "humanitarian" crisis of vast proportions, and it is in the name of humanitarian missions that Israel controls access to Gaza. While humanitarianism offers a framework of rights and redress for multiple communities around the world, it also potentially entrenches power for occupying regimes by creating and sanctioning categories of "natives" and "refugees." Under occupation, as Bhan and Duchinski (2020) suggest, "humanitarianism can be used to whitewash crimes against humanity in occupied contexts and further empire building through discourses of 'participatory militarism'" (p. 3). What is a "separation fence" to Israelis in the West Bank, is after all, an "apartheid wall" to Palestinians. What is a mega security wall for elite landowners in Texas is in fact containment and imprisonment for the indigenous nations that cross the US-Mexico borderlands.

Militarized Regimes and the Politics of Violence in Jammu and Kashmir

The Kashmir Valley (i.e., Jammu and Kashmir) is one of the most highly militarized zones in the world. The Indian government has deployed over 600,000 border security and over a quarter of a million paramilitary forces in the Valley, which has a population of 13 million. This is one of the highest soldier-to-civilian population ratios anywhere in the world (Bhatt, 2003). While much has been written about the history of Indian occupation of Kashmir, and about the way the 1947 partition of India and Pakistan creates and recreates this trauma in Jammu and Kashmir, I am most interested here in the functioning of the Indian militarized state apparatus in the Kashmir Valley, and the way in which it controls and defines identity, community, and subjectivity, especially since 2014, and the rise of a Hindutva State that actively victimizes and dehumanizes Kashmir, and domesticates and punishes all forms of dissent.

The object of three wars, an arms race, and a nuclear race between India and Pakistan, Kashmir has been disputed territory since 1947. It has witnessed the increasingly political role of the military, and of Islamist movements in Pakistan, as well as the rise of Hindu fundamentalism in India. The Kashmir Valley has been treated by India as a state of emergency since 1947. In fact postcolonial India can be analyzed in terms of two contradictory narratives—that of a progressive, anticolonial, democratic, socialist nation post Bandung (1955), and that of a nation that has always exercised violence toward Dalits, Adivasis, women, religious and sexual minorities, Kashmir, the North-East, etc.

in the name of democracy. Since the 1960s, there has been a growing movement against Indian occupation, leading to escalating tensions in the 1980s with the formation of the JK Liberation Front an underground secessionist movement engaged in an armed struggle for selfdetermination.

The nature of the rebellion in the early 1990s changed with the emergence of over 100 separatist organizations, some with explicitly religious and pro-Pakistani politics (Butalia, 2002; Khan, 2009; Duschinski, 2010). In response, India passed the Armed Forces Special Powers Act (AFSPA) in 1990 basically granting the military state impunity to enforce a regime of surveillance and incarceration in Kashmir. AFSPA underwrote the ideological framing of the Kashmir Valley in terms of fear and threat, mobilizing the rhetoric of insurgency/counterinsurgency, and justifying the suspension of constitutional rights and freedoms. The AFSPA in the Kashmir Valley allows the legal suspension of the distinction between legality and illegality. State agents are thus allowed to act with impunity and "protected" by AFSPA. Custodial killings, torture, detention without trial or charge, disappearances, mass rape (as in the villages of Kunan Poshpora), and use of human shields are "protected" by the AFSPA. Nitasha Kaul (2018) claims that in Kashmir, "the funeral and the demonstration do not just look indistinguishable, but are necessarily continuous and the same. The funeral is an act of grief that unfolds into protest, and the demonstration is fired upon and results in funerals" (Kaul, 2018, p. 130). Similarly, Malik (2018) suggests that public mourning rituals are sites of gendered resistance where grieving mothers embody defiance not passive victimization. Kashmir then functions as what activists have called a "constitution free" zone similar to the Texas-Mexico border, and the West Bank and Gaza.

To summarize, in spite of the different histories of colonialism and imperialism, there is a remarkable similarity in the forms of governmentality exercised by the securitized states of India, Israel, and the United States (and now the European Union). Recall that the EU response to the migrant/refugee crisis is framed in humanitarian and religious terms, not in terms of justice, or democracy or equality of all human beings—and that similar securitized regimes, militarization, and forms of governmentality are being enacted at border crossings in Europe. The historical responsibility and the role of European governments in causing, precipitating, or helping to find solutions to the conflicts are largely absent.

Comparing these geopolitical sites allows us to understand the way the "war on terror" and militarized cultures, state violence, and the transformation of civilians into insurgents and illegals through the legal suspension of civil rights is symptomatic of imperial democracies at this present moment. In each context, the sovereignty of the state is predicated on the operation of "constitution free" zones[6] at the borders of the nation. The normalized violence against particular bodies—Muslim, female, immigrant, native, Arab—buttresses the discourses of protectionism and citizenship in each country. In each case, we can identify states of exception whereby the suspension of law is required for the practice of empire. In each context, citizenship remains elusive for the inhabitants of these borderlands, and identity is always in question given the existence of checkpoints, and "I" cards. In these securitized landscapes, identity documents become a form of governance and a part of the state apparatus of surveillance. The process of verifying identity produces what Tobias Kelly (2006) calls "documented lives"— particular forms of subjectivity that are marked by anxiety, uncertainty, and fear. Kelly's work focuses on Palestinians but a similar argument can be made in the other contexts as well.[7]

A bio-militarized gendered body project is evident in each site, and women are impacted in different, albeit similar ways since violence is a part of daily life—as is the presence of paramilitary and police forces. In the Kashmir Valley, women are victims of sexual violence, domestic violence, and rape, and live with increasing trauma, stress depression, miscarriages, and spontaneous abortions (Butalia, 2002). There are increasing numbers of widows and so-called half-widows (women whose husbands have disappeared). In 1947, women's militias were an integral part of the "Quit Kashmir" movement, while many women in recent years have organized under the banner of the Association of Parents of Disappeared Persons (APDP), and under the Kashmiri Women's Initiative for Peace and Disarmament (Khan, 2009). The impact of Israeli occupation on Palestinian women is profound as well. The erasure of the difference between home and battlefield and between civilians and soldiers means that neighborhoods and homes become the battlefield in Gaza. In Israeli official death counts in Gaza, the men are counted as militants, while women and children are counted as "collateral damage" (Johnson, 2010). The occupation shrinks public space, confining women to the household, while long-term unemployment for men in Gaza was at 40 percent before the Israeli invasion in June 2014. Such instabilities translate into changed family dynamics and often a rise in domestic violence in the home.

When the very identities of people come under question, when sexual, ethnic/racial, and political violence becomes normative, as it does in these landscapes, the structure of imperial democracies is laid bare. In fact, the governance practices of securitized regimes are such that security is deeply entangled with citizenship or subjectivation processes. While democratic state projects focus on producing national citizens, in securitized regimes what is at stake is the opposite—the undoing of the very possibility of citizenship for targeted populations like indigenous and Mexican peasant migrant workers, Palestinians in the OPT, civilians in the Kashmir Valley, etc. (Kotef, 2010). These borderlands constitute "shadow" communities at the social and territorial margins of the state—places that exist as part of the formal state, but excluded from it so that the violent realities of everyday life, and the legal and extra-legal networks that support them are caught up in layers of invisibility.

Thus, this logic of violence, containment, and expulsion produces patterns of social abandonment and death with consequences for both communities targeted as enemies and outsiders, and also for the entire political body of rights bearing citizens because it draws them/us into the field of state violence (Gordon, 2007). These forms of truncated subjectivity and non-citizenship are a profound marker of neoliberal global security landscapes at this time.

Walls, Borders, and Connectivities: Enacting Solidarities

> *The first colonization of the "Americas" by Europe dismembered the land and put in motion a process that wiped out Indigenous peoples and their civilizations. Zionist colonization of Palestine has also dismembered the land and attempted to eradicate the Indigenous people's cultural identity and destroy any sign of their previous presence in the land. It wiped over 400 Palestinian villages and dispossessed their residents turning them into stateless refugees in the lands of exile and outsiders and strangers in their own land. The Southwest was subjected to another wave of colonization by American settlers. This act of imperialism divided the Mexican people between two sides of an artificial border.*
>
> Nadine Saliba, 2006 (cited in Platt, 2011, p. 350)

The above quote illustrates the historical and contemporary connectivities forged by feminist and anti-partition activists at the Esperanza Center in San Antonio, Texas. The US Secure Fence Act of 2006 gave the Department of Homeland Security (DHS) unilateral power to waive thirty-six federal laws at the Texas-Mexico international border, and in collaboration with NAFTA partners, begin building a Berlin-style, concrete mega security wall. This waiver of laws led to the militarization of the entire region of the lower Rio Grande, voiding legal rights and protections of indigenous peoples to culture, environment, biodiversity, and sacred sites—a clear example of US imperial policy seen as "rational" through the frame of the war on terror, and an incarceration regime that targets immigrants. The 2006 act authorized hundreds of miles and $1.4 billion worth of additional barriers, checkpoints, border agents, and surveillance technology like drones. In this case, laws (and their suspension) are used as weapons to destabilize, fragment, assimilate, and disappear communities historically residing along the Lower Rio Grande. LAW Defense (founded by mother-daughter, Eloisa Garcia Tamez and Margo Tamez in 2007) focuses on community organization and documentation, and research and education, thus strengthening indigenous peoples struggles against US colonial violence, as well as in relation to legal struggles in tribal, US, and international law courts. The secure fences act also led to the building of a 75-mile border wall on the Tohono O'odham territory in AZ, and the OhDham resistance and organizing against Trump's "new" border wall that led in 2018 to the longest government shutdown in US history!

Capitalist profit-making and corporate agendas (instigated by the United States, NAFTA partners, and corporations with mining interests) operate in full force in Texas and Arizona as waivers work differently for rich landowners and industrialists, and for poor indigenous and Mexican border communities. Rich landowners have waivers from the building of the wall, while indigenous communities have walls built on their land (what activists have labelled a "constitution free zone"). Thus, indigenous peoples and illegal immigrants (poor Mexican peasants) are constructed in similar ways: criminalized and defined as drug lords, terrorists, labor migrants, and civic resisters. It is therefore imperative to disaggregate *both* categories—immigrant *and* indigenous—since at this historical juncture, both are produced by a securitized state engaged in a "war on terror."[8] The continued reinvention of the immigrant and the indigenous and the way in which immigration law, especially laws against the "illegal immigrant" have profound impact in indigenous communities is new. The O'odham and Lipan Apache territory crosses the US-Mexican border. Mexico now requires US passports for the O'odham who travel beyond 12 miles into Mexican territory.

Arizona Law SB 1070 justifies the presence of Border patrol on reservation lands. Check points have been established throughout the territory, thus controlling free movement of the Akimel and Tohono O'odham peoples, especially elders who do not have birth certificates but need to travel across US-Mexico border to Malina/Magdelena in Mexico for religious pilgrimage.[9] Reports by National Public Radio and community organizations like Grassroots Leadership[10] revealed that SB 1070 was funded by the for-profit prison complex. While SB 1070 talks specifically about "enforcement through attrition" of illegal immigrants, it has morphed into the policing of indigenous lands and communities. The check points on the reservation resemble checkpoints in Palestinian territory. People who live on the Tohono O'odham reservation have their everyday lives profoundly shaped by the surveillance and militarization enforced by SB 1070. Along with authorizing the construction of fencing, the 2006 bill also authorized added vehicle barriers, checkpoints, and lighting along the southern border as well as an increased use of advanced technology like cameras, satellites, and unmanned aerial vehicles. Thus militarization[11] is fundamental to the construction of community and identity. The combination of check points, identity verification, and surveillance suggests a specific form of the production of "documented subjectivities." As Naomi Paik (2020) describes, for most of US history borders were both porous and movable. It was only with the nineteenth-century Chinese Exclusion Act that United States began to police its borders. Thus, the building of walls, fences, and resulting documented lives as governance strategies for the creation of white, male citizenship projects has a long history in the United States.

Since 2013 there have been two important mega projects underway across the Texas-Mexico border: (1) a large rail transport system that will traverse over the border wall in lower Rio Grande Valley, and (2) the building of a trans-Texas corridor that connects Alberta, Canada to South Texas, to Mexico that is part of a trans-hemispheric "security prosperity partnership" that entails "priority matters of national security" being transported by a mega heavy rail *freight* bridge over the Lipan Apache territory. And as mentioned earlier, given the fact that Texas and the Rio Grande Valley is home to the largest immigration detention centers, since May 2018 more than 2,300 children have been separated from their parents or guardians while crossing the border illegally or seeking asylum. Since June 20, 2018, when Trump ordered an end to family separations, 2,000 children remain alone in these "processing centers." What this spectacle at the border hides is the US reliance on and *exploitation* of particularly undocumented migrant labor.

As Nadine Saliba suggests above (2006), there are clear confluences between the impact of US colonial and imperial projects, and Israel's colonization and occupation of the West Bank and Gaza. The organizing work of the Esperanza center brings these connections home in terms of the impact of walls, borders, and dispossession in the lives of women in Palestine and the borderlands of South Texas offer a moving and illuminating look at the amazing cross-border, transnational feminist organizing and community building that has occurred over the last five years (Platt, 2011). While the profiteers and state managers in each of these sites share resources and technologies of surveillance and violence, it is the people in the impacted communities who share forms of survival and resistance to the normalized violence of the securitized regimes in the United States and Israel.

In both contexts, social movements focus on environmental justice and land struggles. The militarization of the US-Mexico border and the building of the mega security wall destroys agriculture and livelihoods for peasants and indigenous communities on both sides of the border. The "apartheid wall" and the endless war in the occupied Palestinian territory have destroyed homes, and uprooted olive trees and orchards—a symbol of livelihood and home for Palestinians. These are shared colonial histories of violence and dispossession; they can be mobilized to create connectivities and resistance to partitions and walls in Palestine and South Texas.

What is hopeful here is the way communities organize in resistance. In the US-Mexico borderlands, there are new political formations and alliances between organizations of day laborers, migrant workers, radical high school, and university students, queer and transgender Mexican migrants. Indigenous peasants and migrants, anarchists (Native anarchists), anti-racist white organizations, neighborhood groups (Barrio defense groups), anti-privatization organizations (prisons and detention centers), prison abolitionist organizations, edu-activists, and mainstream alliance organizations like Mexican consulate, legislatures, and unions (*Somos* AZ) work in solidarity. Women of color do the majority of on-the-ground organizing in most of these groups. This coalition is constituted as it is because activists have conjoined a number of Arizona laws that have decimated ethnic studies (HB 2281 passed May 2010, bans Arizona schools from teaching ethnic studies), cast aside affirmative action (Prop 107, Anti-Affirmative action legislation passed 11/4/10), and SB 1070.[12] All of these laws may look like they target separate communities in separate places, which is precisely how the State and hegemonic power wants to have it function, but clearly political organizing has done the work of connecting the links, showing the connectivity within the different kinds of violence to which communities are subjected.

Similar cross-border and cross-community coalitions are evident in the Israeli and Palestinian feminist struggles against the Israeli occupation, and Indian, Pakistani, and Kashmiri women organizing against all forms of state and communal violence across borders, religions, and national loyalties (Bhutalia, 2002). The insurgent knowledges generated by these forms of activism engender the new political subjectivities and visions of citizenship necessary to confront imperial democracies.

While the anatomies of violence in these borderlands are more overt, imperial democracies militarize all domains of social life, and discipline/imprison not just abandoned and criminalized communities, but *all* state subjects. The border after all is not confined to the edges of the nation—it is not a wall or barrier but a logistical infrastructure with its own architecture of surveillance, documentation, and big data technologies that is constitutive of subjectivity and citizenship in neoliberal times. Perhaps we need to be attentive to ever-*encroaching* spread of the "border" and all the violence that it signifies.

Borders and Bridges: On Solidarity

So, what does it mean to decolonize feminism and to envision ethical transnational feminist futures? How do the frameworks/approaches of decoloniality, anti-capitalism, and feminism inform, enhance, contradict, and mutually influence one another? These are urgent and important political and intellectual questions at this time when the rhetoric of "transnational" has been co-opted on a large scale in neoliberal university settings. Administrators are "transnational" since they travel across the globe in search of profitable partnerships with universities in other countries, and for "international" students who can pay for higher education that is no longer available to working-class and poor students in the United States. Academic curricula are also "transnational" since "study abroad" programs now buttress a normative curriculum that supposedly prepares students to compete in a global market. In the US academy then "transnational" often becomes a place-holder for business-as-usual, marked as "progressive" in the face of a conservative, xenophobic backlash. Globalization and transnational knowledge production becomes the new managerial mantra in neoliberal universities.

In addition, the larger geopolitical landscape poses urgent and significant challenges to those of us committed to an anti-capitalist, anti-imperialist, decolonial feminist praxis. While the old/new, constantly shifting political terrain of Trump and Company suggests the consolidation of a white supremacist, ableist, heteropatriarchal, carceral regime with billionaire state managers, the multiple, visible, and persistent uprisings of communities in resistance is truly extraordinary. Since the inauguration of Donald Trump, there have been hundreds of documented demonstrations, rallies, boycotts, and strikes across the country, in small and large cities and towns. The latest post-George Floyd uprising has brought pandemic and protest together in new and deeply hopeful ways. New solidarities have been forged, and feminists of all stripes and colors continue to be in leadership in most of these mobilizations. What lies ahead is the hard work of deepening and consolidating the nascent solidarities that have emerged through these mobilizations, to imagine a decolonized public polity anchored in a horizontal feminist solidarity across borders and divides.

I have always believed that solidarity is an achievement, not something that can be gifted or and assumed lightly. In these neoliberal times, solidarity has been commodified and repackaged as charity or consumption (buying products made by women in impoverished communities to show solidarity with them). A radical vision of connectivity/solidarity requires building ethical, cross-border feminist solidarities that confront neoliberal racism, and militarized gender regimes globally. This framing points toward strategies of resistance that can fundamentally transform economic and social inequalities from the ground up leading to the creation of new political landscapes and visions of solidarity.

I firmly believe that, like in the BLM, the Black and migrant feminist organizations in Europe, the indigenous, undocumented, and anti-racist feminist organizations in the United States, and Dalit feminists making common cause with Muslims in a Hindu fundamentalist regime in India, it is the everyday experiences of marginalized communities, especially women, queer, and trans Black, Brown, Indigenous, and other minoritized folks who so often sustain the networks of daily life that must inform processes of creating radical, cross-border visions for economic and gender justice. I have always believed that radical scholars are made (not born!) and that we are forged within communities and collectives that teach us how to resist the kind of individualized, neoliberal seductions and erasures that result in colonized mindsets or despair. This to me is the essence of living an insurgent life. I remember Audre Lorde saying to the 1989 graduating class at Oberlin College—"remember that the rumor that you cannot fight city hall is started by city hall." So the way to combat neoliberal and authoritarian cultures and institutions is (1) to always question what appears to be normative within our local sites and connect these spaces to larger geopolitical processes of capitalism, racism, sexism, fascism, etc. (i.e., denaturalize and demystify power); (2) to nurture radical communities of dissent in and outside the institutional spaces we occupy at any given moment (i.e. refuse the isolation that neoliberal, commodified cultures thrive on and to actively cultivate mentors, guides, and teachers who inspire us); (3) to seek for what Angela Davis calls "unlikely coalitions" that encourage us to struggle against injustice of all kinds; and (4) to always remember that we are not the first nor the last to engage in oppositional social movements or the hard work of resistance—we stand on the shoulders of many others who came before us. Histories of decolonization, resistance, and revolution are crucial reminders that radical scholarship and activism are legacies we inherit and must claim.

2

The Refugee Crisis Is a Feminist Issue

Sheila L. Macrine and Silvia Edling

Introduction

Inked in our collective memories are the devastating pictures of thousands of global refugees and migrants seeking asylum, most fleeing war, violence, poverty, racial or religious persecution, rape, gender and sexual orientation discrimination, sex-trafficking, including well-documented human rights violations and torture—all in search of safety and better lives. Indeed, there are a number of serious costs and consequences as a result, even a trend in blood and organ trafficking[1] as payment for parts of the journey. Refugee International[2] notes that many of the most vulnerable consist of women and children fleeing war, hunger, and appalling acts of gender-based violence.[3] Furthermore, the depictions of bodies washing up on shores, the barbed wire make-shift holding-pens, and even children in cages[4] have brought a new layer of oppression as the displaced freedom-seekers get turned away or worse incarcerated due to a rise in Nationalism and Conservatism along with the resultant anti-immigration policies. In other words, at every stage of the refugee journey, from the treacherous journey to reception to durable solutions in host countries, gender is an additive factor in oppression (Pittaway & Bartolome, 2018, p. 2). The gendered experiences of refugee women, girls, and those in the LGBTQ communities have amounted to extreme vulnerability to ongoing and systematic rape, as well as other forms of sexual and gender-based violence.[5]

While this unprecedented global "refugee crisis" has received extensive attention, little has focused on the intersecting dynamics of oppression, discrimination, violence, and the subjugation of women and children (Carastathis et al., 2018). In fact, women continue to be "hidden" in the refugee discourse and most data sets (Pittaway & Bartolomei, 2018). On top of this invisibility, there are often very inadequate policies and ineffective legal-political status allotted to many refugees under the United Nations' Immigration and Refugee Protection Regulations (IRPR). Pittaway and Pittaway (2004) argue that the imposed identity label of "refugee women" and the oppressions subsumed within that label are a key element in the failure of protection of refugee women, perpetuating the discourse that confers impunity and social tolerance on perpetuators of sexual violence (ibid.). To further exacerbate conditions, the Covid-19 pandemic is putting added stressors on host countries' health care systems and social safety-net programs, as well as their political and legal systems. Moreover, the global pandemic has created even more dire conditions in refugee camps and challenges our sense of identity in humankind, pitching us back and forth between a spirit of global solidarity and a competition for resources and survival.[6] These tensions play out in our political and legal responses to the pandemic, manifesting the natural human temptation to tribalism in both international and international dimensions.

While the global "refugee crisis" has received considerable scholarly attention, little of it has focused on the intersecting oppressions of women and children, such as discrimination, subjugation, violence, sexual abuse, slavery, and mutilation, to name a few (ibid.). As a result, this chapter looks at the confluences of these oppressions through the lens of feminist intersectional (racial, ethnic, class, and gender) analyses to examine the impact of the refugee/migrant crises on women, and the resultant anti-immigration policies, and emerging political backlash. Clearly, without deliberate consideration and analyses of gender and racial dynamics within the current political climate, governing bodies are more likely to overlook the situation of refugee women and girls' needs in order to ethically and morally promote gender and racially responsive governance, as well as responsive funding services (LaFerriere & Williams-Baro, 2014). Using an intersectional analysis is critical for analyzing and responding to the cultural, economic, social, civil, legal, and political policies and relations' impacts on women refugees.[7] Accordingly, feminist frameworks along with activist orientations, in both transnational and anti-national contexts, are in solidarity with persons displaced by war, capitalism, and reproductive heteronormativity, or when encountering militarized nation-state borders (Carastathis, Kouritowe, Mahrouse, & Whitley, 2018, p. 1).

There are many links that can be made in relation to the failed responses and the backlash against asylum seekers, specifically facing women refugees and migrants within the rise of conservative, authoritarian regimes such as contemporary neo-nationalism. According to Eirikur Bergmann (2020), neo-nationalism represents the move away from liberal democracy and toward renewed authoritative tendencies on both sides of the Atlantic. He adds that neo-nationalism is characterized by three claims of nativist-populism in protecting the interests of native inhabitants: (1) discursively creating an external threat, (2) pointing to domestic traitors, and (3) positioning themselves as the true defenders of the nation (ibid.).

This neo-nationalist turn raises a number of humanitarian and political concerns: for example, the contentious debate about whether refugees are a burden to host and other countries, or a universal responsibility (Pittaway & Bartolomei, 2018). That said, this chapter highlights the inequities and oppressions faced by women refugees in terms of race, gender, class, and sexual orientation within the current wave of (forced) displacement. While this is a global concern, this chapter examines conditions in two countries and the impact on asylum seeking policies as they take tough steps to limit refugees. First examined is the United States to show the plights of women refugees from Latin America to the United States as a result of the political climate and the other exposes the ramifications of the refugee crisis on women and politics in Sweden from the Global South. Since the end of the Second World War, Sweden has actively worked to promote social justice, and presents it as an interesting European country to highlight in relation to the immigrant crisis. We believe that by exposing the existing (or lack of) research on refugee/migration of women can both make visible and inspire action against the gender-based violence and oppressions of women refugees/migrants. The chapter begins by describing selected dimensions of the refugee situation from a global perspective, the rise of neo-nationalism, the refugee crises as a feminist issue, the impact of refugee crisis in the United States and in Sweden, and some obstacles in relation to the much-needed safeguard-protections for refugee women and children.

Global Background on the Refugee Crisis

The recent media coverage of the "refugee and migrant crisis" has deeply emblazoned the human tragedy of forced displacement of peoples in our thoughts forever. Today there are more refugees and displaced people worldwide than ever before (Edwards, 2016; Pittaway & Bartolome, 2018). Tragically, this same media coverage along with right-wing political rhetoric has whipped up "negative refugee/migrant stereotypes" and resulted in serious polemical debates. Furthermore, the hegemony of the media coverage in Europe and the United States has constructed a largely dehumanized image of refugee/migration, focusing on increasing numbers of migrants and clandestine methods of entry (see for instance Berry et al., 2015; Cohen, 2006). For clarification, with close to 100 million people globally who have been forcibly displaced, the terms "refugee" and "migrant" are frequently used interchangeably in media and public discourse. Yet the conflation of these two terms can have grave consequences for the lives and safety of refugees.[8]

In accordance with Article 1 of the 1951 Geneva convention (modified in 1967 through the New York protocol), a "refugee" is someone who is unable or unwilling to return to their country of origin owing to a well-founded fear of being persecuted for reasons of race, religion, nationality, membership of a particular social group, or political opinion (p. 5). It implies a group of people who have been displaced and forced to escape persecution and/or the horrors of war in order to save their and their families lives; migrants lack this dimension of desperation.[9] The Convention also provides a codification of the rights of refugees at the international level.

The UN's International Organization for Migration (IOM) considers the term "migrant" as an umbrella term, and not defined under international law. The IOM adds that it reflects the common lay-understanding of a person who moves away from his/her place of usual residence, whether within a country or across an international border, temporarily or permanently, and for a variety of reasons. However, they write that the term is inclusive of a number of well-defined legal categories of people, such as migrant workers; persons whose particular types of movements are legally defined, such as smuggled migrants; as well as those whose status or means of movement are not specifically defined under international law, such as international students.[10]

Being a migrant, on the other hand, is described as the desire to change one's environment to a better one regarding, that is, job opportunities, education or simply to reunite with family that live abroad. Contrary to refugees, migrants have a home to return to and as a result do not qualify for international recognition of being in need of protection.[11] Whereas immigrants are "Others" within a contract of citizenship created in-between nations, being a refugee is considered "Other" and forced to give up this contract thus ending up in a no-man's-land, without a sense of belonging or feeling welcome to any nation (Benhabib, 2004), thereby becoming stateless persons.

The refugee crisis of 2015 exploded around the world mainly due to the brutal civil war in Syria and there are nearly 13 million Syrians who have been forced to flee their homes because of war.[12] Adding to this there about 6.2 million people are displaced within Syria itself. The UNHCR reported more than

6.7 million Syrian refugees and asylum seekers during 2018. Children and families have suffered from targeted violence as well as indiscriminate attacks. The communities they had built and enjoyed are destroyed. The actual rate of people fleeing war and persecution has soared globally from 6 per minute in 2005 to 24 per minute in 2015 according to UNRA. Indeed, political, social, and economic instability and conflicts in Syria, Iraq,[13] South Sudan, the Democratic Republic of Congo (DRC), Central African Republic, Myanmar, and South America, to name a few, have caused millions to flee their homes.

While most refugees come from Syria, other countries generating refugees are Afghanistan, South Sudan, Myanmar, and Somalia (in addition, the countries with the highest increase in refugees during 2018[14] were from Syria [343,850], Democratic Republic of Congo [99,500], Afghanistan [57,230], Central African Republic [45,350] and Nigeria [37,850]).[15] Whereas the United States is one of the strongest immigration countries in the world and Sweden is well known for its humanitarian work, the host countries who have accepted most are also economically weak: Turkey, Pakistan, Uganda, and Sudan (see Table 1).

This increasing global tragedy has reached some of the highest levels of refugees in history with approximately 78.5 million men, women, and children escaping protracted wars, persecution, and political turbulence.[16] Take, for example, the Middle-East Syrian refugee crisis, which is now entering its ninth year. The Rohingya refugees, a Muslim ethnic minority group, have fled persecution, fueling a historic migration crisis numbering close to 855,000 in thirty-four overcrowded camps in Bangladesh. Like many refugee camps, they have little access to health care or hygienic facilities.[17] Another example can be seen in the United States where refugees are walking through Mexico from the Northern Triangle of Central America (NTCA), composed of El Salvador, Guatemala, and Honduras refugees, which is now considered one of the most dangerous places on earth (Mathema, 2018). Globally, there are now more refugees and displaced people worldwide than ever before creating a "refugee

Table 1 2018 UN Refugee Agency—countries who host the most refugees.[18]

Host country	Refugees
Turkey	3.68 million
Pakistan	1.40 million
Uganda	1.17 million
Sudan	1.08 million
Germany	1.07 million

crisis" (Edwards, 2016). The UNHCR writes that, as of 2018, 1 in every 113 people on the planet as of 2018 internally displaced in a home country is a refugee, or an asylum seeker. For the first time in UNHCR's history, since the Second World War, the threshold of 100 million-displaced has been surpassed.[19]

Today, the global refugee crisis has reached unprecedented levels across the Western Hemisphere. Out of approximately 79.5 million refugees, around 50 percent are women or girls.[20] While there are also individual differences between countries, the UN Refugee Agency reports that up to 86 percent of Africa's Sudanese, Ethiopia, Eritrean refugees are made up of women with approximately 26 million children under the age of eighteen.[21]

Women and the Refugee/Migration Crisis

In June 1993, the World Conference on Human Rights stated that women all over the world were to be protected by "rights against violation and gender discrimination" and stresses that the term "human rights" is not sufficient in protecting the rights of women (Sullivan, 1994). Recognizing that women belong to a particularly vulnerable group, these changes imply an extra protection for refugee women. However, the way that these rights are recognized and implemented depends on how each host country interprets and puts them into action (SOU, 2004, p. 31; Akram 2013). The UN Convention on the Elimination of All Forms of Discrimination Against Women (CEDAW), adopted by many countries in 1979, was the only international human rights treaty that exclusively focused on the rights of women. CEDAW has been ratified by 186 of 193 UN member states worldwide. Becoming more specific, the UN Security Council adopted a new resolution in April of 2019, which recognized the need for a survivor-centered approach to inform all measures to prevent and address sexual violence in conflict and post-conflict situations.[22]

While, for the most part, men outnumber women as refugees and asylum seekers, their situations are radically different from one another. Indeed, the processes to establish asylum in many countries are usually based on male perspectives and values. Typically, a refugee tends to be viewed as a politically active man who is persecuted due to his political activities (Segenstedt, 2015). The UN's refugee organization (UNHCR) has emphasized the importance to have a gendered perspective in any processes for judging refugee status and it also requires a stronger sensitivity for the needs of refugee women (UNHCR, 2001). This devastating humanitarian situation also puts the most vulnerable (women and young children) at significant risk of being victims of gender-based violence, sexual exploitation, and radicalization, including trafficking. UN National Security Advisor (2017) added, "We have received bone-chilling accounts from those who fled—mainly women, children and the elderly."[23]

In the face of these overwhelming odds, there are examples of refugee-women actively taking responsibility to change in their horrific situations.[24] Yet, their needs are so great and with little adequate support, there are particular procedures that need to be put in place that acknowledge the differences in the violence faced by women refugees as opposed to men refugees. Oppressions faced by women refugees can be categorized into: (1) systematic oppression on a society level, (2) oppression and violence in their homes, (3) vulnerability during the escape and journey, and (4) vulnerability in host countries.[25]

In terms of "systematic oppression" on a society level, many refugee women are escaping the gender-based violence in their home countries, such as "rape, forced impregnation, forced abortion, trafficking, sexual slavery and sex trafficking, forced early marriage, female genital mutilation ('FGM') and, more recently, the intentional spread of sexually transmitted infections" (Akram, 2013, p. 287). The "oppressions and violence" that these women face in their own homes can be linked to the patriarchal social-patterns that deem women as "low-status" rendering them exclusively dependent on their male relatives or husbands. Of note, during 2012, approximately half of the gender-based murders of refugee women were perpetrated by intimate family members or husbands.[26] In addition, the rise in armed conflicts is accompanied by gender-based violence, that is, the rape of women and girls used in war for ethnic-cleansing. For example, in the Bosnian War in the 1990s between 20,000 and 50,000 women were raped for such strategic purposes (Akram, 2013).

While women face "vulnerability during escape and journey," then again in refugee camps where many unaccompanied women often lack access to self-identification containing identity, marriage, family names, and so forth. Many of these documents are withheld or deliberately hidden by their male relatives and husbands. Without identification papers, the process of asylum becomes even more difficult, and refugee women tend to be labelled as economic-migrants or seen as participants in trafficking schemes that go under different laws and regulations. Besides identification documents, refugee women often lack money which makes it difficult to pay smugglers. Consequently, women, young girls, and LGBTQ persons are forced to pay for their escape through sex, called "survival sex."[27] They are frequently sold off to trafficking groups and, as a result, enter a life in involuntary prostitution. For instance, in Jordanian many hundred women have been sold in the form of temporal marriage. Unaccompanied girls tend to disappear during the asylum process. Over 1.2 million children worldwide are being sexually exploited in trafficking organizations—all of these are not refugees but refugees are particularly vulnerable to these kinds of exploitations. In fact, many young male refugees pretend to be gay or to have converted to Christianity to help strengthen their case for asylum. Because of women's low status and the traumas from wars—even accompanied refugee women tend to experience violence from their husbands during the escape and stay in camps (ibid.).

Finally, refugee women's "vulnerability in host countries" comes from a lack of knowledge about host country situations, and as a result they receive inadequate support without competent representation and counselors during the refugee process. Many refugee women have historical negative interactions with men, in general and thus less inclined to talk to male interpreters and counsellors. While in host countries, many unaccompanied women and girls are forced to take responsibility for both the home and obtaining money, making it difficult to learn new cultures and languages—creating more isolation and marginalization. Furthermore, unaccompanied women and girls tend to live in low-standard housing in urban areas making them vulnerable to slave labor and at the mercy of slum-landlords. Refugee women also often lack access to social services like education, health care, and so forth. That said, every step of a woman refugee's journey becomes a heightened-risk, demonstrating an alarming need for society to act on a humanitarian level to collectively prevent the threat of assault, sexual abuse, harassment, and trafficking, among others (ibid.).

Accordingly, the humanitarian disaster of the current refugee crisis has become weaponized as political-weaponry tool in many countries, and at issue is the omission of the feminist perspective.[28] The construction of refugees/migrants as "Other" or as cultural and security threats, particularly in the case of Muslim and women refugees, not only assists in their dehumanization, but also legitimizes actions taken against them through the perpetuation of a particular discourses (Sajjad, 2018). Furthermore, such dynamics highlight the long-standing struggles of Western countries to articulate its identity within the economic, demographic, and cultural anxieties produced by the dynamics of neoliberal globalization (ibid.). Pocock and Chan (2018) add that there are the numerous risks and threats that refugees face with growing anti-refugee and anti-migrant sentiment, discrimination, and violence, which have profound implications for refugees' social welfare and health care entitlements as they migrate to and settle in new host communities. The UNHCR is the largest organization with mandated responsibility, position, and capability to shape discourse and influence policy to the protection of refugees/migrants and finding solutions for their plight, position, and capability to shape discourse and influence policy (Shinn, 2017).

Political Backlash: The Rise of Neo-Nationalism and Post-Democracy

Exacerbating the political backlash against refugees has been the rise in neo-nationalism with its protectionist attitudes that reject liberal democracy in favor of authoritarian tendencies, while conflating democratic ideology with a populist discourse. For example, Cas Mudde has posited that the term "nativism" is xenophobic nationalism that gives exclusive priority to the native group (nation) and treating non-native elements as a threat to the nation-state (Cas Mudde, 2007, p. 13). Furthermore, Alexander Svitych describes *neo-nationalism* (or *populist nationalism*) as the ideology articulated by political parties often described as radical, populist, or nativist.[29] This turn toward right-wing nativism and nationalism has created additive oppressions against refugees in general, and more specifically women refugees.

Parallel with neo-nationalism Ludwig (2018) draws on Crouch's (2004) book, *Post-democracy* to describe how modern democracies present a façade of democracy that is often driven by capitalist interests. Post-democracies are characterized by a focus on male values, as well as a division between the private and public sphere. As such, post-democracies focus on feigning democratic procedures, while ignoring processes and conditions, including aspects of power and privilege, that allow for the possibilities for democratic participation and influence. With this definition at hand, post-democracies are easily deepened by neo-nationalism and hence radical-right movements. In stable democracies all around the world, the radical-right's conservative attitudes and values have increased significantly the last two decades. As a result, many of those living in liberal democracies are choosing to vote for political candidates and parties that do not promote equal conditions, but rather stimulate xenophobia, racism, gender discrimination, authoritarianism, protectionism, and ethno-nationalism.

This phenomenon has gained interest among researchers and one central explanation of the *ethnic competition thesis* is directly linked to issues concerning migration and refugees (Rydgren, 2007) creating an anti-immigration hegemony. It is by far the primary raison d'etre for voters supporting radical-right ideologies, candidates, and groups (Lubbers et al., 2002; Arzheimer, 2018). Those who turn to radical-right wing parties hold that immigrants and refugees are in competition for limited resources like housing, benefits from the state, and labor market. As a result, certain groups of people (many of them lower educated males) who live near immigrants feel threatened by them and are most likely to vote for radical-right parties (Lubbers et al., 2002; Van der Brug et al., 2005).

The wave of refugees has not been as strong since the Second World War, the rhetoric of radical-right, promoting ethno-nationalism through a false sense of nostalgia and belonging, claims that the elites in liberal democracies inevitably overlook the interests of the native people in favor of cherishing multiculturalism/internationalism (Rydgren, 2018). Some of the anti-immigration arguments stress: (a) refugees//immigrants are competing of meagre resources, (b) welfare benefits go to refugees and immigrants rather than natives, (c) immigrants/refugees threaten ethno-national identities, (d) immigrants/refugees generate various forms of social turbulence like criminality, and (e) particularly Muslim immigrants/refugees are seen as a threat to liberal democracy. Especially (c) and (d) have been successful arguments for the right wing (Elgenius & Rydgren, 2018). A prime example of this move towards neo-nativism is Hungary's' illiberal Democracy move.

Moreover, it is important to recognize the rise of the far-right values that tap into the structural oppression of women that many refugee women faced in their home countries. Often the far-right support a hyper-masculinity that favors violence and maintains hierarchical relationships between men and women, positioning women as subordinated to men (Kinnvall, 2016; Korolczuk & Graff, 2018). At the same time, Muslim refugees are perceived as homogenous cultural groups, which renders them a threat to liberal support systems (Kuby, 2015). The rise of the far-right politics and policies creates a limbo for refugee women in-between world of an acceptance and enhancement of a systematic oppression of women, both considered a threat to liberal values seemingly reflective of aggressive (Muslim) cultures.

The 2018 UN Security Council has reported on the excessive violence and serious violations of human rights, including indiscriminate firing of weapons, the use of landmines against civilians, and sexual violence.[30] The hostile political climate, public debates, and discourses on migration-tightening border[31] regimes, encompassing the deterritorialization of border control, the fortification of nation-state borders, and the domestication of borders (Filippi, 2018). Finally, given the number of refugees worldwide has reached the highest levels since the Second World War,[32] the plight of refugee women demands attention to the ongoing gender-based violence, as well as consideration of the additive oppressions created by the increase of far-right politics. In the following, we shed light on how the situations for women refugees in the United States and Sweden have handled these situations.

A Tale of Two Countries: The United States and Sweden

Here, we discuss two different responses to the refugee crises, one in the United States and one in Sweden. We examine the plight, consequences, and support or lack thereof for refugee women, particularly in light of the dramatic shifts in policies as a result of Trump's conservative values and the rise of far-right politics in Europe. The situation in the United States is interesting because it has been one of the leading immigration host countries in the world (rooted in its Constitution), and played a crucial role as an advocator for and protector of democratic values after the Second World War. Sweden, a smaller European country, has made a commitment to protect and empower women and girls, and is at the forefront in efforts to advocate for refugee women's and girls' rights, strengthen gender equality, and combat sexual and gender-based violence.[33]

Refugee Women and the United States

During the past five years, the United States has experienced the election of an autocratic president, which ushered in an unprecedented onslaught of refugees seeking asylum. Millions of Latin Americans are being displaced as they walk to the United States and neighboring countries. For example, by the end of 2019, the total number of Venezuelan migrants and refugees was estimated at 5.5 million, according to the UNHCR. Trump's protectionist rhetoric and his push for building border-walls with Mexico follow in the footsteps of authoritarian leaders throughout history where walls have been used for centuries to spread fear, closed-mindedness, and isolationism.[34] The US-Mexico border wall is aimed at preventing asylum seekers and to apprehend refugees/migrants from El Salvador, Guatemala, and Honduras (known as the Northern Triangle of Central America). At the same time, many of the refugees and migrants from the Northern Triangle are turning themselves in to authorities to apply for asylum rather than attempting to cross illegally.[35]

All humans deserve to be treated with dignity and respect, as well as the basic human rights of refugees/migrants guaranteed, yet the refugee crisis has created a severe political backlash that threatens these protections. Blurring terms ("refugee" and "migrant") have also contributed to the diverting attention to the legal protections for refugees as asylum seekers who need protections more than ever before.[36] In the name of justice, it is imperative to provide appropriate legal responses to refugees' particular situations, such as gender, points of entry, and host countries. Indeed, the politics of labelling, criminalization, and the securitization of refugees undermines the protective frameworks for the globally displaced (Sajjad, 2018). Sadly, the refugee crisis has fermented fear; Trump even called Latin American refugees *Murderers, Rapists, and Bad Hombres*.[37] Similarly, in Europe political and media rhetoric has whipped up fear of terrorists' infiltration. These hyperbolic racist and sexist responses have produced a vacuum nurturing the rise of hardline stances including "nationalist fixes" and calls for "genetic purity" resulting in protectionists policies. In terms of securitization, Beck posits three prominent arguments: (1) the link between migration and terrorism, (2) the allegation that immigrants drain a nation's resources, and (3) the claim that immigration threatens a society's cultural achievements and genetic purity.[38]

While the declared global "refugee crisis" has received considerable scholarly attention, little of it has focused on the intersecting dynamics of oppression, discrimination, violence, and subjugation of women and the LGBTQ community. The issue at hand is that border and forced migration studies proliferate, but the problem noted by feminist theorists is the absence of intersectional analyses that examine the multiple layers of oppressions faced by women refugees (Carastathis et al., 2018).

To make a case for his border wall, Trump has been known to discuss the violence that refugee and migrant women and children face on the journeys. Yet, paradoxically, Trump's motivation in telling these stories is not to provoke empathy for them, but to drive home the message that these women should have never left home in the first place.[39] In other words, Trump is selling his border wall on the backs of oppressed women but he never addresses the violence that forces these women to flee. In a recent UN report, 85 percent of the 160 Central American women interviewed lived in neighborhoods controlled by armed groups and gangs. Many reported barricading themselves and their children in their homes—choosing to stay home from school and work in order to avoid gunfights.[40]

The violence, poverty, and political instability in the Northern Triangle make women and children particularly vulnerable. While the media has focused on the great numbers of unaccompanied minors to the US border in startling numbers in 2014, little attention has focused on the gendered experiences of women and girls forced to leave the region. These savagery of their conditions and personal insecurity directly contribute to women's decisions to seek asylum and migrate. Sadly, a 2018 study by OXFAM reported that male violence against women has been historically normalized in Latin America and persists in their daily lives. Compounding these conditions are the traditional social norms and legal precedents that routinely allow gender-based crimes to go unpunished with some of the highest femicide rates in the world.[41] While these figures are frequently attributed to general or domestic violence and organized crime, femicide is perpetuated by deep-rooted social and systematic factors such as a widespread *machismo* culture that favors: men over women, low degrees of institutional capacity due to corruption, and high degrees of impunity—an exemption from punishment and the failure for perpetrators to be brought to justice (Pérez Arguello, & Couch, 2018).

Such deplorable conditions force many desperate women and children to flee with only the clothes they had on. And their children are out of school, making them vulnerable to violence and health issues from unstable and unhygienic living conditions. Needless to say, women and girls also face extreme hardships on the journey northward with disproportionately high rates of sexual violence, and being victimized at the hands of smugglers (*coyotes*), gangs, cartels, and police. Clearly, more attention needs to be paid to the violence, gender inequality, and oppression of female refugees/migrants. In other words, we need international long-term policies that can put safeguards into place to protect women and girls, as well as boys and men. If the international community ignores and overlooks this crisis, then they are complicit in perpetuating femicide, hindering development, providing safety for women and girls, and for destabilizing the regions (ibid.).

Refugee Women: The Increase of Conservatism in Sweden

Swedish migration policies and legislation are based on human rights, its cornerstone, as well as international agreements that it has signed. Sweden has a commitment to asylum seekers as protecting the right of fleeing people to seek refuge/asylum. For example, in 2015, the Syrian war created the highest number of refugees ever who sought asylum in Sweden (160, 000), a significant number when compared to the 30,000 in 2000 and 22,000 in 2019. Responding, a number of harsh political decisions to make it much more difficult to travel to Sweden as a refugee have led to a drastic decrease of asylum seekers.[42] On the other hand, Sweden overall tend to accept refugees specifically chosen by UN's refugee organization UNHCR's (kvotflyktingar) *Resettlement* policy in Europe.[43] In terms of gender disparities, generally more men than women applied for asylum in Sweden during the first two decades of this century; this was particularly evident during 2015 when only 30 percent of women applied. Since 2016, the gender divisions have remained relatively stable with 40 per cent women and 60 percent men. Most refugees come from Syria (2649) followed by Iran (1090), Iraq (1054), Uzbekistan(1052), and Georgia (975).[44]

Resultantly, in a growing number of Nordic countries, there is a turn toward neo-nationalism fueled by ideals of radical right-wing parties. Their ideologies are basically founded on ideas of nationalism, anti-immigration, and the superiority of assimilation over integration. The political framework of nationalism promotes strong family values grounded in conservatism, religion, and patriarchal systems with commitments to law and order (Elgenius & Rydgren, 2018). Implicitly, there is a conviction that gender roles need to be separated in a hierarchical fashion where men are to rule in the public, and women take responsibility for private matters like the home and family (Norocel, 2013). In Sweden, this has led to a wave of anti-genderism linked to opposition to gender studies described as something outside the field of serious science and viewed as a phenomenon that threatens traditional values (Francia, in this volume). While promoted a so-called gender-equality stance, it has "served as a means to silencing the violence (of men) occurring within Swedish families, the purchase of sex by Swedish men, and the generally claimed but rarely assumed gender equality practice coupled with a tacit reinforcement of patriarchy by Swedish men" (Norocel, 2013, p. 141).

A little more than three decades ago, Sweden's the far-right party *the Sweden Party* (Sverigepartiet) was established in 1986, and it regrouped as the *Sweden Democracy* (Sverigedemokraterna) in 1988. The *Sweden Democracy* party was considered a hybrid between *Keep Sweden Swedish* (Bevara Sverige svenskt), an explicit racist group, and the *Progress Party* (Framstegspartiet) (Jungar & Jupskås, 2014). During the 2002 election, the Sweden Democrats got only 1.4 percent of the votes probably due to their racist positions and façade. Over the years the *Sweden Democracy* party has actively struggled to polish its frontage replacing their racist-rhetoric with ethno-nationalism and ethnic democracy that stressed ethnic purity for a clean country. This repackaging has led to an increase in support, and during the 2014 election the *Sweden Democracy* party jumped to 15–20 percent of the votes (Elgenius & Rydgren, 2018). Central to Sweden Democracy's platform is the *ethnic competition thesis* in which the influx of immigrants and refugees leads to the destruction of Sweden's cultural and genetic identity as a nation, and competition for scarce resources, and the overtake the newly marginalized native Swedes (Gasslander, 2015).

In a very short time, the radical far-right party has drastically increased its presence in Sweden where they have fought and gained positions as leaders of the country. In a country considered one of the leaders in gender equity, the right-wing political parties are actively working against multiculturalism and the acceptance of traditional family values based on a hierarchical relationships between men and women in ways that risk harming not only refugee women in Sweden but women in general, who all strive for equal treatment.

Conclusion

At issue is the plight of refugee women and the absence of intersectional analyses that warn about the inextricably linked among racial, gendered, ethnic, sexual preference, and class relations as an entry point for future interrogations. While much work is needed, this chapter highlighted how the women refugees have been exploited, re-constructed, ignored and concerns for the lack of health and welfare safeguards that need to be contested. Utilizing intersectionality helps to expose the gendered, raced, and ethnic representations that have been powerfully written-upon, and experienced within the bodies of refugee women. It also challenges the insidious hegemonic discourses and right-wing politics that have created and contributed to the additive oppressions faced by women refugees in transnational diasporic spaces. In other words, a critical intersectional theory asserts that people are often disadvantaged by multiple sources of oppression: their race, class, gender identity, ethnicity, sexual orientation, religion, and other identity markers. Intersectionality also recognizes that identity markers (e.g., "female, brown, black, disabled") do not exist independently of each other, and that each informs the others, often creating a complex convergence of oppressions.

In sum, this chapter presented an integrative review of the feminist work in refugee/migration studies as it engaged with intersectionality as a critical analytic. Intersectionality principles were applied to examine the inequalities and oppressions of women in general, and more specifically women refugees and those in the LGBTQ populations. It also takes into account people's overlapping identities and experiences in order to understand the complexities and prejudices they face. Understanding intersectionality is essential to combatting these interwoven prejudices people face, and more specifically refugee women and children in their daily lives.

Clearly, the international community of host and asylum countries have seriously failed to implement protections and policies to address needs of women and girls, as well as to promote gender equality resulting in serious human rights abuses. At the same time, the enormous potential and social capital that women and girls can bring to achieving such solutions have been squandered. The UN member states, led by the UN Refugee Agency (UNHCR), have created a global compact on refugees to examine the reasons for this failure, and its impacts for women and girls, men and boys, youth, families and communities, in host countries and countries of asylum. It is both a humanitarian and a political issue, and includes the contentious debates about whether refugees are a burden in host and other countries, or a universal responsibility. More is needed!

We conclude that forced migration/refugee and displacement today are a crisis of epic proportions and creates additive oppressions of women. In addition, our analysis suggests that the negative racial and gender environment, lack of institutional support, and race and gender stereo-typing have been shown to have more harmful and harsher effects on women and children. As a result, the "refugee/migrant crisis" has accelerated conditions of oppression for women and children, and is inextricably rooted in the rise of neo-nationalism, globalized capitalism, histories of colonialism, and contemporary imperialism. The prescient words of Paulo Freire (1978) still ring true today, *"The true focus of revolutionary change is never merely the oppressive situations which we seek to escape, but that piece of the oppressor which is planted deep within each of us, and which knows only the oppressors' tactics, the oppressors' relationships."* We need to rise up and advocate for the protection of women and girl refugees/migrants.

In addition, our analyses suggest that the negative racial and gender environments, lack of institutional support, and race and gender stereo-typing, that we believe to manifestly xenophobic, have been shown to have harmful and harsher effects on women and children. As a result, the "refugee/migrant crisis" which are products of war and state violence are inextricably rooted in authoritarianism, globalized neoliberal capitalism, histories of colonialism, and contemporary imperialism. The time has come to not only recognize the plight of women refugees but also demand that host countries and refugee camps, who are obliged to protect refugees within their territory, abide by the IRPR legal protection to all refugees. These remarkably strong women and girls are anything but victims; therefore, we need to raise awareness about the inequalities and structural problems that continue to oppress women. We need to stand with these women and girls, to be heard and demand the right for all people to live with dignity and respect.

We conclude the need to stand in solidarity with all of our sisters, and anyone who can advocate for the rights and protections for women refugees worldwide in their pursuit for asylum, freedom, liberty, and human rights. One clear pattern emerges from this examination of the women refugee/migrant crises, and that is the lack of safeguards to protect women and girls from perpetrators of violence at all phases of their journey to hold the perpetrators accountable, legal and institutional reforms and improvements in host countries. Viewing the female refugee/migrant crisis through a gendered perspective helps to illuminate how various legal protections need to be put in place, as well as the need to eliminate anti-gendered cultural norms that disproportionately affect specific groups, in particular women and girls.[45] A Herculean task to say the least!

3

How the Neoliberal Ultraconservative Alliance in Brazil Threatens Women's Lives: Learning to Fight and Survive

Inny Accioly

Introduction

Neoliberal global trends in education reforms, including standardized curriculum and marketization of public education, restrict and reduce working-class education to the rudimentary skills aimed at adapting workers to the new demands of late capitalism. In Brazil, this dynamic has also resulted in severe exploitation of labor and the natural ecosystems. Promoting such reform agendas weakens environmental protections and removes the remaining public safety nets and labor rights. While these concerns have wide-reaching impacts, they disproportionately impact rural communities, in particular, peasant and indigenous women.

This chapter argues that the latest stage of capitalism that links neoliberalism, authoritarianism, and conservatism has had significant negative effects on women's rights. It further explicates how the relationship between neoliberalism and conservatism has negatively impacted educational policies and curricular reforms in basic education in Brazil. The chapter confronts approaches to neoliberalism, imperialism, racism, sexism, and more specifically the hyper-exploitation of women of color, peasant women, and indigenous women in Brazil.

The historical importance of supporting the rights of women of color, peasant women, and indigenous women's struggles is highlighted in the defense of democracy, human right to life, and the possibilities for emancipatory movements. Finally, the chapter demonstrates the positive impact on children and youth when exposed to women's struggles and social movements as part of the school curriculum.

The Latest Stage of Neoliberalism in Brazil and Its Impacts on Women

In Brazil, thirteen years of a progressive policy cycle enacted by the Workers Party (*Partido dos Trabalhadores*—PT)—with income-redistribution and affirmative policies combating racism and intolerance—was dashed by a parliamentary coup, in 2016.

The coup against President Dilma Rousseff (affiliated to PT) resulted in the consolidation of the efforts to carry out aggressive neoliberal reforms. It is not that PT was averse to neoliberalism, but the option to conduct politics of coalition that both satisfied demands of businessmen and workers limited the scope of most neoliberal reforms.[1]

The turning point began in 2013. What started as a financial crisis and discontentment with the bus fares opened the door to a cycle of protests and demonstrations across the country. However, the street-rioting was conducted by a convergence of very diverse political sectors with a leading role of the Right.[2]

Historically, different right-wing cycles emerged in Brazil.[3] For example, from 1964 to 1985 the cycle of Dictatorial Right was characterized by an authoritarian military dictatorship with conservative forces that stifled freedom of speech and violently suppressed opposition.

The eventual movement for re-democratization coincided with the emergence of a new cycle—associated with the Neoliberal Right led by the structural adjustment and the Washington Consensus—that appeared and extended from 1985 to the present. This Neoliberal Right approach combines some respect for institutional frameworks (but not in cases when dealing with lower classes and Black communities), with heavy-handed security policies.

Today, the Neoliberal Right, updated with a very conservative or post-political approaches, has led to the emergence of a Radical Authoritarian Right that maintains ambiguous relationship with neoliberalism, while proposing a return to hierarchical values and traditional binarisms.[4] These conservative and authoritarian values have never disappeared in this country which historically employed the major number of African slaves and that was the last to abolish slavery. Although the slaveholder's mentality did not disappear during the progressive cycle, racists and elitists were uncomfortable in expressing their hatred toward people of color or LGBTQ.[5]

The victory in 2018 of President Jair Bolsonaro, a far-right congressman and former military officer, demonstrated a call to restore traditional moral values and the deposed hierarchies. A new political option emerged: a populism of the extreme right with generalized anti-progressive reaction and fascist features. Here, the appeal to a classical/authoritarian capitalist order converges with the call to the traditional patriarchal order.

This new Radical Authoritarian Right proclaims a defense of the traditional family against the state, arguing that the prior progressive cycle of policies demolished the Christian morality. Some of them criticize human rights policies, express aversion to social movements, or prosecute teachers for allegedly indoctrinating students. Some put forward the defense of military dictatorship and the justification of torture.

Bolsonaro's government is an expression of the affinities between the Neoliberal Right and the Authoritarian Radical Right. Almost all ministries and many government agencies are now run by armed military officials.[6]

The further liberalization and deregulation of labor and environmental protection coupled with anti-indigenous, anti-human rights, and anti-environmentalist rhetoric lead to the intensification of extractivism in all its modes (agribusiness, mining, fracking, mega-dams, among others).

While President Bolsonaro stimulates neoliberal free-market to advance on communities' lands, traditional territories, water, soil, and forests, the transnational extractive industries expand their business implementing a neo-colonial system that provokes environmental and social deterioration.

This reinforces the principle that capitalism, in order to continuously advance, must reenact the elements of what Marx called "the primitive accumulation," the separation of the producer from the means of production. The barbarism of primitive accumulation has always been part of the daily life of the peripheries of capitalism where peasant and traditional communities are dispossessed from land in the name of development.[7]

In these regions, the state apparatus is largely used in defense of capital accumulation since territories are militarized to safeguard the capitalist' interests against people. This directs Brazil to be at the top of world rankings for murders of human rights and environmental activists.[8]

Extractivism is the face of the latest stage of capitalism in the peripheral territories and countries. It is deeply connected to the financialized global economy since "financialization concerns both finance and production, making it indissociable from contemporary 'actually existing' capitalism."[9]

Therefore, extractivism is based on the international division of labor that assigns some countries the role of exporters of cheap raw materials while the importers profit developing new technologies. Its roots are on the structural racism (remaining from colonial times) that manifests itself in the dispossession of ancestral territories, the denial of cultural practices and traditional ways of caring for the environment.

The radicalization of the international division of labor in the twenty-first century deepens the situation of dependency in Latin American countries and directly impacts the sexual division of labor. According to Federici, the appropriation of women's bodies and their reproductive capacity was fundamental to the control of labor force and the further development of capitalism.[10]

During the colonial period, the wealth transfer was made from the colony to the metropolis by means of taxes, land exploitation, and pillaging of metals and other riches. The indigenous and the Afro-descendant women bodies were also considered as wealth to be looted and exploited.

The first document written by the Portuguese colonizers about Brazil describes in details the body and genitals of native women. Colonizers considered their naked bodies as an invitation to sexual abuse and exploitation.

The African slave women, in addition to working hard in agriculture, were exploited in the colonizers' domestic spaces being doubly sexually abused: either by doing the caring labor of house and children or by having forced sexual relations. Besides that, they usually had to find time to take care of their own children and living places.[11]

In the twenty-first century, extractivism reinforces neo-colonialism and economic dependency of Latin American countries by mechanisms of "unequal exchange." While the exporters of raw materials take the social and environmental damages selling low value-added goods, the central economies exercise monopoly of technologies and knowledge.[12] This exposes Latin American countries to recurring economic crisis that acts as means of justifying austerity measures (privatizations and lower public investments on social policies) and increased public debt. Here, state plays an important role on feeding the growth of interest-bearing capital.

> The parasitical traits of interest-bearing capital intuited by Marx and later emphasized by Lenin permeate the operations of all money, commercial, and industrial capital alike. As one leaves the inner circle of finance capital, the pre-eminence of banks and funds over firms begins to assert itself. [...] When one moves to the periphery of the world system analyzed in its dimension of financial globalization, notably to the US's 'backyard' in Latin America, the weight of financial capital is striking, as inflowing financial investment interfaces and merges with domestic capital accumulation, consolidating oligopolies based on the predation of natural resource endowments in agribusiness and mining.[13]

Thus, it is not just the hoarding of industrial profits that feeds the growth of interest-bearing capital. The power of banks and funds is also based on their capacity to centralize money coming from land rent and workers' savings.[14] This leads to a situation in which workers pension funds from the central capitalism fuel deforestation and social degradation in peripheral countries.

> It may come as a shock to Harvard students, faculty, and alumni, as well as the millions of educators and others in the United States whose pensions are managed by TIAA, to learn that these two institutions are deeply and directly invested in this destructive expansion of agribusiness. Over the past twelve years, TIAA and Harvard University have collectively spent over $1 billion on Brazilian farmland, making them two of the largest owners of farmland in the Cerrado.[15]

Extractive industries induce violent displacement and resettlement of families, while privatize place and natural resources—which characterizes what has been denounced as "land grab" (Accioly, 2018).[16] The increase of agrarian conflicts goes *part and parcel* with repression of protests, criminalization, and murder of community leaders, especially women.

According to the peasant women marching in the Marcha das Margaridas 2019:[17]

> Sexist violence is one of the main instruments of the neoliberal offensive, for which the control of the territories and the women's bodies are central elements, and whose agenda is based on a moral that seeks to recover the paradigms of the patriarchal family and the subservient woman, which is expressed in violence against women.[18]

In contexts of mining, oil exploration, and hydroelectric installation, there is a "masculinization" of the territories due to the migration (nationally and internationally) of men to work in these sectors. In addition to the population increase that burdens public health and education services, community spaces and daily life are reconfigured around the desires and values of a hegemonic masculinity.

The colonial mentality is still propagating a hyper sexualized image of Brazilian women, who (in the patriarchal imagination) mix the "seductive" characteristics of indigenous women with the "lovingness" and the broad hips of African women.[19] These qualities make Brazilian women valuable commodities, including in the advertisements of the Brazilian State Agency of Tourism Promotion in the 1970s and 1980s.[20]

Thus, reports of increased violence against women, sexual exploitation of girls, and sex trafficking are frequent in the areas where extractive industries are situated.[21]

Women's vulnerability increases when their communities are displaced. Because resettlement policies do not have a gendered approach that allows women to be included as autonomous subjects, it leaves them subjected to customary patriarchal norms.[22] For women, land tenure is a means of emancipation as it enables income generation through agricultural activities. Women's economic independence enables them to participate in decision-making spaces. Thus, when losing the land property, they become more subject to unpaid, low-wage work, or prostitution.[23]

The contamination of land, air, and water by extractive industries drastically affects biodiversity and provokes loss of food sovereignty. This is particularly serious for women because they are usually responsible for food production for self-consumption as they play a fundamental role in the care of native seeds.

The privatization of water—whether due to the limitation of access or the contamination of available sources—generates an overload in women unpaid-labor, making them travel longer distances to access water.[24] In most cases, women are responsible for taking care of house, children, the ill family members, and often their partners.

It should be highlighted that extractivism in Brazil was intensifying during the progressive cycle of policies and that the PT government was also conniving with the repression of protests. However, the latest stage of neoliberalism inaugurated by the neoliberal ultraconservative alliance represents the unlimited advance of capital over the social rights, making women more vulnerable—especially indigenous, Afro-descendants, and rural women workers.

Neoliberal and Conservative Reforms and Its Impacts on Gender and Sexuality

Since the parliamentary coup in 2016, it seems that the neoliberal and the conservative agendas are increasingly joined in expanding the capital control over land, labor, and the people's customs. The broad range of dispossession is intensifying due to a roll of neoliberal reforms that are increasing unemployment, impoverishment, and social vulnerability.

In 2016, a constitutional amendment (Constitutional Amendment 95) put strict limits on public expenses aiming to reduce investments in social policies, which is drastically affecting the budget for public universities.

The cuts to funding are coordinated by the Bolsonaro's Minister of Education with false denouncements against professors.[25] False accusations are largely used as part of the post-truth politics aimed at gaining popular support for privatizing reforms.

The neoliberal reform package includes the labor legislation reform (enacted in 2017), the high school reform (enacted in 2017), the pension system reform (enacted in 2019), the public administration reform (that can be voted in 2020 by parliamentarians aiming to enable the dismissal of public servants), among others.

The high school reform deeply transforms the Brazilian high school system to enable credit-based modular curriculum, choice-based credit system, competence-based curriculum defined in the new Common National Curriculum Base (*Base Nacional Comum Curricular—BNCC*) and the implementation of distance learning. Since this legislation mandates increased instructional hours in the school year and the public school systems are underfunded, it opens the doors for expanding the private education market.

The conservative agenda has advanced concurrently with neoliberal reforms. As soon as Bolsonaro took over presidency in 2019, he remodeled the Ministry of Education in order to extinguish The Secretariat for Continuing Education, Literacy, Diversity and Inclusion (created in 2004 by the PT government) whose function was to guarantee that educational policies took into account issues of race, ethnicity, gender, and disabilities. This Secretariat had an important role in the program "Brazil Without Homophobia" launched in 2004 to combat violence and discrimination against the LGBTQ population.

While he was still a deputy, Bolsonaro repeatedly attacked the project "School without Homophobia" (elaborated by the Ministry of Education in 2011) which included the development of informational materials to be distributed in public schools. The materials were never distributed due to Bolsonaro and his supporters' reactions, who pejoratively called it as "gay kit."[26]

At least since 2014, conservative parliamentarians had been gaining strength in educational debates. They managed to direct the discussions about the 2014–24 National Plan for Education in a way that all mentions of gender and sexuality have been excluded from the text.

The previous education plan enacted in 2001—the 2001–10 National Plan for Education—mentioned that the government would consolidate the Textbook Evaluation Program, also establishing among its criteria the appropriate approach to gender and ethnicity issues and eliminating textbooks that reproduce stereotypes about the role of women, Blacks, and indigenous. The

2001 legislation also mandated the inclusion of themes such as sexual education in the curricular guidelines for teacher education.

Because of conservatives' pressures, the Common National Curriculum Base (enacted in 2018) also does not mention gender or sexuality. BNCC represents in Brazil the global trend to standardize school curriculum. As mentioned before, the instructional hours in the school year of high school must be increased. The exclusion of sexual education and the debate on gender issues does not contribute to reducing the dropout rates due to early pregnancy or sexual orientation discrimination.

Some conservative parliamentarians support the movement "School without Party" (*Escola Sem Partido*) which combats what they consider ideological indoctrination, gender ideology, and cultural Marxism within schools. The movement aims to criminalize teachers by encouraging parents and students to record classes and denounce their work.[27]

The conservatives argue that gender identity and behavior should be based on biological sex. Thus, they repudiate what they call "gender ideology" which allegedly states that gender identity is a social construct and therefore can be a personal choice. One of the leaders in Bolsonaro government combating the "gender ideology" is the Evangelical pastor Damares Alves, who took over the newly created Ministry of Women, Family and Human Rights. During the inauguration speech in 2019, she stated that "we are in a new era in Brazil" where "boys wear blue and girls wear pink" and "girls will be princesses and boys will be princes."[28]

When combating the "gender ideology," the government reaffirms the gender roles designated in a patriarchal society where men are educated to dominate while women are told to be demure and obedient. The consequences are the increased rates of violence against women and feminicides, which express misogynistic hatred and cultural contempt for women. In 2017, 4,936 women were murdered in Brazil, an average of thirteen women murdered per day.[29]

> Femicide, therefore, is part of the mechanisms of perpetuation of male domination, being deeply rooted in society and culture. Expressions of this rooting are the identification of men with the murderers' motivations, the ways in which the press covers the crimes and the ways in which the justice and the security systems deal with these crimes. The fact that women often deny the existence of the problem is attributed to the repression or denial produced by the traumatic experience of sexist terrorism, in addition to gender socialization, in which the gender ideology (here ideology is considered in its negative aspect) is used to naturalize the differences between the sexes and impose these standards and roles as if they were natural or constituent of human nature.[30]

These data reinforce how femicide is a crime related to power and domination that affects the most vulnerable groups and it is more frequent in places where there is impunity.[31]

Women in rural areas frequently are exposed to symbolic and material violence as their economic contributions to society are disregarded. In general, their activities are classified as a "helping hand" or a "complement" to men work. This sexist perspective limits women's access to income and, therefore, subjugate them to male control and also exposes them to physical and psychological violence. Indeed, women living in remote regions are far more vulnerable to sexist violence since they lack access to health care and social policies, such as contraception and HIV/AIDS prevention programs.

The current scenario of neoliberal and conservative reforms exacerbates these problems. In February 2020, the Ministry of Family, Women and Human Rights launched the National Campaign for Prevention of Adolescent Pregnancy which promoted sexual abstinence as a contraceptive method. The campaign never mentions the use of condoms or any other contraceptive method despite of the fact that Brazil is facing an explosion of HIV/AIDS among the youth. According to the United Nations, between 2010 and 2018, infections increased 21 percent in Brazil.[32]

Likewise, the rural-school closures are factors that deeply affect rural women safety. While participation in education is a key determinant for child exploitation, during the period between 1997 and 2018, almost 80,000 rural schools were closed.[33] In rural areas, lacking school systems, children are more exposed to child labor. It's not uncommon for parents to send their children to be adopted by aunts, uncles, friends, or acquaintances who live in urban areas hoping for better opportunities. In these cases, girls often do babysitter and house cleaning services in exchange for housing, food, and education.[34] Most of them become vulnerable to sexual abuse, exploitation, and even trafficking.

The authoritarian-reactionary camp has played a leading role in current education policies. While Bolsonaro's government cuts funds for education programs that benefit rural workers, LGBTQ, indigenous, and other minority groups, it promotes a program to implement civic-military schools.

> The National Civic-Military Schools Program is an initiative of the Ministry of Education in partnership with the Ministry of Defense. It presents a management concept in the educational, didactic-pedagogical and administrative areas which involves the participation of the school's faculty and the military. The proposal is to implement 216 Civic-Military Schools across the country by 2023, 54 schools per year.[35]

This model consists of delegating the school administration to military personnel, who are responsible for imposing strict disciplinary rules on students, as well as military notions of hierarchy and behavior. Besides the mandatory use of school uniforms, there are restrictions on hairstyles and haircuts, color of the glasses, nails and harsh restrictions on behavior.[36]

In Brazilian states where civic-military schools exist, military officials are denounced for moral and sexual harassment. For example, in 2020, a civic-military school administrator, in the state of Rondônia, removed ten teachers because they indicated an interest in participating in the teachers' union.[37] In the state of Amazonas, about eighty mothers accused military officials for moral and sexual harassment against their daughters. Currently, there are at least 120 cases of violence reported to the state public prosecutor's office.[38]

Thus, in addition to putting limits on teachers' and students' freedom of expression, the Program—which is the main education policy of Bolsonaro's government—implements its quasi-fascist and sexist orientation.

There are numerous examples that demonstrate how Bolsonaro's government is an ongoing threat to women lives, particularly the Afro-descendant, the indigenous, and the peasant women.

The Pedagogical Dimensions of the Indigenous and the Peasant Women's Struggles

Let's start this section with a question: *What if children and youth could study about women's struggles and social movements as part of the school curriculum?*

Women play a central role in social struggles because they are those most affected by environmental degradation and dispossession.

> Many recent studies on the impact of ecological deterioration on women, particularly the poorest women in the South, have highlighted not only the fact that women and children are the main victims of this war against nature but also that women are the most active, most creative, and most concerned and committed in movements for conservation and protection of nature and for healing the damage done to her.[39]

It is women who must deal with those who become sick due to petroleum contamination or because the water they use to cook and clean is toxic, and who cannot feed their families because of the loss of land.[40] In many cases, women head households alone when men become addicted to alcohol or drugs due to unemployment and poverty.

Since women are the primary subjects of this important work—the reproductive work—historically and in our time, they have depended on access to natural resources more than men and have been most penalized by their privatization and, therefore, most committed to their defense.[41]

Thus, women have directly suffered from the effects of the neo-conservative public policies in their everyday life. That's why women today stand on the front lines against extractivism, struggling for the commons.

> The ancient voice that speaks to us of community heralds another world as well. Community—the communal mode of production and life—is the oldest of American traditions, the most American of all. It belongs to the earliest days and the first people, but it also belongs to the times ahead and anticipates a new New World.[42]

Commons are related to the necessary means of production and reproduction of life, in the form of a shared natural or social wealth—lands, waters, forests, systems of knowledge, capacities for care—to be used without any distinction. Because they are essential to the existence of life, in all its forms (human and non-human), they unveil how unsustainable and disastrous is the private property system and how wicked is the capitalist mode of production. Being understood in this way, commons refuse any kind of hierarchy of gender, race, or ethnicity. Above all, this concept is averse to class divisions.

This apparently archaic idea has come to the center of political discussions in contemporary social movements, especially those popular movements fighting for subsistence.[43] In these movements, there is an understanding that the "subsistence perspective" is the only guarantee of the survival of all.[44]

> Subsistence work as life-producing and life-preserving work in all these production relations was and is a necessary precondition for survival; and the bulk of this work is done by women. With increasing ecological destruction in recent decades, however, it becomes obvious that this subsistence—or life production—was and is not only a kind of hidden underground of the capitalist market economy, it can also show the way out of the many impasses of this destructive system called industrial society, market economy or capitalist patriarchy.[45]

According to Mies, the subsistence perspective demands a new paradigm of science, technology, and knowledge.[46] Instead of the prevailing reductionist science and technology—which have constituted and maintain dominations of class, gender, race, and ethnicity—a "feminist subsistence science and technology" must be developed in participatory action with the people.[47] Such people-based science would lead to a re-evaluation of older survival wisdom and traditions and also utilize modern knowledge in such a way that people maintain control over their technology and survival base.

Federici highlights women's role in preserving and transmitting traditional knowledge.[48] This points to the fact that despite all the attacks on "witches" aiming to erase women's traditional wisdom, female resistance (especially from indigenous people in Latin America and non-Western countries) managed to preserve much of that knowledge.[49] The movements of indigenous women, who bring with them a vision of the future shaped by a connection with the past and a strong sense of the continuity between human beings and nature, are crucial in this context. "With reference to the 'cosmovisions' that typify indigenous cultures in Latin America some feminists have coined the term 'communitarian feminism,' where the concept of the common is understood to express a specific conception of space, time, life, and the human body."[50]

For all those reasons, women have played a greater role in social struggles and collective self-organization processes for several decades. Once women's long-standing resistance strategies became more visible, they caught the attention to what has been called by "feminization of struggles."[51] These women developed strategies such as formative meetings and assemblies in local and national levels, self-defense workshops, and nonviolent direct actions that challenge governments and police.

Because they feel the social and environmental damages caused by extractivism, women are the main social force fighting against the commercialization of nature and also supporting the subsistence-oriented agriculture. This defense is made by Federici, who argues that women are less easily co-opted by extractive industries than men, who are often seduced by the wages—which give them more power over women, feeding into a macho culture that instigates violence against them.[52]

Above all, fighting for subsistence and survival means stop violence against women. For example, the rate of violence against women in agrarian conflicts in Brazil increased 377 percent between 2017 and 2018.[53]

Stopping violence was the main purpose of those women from forty-nine different countries that gathered during December 2019, in the Zapatista territory, in Mexico, at the "Second International Meeting of Women Who Fight."

> We think that in order to fight for our rights—the right to live, for example—it's not enough to fight against machismo or the patriarchy or whatever you want to call it. We have to fight against the capitalist system. They go together as we

Zapatista women say. [...] What matters is that we fight for our lives, which now more than ever are at risk everywhere and all the time. Despite the fact that they declare and predict that women have made great strides, the truth is that never in human history has the fact of being a woman been so fatal. [...] But you and we know that the most dangerous thing in the world to be right now is a woman.[54]

In August 2019, women from more than 130 indigenous ethnic groups gathered in Brazil's capital for the First Indigenous Women's March under the theme "Territory, Our Body, Our Spirit" which was held in conjunction and solidarity with the *Marcha das Margaridas* led by women rural workers. They denounced the different kinds of violence suffered by the indigenous and pointed out machismo as an epidemic brought by the Europeans colonizers.

The Indigenous Women's March was conceived as a process, started in 2015, with the purpose of educating and empowering the indigenous women. [...] The movement produced by our dance of fight considers the need for a return to the complementarity between the feminine and the masculine, without conceiving an essence to man and woman. [...] We need to dialogue and strengthen the indigenous women's power, taking up our matriarchal values and memories in order to be able to advance in our social claims related to our territories. [...] To fight for the right to territory is to fight for our right to life. Life and territory are the same, because the land gives us our food, our traditional medicine, our health and our dignity. To lose the territory means losing our mother. [...] When we take care of our territories—which is part of our culture—we are guaranteeing the well-being of the whole planet, since we take care of the forests, the air, the water, and soil. Most of the world's biodiversity is in the care of indigenous peoples and, thus, we contribute to sustain life on Earth.[55]

The *Marcha das Margaridas* brought together around 100,000 peasant women in the capital. Their purpose was to charge the government for the setbacks and to demand policies that meet their needs.

For us, women in the countryside, forests and waters, the *Marcha das Margaridas* has been a collective way of building a project of society that proposes Brazil without violence, where democracy and popular sovereignty are respected, based on fair and egalitarian relationships. We believe that it is possible to build new social relationships based on the values of ethics, solidarity, reciprocity, justice and respect for nature.[56]

During this march, the peasant women presented their political platform which included demands for better conditions in the field, also voicing their disapproval of far-right President Jair Bolsonaro. These demands have been discussed in all Brazilian regions since 2017. The political platform was organized around ten axis of struggles: for land, water and agroecology; for people's self-determination, with food and energy sovereignty; for protection and conservation of socio-biodiversity, with unrestricted access to common goods; for economic autonomy, work and income; for public and universal social assistance; for public health; for non-sexist and anti-racist education, with the guarantee of the right to rural education; for women's autonomy and freedom of their body and sexuality; for a life free of violence, without racism and sexism; for democracy, equality, and the strengthening of women's political participation.

What seems to be a common factor in all these women's movements is that they are far from being concerned solely with their local cultivation rights or their families' well-being. Their concerns are long-range, not exclusionary and, therefore, encompass all present and future forms of life. This can be observed in the final declaration of the Indigenous Women's March:

> We have the responsibility to plant, transmit, transcend, and share our knowledge, just as our ancestors and all those who preceded us have done, helping us to strengthen, together and on an equal footing with men—who were brought to life by us—our power of struggle, decision, representation, and care for our territories. We are responsible for the fertilization and the maintenance of our sacred soil. We will always be warriors in the defense of the existence of our peoples and Mother Earth.[57]

At this point, it can be concluded that the history of women's struggles—particularly from the indigenous and peasant women's perspectives—can and should be added to school curriculum to help address the socio-environmental crises that currently challenge peoples and governments. Connecting the wisdom from the past and concerns for the future can nurture our children and youth with the necessary hope to transform the oppressive ultra-conservatism in our late-capitalist society.

Final Considerations

The current neoliberal ultraconservative alliance in Brazil unveils the fact that in order for capitalism to advance, it always comes with serious costs and sacrifices to the people, especially this who live in the peripheral countries, as a result of looting, exploitations, and genocide. The control of territories and women's bodies have historically been central elements for capital accumulation and, therefore, this must be radically re-considered by those concerned with social transformation.

Recognition of these concerns relies on the recognition of the historical importance of the struggles faced by indigenous and peasant women. Their plight, activism, and social movements should also be added to the school curriculum—particularly in places where people face extractivism. These actions can create the hope, possibilities, and bravery necessary to fight against all forms of oppression, domination, and exploitation. Unfortunately, for Brazil in order to overcome the conservativism and authoritarian rule, we will need long-term activists' efforts, strategies, and education—considering the polarizations within the current fractured social order.

4

The Antidemocratic Fantasmatic Logic of Right-Wing Populism: Theoretical Reflections

Gundula Ludwig

Introduction

Gender and sexual politics have always played a significant role in the agenda of right wing's politics. Propagating a racially unified "people" relies upon the naturalization of heteronormativity and gender "differences."[1] Also, in the current political strategies of Germany's right-wing party *Alternative für Deutschland* (AfD), sexual and gender politics are key elements. The AfD was founded in 2013. In Germany's federal election in 2017 they gained 12.6 percent. On the level of state parliaments, so far, their biggest successes have been in Sachsen and Thüringen in 2019: in the election in Sachsen they gained 27.5 percent, in Thüringen 23.4 percent. Their politics are openly nationalistic and they have a strong anti-migration course. In their affirmation of the "German nation" and the "German Volk," they not only deny the responsibility for the Holocaust, but also aim at rehabilitating and normalizing national-socialists' notions and ideas such as "Volksgemeinschaft."[2] Attacking feminist and queer political principles is crucial for their politics.[3] They aim to reinstall a masculinist authoritarian political style of leadership[4] and advocate the need to rescue the ideal of the heterosexual, patriarchal family.[5] Feminist achievements, equality policies, as well as gender and queer studies are cast as threats to the supposed natural order of society.[6]

According to Birgit Sauer, the right-wing occupation with gender and sexuality has become a catalyst in the move toward a masculinist identity politics in efforts to not only restore traditional gender regimes but also push forward an anti-democratic project.[7] Anti-feminist and anti-queer politics have gained such an importance, because they make right-wing ideas acceptable at the core of society. In a similar manner, Franziska Schutzbach[8] argues that anti-feminist and anti-queer politics allow right-wing ideas easy access to the middle of society. Anti-feminism and anti-genderism "have become central idioms for establishing right-wing world-views, i.e. rendering right-wing positions socially acceptable in various political settings. Unlike xenophobia or clumsy nationalism, the rejection of feminism or gender does not immediately appear to be right-wing per se."[9] This is because antifeminist and anti-queer rhetoric can be used to delegitimize democratic premises without *explicitly* using extremist right-wing rhetoric.[10]

Building on the large body of feminist and queer analyses of the interplay between right-wing populism and sexual and gender politics, this chapter aims to add theoretical reflections on the question of how gender and sexual politics have become such impactful issues within current attempts of right-wing actors to gain hegemony. For this purpose, the chapter refers to theory of hegemony and asks what kinds of *fantasmatic logic*[11] do right-wing populists deploy in their attempts to assert their political views as hegemonic.

My geopolitical focus is Germany and my examples focus on the right-wing party AfD. I take up Sauer's and Schutzbach's argument that gender and sexual politics are key in organizing hegemony and I add that in order to fully grasp right-wing hegemonic strategies, it is necessary to also take the fantasmatic realm into account. After introducing my theoretical frame in the subsequent section, I discuss three figures who are central to the current right-wing fantasmatic logic. The overall aim of this chapter is to bring to the fore how right-wing politics are deeply anti-democratic not only in terms of their content but also in their fantasmatic logic.

The Fantasmatic Logic in the Struggle for Hegemony

According to Ernesto Laclau, hegemony needs to be a key concept of political analysis.[12] He bases this on the radical democratic theory premise that the social is founded upon a radical contingency.[13] The social is discursively constituted according to the logics of difference and equivalence. Hegemony is a temporal and partial fixation of a political order.[14] It is not the imposition of a pre-given set of ideas and interests, but emerges from the political interaction of social actors, and exists within social struggles. Politics then is a continuous struggle for hegemony. Consequently, democracy does not mean to once for all define and fixate the political but rather to enable a contestation of a "given" political order and to politicize fixations that are built upon exclusions and disclosures.

Given that "radical undecidability"[15] is a constitutive element of democracy, we can differ between democratizing and anti-democratic struggles for hegemony: The former accepts that the social is built upon contingency and aims at opening up political contestations, allowing the politicization of "truth claims" and the exclusions and disclosures behind them. The latter promises to fixate the political order through "truth claims' that are built upon exclusions. In anti-democratic struggles for hegemony, a fantasmatic promise is at work, which offers a promise that the social could be ultimately fixed. Anti-democratic struggles for hegemony then carry out the filling of that lack."[16]

It is not difficult to see the influence of psychoanalyses in Laclau's thoughts here, which he brings into the political realm: what is the fantasma of restoring the myth of an original unity between the primary care-giver and the child within psychoanalysis is also a crucial dynamic within hegemonic struggles that promise to suture the constitutive cracks and ruptures of the social, and to overcome contingency. However, the promise to restore any "original myth" fails, not only in psychic life but also in the political. "For if such a total suture was possible, it would mean that the universal would have found its own undisputable body, and no hegemonic variation would any longer be possible."[17]

This perspective on hegemony sheds light on the importance of the realm of fantasmatic promises. This is what—among others—Jason Glynos and David Howarth have brought to the fore by arguing that any analytical engagement with hegemony needs to take not only the social and the political but also the fantasmatic logic into account. Fantasmatic logics entail the ideological rationales that lead individuals to immerse themselves in the political practices at hand. Looking into the "logic of fantasy" enables us to investigate "how subjects are rendered complicit in concealing or covering over the radical contingency of social relations."[18] Fantasies are a "framing device that subjects use to protect themselves from the anxiety associated with the idea that there is no ultimate guarantee or law underlying and guiding our social existence. This guarantee has been given many names, certainly when one takes the long historical view: God, Reason, the Senses, the Laws of History, and so on."[19] The inclusion of fantasmatic logics thus expands the analytical scope for understanding how hegemony is organized. It allows one to also investigate how phantasies are evoked and which fantasmatic promises are articulated within struggles over hegemony.

The Fantasmatic Logic of Right-Wing Populism

In the following section, I make use of the analytical tools by Glynos and Howarth and look at the fantasmatic logic that the AfD deploys in their struggles for hegemony. I present three figures I consider crucial in the contemporary right-wing fantasmatic logic with regard to their gender and sexual politics: the fantasmatic logic of unity as sameness, the fantasmatic logic of securitization, and the fantasmatic logic of autonomy.

The Fantasmatic Logic of Unity as Sameness

A key rhetorical strategy of right-wing actors is to address "the people" as a natural, homogenous, and pure entity. Referencing a presumably given "culture," nationality, religion, and gender order constructs "a people" on the basis of an assumed homogeneity. What binds the members together and to "their" nation is sameness. Consequently, heterogeneity and plurality appear as an imposing threat, along with anything else that is configured as "Other," including migrants, racialized Others, queers, and people affiliated with religions other than Christianity. In their statement of principles, the AfD declares: "The AfD considers the ideology of multiculturalism, which equates imported cultural trends with the local culture in a history-blind way [...] as a serious threat to social peace and to the continued existence of the nation as a cultural unit. The state and civil society must confidently defend German cultural identity as 'Leitkultur' against it [multiculturalism]."[20]

Viewed from the perspective of a post-foundationalist theory of democracy, such a construction of "the people" as a homogenous unity can only be a fantasm. It is a fantasm that promises to overcome the fundamental contingency and impossibility to define and determine once and for all who belongs to "the people" and what *is* the people.[21] References to German "*Leitkultur*," whiteness, Christianity, and heteronormativity are in themselves a fantasmatic promise to ultimately fix what cannot be fixed. The promise of reestablishing or defending any "original myth" is a fantasmatic promise that something does "exist," which cannot exist.

I interpret the logic of this unifying fantasy of "the people" as both androcentric and Eurocentric. Already in the 1970s, feminist scholars like Helene Cixous and Luce Irigaray argued that patriarchal societies rest upon a "phallic economy"[22] that defines "the masculinist" as the One, the norm, the universal point of reference. Despite the extensive debates within gender and queer studies that question the (possible) essentialist premises within Irigaray's work and in particular her references to the "sexed bodies," for the purpose of my argument I consider Irigaray's work useful for demonstrating the fundamental *logic* in the social and imaginative structures of patriarchal societies. What Irigaray calls phallogocentrism denotes a *logic of society* that does not rely on biologically given bodies. Within a "phallic economy," the logic of the social order is based upon the logic of singularity. As symbol for truth, the phallus signifies the norm and functions as the central point of reference. All other *objects* can only be defined hierarchically and in relation to *the One*. They can only be represented as what is defined as "Other" according to masculinist terms—that is, as deviation from what has been set as the One. Since it is impossible to define the Other outside the terms of the One, the Other can only be constructed in hierarchical difference to the One.

In a society that is structured through a "phallic economy," community and collectivity do not and cannot rest upon plurality, but are structured according to the logic of One. The One defines belonging and defines the Other who is either excluded or integrated—assimilated—as the other-ed Other[23] on terms that are defined by the One. Belonging can only be defined in relation to the androcentric One as sameness. Phallogocentrism installs a community that is structurally incapable of including a plurality that allows the Other to become the Other on terms that are not fixed by the One.

This logic is not only androcentric, it is at the same time Eurocentric. As Aníbal Quijano has argued, a binary, dualistic logic is constitutive for colonialism and continues to be hegemonic in the ongoing "coloniality of power."[24] Colonialism installed Eurocentrism as the epistemic norm, whereby Europeans rendered themselves the exclusive "bearers, creators and protagonists of modernity,"[25] while the colonized people became the other-ed Other. The effect of this Eurocentric dualism is that only *one position* is legible as the determiner of norms, rationality, modernity, progress, and on the basis of this anything "Other" is defined according to Eurocentric terms. Quijano illuminates that this dualism is a "nuclear effect [...] of Eurocentrism"[26] and racism.

The invention of "races" led to the creation of this dualism in the first place, "for underneath that codification of relations between Europeans and non-Europeans, race is, without doubt, the basic category."[27] The "Other" is not recognized as equal Other but either as someone who belongs to the community through an ascribed sameness or as someone who is constructed as stranger who is a threat to the community because of its Otherness. As Sara Ahmed argued, whoever is constructed as stranger is constructed as someone who does not belong to the community. Strangeness is not what remains as unknown but as whatever is recognized and takes form on the terms of the hegemonic norm.[28] Strangers are "those who are, in their very proximity, *already recognised as not belonging*, as being out of pace."[29] Thus, not only is Otherness equaled with strangeness but also is strangeness equaled as threat "which must be expelled from the purified space of the community."[30]

Bringing back these insights to the fantasmatic logic of current right-wing populism, I argue that addressing and instating a longing for a "pure people" is masculinist, heteronormative, and racist not only in terms of its *content*, but also in its *fantasmatic logic*. The fantasm of "the people" as a unified entity is in itself an effect of a *phallogocentric and Eurocentric, white logic*. The fantasmatic logic of a reinstatement of an "original myth" of "the people as a unified entity" relies on the idea that the relationship of people within a community requires *sameness* and is *threatened by* "Otherness." The fantasm of the "pure people" promises a closure and fixation of what cannot be fixed. It can only be fixed through using a white, Eurocentric, masculine logic of what a community *is* and should be. If, following Glynos and Howarth, enjoyment is an important element of any fantasmatic logic, it can be argued that the "enjoyment" offered by the right wing's re-activation of "the people" is the prolongation of a Eurocentric, masculinist dualism that enhances and stabilizes those who resemble sameness at the price of discriminating and excluding other-ed Others.

The Fantasmatic Logic of Securitization

The second figure I identify as central to the current right-wing discourses is the promise of securitization through referring to what is defined as natural laws. For this trope, right-wing gender and family politics are paradigmatic because at their core lies the promise to rescue heterosexuality and the gender binary as *the natural foundation of society and the state*. AfD members and affiliates identify these "natural foundations" as under threat due to the existence of feminism, equality, and diversity politics—in particular gender mainstreaming—and gender and queer studies. Consequently, AfD rejects "all attempts to extend the meaning of the word 'family' in Article 6 Abs. 1 of the Constitution to other communities."[31]

The accusation that "gender ideology" aims at destroying an assumed natural gender order is one of the key charges they make against feminist and queer activists and scholars. "Gender ideology marginalizes natural differences between the sexes and calls gender identity into question. It seeks to eradicate the classic family as a life model and role model."[32] As a consequence of the assumption of "natural" gender differences, the AfD propagates to protect patriarchal gender stereotypes that construct women and men as opposites. They promise to put an end to the "stigmatization of traditional gender roles" that they see at work in the feminist critique of motherhood as an ideological construct to secure social reproduction at the price of gender inequality and exploitation. Already in 2013, AfD deputy spokesperson Beatrix von Storch criticized this: "Gender mainstreaming does not aim at attaining equal rights for men and women, it is the doctrine that men and women do not exist. According to the gender ideology, the gender of a person does not determine biology, but is created through education and society. That is why gender is now gradually being officially done away with."[33] Instead of doing away with what von Storch claims to be a naturally given gender, she promises to rescue the natural institution of the family. Consequently, von Storch fights to replace gender mainstreaming with "family mainstreaming."[34]

In order to better understand the fantasmatic logic here, let us return to radical democratic theory. Radical democratic theorists have highlighted that democracy cannot be grounded in pre-political, ontological truth claims; it can only be grounded in indisputable contingency. As Claude Lefort has argued, democracy is the "dissolution of the markers of certainty."[35] In a similar manner, Laclau illuminates that "radical undecidability"[36] is a constitutive element of democracy. Every form of instituting implies that the "original contingency fade"[37] and the "instituted tends to assume the form of a mere objectivity."[38] Laclau relates the constitution of "objectivity" to myths. Any objectivity is "merely a crystallized myth,"[39] and the "'work' of myth is to suture that dislocated space through the constitution of a new space of representation."[40] Since the idea of objectivity is based on—at times also violent—exclusions, "the traces of that exclusion will always be present."[41] But even though every act of instituting makes its own powerful and violent origin invisible, these exclusions are still sedimented.[42]

In line with Judith Butler,[43] I argue that gender as a binary heteronormative construction operates as a myth that helps to constitute the fundamental "objectivities" of modern Western societies. This myth of gender entails a fantasmatic "objectivity" that assumes the existence of a natural binary of bodies and subjects. As Butler argues, it is precisely an effect of the embodied performativity of gender to create this illusion of a "natural sex."[44] Furthermore, gender as a binary, heteronormative construction constitutes the fantasm that naturally equates "family" with heterosexual family. In this sense, gender operates as a powerful myth that sutures the contingency of subjectivities, social order, and institutions. The naturalization of gender is a promise of assurance in a fundamental contingent social world and a promise to silence struggles to define and imagine gender, subjectivities, bodies, desires, families, and reproduction in a different way.

If democracy is the ongoing contestation of "markers of certainty" and not their[45] fixation, deploying gender as naturalizing myth is *anti-democratic as such*. Referencing the binary of bodies, heterosexuality, and heterosexual reproduction as to be one of Western society's core natural laws promises a fantasmatic stability and "objectivity" that aim to push back democratic struggles concerning ways of living, caring, reproducing. Thus, not only is the reference to gender and heteronormativity in right-wing politics anti-democratic because it aims to discriminate against non-heteronormative, non-binary ways of living that "deviate" from "natural gender roles" and "natural family" referenced in AfD's quotes. From the perspective of radical democratic theory, it is also *anti-democratic in its fantasmatic logic*, because gender is deployed as a naturalizing myth, as a "marker of certainty." As a mode of fixation, the heteronormative fantasm of gender thus suspends a fundamental precondition of democracy: the ability to accept that the social is built upon contingency.

Furthermore, deploying gender as a "natural truth" reenacts the inherent violence that enables gender to operate as naturalizing fantasm in the first place. As Butler has argued, to define gender as "naturally binary" is a form of normative violence.[46] It requires that other imaginations and materializations of genders, bodies, sexualities, desires, and subjectivities be punished,[47] rejected, and that they remain unimaginable and unlivable.[48]

Postcolonial feminist scholars have also addressed the violence inherent in the heteronormative construction of the gender binary. María Lugones highlighted that gender as naturalizing binary construction is in itself a colonial invention. An integral element of colonialism was to eradicate gender and kinship practices that did not correspond to the European heteronormative ideal of a binary, hierarchical gender.[49] According to Lugones, this annihilation and the violent destruction of all other forms of sexual life, bodies, sexualities, and kinship systems were the prerequisite for the heteronormative gender to become globally hegemonic.[50] Thus, deploying gender as a naturalizing fantasm continues its violent origin while simultaneously rendering it invisible.

If right-wing politics that defend gender as naturally given can be interpreted as employing an anti-democratic fantasmatic logic, it further comes as no surprise that gender and queer studies are specifically targeted on the right-wing agenda.[51] The AfD regularly calls gender and queer studies into question in numerous statements, party programs, or in requests for parliamentary debates in both state and federal governing bodies. Gender and queer studies are accused of being ideological, dogmatic, totalitarian, and unscientific (Hark & Villa, 2015, p. 20). In the manifesto for the national election in 2017 the AfD proclaimed: "'Gender research' is not a serious science, because it is based on the ideological precept that natural sex and social gender are completely independent from each other. The ultimate goal is to abolish the natural gender difference. The federal and state governments should no longer provide funding for 'gender research' and be forced to step down from so-called 'gender professorship.'"[52]

Despite the fact that the percentage of professorships that actually carry the title of "gender studies" is very small in Germany—less than 1 percent[53]— gender and queer studies still draw a considerable amount of attention in right-wing discourse. One reason for this is that they can be interpreted as paradigmatic antipodes of the anti-democratic gender politics that right-wing actors pursue. Being based on the feminist premise that there simply is (and cannot be) any neutral and objective science, (critical) gender and queer studies are built upon a *democratic epistemology*.

The production of knowledge is not considered to be a search for objective truth claims, but rather as invitation to question hegemonic power formations and their disclosures, and to initiate inquiries on the genealogy of what is considered as "given." In gender and queer studies, the category of gender does not function as a naturalizing myth, but as mode of questioning. Gender is "never the answer, it is the question that opens up inquiry."[54]

The right-wing attack on gender and queer studies is therefore an attack on "science and university as places of an unconditional questioning and negotiating reality,"[55] as Sabine Hark and Paula-Irene Villa state. "For there is hardly any other contemporary theory that entails the very essence of critical thought [as gender and queer studies,] namely a high degree of willingness and ability 'to question one's own political and epistemic foundations' (Knapp, 2013, p. 106)."[56] Thus, defaming gender and queer studies as unscientific is actually an assault on the underlying democratizing epistemic basis that does not dismiss contingency and openness, but takes them as a starting point in analyzing power relations and thinking about different social imaginaries that needs to be destroyed from a right-wing point of view.

The Fantasmatic Logic of Autonomy

The third fantasmatic promise I identify is the promise of autonomy. The fantasmatic logic of autonomy promises to overcome that living implies being related to and being dependent on others.

A key feature of AfD's political performance is their self-definition as the party of the "common man." The construction of representing the "common man" and defending his [sic] true interests against the elite is a crucial element of populism.[57] One would assume that a party that portrays itself as representing "the common man" would reflect this in its social policy. However, this is clearly not the case given AfD's lack of solidarity along with its outright neoliberal social policy. In her analysis of AfD's social policy both on the state and federal level, Katharina Nocun reveals that AfD's social policy clearly has a neoliberal agenda. They condone further cuts to the welfare state and view privatization as key to social policy.[58]

AfD's social policy places a neoliberal emphasis on the individual and on the notion that the individual carries the sole responsibility in creating security in one's own life and thus, negates social structures. The AfD's statement of principles claims: "The more competition and the lower the state ratio, the better for everyone."[59] And in the party's program for the Hamburg state election in 2015 they announce: "It should never be worthwhile to receive social benefits from the state without putting forth efforts, instead of working, as far as age and health permit."[60] Consequently, the AfD has rejected the idea of a legal minimum wage[61] and proposed the privatization of the unemployment insurance.[62]

That same emphasis on the individual and a negation of discriminatory social structures is present in AfD's gender policies. AfD's program policy on gender aims to restrict or eradicate diversity and anti-discrimination measures.[63] They clearly deny the existence and persistence of structural inequality and discrimination. Consequently, they "reject gender quotas in studies or in the labor sector, as quotas are hostile to merit and unfair and create other disadvantages."[64] It also goes without saying that disregarding the existence of social power structures also shapes AfD's stance on (im)migration. In a recent statement, Wolfram Keil, AfD deputy-representative in the Saxion parliament, sums up the key assumption underlying AfD view on (im)migrants: "It is an irrefutable fact that asylum seekers who come from Africa to Europe are economic refugees and have no right to stay."[65]

By employing the figure of the "economic refugee," the AfD reduces migration to a will-full and individual decision to seek a better life, because the individual feels like it. Employing a discourse that equates migration with economic migration disarticulates the social power structures in the migration process. Such a discourse obscures post- and neocolonial structures of global inequalities and exploitation, colonial legacies that give rise to wars in non-Western regions, and global effects of climate change in the global South—largely due to the capitalist demands from the global North. Consequently, instead of understanding these issues as a matter of human rights, AfD believes that the state should completely refrain from ensuring fair asylum processes or from rescuing refugees, for instance in the Mediterranean Sea.[66]

The common denominator in AfD's stances on various issues briefly cited here—from migration, to gender, to social policy—is understanding "the human" as a solipsistic, self-responsible monad. Such discourses ignore that every individual is embedded within social structures, and that no one can ever be fully autonomous. Therefore, the need for support—be it for people seeking to escape war or ecological destruction, those who are unemployed, or women, lesbians, gays, transgender and queer people who are structurally discriminated, for example, on the job market—is framed as a result of individual failure or fate, instead of as bound up with social power structures that privilege some and discriminate others.

What fantasmatic logic undergirds such politics? In *Precarious Life*,[67] Judith Butler elaborates on the need to dismiss the fantasm of autonomy. Butler argues for an understanding of precariousness as a general condition of each and every life. "Precariousness implies living socially, that is, the fact that one's life is always in some sense in the hands of the other. It implies exposure both to those whom we know and to those we do not know; a dependency on people we know, or barely know, or know not at all. Reciprocally, it implies being impinged upon by the exposure and dependency of others, most of whom remain anonymous."[68]

Even though precariousness is a fundamental condition of all lives, not all lives are precarious in the same way. Butler uses the notion of precarity[69] to highlight that heteronormative, racist, nationalist, capitalist, ability-oriented power relations protect and safeguard vulnerability in different ways. Through gender, heteronormativity, race, nationality, class and ability, demarcations of power are drawn between the lives of those whose precariousness is considered worthy of protection, and those lives whose precariousness is not protected.

Reflecting on the ethical and political consequences of this social ontology, Butler argues "the precarity of life imposes an obligation on us" (Butler, 2010, p. 2). This obligation is not and cannot be to secure or overcome the socio-ontological precariousness. This is, as Butler states, simply not possible. Neither can precariousness "be properly *recognized*."[70] Rather, "there ought to be recognition of precariousness as a shared condition of human life (indeed, as a condition that links human and non-human animals), but we ought not to think that the recognition of precariousness masters or captures or even fully cognizes what it recognizes."[71] Although precariousness cannot be overcome, we must still strive to take it into account—as a condition of life that cannot be ascertained.

Drawing inspiration from Butler's thoughts, how might we interpret the fantasmatic logic at work in the right-wing imagination of human beings as autonomous monads? Given that the social-ontological precariousness is constitutive of every life, right-wing politics can be interpreted as a fantasmatic promise to overcome this fundamental precariousness as well as the fundamental exposure to other human beings. Hailing the subject as autonomous ascribes an imagination oneself as capable of securing what cannot be secured. The fantasmatic promise to escape fundamental precariousness as a shared condition of human life implies a further promise: to deny the fundamental dependency and relationality with others, both known and unknown. It promises a way of escaping the social ontological premise that being human means being exposed to others, and thus, to an alterity we cannot know.

The right-wing's re-activation of the liberal subject entails a promise of overcoming that being human means to be given over "to the world of others."[72] It is ultimately the fantasy of omnipotence that denies the fundamental dependency, relationality, and dispossession. This fantasmatic logic requires a projection of that which is denied onto Others. In other words, dependency and dispossession are projected on to those constructed as Other through race, gender, sexuality, disability, class, nationality, and religion. Rallying against providing support to asylum seekers, unemployed people, or against equality measures is a symptom of this denial. The right wing does not consider these measures as an attempt to rectify structural discrimination that brings about different forms of precarity in the first place, but instead as unjust rules for eligibility to benefits and unjust forms of preferred treatment. This denial of the fundamental dependency of human beings and the preservation of the fantasm of one's own autonomy are made possible by projecting precariousness and vulnerability through racializing and gendering Others while simultaneously neglecting to politically address it.

This white, masculinist, Eurocentric fantasmatic promise of autonomy that denies fundamental precariousness is clearly not an invention of current right-wing politicians. Rather, it is the reactivation of the white, masculine, Eurocentric liberal fantasm of "human beings" as autonomous monades.

Conclusion

From the perspective of radical democratic theory, democracy is a process that cannot be built upon any kind of fixation. When ontological truth claims enter the political realm, democracy is stripped off its democratic character, it becomes post-democracy that, according to Jacques Rancière, is a state of the "disappearance of as politics."[73] This, however, is precisely what the right aims at with its project of hegemony that promises to suture contingency and enables whoever is part of "the people" to reach a state of social fullness. From the perspective of radical democratic theory, this can only function through fantasmatic promises. As I have shown above, the fantasm of gender as a naturally given binary entity along with masculinist and colonial legacies plays a crucial role here.

Right-wing politics are deeply anti-democratic not only in terms of their content but also in terms of their fantasmatic logic: they are not merely anti-democratic by excluding and discriminating people through their use of racializing, nationalistic, heteronormative, misogynist, gender-binary-focused discourses, and because they aim at eradicating emancipatory accomplishments attained through social struggles, such as anti-discrimination laws, gender equality measures, or the legal establishment of a "third option" for gender markers on official documents. They are also anti-democratic because their fantasmatic promises aim to install a social order that denies the democratic foundations of contingency and the openness of the social. Because of their fantasmatic logic that is based upon a denial of openness, dependency, and precariousness, they aim at the "disappearance of politics" as such.[74]

Anti-feminist politics and the fantasmatic naturalization of gender and heteronormativity have always been part of modern Western societies and they have been radicalized with neoliberalism in the last decades. Neoliberalism has led to a broad precarization of wage work and ways of living and to a profound "*de-democratization of the state and society*" and a "far-reaching yet subtle de-democratization of *everyday forms of living and subjectification.*"[75] The success of right-wing politics is built upon both, neoliberalism's erosion of democracy and its precarization of ways of living. Both have served as discursive prelude of the success of the right-wing's fantasmatic logic because neoliberalism has laid the basis by normalizing anti-democratic politics in people's everyday lives. Against this background, right-wing fantasmatic logics that aim to suspend the foundations of democracy can spread so easily.

The fantasmatic promises of right-wing politics are neither a break from nor an antipode of the (neo-)liberal social order. They are an intensification of anti-democratic roots inherent in the fabrics of modern Western liberal democracy. The fantasmatic logic of right-wing politics and their masculinist Eurocentric legacies are a radicalization of the structures of liberal democracies that entail not only exclusions and hierarchies but also fantasmatic logics that make a *democratic* democracy impossible. Thus, to counter the right-wing undemocratic fantasmatic logic it is indispensable to re-democratize democracy by struggling for an entirely different understanding of democracy than the liberal understanding: a democracy that becomes able to deal with the fundamental contingency of the social, has the capacity to encounter others in their alterity, and to grasp precariousness and dependency of human beings as its *non-foundational basis* of the political.

5

Technologies of Surveillance

A Transnational Black Feminist Analysis

K. Melchor Quick Hall

My hair started being searched at airports after the September 11, 2001, attacks on the World Trade Center. I never had a problem with the metal detectors, but the new body scan technology regularly raised suspicion among airport workers. With dread, I would wait with my back to the screen, to find out whether they were going to insist on searching my hair. My hair is natural, worn in cornrows, braids, or twists. There are no large sections in which I could hide anything, nothing suspicious looking. When I inquired about the searches, I was told that the problem was the shape of my head. Apparently, my head was not the "regular" head shape. When I asked what norm was used, the responses were dismissive; they would repeat what they had already said about my head (with hair) not being the regular shape.

Airport security officials were also dismissive when I said that their standard was based on white bodies and hair. My hair, and that of other African Americans with thick, kinky hair, would not lay flat. In other words, I made clear that their technology was racist, assuming that people with stringy hair are normal, and those with kinky hair are abnormal, and worse suspicious of engaging in terrorism. As Browne (2015) described, "Where public spaces are shaped for and by whiteness, some acts in public are abnormalized by way of racializing surveillance and then coded for disciplinary measures that are punitive in their effects" (17). I insisted on speaking with supervisors, and going to private screening areas to undo my own cornrows, braids, and twists. In defiance of these dehumanizing searches, I insisted that my hair could not be touched by these government agents, trained by racist technologies. When questioned, I declared it as a central part of my spiritual practice, one that was rooted in claiming my Black humanity, as both normal and unsuspicious. This is just one kind of encounter with technologies of surveillance. In the following chapter, I explore the ways in which this encounter is part of a larger system of biased technologies of surveillance deployed in the context of a neoliberal state.

Technologies of Surveillance in International Relations Perspective

This volume explores the varied impacts of a triangulation of neoliberalism, conservatism, and nationalism. In this chapter, I offer a transnational Black feminist (TBF) analysis rooted in the guiding principles of intersectionality, scholar-activism, solidarity, attention to borders/boundaries, and radically transparent positionality (Hall, 2016; Hall, 2020). Under the Trump administration, international attention has been given to current movements, highlighting a history of state violence that has long targeted African Americans. Contemporary policing involves surveillance technologies and predictive software. While public policy that criminalizes poverty, resulting in the targeting of African American communities, is the hallmark of Republican politicians and conservative politics, complicity among liberal politicians must not be ignored. Although Trump exemplifies white supremacist nationalism, it is important to attend to the structural issues that were in place long before the current administration. This chapter is organized to engage the framing of neoliberalism, (neo)conservatism, and nationalism, while also attending to the continuity of the mistreatment of Black communities in the United States.

As an international relations scholar, I am always compelled to make the important distinction between state (used here synonymously with country) and nation. In the past, scholars have used the term "nation-state" to refer to states that were relatively homogenous, in terms of ethnic identity.

> Today there is virtually nowhere in the world in which such a pure nation-state exists, if it ever did, and therefore there are always settled residents (and usually citizens as well) who are not members of the dominant national collectivity in the society. The fact that there still exists this automatic assumption about the overlap between the boundaries of the state citizens and 'the nation', is one expression of the naturalizing effect of the hegemony of one collectivity and its access to ideological apparatuses of both state and civil society. This constructs minorities into assumed deviants from the 'normal', and excludes them from important power resources. Deconstructing this is crucial to tackling racism.
> (Anthias & Yuval-Davis, 1992, pp. 21–2)

The United States is not, and has never been, made up of one nation. Contrastingly, its "founding"—if that's how we want to describe the country's violent history—is rooted in the active erasure (read: genocide) of indigenous peoples and enslavement of Africans and their descendants. Thus, any brand of so-called US American nationalism is rooted in a white supremacist ethic that intends to erase indigeneity and devalue Blackness.

In this chapter, I want to focus on the realities of technologies of surveillance in such a context. Having studied computer science, I am acutely aware of coded (i.e., algorithmic) bias and many people's assumptions of the neutrality of technology. In the sections that follow, I discuss the relationship of a US American (read: white supremacist) nationalism, (neo)conservative politics, and a neoliberal agenda. Importantly, I call attention to the detrimental impacts of liberalism that often continue (neo)conservative policies, and do not offer any radical (i.e., addressing root cause) solutions. Next, I focus specifically on the racialized dangers of neoliberal surveillance, before introducing a TBF analysis. Importantly, I engage ideas about resistance to these technologies, by engaging the idea of dark surveillance (Browne, 2015) before concluding.

US White (Supremacist) Nationalism, (Neo)conservative Politics, and Neoliberalism Social Solutions

If we understand that the United States is a country of many (indigenous and non-indigenous) nations, the question of nationalism is not about any "authentic" claim to US territory, which goes by many other indigenous names. Instead, what is at stake is "how sections and groupings from the civil society gain access to the state's coercive and controlling powers" (Anthias & Yuval-Davis, 1992, p. 23). Since its inception, the government of the United States has had a white supremacist ethic, with conservative politicians often taking the opportunity to develop structures that will deepen and normalize inequitable practices. Roberts (2011) wrote about the an ever-evolving anti-Blackness of conservatives:

> When eugenics was discredited after World War II, most conservatives developed an alternative explanation based on black cultural depravity and individual irresponsibility. The new racial science based on genetics has rejuvenated the biological rationale in a modern version that does not appear to be racist—and is all the more insidious for it. Some conservative proponents of social color blindness have eagerly embraced the new genetic definition of race as well as genetic explanations of health disparities and racial medicine.
>
> (291)

Brown (2006), who distinguished neoconservatism from conservatism by its greater international imperial ambitions, described US-based neoconservatism as an ideology that "looks backward to a national and nationalist order contoured by a set of moral and political attachments inflected by the contingent ambition of Empire" (Brown, 2006, p. 699). Embodying both neoliberalism and neoconservatism in the United States, the Republican Party aims to be both "the Party of Moral Values and Party of Big Business" (Brown, 2006, p. 698). However, the morality foregrounded is one that protects white life and property. Brown (2006) eloquently described the contradictions of corporate morality as follows:

> And the upright, patriotic, moral, and self-sacrificing neoconservative subject is partially undone by a neoliberal subject inured against altruism and wholly in thrall to its own interest: the neoliberal rationality of strict means-ends calculations and need satisfaction (and the making of states, citizens, and subjects in that image) clashes with the neoconservative project of producing a moral subject and moral order against the effects of the market in culture and oriented to the repression and sublimation rather than the satisfaction of desire.
> (Brown, 2006, p. 699)

Morality in this context is white (supremacist). If we consider questions of morality with attention to the indigenous or Black subject, there is never in pretense of state morality, only state erasure, capture, and control.

Although (neo)conservatives play an important role in the creation and expansion of discriminatory laws and policies, they also have a way of masking these practices with colorblind language: "With the new distinction between biological and social race, conservatives now have a way to speak about racial difference while maintaining a color-blind approach to social policy. They find it acceptable to refer to race explicitly as long as it has biological meaning because that use of race is purportedly scientific and unbiased" (Roberts, 2011, p. 292). This colorblind language is shared with liberal politicians, who are frequently complicit in the maintenance of racist policies in their unwillingness to enact radical change that would upend it. For that very reason, "combating liberalism with principled struggle" is one of the three collective commitments of contemporary social justice movements (Carruthers, 2018, p. 64). In the end, (white) conservatives and liberals have a frightening amount of common ground when it comes to questions of race.

> Liberal Americans have bought into the new racial science in part because it is science. Many believe in the inherent progress of science and have faith that scientists conducting research on race and genetics must be advancing

knowledge in an objective, rational, and ultimately beneficial way. ... The liberal faith in scientific objectivity has generated an approach to the genetic definition of race that sounds remarkably similar to the conservative one. Like conservatives, liberals separate racial science from racial politics to retain a supposedly scientific concept of race as a genetic category. Liberal scientists erect a wall between their objective study of racial difference in the lab and racial politics at play in the outside world.

(Roberts, 2011, p. 293)

This complicity with dangerous—and in fact lethal—racist thinking explains why many activists view liberalism as "one of the greatest threats to movement building" (Carruthers, 2018, p. 79). Sharing colorblind politics with conservatives, liberals adopt an "identity-neutral" approach that is counter-productive to the profound change required for a deeply racist system. As Carruthers (2018) wrote, "Liberalism dominates discourse about progress in the United States, and our movement must combat it and advance radical agendas for the sake of our collective liberation" (Carruthers, 2018, p. 79).

While both conservatives and liberals maintain racist policies, conservative politicians notoriously have advanced many of the policies that govern the surveillance of marginalized groups. One example is the drug war, started by US President Richard Nixon in the 1970s and taken up by President Ronald Reagan in the 1980s, resulting in the incarceration of many Black and Latinx people (Khan-Cullors & Bandele 2017, p. 44). There is also the DNA Fingerprint Act of 2005, signed into law by George W. Bush, which allowed for the widespread retrieval and storage of DNA data for people arrested and detained, even when not convicted or charged of anything (Roberts, 2011, p. 266). This data, once collected, can be used for a form of "genetic surveillance," being compared to genetic data found at crime scenes. Similar to other technologies of surveillance, its use can be discriminatory: "Why would we expect DNA to eliminate the corruption in law enforcement that led to the framing of these innocent people? To the contrary, it gives dirty lab analysts, police officers, and prosecutors a simpler and more effective tool to use in building a false case against someone they want to see behind bars" (Roberts, 2011, p. 273). Embedded with a white nationalist bias, (neo)conservative administrations have created an infrastructure that can create "a nearly universal database for urban black men" (Roberts, 2011, p. 278). The long-term consequences can create significant harm even after (neo)conservative politicians leave office: "Racial disparities in DNA databanks make communities of color the most vulnerable to state surveillance and suspicion. The disproportionate odds faced by blacks and Latinos of having their DNA extracted and stored will, in turn, intensify the racial disparities that already exist in the criminal justice system" (Roberts, 2011, p. 281).

Once the conservative (or liberal) politics within a state give rise to the control of state power, a neoliberal ethic can then result in the export of repressive (and militarized) practices. Certainly, US (militarized) domestic policing stands as a model for other countries working to control ethnic minorities within the state. Its reliance on a (capitalist) market logic, applied to domestic "security" (understood narrowly as the protection of white property), exemplifies the neoliberal ethic. While neoliberalism is characterized by its attention to (capitalist) markets and privatization of services (especially those previously managed by the state), it is important to understand its impact beyond the traditional marketplace: "its organization of governance and the social is not merely the result of leakage from the economic to other spheres but rather of the explicit imposition of a particular form of market rationality on these spheres" (Brown, 2006, p. 693). In this context, social problems get market-based "solutions" that extend beyond the borders of any one state. In the 1970s, one of the major "problems" of the US government was the race problem:

> The Negro—America's greatest problem—would be the new computer society's first major problem to solve. Government, industry, and higher education institutions collaborated, designed, built and deployed automated policing systems, networked databases, and algorithmically driven predictive policing imperatives. Six hundred criminal justice information systems were being used by police, courts, corrections, and other criminal justice agencies up through 1980.
>
> (McIlwain, 2020, p. 249)

Later tools were more sophisticated, but the target was the same: "The escalation of genetic surveillance is part of a broader practice of experimenting with solutions to social problems at the expense of minority group freedom" (Roberts, 2011, p. 285). Of course, true resolution of social problems of a country is at odds a structure that places state power in the hands of a small, powerful elite. Our social and political consciousness must stretch beyond colonial borders to deeper questions of our shared humanity. As Fanon wrote, "If we really want to safeguard our countries from regression, paralysis, or collapse, we must rapidly switch from a national consciousness to a social and political consciousness" (Fanon, 1963, p. 142). Below, I explore some of the dangers of a corporatized, state system of surveillance.

The Dangers of Neoliberal Technologies of (Mis)identification and Surveillance

One of the tragedies of neoliberalism is a "criteria of productivity and profitability, with the consequence that governance talk increasingly becomes market speak, businesspersons replace lawyers as the governing class in liberal democracies, and business norms replace juridical principles" (Brown, 2006, p. 693). This tendency has resulting in a corporatization of policing, and a market for predictive policing technologies. These technologies are not produced by governments, but rather are sold by corporate technology companies to local, state, and federal governments. Brown (2006) wrote about this "neoliberal de-democratization" resulting in "the transformation of political problems into individual problems with market solutions" (703). Corporate-run policing technologies exemplify this trend.

However, surveillance technologies are spread throughout government and private industries, in what Zuboff (2019) labeled "surveillance capitalism." According to Zuboff (2019), "Surveillance capitalism found shelter in the neoliberal zeitgeist that equated government regulation of business with tyranny." Poster (2019) referred to the infrastructure that supports various online transactions and interactions with the term "platform capitalism," which is described as "activating (or enabling) consumers for surveillance. Here, racial proclivities and assessments are given a space within the digital infrastructure, and then have a significant impact on economic transactions" (Poster, 2019, p. 137). Whether the focus is on the infrastructure (vis-à-vis platform capitalism) or on the resultant monitoring (vis-à-vis surveillance capitalism), public services must be understood in this context as racially biased and corporate-driven. Furthermore, the systems build upon data collected in a context of virulent racism. As Scannell (2019) wrote, "The racist history of American policing means that any predictive system's data is garbage. Therefore, predictive policing programs will be racist garbage" (Scannell, 2019, p. 107).

Thus, we must understand technologies of surveillance that target communities of color do not do so by accident, but instead are part of a long history of racist overseeing and an important part of a neoliberal and digitized approach to social services: "racialized surveillance is an integral and routine part of the U.S. service economy. As interactions between consumers, workers, and firms have moved to online platforms, cell phone apps, digital satellite communications, and artificial intelligence, racial discrimination is an everyday activity"

(Poster, 2019, p. 133). These technologies codify the biases of a white supremacist state, as Noble (2018) described when discussing search engines. As Duster (2019) wrote, "algorithms can be as racist as the designers of the generated computer programs" (Duster, 2019, p. xii). Buolamwini (2018) referred to this embedded bias of technology as "the coded gaze," which sometimes mistakes Black people for gorillas. This dehumanizing view is not surprising for the United States, a country that has yet to reckon with its history of enslaving Africans. There have been no reparations, and no radical change in the power structure.

Alexander (2012) has written about how the carceral state is a continuation of the government's practices of restricting the freedom of Black people. Similarly, Carruthers (2018) wrote, "Anti-Blackness is inextricably tied to the mass criminalization of Black people" (27). Digitizing the decision-making of the carceral state only broadens and deepens its violence (Scanell, 2019, pp. 107–8). According to Benjamin (2019), technology "actually aids and abets the process by which carcerality penetrates social life" (2). Roberts (2011) described how genetic surveillance is similarly a continuation of an anti-Black and white supremacist culture:

> Black people in America have long belonged to a "nation of suspects," reinforced with the explosion of the prison population since the 1970s and more recently with the escalation of government DNA data banking. This is not a reason to stretch the civil liberties violations to more people. It is reason to be concerned about the police state that already exists in inner-city neighborhoods. The burgeoning government databases of genetic profiles reflect a broader political trend at work in America today. The latest science and technology that has redefined race as a genetic reality could facilitate brutal government policies that threaten disaster for this nation—what I call the new biopolitics of race.
> (Roberts, 2011, p. 286)

Contemporary surveillance technologies (dis)embody this new biopolitics of race. The inability of a white supremacist state to see Black humanity is exemplified by the deployment of these racially biased technologies: "This matters because misidentification can subject innocent people to police scrutiny or erroneous criminal charges" (Buolamwini, 2018). Even when surveillance technologies correctly identify people, Buolamwini (2018) pointed to the potential for misuse, including arresting participants in protests against police misconduct. Roberts (2011) wrote about the risks in relation to genetic surveillance:

> The problem is not only that all of these harms are visited disproportionately on people of color; the dangers of state databanks are multiplied when applied to

blacks and Latinos because these groups are already at a disadvantage when they encounter the criminal justice system. They have fewer resources than whites to challenge abuses and mistakes by law enforcement officers and forensic analysts. They are stereotyped as criminals before any DNA evidence is produced, making them more vulnerable to the myth of DNA infallibility.

(Roberts, 2011, p. 282)

Scholars have expressed similar concerns about facial processing technology (FPT), and related surveillance technologies: "The reality of FPT deployments, however, reveals that many of these uses are quite vulnerable to abuse, especially when used for surveillance and coupled with predatory data collection practices that, intentionally or unintentionally, discriminate against marginalized groups" (Raji et al., 2020, p. 1). In San Diego, California, police have taken photos of people they stopped and run the images through a facial recognition service that compares the images to those in a database of "criminals and suspects" (O'Neill, 2016, p. 100). Given the inaccuracy of non-white facial recognition, this undoubtedly puts people of color at disproportionately high levels of risk. While misrecognition of Black (and other non-white) bodies is based on the initial (white) bodies used to train the software, attempts to gather more information can also result in discriminatory behavior.

Privacy and consent violations in the dataset curation process often disproportionately affect members of marginalized communities. Benchmark dataset curation frequently involves supplementing or highlighting data from a specific population that is underrepresented in previous datasets. Efforts to increase representation of this group can lead to tokenism and exploitation, compromise privacy, and perpetuate marginalization through population monitoring and targeted violence.

(Raji et al., 2020, p. 4)

Especially in places where all bodies are subjected to surveillance, such as airports, the learning curve for technology companies wears heavily on the "abnormal" body. In a patriarchal, white state, these technologies render Black female humanity (and hair) illegible, abnormal, and suspicious. These deeply racist technologies are reminiscent of the days of phrenology and have only been modernized through contemporary genetic surveillance: "the massive genetic surveillance we are witnessing threatens to reinforce the racial roots of the very injustices that need to be corrected" (Roberts, 2011, p. 284). In order to attend to these injustices, we must change how we talk and think about technology.

A Transnational Black Feminist Analysis

Elsewhere, I have developed a transnational Black feminist (TBF) framework (Hall, 2016; Hall, 2020) as a way to re-orient studies toward the transnational lives of ethnoracial groups, specifically attending to the lives of Black and indigenous people. The guiding principles of the TBF framework are intersectionality, scholar-activism, solidarity, attention to borders/boundaries, and radically transparent positionality. A TBF approach is rooted in a Black feminist tradition that embodies a "radical humanism committed to liberating humanity and reconstructing social relations across the board" (Kelley, 2002, p. 137). This is an appropriate framing for this discussion that intends to confront technology that dehumanizes and devalues Black bodies in the ways described above. The approach is also fitting because of the long history of Black activists and intellectuals targeted by US government surveillance. As Browne (2015) wrote, "Surveillance is nothing new to black folks. It is the fact of antiblackness" (10). The TBF framework provides principles for a nuanced analysis, focusing on concepts that are important to the understanding of the lives of marginalized peoples.

Because women are rarely centered in discussions of nationalism (Anthias & Yuval-Davis, 1992, p. 28; Manchanda & de Haan, 2018, p. 91), we have the opportunity to gain some important insights in the context of a gendered analysis of the impact of (white) US American nationalism on Black communities. If we understand the United States as a country with many nations competing for control of state power and resources, we can understand the significance of this analysis even beyond the state: "state power and sovereignty are not only embedded in the structures, cultures, and social relations of locally and nationally organized communities, but are also always grounded and mediated on a transnational scale" (Chowdhry & Nair, 2002, p. 6). For that reason, in order to understand how state power is yielded in a neoliberal context, we must examine the porosity of colonial borders and conventional boundaries. Below, I engage each of the TBF principles with attention to its relevance to the discussion of surveillance technologies.

Intersectionality

Intersectionality requires an understanding of how multiple hierarchical social structures impact realities. Commonly, it highlights how people who lack race, gender, and class privilege are impacted by policies created in a society designed for white, wealthy, men. Browne (2015) described "racializing surveillance" as "a technology of social control where surveillance practices, policies, and performances concern the production of norms pertaining to race and exercise a 'power to define what is in or out of place'" (Browne, 2015, p. 16). My opening story is about Black hair, which is a notoriously important social and political expression for Black women. Through a gendered analysis, we can see how certain braided and cornrowed hairstyles, popularized by Black women, are coded as suspicious by surveillance technologies.

Browne also uses the term "intersecting surveillances" to describe the "the interdependent and interlocking ways that practices, performances, and policies regarding surveillance operate" (Browne, 2015, p. 9). Before my father passed away, he was in a wheelchair, which meant that he was not able to be scanned with the newer airport scanners, requiring that a person stand with hands raised. In that way, we can see how a technology is built for some (able) bodies and not for others. Although he was a tall, Black man, the surveillance technologies rendered him unsuspicious because of his differently abled body. We had sufficient resources and professional status that he never had to travel alone, but the existing corporate technologies target people with few economic resources in the creation of what Eubanks (2017) called a "digital poorhouse." Whether systems of public assistance or airport travel, the everyday digitized system of our lives disproportionately impacts and monitors marginalized communities whom a small elite intends to control. Referring to the digital poorhouse, Eubanks (2017) wrote, "Its integrated data systems and digital surveillance infrastructure offer a degree of control unrivaled in history" (Eubanks, 2017, p. 200). Realizing that the system is set for the control of many by a few, the work to be done is not simply scholarship.

Scholar-Activism

What, then, is the work of the scholar-activist in relation to such surveillance technologies? The responsible scholar should highlight "the capabilities of noncooperative biometric tagging" (Browne, 2015, p. 128). Much of the general public is unaware of the extent to which they are being surveilled at political protests, country borders, and airports. Furthermore, these practices disproportionately impact people of color:

> Marginalized groups face higher levels of data collection when they access public benefits, walk through highly policed neighborhoods, enter the health-care system, or cross-national borders. The data acts to reinforce their marginality

when it is used to target them for suspicion and extra scrutiny. Those groups seen as undeserving are singled out for punitive public policy and more intense surveillance, and the cycle begins again. It is a kind of collective red-flagging, a feedback loop of injustice.

(Eubanks, 2017, pp. 6–7)

A scholar-activist orientation requires more than simply researching injustice. It requires an appropriate justice-oriented response. When I discuss an intersectional scholar-activist identity, I mean for scholars to engage activism in the locations where they have the most power and privilege. Thus, a scholar-activist position would require engaging questions of university surveillance and data collection, in order to advocate for equitable practices. In what circumstances is it possible for students and staff to opt out of surveillance? Are students unable to access basic services (e.g., health and dining services) without being subjected to surveillance or submitting genetic information? In what ways are students without class privilege subjected to increased monitoring (possibly through financial aid records and reporting)? Understanding that data collected can be (and has been) used to harm individuals, we must work to challenge inequitable surveillance practices, and also to create opportunities for escape from them.

Solidarity

One way to think about solidarity as it relates to surveillance is to consider the disparate ways in which (racially and economically segregated) communities are surveilled. White and wealth-privileged communities can and should use their access to structural power to dismantle forms of policing that cause disproportionate harm for people of color living in poverty. In parts of Atlanta, Georgia, the city is "engineering innovative technologies that animate a drone imaginary of future war" (Miller, 2019, p. 93). The city, known as a Black Mecca because of its African American professional class, has been a test case for predictive (and predatory) policing: "Atlanta-area police have historically used the city as a laboratory for the development and testing of new policing technologies, including PredPol predictive policing software, surveillance drones, and social media monitoring" (Miller, 2019, p. 94). When police departments adopt the software, they make a decision about whether to use information about minor crimes (e.g., vagrancy and panhandling); the inclusion of such data results in more data and more arrests (O'Neill, 2016,

p. 86). Unfortunately, those arrests are concentrated in neighborhoods that have a history of being highly policed. "So even if a model is color blind, the result of it is anything but. In our largely segregated cities, geography is a highly effective proxy for race" (O'Neill, 2016, p. 87). Solidarity requires an understanding of the unevenness of policing strategies and a commitment to humane practices in all communities.

Attention to Borders/Boundaries

Surveillance technologies challenge how we think about spatial relations because they allow someone who is physically distant to watch and/or monitor a person in a different location. At the same time, these technologies are coded in ways that reify conventional boundaries: "Racializing surveillance is a technology of social control where surveillance practices, policies, and performances concern the production of norms pertaining to race and exercise a 'power to define what is in or out of place'" (Browne, 2015, p. 16). In this way, racial boundaries (and categories) are reified through surveillance technologies as spatial and geographic boundaries. According to Browne (2015), "'racializing surveillance' signals those moments when enactments of surveillance reify boundaries, borders, and bodies along racial lines, and where the outcome is often discriminatory treatment of those who are negatively racialized by such surveillance" (Browne, 2015, p. 16). Thus, attention to these borders and boundaries leads us to challenge racialized borders and boundaries. Who do they serve? How is power implicated in their reification?

Also, surveillance technologies challenge the conventional separation between online and offline behavior. In that sense, "racializing surveillance" is "part of the digital sphere with material consequences within and outside of it" (Browne, 2015, p. 17). Often, surveillance algorithms map onto colonial geographies in a way that reinforce racist histories and realities so that "geographic and racial imaginaries remain deeply intertwined, the former naturalizing the latter, whereby 'desirable' and 'undesirable' serve as euphemistic codes for valuable and disposable people" (Benjamin, 2019, p. 13). PredPol predictive policing technologies, deployed in Atlanta, Georgia, exemplify such practices:

> First PredPol utilizes predictive analytics to purportedly generate locations of imminent future threat. As with preemptive strikes in drone war, these predictive capacities are fueled through discourse of risk management that seek to contain racialized threat. Second, implementation of PredPol follows a discursive logic of the war on terror whereby the language of technological

precision and innovation is used to mask the force of state violence and its historical trajectories.

(Miller, 2019, pp. 94–5)

With such technologies, entire neighborhoods can be mapped as "criminogenic regions" that are "so saturated with racialized threat that persons within those spaces cannot be otherwise than suspect" (Miller, 2019, p. 96). In this way, Black neighborhoods can be coded as policing threats and targeted as hotspots for intervention. As Scannell (2019) wrote, "Prediction, presented as a method of harm reduction, makes no effort to change the structural inequalities and violence of the American carceral state" (Scannell, 2019, p. 117). These technologies only stand to make these inequities more profound.

Radically Transparent Positionality

Feminist scholars are accustomed to positioning themselves in relation to their topics. In this case, it may be useful to know that I am a cisgender, able-bodied Black woman, who was raised with relative (middle) class privilege by a single African American mother. Often, I find that these characterizations do not provide sufficient explanation of the scholar's relationship to the particular issue being explored. Rarely do scholars reveal an inside track that may have provided them with greater access to the research topic than others. It can be considered unprofessional to reveal one's motives. My belief is that revealing these things actually demystifies academic writing, and provides much needed transparency.

This chapter is directly related to my experience as a (very frustrated) computer science graduate student. At the time when I was studying, there were many fewer discussions about the moral and ethical implications of technology. When those conversations did happen, it was rare that they were taken up by the actual coders. Since I was learning to build technology, the expectation was that I should accept specifications given to me by others. However, this chapter is also written from the perspective of someone born into a community of Black resistance. As long as I can remember knowing anything of US history, I have known that the government repressed and killed Black revolutionaries. I am committed to the world of Black technologists who are working on behalf of this kind of resistance to government surveillance. Resistance will likely come in the form of that Simone Browne (2015) called dark sousveillance.

Resisting Neoliberal Surveillance: Exploring Dark Sousveillance

Lisa Nakamura (2008) suggested that "an examination of the deployment of the Internet as a racial and gendered visual cultural practice might help us to take a closer look at the ways that cultural resistance to normative gender, racial, and national narratives might be enabled in new digitally interactive spaces" (34). While some people think of surveillance as unidirectional, the perspectives explored in this section engage digital responses that allow us to see surveillance as a "digitally interactive space." In *Black Software*, McIlwain (2020) asked, "will our current or future technological tools ever enable us to outrun white supremacy? After all, this is not just our country's founding principle. It is also the core programming that preceded and animated the birth, development, and first uses of our computational systems" (8).

Building on that history, Browne (2015) highlighted "how racism and antiblackness undergird and sustain the intersecting surveillances of our present order" (Browne, 2015, pp. 8–9). People often think of technology as only computerized or digital, when in fact, newer inventions are often borne out of prior practices and older non-digital technologies. If we understand white nationalist and neoliberal intentions to be the underlying logic informing US surveillance, we are able to place recent technologies in a broader historical context: "How things get ordered racially by way of surveillance depends on space and time and is subject to change, but most often upholds negating strategies that first accompanied European colonial expansion and transatlantic slavery that sought to structure social relations and institutions in ways that privilege whiteness" (Browne, 2015, p. 17). Thus, we should understand a genealogy of contemporary surveillance technologies that is an extension of the enslavement of Black bodies.

Accordingly, we can connect various forms of resistance to an ongoing struggle for liberation. Browne (2015) used the term "dark sousveillance" to describe "the tactics employed to render one's self out of sight, and strategies used in the flight of freedom from slavery as necessarily ones of undersight" (Browne, 2015, p. 21). In this way, we can understand Black people's resistance to surveillance in a much longer trajectory: "Dark sousveillance is a site of critique, as it speaks to black epistemologies of contending with antiblack surveillance, where tools of social control in plantation surveillance or lantern laws in city spaces and beyond were appropriated, co-opted, repurposed, and challenged in order to facilitate survival and escape" (Browne, 2015, p. 21). In the 1960s, a form of dark sousveillance happened within robust networks of Black people who were developing computerized resistance to racial violence:

> They manipulated algorithms to influence search outcomes. They enhanced public visibility and compelled attention to racial justice causes and actions. They used digital hardware and software to obfuscate state surveillance systems and watch the watchers. They created digital stylistics and protected spaces that produced personal and collective pleasure, instigated conversation and debate, and established community.
>
> (McIlwain, 2020, p. 6)

These discussions of Black resistance extend beyond conversations about how increased participation might change notions of race in online environments (Nakamura, 2002, p. 109). It is important to consider the existence of online participation, but also the various ways communities choose to participate, or not.

Elsewhere, I have explored the design possibilities of "technology in Black feminist world" (Hall, 2019). Contemporary examples of dark sousveillance engage many forms of resistance: "Hyphen-Labs, an international team of women of color working at the intersection of technology, art, science, and futurism, is experimenting with a wide array of subversive designs, including earrings for recording police altercations, and visors and other clothing that prevent facial recognition, all part of their Not Safe as Fuck project" (Benjamin, 2019, p. 11). As Black digital practice has become mainstream (Brock Jr., 2020, p. 1) and is "decentering whiteness as the default internet identity" (Brock Jr., 2020, p. 5), the possibilities for dark sousveillance are increasing. Black digital practice "upends technocultural beliefs about how information, computers, and communication technologies should be used" (Brock Jr., 2020, p. 6). There are many ways to resistance neoliberal technologies of surveillance, both online and offline.

Conclusion

The dark—and Black—truth is that government technology in the United States has never accounted for the natural lives and bodies of Black people. The US government has never intended to correctly identify our humanity. To the contrary, the information that is listed on our government (white) "identification" cards tends to list information that varies primarily for white people. For most of my Black family, eye color and hair color are brown. Any Black girl or woman who has ever had braided extensions can tell you about the many shades of brown hair to be found in a beauty supply store. However, my driver's license makes no such distinction, and there is no information about texture. (If there were, maybe I would not have faced hair harassment at the airport.) This is a (white nationalist) government's complicity in the erasure of diverse Black humanity.

Somewhat ironically, state (mis)identification cards have been central to voter disenfranchisement in states with Republican governors (Duster, 2019, p. xii). Conservatives and neoconservatives have played an important role in developing state mechanisms for the disenfranchisement of communities of color, even while liberals maintain them in a colorblind daze. Given this context, it is no wonder that the (white and patriarchal) neoliberal state is incapable of responsibly identifying, tracking, or securing the safety of Black citizens. This state has always had the goal of control and containment for Black communities.

Understanding the experience of surveillance through the history of Black people in the United States provides a unique perspective: "Routing the study of contemporary surveillance—whether that be biometric technologies or post-9/11 security practices at the airport—through the history of black enslavement and its attendant practices of captivity opens up the possibilities for fugitive acts of escape, resistance, and the productive disruptions that happen when blackness enters the frame" (Browne, 2015, p. 164). This chapter aimed to both name the violence of the current neoliberal state and give voice to the ongoing struggle for various forms of escape and resistance. It is dedicated to those revolutionaries working in dark sousveillance.

6

Hot Rockin' Vampires on Skateboards

Neoliberalism's Feminism

Robin Truth Goodman

This chapter considers how neoliberal ideology is appropriating feminism's oppositional rhetorics to gloss neoliberalism as oppositional to imperialism, religious conservativism, and authoritarianism. In other words, feminism is being used for neoliberalism's purposes in order to make neoliberalism seem as though it is oppositional to the global *Realpolitik* that it practices.

For this, I turn to a moment where Iran is building toward a 2015 agreement about restricting its nuclear enrichment and reprocessing capacities with the member states of the United Nations Security Council. In US political positioning of the time, Iran called up a figure of a nation-state that denied individual and market freedoms through a religious fundamentalism held in place by economic stagnancy and regression that only market fundamentalism could resolve. Whereas the Obama administration and its allies negotiated to bring Iran more in line with mainstream liberalization and peace initiatives, including in controlling energy markets, the Trump administration subsequently surrendered such an alliance, following instead the preferences of their more right-wing Saudi and Israeli counterparts simultaneously by continuing instead an Iran policy based in economic and political marginalization. The Obama-era treaty may have opened Iran up for financial investments and the advancement of credit, while Trump's policy, ushering in a draconian regime of sanctions, bolstered up the more conservative wing of the Iranian political establishment. It is too early to tell how US Iran policy will proceed during the Biden administration, but it looks like the Biden administration is threatening to continue Trump-era policies and strict sanctions unless Iran first gives up the advances it has made in its nuclear program after the United States broke its side of the agreement. The period I am considering is before Trump changed the US course.

In my argument, culture plays an important role in creating consent and implementing neoliberalism's hegemony, showing that neoliberal reforms make sense only after intervening in and asserting dominance over the prevailing mix of political ideas. Culture envisions a substantial difference between liberalism and authoritarianism through the figure of the liberal woman. In this, the feminist in her quest for freedom is positioned as directly resisting the regime's economic, industrial control by means of her sexual autonomy in the same way that neoliberal reforms promised by the signing of the treaty were supposed to break up the old Iranian power block. At the same time, the woman acting freely turns into an alibi for political control, meaning that the difference that the sexually liberated woman injects between fundamentalism and its opposition in free markets collapses. Contingently, feminism is defanged, so to speak, from resisting neoliberalism's platforms that have been instrumental in impoverishing women, subjecting them to debt and austerity, and making them responsible for the care of population in the absence of social supports.

In this chapter, I discuss liberal feminism's visibility as it is appropriated to shape neoliberalism's self-image. While in the late seventies we may have learned from Laura Mulvey that the masculine cinematic gaze fetishizes woman-as-image, we are now seeing neoliberalism itself fetishized as feminist by the woman in the image. In *A Girl Walks Home Alone at Night*, the woman-in-the-image—a death-dealing seducer and destroyer of populations—poses autonomous sexuality—and therefore, feminism—against the political and economic control of an authoritarian regime. *A Girl Walks Home Alone at Night* is a 2014 début feature film by Ana Lily Amirpour, a British filmmaker of Iranian descent and a US resident whose parents fled from Iran to Kent after the 1979 Revolution and then moved to Miami when she was eight. Her first trip to Tehran was in 2003. The movie, funded through crowd-sourcing on *Indiegogo*—where Margaret Atwood was one of the first to donate part of the initial $57,000 budget—was shot in Farsi in Taft, California.[1] A critique of the policies responsible for what the movie envisions as a corrupted and authoritarian Islamic state, *A Girl Walks Home Alone at Night* captures, in the mode of the Iranian New Wave, the postindustrial landscape of post-Revolutionary Iran in a spaghetti-Western, ghost-town, black-and-white, avant-garde, soft-porn aesthetic with a vampire theme.

I argue here that *A Girl Walks Home at Night* draws on the popular appeal of feminism to celebrate neoliberal market integration as a heroic feminism that will save us from regressive, parochial, patriarchal authoritarianism. The film therefore participates in a marked uptick in feminism's current popularity which is fueled forward partly on the basis of feminism's appearances as world-formative. As Susan Watkins explains, feminism has been absorbed as "a mantra of the global establishment" (5), becoming a rallying cry for the expansion of global power and losing some of its critical edge even as its following surges. Not only is there a clamping down on or at least an enlivened awareness on what is called "rape culture" in the United States and elsewhere as well as a rise in Title IX enforcement, but also a number of social movements have arisen around the world that reference feminism and women's rights, including one in Saudi Arabia, where women were finally allowed to drive, to travel without permission, and to jog in public (even though women's rights activists remain incarcerated with its leading activist, Loujain al-Hathloul, only released in 2021 after nearly three years in prison). The *New York Times* celebrates Saudi Arabia's embrace of "women's rights" in an article that lauds women's entry into the workforce as baristas, low-earning, and low-skilled service to a cosmopolitan consumerist elite, a change that the *New York Times* recognizes, using feminist vocabulary, as a boost to "self-esteem" (Yee) because it gives the women a choice of what to wear. With sexual harassers being called out and women "leaning in" to achieve work/family balance, with more women being elected to political office, more women CEOs, and superheroes like Wonder Woman, Furiosa, and Katniss Everdeen kicking the world's butt to secure the world's survival, why are women still earning less around the world, more subject to violence, more subject to debt, more impoverished, and why is it so easy to agree with Andrea Long Chu when she defines "female" as the part of ourselves that we hate most, that is, "any psychic operation in which the self is sacrificed to make room for the desires of another" (22)? Why, that is, would the idea that the female subject is made in isolation from the desire of others be blogged as a feminist idea? Although Catherine Rottenberg recognizes that feminist themes have become "increasingly compatible with neoliberal and neoconservative political and economic agendas" (11), fostering a calculative rationalism in lifestyle choice, a neoliberal use of feminist themes must also be situated within our current geopolitical context and our broad, political self-image.

Neoliberalism's Feminism

Neoliberalism today promotes its version of feminism around the world, as feminism can help enforce its policies and social ideologies, and the feminism promoted by neoliberalism does not usually add up to better living conditions around the world. "[A]dvances in gender equality," Watkins shows, "have gone hand-in hand with soaring socio-economic *inequality* across most of the world," testifying to "mainstream feminism's collusion with the neoliberal order" (7). Much of the reason for this is that a vital concern for feminism—social reproduction—is quickly becoming reconstructed for more massive appropriations as public welfare is cut and education is infused with profiteering technologies. Indeed, feminism's "Second Wave" gained steam at the same time as neoliberalism in the seventies, when women were entering the workforce while public sector supports for them were being divested, financial speculation was an increasingly bigger piece of the economic picture, and when, as Nancy Fraser has shown in her many books and articles, the feminist critique of patriarchal statism was appropriated and reprogrammed to support expansive capitalization, deregulation, and public spending cuts.[2]

Today, the tasks of social reproduction are being increasingly left to the individual with a corresponding ideological make-over of a superpowerful individual responsibility divorced from social bonds or supports. This dovetails with a feminist message of "empowerment" that makes women appear "feminist" for taking on by themselves responsibility of global political failure. Neoliberal realignments of gender within reproductive economies, as Aihwa Ong has shown, have allowed for manipulation and seizure of profits by constructing private, domestic, reproductive identities as privatized "work," especially in the face of national economic need. As women professionals in the tech economy have been absorbed into production in tech-rich countries like Singapore, women "care" workers are recruited from poorer nations like Malaysia and the Philippines, their identities re-envisioned with "moral guarantees of biological welfare" (179) by prohibitions on sex and policed leisure time. As Fraser, Bhattacharya, and Arruzza phrase it, "the making of people is treated as a mere means to the making of profit" (22) as this system "free-rides on nature, public goods, and the unwaged work that reproduces human beings and communities" (17). Dumping responsibility for socialization singularly on mothers and their care-giver surrogates overburdens women with securing the promise of future social well-being both nationally and internationally.

Population

In addition, though, and perhaps less visible in academic treatments of neoliberalism, feminism has also participated in a neoliberal framing of population. Even though both Angela Davis and Adrienne Rich warned that a feminist movement for reproductive rights needs to be careful to disassociate itself from the eugenic racism of "population control" in sterilization campaigns (Rich, xix) like the one in Bolivia, today population as a pressure on the environment has elicited a feminist response as part of global feminist agendas. A feminist as prominent as Donna Haraway has saddled feminism with reducing population in the face of environmental collapse, burdening feminism with the onus of planetary redemption by advancing the slogan "Make Kin Not Babies!" (102). In the face of structural adjustment programs enforced by the International Monetary Fund (IMF) and the World Bank as well as credit crunches under the Volcker plan—worsening economic conditions disproportionately to women— World Bank and US policy has sought to use "women's empowerment" as a mechanism for boosting economic growth by reducing fertility rates. While First World feminism's emphasis on liberation through sexuality ushered in population control through birth control to the benefit, as Susan Watkins points out, of Big Pharma (45), sterilization was often imposed on women of color or women in poorer countries to control the numbers of what Marx called "the reserve army of labor" and to diminish state responsibility for the economically marginalized and the dispossessed. Concern over population, as Hannah Arendt pointed out, involves a decision over "who should and who should not inhabit the world" (*Eichmann*, 279). Arendt was protesting Eichmann and the Nazis' illegitimate sovereign appropriation of this decision, leading into her life-long thinking on participatory politics. Twisting feminist politicization of reproductive rights issues, neoliberal ideology has refashioned this sovereign decision over population as a responsibility of mothers and the excessive fecundity of their reproducing bodies, thereby positioning mothers as blamable for social failure.

In neoliberalism's framing of overpopulation as a problem, feminism has become an alibi for public disinvestment. According to Susan Watkins, the belief that the United States led global feminism is a myth; actually, during a time in the early seventies when the price of oil was high and the United States was still reeling from defeats in Vietnam, African and Arab feminist movements initiated calling for national control over resources to defend against the incursion of foreign corporate interests. A corporate backlash and appropriation ensued, consisting of a World Bank "feminist turn" focused on private-sector growth with the extension of micro-credit and contraception as its stated goals, thereby targeting religious states primarily. "'[W]omens empowerment,'" she sums up, "would boost economic growth and could help to reduce fertility rates" (41).

In particular, the 1994 Cairo Programme "directed the bulk of funds towards long-acting contraception programmes" (44) without any improvements to health care, child mortality, or social services. In this logic, women's bodies as reproductive capacities are at fault for the bloated budgets that have led to both economic and ecological decline, not corporate-favored policies of upward redistribution, tax cuts, social spending cuts, privatization, deregulation, and the like. The solution is to put onto women the responsibility for securing the future productivity by bearing fewer children.

There have been a number of critics who have interrogated how maternity circulates as an ideological lever for neoliberal cuts and economic restructuring. As Jacqueline Rose asks, "what are we doing to mothers—when we expect them to carry the burden of everything that is hardest to contemplate about our society and ourselves?" (1). Catherine Rottenberg has, too, noticed a corporate messaging seizing feminism within neoliberal ideals in "the commodification and the depoliticization of motherhood" where "parenting problems are the result of problematic individual choices" (113). Particularly non-white mothers, Sophie Lewis adds, "can practically do no right and carry the blame for every social problem even as they receive no economic incentive whatsoever to perform motherhood 'better'" (114). Angela McRobbie, meanwhile, equates the "rehabilitation of feminism" (120) under neoliberalism with a maternalism that emphasizes "self-responsibility, entrepreneurialism" to "enhance the core values of the neoliberal project" (121). McRobbie understands the feminist mother as advancing neoliberalism's corporatism by making mothers responsible for the insecurities ensuing from the gutting of the social safety net. McRobbie specifies that the "empowerment" of the entrepreneurial mother is in part, after 9/11, formed in opposition to "the imagined other, the Muslim woman assumed to be oppressed and subjected to various forms of domination and control" (121-2). In this view, the entrepreneurial mother is envisioned as a hierarchical, even evolutionary step above the woman whose choices and mobility are the targets of religious fundamentalist regressive patriarchies with their regulation on the family; she is the proof of secular progress promised in market integration.

There have been fewer treatments of how the birthrate and population controls are filters for neoliberal ideas, where women's bodies are invested with the interests of capital in removing the birth of the unwanted and the dependent from habitation in the world.[3] One exception may be Penelope Deutscher. She asks, "how does reproduction come to present as a mode of responsibility toward 'population' or its future?" (78). Her interest is in the production "of female subjects understood as having the capacity to propagate death" (65) that she links to biopolitics. She goes on, "I have argued that to see reproduction and parenting taking shape as technologies targeting the health and optimization of individual and population futures is to see them concurrently taking shape as parallel technologies of death, with corresponding conducts including averting, managing, gridding, stimulating, predicting, distributing, and proliferating" (114). Deutscher's focus is on understanding reproductive rights politics as not just about a transfer of sovereign decision from the state to the individual but also as a biopolitics built through a politics of death (thanatopolitics). "[T]he family," she writes, "is a zone of risk. As the space of the child's desirable survival, it also becomes the context for calculating its likelihood of death" (93). Although Deutscher moves on from there to talk about attributing unhealthy situations to "deficient mothering" (93), she also interprets thanatopolitics as enhancing "the quality of the population and the nation's strength" (96), thereby foregrounding the role of the mother in making lives precarious. Women's reproducing bodies here constitute a division between desirable and undesirable lives, and women can be blamed for economic scarcities—particularly ones that target populations like immigrants—that should be laid in the lap of bankers and financers. My interest here is in how such a biopolitics of death—"thanatopolitics"—is used to control transnational productivities by creating a heroic narrative around the capacity of women's bodies to reproduce death.

A Girl Walks Home Alone at Night

A Girl Walks Home Alone at Night stages, on the body of a woman, an epic battle between the forces of neoliberal imperialism and the authoritarian state. From the very beginning, *A Girl Walks Home Alone at Night* links a barren industrial economy to barren reproduction. The barren industrial landscape can be blamed on the political barrenness of the regime. However, reproductive barrenness is a different and more complicated story: it relates to a changing social context of family dissolution that allows women both economic and sexual mobility. The movie favors this sexual liberation as a defining trait of its hero. The familial dissolution brings to light an association between women's freed sexuality and the demise of the regime which builds its power in part through familial control. Women embody the historical border between the regime's authoritarian politics, on the one hand, which are a regressive sovereign power that decides to let live or to give death, and, on the other, a neoliberal advance that gives bodies over to "free" exchange and individual sovereign decision by alienating them from social supports and the state (as represented in the heavy-equipment-laden dead landscape). The demise of the regime underlies the condition of possibility for liberal feminism—the exercise of free sexuality on the part of the individual woman as the condition of possibility for (neoliberal) free (entrepreneurial) labor (microcredit or the like).

The opening sequence establishes this central political conflict between the sovereign Islamic state (represented as family) and the sovereign individual (woman and feminist) in a montage of death scenes relating to old industrial equipment and to women. A series of spliced-together shots tracks Arash on his way home with a found cat: deserted streets lined with shuttered middle-class homes; a fenced-in work site with trucks, barrels, and other equipment but without workers; in front of the fence, a close-up of a prostitute, her lipstick applied, shadows over her face, her eyes lifted seductively in reaction to Arash and her eyelids blinking over a half-smile as he passes; the camera pulls back on three white silos in back of her, dwarfing her. The juxtapositions of nearly still shots ally metaphorically the deadened, emptied industrial landscape and the childless woman. The next shot reveals, on the side of a highway, a pit strewn with dead bodies, curving around, with a set of electrical wires crisscrossing overhead, followed by another shot of the same setting with Arash walking in the opposite direction to reveal a population in death behind him. Indications of industrial work and power poles without actual workers here hang over a pile of corpses, as though industrial development had been death-inflicting rather than life-enhancing. Later in the movie, we learn that the sucking machines are not the corpse-maker but the vampire is, linking the two. The movie is shot with sharp black-and-white contrast and deep shadows, creating an eerie, after-life quality to the industrial landscape.

The critics of *A Girl* have mostly been interested in Amirpour's experiment with genre translated into a new and exotic national setting. Mary Ann Johanson of *Flick Filosopher* excitedly comments: "The Iranian skateboarding vampire feminist spaghetti western we have all been waiting for, creepy cool and gorgeously sinister, engorged with suspense and desire."[4] And Sheila O'Malley says, "They all live in Bad City, an Iranian town filled with bad bad vibes, surrounded by pumping oil drills, seen like galumphing prehistoric beasts, going up and down, up and down."[5] The film, however, does more than just play off the strangeness of seeing a Muslim culture within a familiarly sexualized genre (in the rhythm of a Kurt Vonnegut novel?), an interpretation that would single out the film's conventional Orientalism. The film uses the deathlike quality of the industrial landscape to highlight the failures of the authoritarian

Islamic Republic. At the same time, it raises depopulation as a result and social fallout caused by the failing economic policies of the Islamic Republic's authoritarianism. Islamic fundamentalism with its death machines creates the death-landscape of industrialism, but so does the liberated woman. This is a far cry from the "reproductive futurism" that Lee Edelman says repeats the future in the oppressive social and cultural hierarchies of the present;[6] instead, the future is premised on the woman's capacity to deny reproduction and interrupt the nation, to set it on a different path. Non-reproductive, the vampire embodies independence and becomes a figure of rejuvenation, a feminist hero freed up from the stagnation of authoritarian nationalism, religious dogmatism, economic retrenchment and sluggishness, and familial and cultural traditionalism in order to pursue a new entrepreneurial adventurism.

The film's invocation of cultural difference only really appears through its remaking of character plotlines into the particular plotlines of the nation-state. Emphatic within its *mise-en-scène*, the film's historical moment looks back to invoke the beginning of the regime as the start of its narrative and at the same time as the starting date of the protagonist's work-life and the concurring decline of industrial labor. This coinciding of timeframes—for the regime, the film's story, and the character—points to the film's movement as freeing the present from its past and therefore freeing the characters from the national plotline that assures decline. The film is very specifically citing popular genres from the eighties in order to explore the economic fallout of post-Revolutionary Iran. So Mayer, from the British Film Institute's (BFI) *Sight and Sound*, points to cultural references like Jim Jarmusch's *Only Lovers Left Alive*, which alludes to the early eighties in its score, but also to *Down by Law* and Gus Van Sant's gritty queer cult flick *Mala Noche*, both from 1986,[7] and as well there are turntables, cassette tapes, posters of Michael Jackson's *Thriller* (1983), Madonna, and the Bee Gees collaged on the lead female character's bedroom wall, and the vampire's confession that her favorite song is Lionel Richie's 1984 release *Hello Hello* (a song that might not easily be associated with vampires) and the song in the almost-sex scene: a 2009 White Lies piece called *Death*, part of a British goth revival of early eighties sounds produced by bands like Joy Division. After the opening credits, when Arash walks to his car still holding the cat, a boy approaches him to ask for money which he says he does not have. "Do you know how many days I've worked for this car?" he asks the boy, "2,191 days"—exactly six years, dating his working life, as of 1986, from the time around the Revolution. Yet, in the next scene, when the pimp takes his car to pay for his father's heroin debt, the film signals that his days of work productivity are behind him.

The vampire's body is a zone of precarity where she embodies the fate of national revival in her capacity to give death. She can kill like the regime's machines can, but the machines are rooted in the ground that grips their base, while the vampire is unattached, sometimes seeming to float in on her victims on the wings of her veil. The vampire is responsible for the piles of corpses and industrial waste as she is responsible the population deaths caused by her sexual predations. Visual analogies between fruitless industrial penetration and female unreproductiveness saturate the dystopic imagery even beyond the introduction. Amirpour treats the failures of the regime's industry as castration. The cut after the opening sequence reveals a smoky dark sky bearing over giant drills pounding into the black earth, the equipment in dark silhouette. The presence of oil extraction returns in scene after scene as still, smoky, inhuman transition shots, deathlike, with the monstrous machines bearing into the ground like rapists. This exploitation of the earth is echoed in the murder scenes when the vampire replicates the motion of the borer. In the first murder, like the phallic mother of psychoanalysis she bares her teeth, sticks them deep into his finger flesh for a cut, sucks the pimp's finger as though giving him *fellatio*, and then bores her sharp incisors down into him (like the oil drills) till he falls away screaming, and she slowly slides the severed finger from her mouth. The pimp dies in that scene. A typical feminist reading might interpret this scene as instigating a psychic terror caused by the female reversing the order of gender domination and seizing the phallus, where the narrative trajectory would be to punish the woman in order to restore the correct order of power. The film, however, sides with the vampire as she rises in a feminist victory of revenge for the pimp's abuse of women. The killing sets the stage for releasing the woman as independent from the figures of control and stagnation that induce the moral and economic decline associated with the violence of the industrial machines.

This imagery can be seen as a reversal of Iran's film codes and a direct critique of the regime. Iranian post-Revolutionary film has, as Negar Mottahedeh convincingly argues, used the veiled woman to counter the imperialist gaze. One method of changing what Ayatollah Khomeini objected to as the imperialist gaze in realist film conventions and to purify the Islamist body was by covering women, blocking the gaze that Laura Mulvey had argued allowed identification with the camera through a non-narrative interruption, a dense black mark, a fetish. "[V]eiled female bodies," Mottahedeh notes, "were generated to stand against the contaminating influences previously introduced into mediating technologies" (2). Yet, Amirpour restores castration in the gaze to oppose the logic of the regime, using the veil as a screen that gives away the secret. The chador that the vampire wears could read as Orientalist exoticism but it also, more glaringly, with the veil in silhouette, gives the back of her head the same shape as the industrial grinder biting into the soil for its life-blood. The vampire-woman often appears out of nowhere, accompanied by a drumbeat, landing when an unaware character turns around, or breaking the continuity of a street or a wall, creating an eerie shadow, stopping the motion with her speechless stare. The camera takes her in as a break in the stilled, regularized rhythm and symmetry of the industrial *mise-en-scène*, an opening within the shot that suggests something else not in the shot and outside of its pattern, a dark empty break. Amirpour teases with the veil and then removes the veil, emphasizing the body's sexual empowerment underneath the regime's-imposed façade and its controlled social program, as much economic as sexual.

The unproductiveness of production directly corresponds to the unreproductiveness of reproduction, the decline of the family, sexual autonomy or feminism. Inviting the prostitute into the car he just took from Arash, the pimp, for example, scolds her for not having a family as he slips his finger into her mouth (the same finger the vampire will later sever), pays her in cash, and guides her head down toward his lap, reminding her that she is old and should want children, when the vampire appears in a series of jump-cuts and terrifies the pimp into quitting. The film suggests that cash is the visual counterpart to this vampiric feminism as the frequent presence of piles of cash and jewels calls into visual play (as in this scene) insinuations of female domination, female choice, female seduction, female desire, female reason, and female autonomy: "Your husband brings home the money," intones the TV as Ashram's father shoots up at the beginning of the film. "But be prepared. One day, everything changes." In the only scene showing anyone working, Arash, is employed as a groundsman for what looks like a ruling class family with impressive jewelry and a luxurious compound, when the TV breaks and the daughter invites him up to her room to fix it. As she lounges on her bed in a loose-fitting slip, he asks that she leave, as her parents (though apparently not home) would think it inappropriate for the two to be alone. She laughs, teases him, touches him from behind. The cash relation frees her from family controls. This is the only work scene in the film, but it is not a scene of workers making things but rather, as a scene of unveiling, it is a scene of a worker seemingly (though unconvincingly) trying to fix broken things—including the family as a regulative principle, and the veil—and failing.

Even if feminism and Islamism make odd bed fellows, feminism continues to be treated as the outcome of the regime's industrial demise, in that it tears apart the family in the same way that extraction tears apart the earth. Arash's father, sick with addiction, flings the photograph of Arash's missing mother across the room, breaking the glass. Meanwhile, the vampire's veil conceals a secular feminist: cropped-haired young rock 'n' roll sex-seeker, living alone, wearing a tank-top or nothing at all, with lipstick and eyeliner, seductive eyes (often in close-up), and hip-waving dance moves. When Arash approaches her from behind over the turntable, embraces her, and caresses her neck, the scene cuts to the prostitute dancing with a balloon in industrial wreckage, suggesting death, dispossession, and developmental decline as the *sexual* byproduct. Most terrifying of all, the vampire accosts a boy alone on the street at night and blocks his way, appearing right in front of him no matter which way he turns; she asks him multiple times if he is a good boy, and when he insists that he is, she puts her face up to his, tells him not to lie, bares her incisors, and steals his skateboard, threatening—in an echoing, devilish whisper—to take his eyes out of his skull and feed them to the dogs, while he runs away and she licks her lips. As the inverted mother, the title character shatters any sense of a naturalized reproductive femininity, showing instead feminist femininity as destructive, petrifying and murderous, especially to children. Female sexuality detaches women from the reproductive family in as much as the Revolution detaches the fruits of industry from enriching the cultural ground on which it intimately stands.

A Girl Walks Home Alone at Night ends in the dead of night, with Arash, the vampire, and the cat driving off in the car into what should be the sunset but is not. There are no repercussions for the girl having murdered the pimp and Arash's father because industrial automation and vampiric fear take the place of any semblance of government presence, state regulation, or police. In the deadened landscape, the film gives no sense of the road ahead offering anything but more of the same. "If there were a storm coming right now," Arash asks her under the smoke from the refining station, "a big storm, from behind those mountains, would it matter? Would it change anything?" With the family and the local economy both left in ruins, the film's concluding nihilism could be read as an invitation to neoliberal reform, that is, a menacing warning that the industrial economic policies of the authoritarian Revolutionary regime with its Muslim cover needs to turn the page from small-town national inwardness toward an outward, expansive, opening to the world, or else face a deadly blood-sucking. This opening to the unknown future begins with feminism and economic liberalization, as we watch the two main characters through the windshield, the male worker and the smiling veiled female vampire now settled in the machine travelling forward on the open desert road.

Neoliberalism has developed practices of exploiting reproductive economies as much as productive economies, finding methods of reconceptualizing domestic spheres as work sites, places of subject formation and social organization, networks of consumer demand, ideological pressure-points, or points where agents of global profit directly extract surplus from local poverty. In industrial economies, as feminist scholar Leopoldina Fortunati observes, "while production both *is* and *appears as* the creation of value, reproduction *is* the creation of value but *appears otherwise*" (8); yet, neoliberalism has remade reproduction—in this case the reproduction of death—to *appear as* the creation of value. *A Girl Walks Home Alone at Night* justifies neoliberalism's transfer of the profits labor earns to globalization's expansive adventure by presenting a sterile coupling of the feminist and the service worker no longer bogged down by reproduction or production. Just as work is now under the control of the worker rather than the responsibility of the industrial state, population control is imagined as a strategy for better living that the individual can take responsibility for in the face of incredible violence and ecological catastrophe, as a project of empowerment.

In neoliberal ideology, the state can only act violently and restrictively against people and their freedoms (like the Iranian Revolutionary state), and the absence or invisibility of such state in political representation means progress. The authoritarian state—as the sole possible form the state can take (in neoliberal logic) and the sole legitimate purveyor of violence—has dissolved into the natural and psychological landscape, and as such is the invisible rationality of social life. *A Girl Walks Home Alone at Night* shows the woman's body alone mitigating life's precarity, risk, and death against such a state, as the woman, as the purveyor of death, takes the place of the state at the same time as she accounts for the state's failings. The social here, in Hannah Arendt's sense, has been reconceived as a space of anti-politics. As Penelope Deutscher explains, "The decision making transferred to women has taken a new kind of responsibilization: for physiologically and psychologically healthy choices become a new kind of biopolitical obligation" (161). In this context, neoliberalism thrives by twisting feminism's concern about reproduction and reproductive rights into an ideology of population control through individual responsibility as an answer to dire economic and political retrenchment. By appropriating feminism as its concern, neoliberalism makes itself appear like it is other than the authoritarianism that it repeats. It should be clear that an espousal of independent sovereign (feminist and worker) resilience at the expense of social attachment does not oppose authoritarianism but rather gives it another life, sucking the blood of others. Biting through the logic of castration, feminism needs to make an opening on the screen of ideology that cuts in a different direction.

Religious fundamentalism positions women as the internal culture that imperialism threatens while imperialism, like neoliberalism, by justifying itself on freer markets and more micro-credit loans to women, promises to lift up women away from the injustices of a violent, "backward" patriarchal indigenous culture and its oversized authoritarian state. By now, we know where this leads. The polarization of wealth and income globally, which was the result of neoliberal reforms, has not catalyzed women's enrichment, but rather has further and more directly put them in debt to financial elites, where corporations and banks can manage and control their community's organization and production without, in turn, being responsible for their well-being. The dichotomy between the so-called freedom of neoliberal imperialism and the unfreedom of authoritarianism seems to bracket the "woman question" for the contemporary age, giving very little sense of a viable agency or future opening beyond domination by either markets or the state and not offering any treatment of the state or of politics that is anything but a constant return to authoritarianism, no matter which way we turn. To rescue feminism's political edge, feminism needs to wrest itself from being used as an ideological bulwark in the geopolitical struggle between fundamentalist nationalism, on the one hand, and neoliberal market fundamentalism on the other.

Part Two

Contextualizations: Education and the Teacher Profession

7

Feminism and Anti-feminism in Sweden, in the wake of #MeToo

Sarah Ljungquist

Introduction

The revelation of media mogul Harvey Weinstein as a sex offender in the *New York Times* 2017[1] was the starting shot for the global and viral action #MeToo where millions of women testified about their experiences of sexual harassment and abuse. Women's own stories, posted on social media, were closely interlaced with the reporting and attention in traditional media, whereas media's broadcasting of women's testimony made it abundantly clear that sexual violence, abuse, and harassment still are a highly structural problem in societies all over the world (De Benedictis Orgad & Rottenberg, 2019). The movement was rapidly shaking the world. In country after country, politicians and other famous men were forced to leave their positions after accusations and revelations about sexual harassment and abuse of women. However, the #MeToo phenomenon is not just a feminist success. Like previous feminist movements, #MeToo is also fraught with setbacks. Media reports about structural problems with sexual abuse of women that #MeToo has revealed, alternately with reports of angry voices and criticism that men are publicly accused before they have had the chance of being legally investigated and judged guilty.

With this as a starting point, the purpose of this chapter is to discuss tensions and conflicts that arise when a feminist movement like #MeToo challenges structures that legitimate gendered sexual violence and harassment using Sweden as a case. Sweden is a country known for its strong gender equality legislation rendering it particularly interesting to look into more thoroughly. The ideological conflict which characterizes the clash between feminism and anti-feminism at any time in history serves as a background to this discussion (Faludi, 1991).

The chapter is divided into four sections. To begin with, a brief overview of the #MeToo emergence in the United States is presented, followed by a discussion of the #MeToo movement in Sweden based on three different cases illuminated in media. The cases make visible tensions and conflicts linked to the phenomenon backlash, defined as a mechanism triggered by any advance toward justice by the women's movement (Faludi, 1991). In the third section, the place of #MeToo in the Swedish feminist movement is highlighted, through a brief historical overview of its advances and setbacks. Finally, the results are discussed against the background of the literary scholar Kate Millett's theory of patriarchy. The concept of feminism is used here in accordance with a basic definition, the common core being the notion that women are subordinate to men, and that this condition should be changed (Gemzöe, 2006). Feminism is in this text understood as a phenomenon that has existed for as long as the patriarchy. Feminism as a concept was though first used at the beginning of the 1890s, to describe the women's movement for gender equality (Clayhills, 1991).

#MeToo Worldwide

October 2017. An article in the *New York Times* reveals the Hollywood mogul Harvey Weinstein's numerous sexual violations of women, during several decades. A few days later, in an article in the *New Yorker*, thirteen women accuse Weinstein of sexual assaults. This was followed by the most widely reported event, a plea by the actress Alyssa Milano, addressing all women who had been exposed to sexual violation or assault, asking them to answer her tweet with "me too," as way of bringing attention to "the magnitude of the problem."[2]

However, Milanos' initiative did not occur in a historical vacuum. The struggle against sexual violence in the United States began in connection with the foundation of the Women´s Liberation Movement (WLM) at the end of the 1960s (Eduards, 2002). Nor was the use of the phrase "me too" new as a way of sharing experiences of sexual assaults. As early as 2006, the women's rights activist Tarana Burke launched a #MeToo movement, involving young colored women from socially disadvantaged areas, who had been sexually abused.

In fact, the earlier #MeToo movement caused a conflict between Milanos's and Burke's followers, the latter being critical to a famous white woman taking credit for a movement headed by a (at the time) lesser-known colored woman. The criticism is still current, in that it reveals how power hierarchies are still created between women's groups, on the basis of gender, class, and ethnicity (Mohanty, 1988; Bloomfield, 2019). But the conflict was played down, as the key figures behind #MeToo made friends. As soon as Milano was made aware of Burke's earlier initiative, she wrote a tweet praising Burke's campaign: "I was just made aware of an earlier #MeToo movement, and the origin story is equal parts hearth breaking and inspiring." The tweet was linked to Burke who responded favorably and came to see Milanos' initiative as a reinforcement of the movement she had started eleven years earlier.[3]

#MeToo Spreading around the World

The struggle against sexual violence, long-standing though it may be—not just in the United States but in large parts of the world—became global with #MeToo. It is true that so far, #MeToo has made its greatest impact in the West, but it has also made a mark in other parts of the world, in a similar manner.[4] Image 1:1. Millions of testimonies of sexual abuse—without the perpetrators being *named*—have contributed to the reinforcement of legislation on sexual crime. However, these testimonies have also caused verbal and physical attacks against the women—individuals and groups—who have brought these issues to the attention of the public.[5]

In all countries where #MeToo has had a large impact, allegations against men in powerful positions have received the most attention. Media coverage, in many cases fueling the cases, has always had consequences, but not necessarily for those accused. While the case against Harvey Weinstein resulted in a long prison sentence for the perpetrator, the allegations against Brett Kavanaugh led to death threats against the woman who accused him of rape; she had to go into hiding. Brett Kavanaugh was later sworn in as a judge in the United States Supreme Court, under President Donald Trump. In a speech at a rally in Mississippi a few weeks later, Trump commented the event:

> I say that it's a very scary time for young men in America, when you can be guilty of something you may not be guilty of. This is a very, very, very difficult time.[6]

The #MeToo movement instantly reached Sweden; the first testimony was posted on social media an hour after Alyssa Milanos's tweet #MeToo.[7]

#MeToo in Sweden

In Sweden, considered one of the countries with the greatest equality worldwide,[8] the impact of #MeToo was huge. In relation to its population, just over 10 million, the number of #MeToo hashtags in Sweden was the largest in the world.[9] Only days into the movement, thousands of well-known women, such as Foreign Minister Margot Wallström, and Åsa Regnér, Minister for Children and the Elderly, along with a host of unknown women, testified to sexual harassment and abuse, in various networks on social media (Askanius & Møller Hartley, 2019).

On November 8, 2018, women in theatre and the film industry issued a joint call: #quietontheset (#tystnadtagning), with 703 signatures. This call testified to sexual harassment, assault, rape, and a systematic silencing of such acts in the industry. This was soon followed by a number of similar appeals with the same purpose, by various occupational groups, often punning on their profession. Women in the legal profession, for instance, used the hashtag #withwhatright (#medvilkenrätt), and women in the music industry, #whenthemusicisover (#närmusikentystnar), women in the medical profession, #withoutprofessionalsecrecy (#utantystnadsplikt), and so on. By the end of the month, 62,931 women in sixty-five different occupational groups had issued their own appeals to call attention to sexual harassment and abuse within their professions.[10] The extent of these calls should be related to the fact that 80.4 percent of women in Sweden are part of the labor market.[11]

Cases of Media Reporting

Timell and Virtanen

Inspired by the events involving Harvey Weinstein, the broadcaster Lulu Carter accused her former colleague, the anchorman Martin Timell, of groping her during work hours and of sending her pornographic movies at night, on Instagram, November 13. A day or so later, another colleague of Timell's accused him of having raped her in a hot pool during a staff party in 2008. Around the same time, the journalist Cissi Wallin stated on her private Instagram account that Fredrik Virtanen, journalist at the evening daily paper *Aftonbladet* had drugged and raped her in 2006. In this case, too, several other women joined her, testifying to sexual harassment, one of them also stating that she had been drugged and raped by Virtanen[12] (Mendes, Ringrose, & Keller, 2018).

Several public figures and celebrities were accused of sexual crimes, but Timell and Virtanen drew most attention during the first two years of #MeToo in Sweden (with the exception of Arnault, whom I will discuss below). The media coverage of Timell and Virtanen was extensive, not least in traditional national media that, in many cases, published their names and portraits. As a result, both Timell and Virtanen lost some of their commissions. TV 4, Timell's employer, immediately suspended their collaboration with them, and *Aftonbladet*, Virtanen's employer, commissioned an external investigator, specializing in sexual crimes, and Virtanen was pressured to take time-out.

After the allegations, both Timell and Virtanen gave several interviews where they apologized for their behavior. Timell denied the allegations of sexual assault but admitted to "his behaviour [being] seriously out-of-date" and that his actions could have been perceived as sexist. He also stated that he would "get therapy in order to change his behaviour."[13] Even Virtanen denied the assault allegations but admitted that his behavior toward women, during a time in his life when he had problems with drugs and alcohol, had been "like shit, rotten, boorish." He was also held liable for having asked a fourteen-year-old girl who applied for an internship with him if she wanted to have sex with him; his response to this allegation was that he did not know she was fourteen: "I think it was boorish of me to write this, and I understand that it made her uncomfortable, since she was only 14, which I did not know at the time."[14]

The Arnault Case and the crisis in the Swedish Academy

The Swedish Academy is a Royal Academy established in 1786 by the Swedish king and is known worldwide as a Royal academy who nominates and selects the Nobel Laureate in Literature each year. On November 22, 2017, an article entitled "18 women: We Were Abused by a Cultural Personage" was published in one of Sweden's largest daily papers, *Dagens Nyheter*. In a well-documented survey, the journalist Matilda Gustavsson exposed the man in the cultural sphere whose abuse of women had been rumored for decades. There were eighteen women who reported how this man had subjected them to sexual harassment and abuse from 1996 to 2017. The article reveals how the man, called "the cultural profile," had close ties with the Swedish Academy through his wife, and that he was the artistic director of one of Sweden's most exclusive cultural venues.

Through detailed testimonies by the eighteen women, the article also reveals that several of the alleged assaults had taken place in flats owned by the Swedish Academy, one in Stockholm, one in Paris.[15] As a result of the disclosure in *Dagens Nyheter*, the Swedish Academy called an emergency meeting, after which its Permanent Secretary, Sara Danius, stated before a gathering of Swedish media that the Academy had made the unanimous decision to terminate any collaboration with "the cultural profile," for two reasons:

On the one hand, *Dagens Nyheter*'s survey, which we welcome, and on the other hand, it was revealed during our meeting that some members, their daughters, wives and members of the staff, have been subjected to unwanted intimacy and inappropriate treatment by the man in question.

(Gustavsson, 2019, p. 52)

In her book *The Club* (2019), where Matilda Gustavsson adds depth to her survey about "the cultural profile" and his connections with the Swedish Academy, we learn more details about the incidents involving the man who figures here with his real name: Jean-Claude Arnault. It is clear, for instance, that the purportedly "unanimous decision" covered tensions among the group, as opinions about the management of the Arnault case differed widely. According to Gustavsson, this was revealed by an e-mail conversation that took place before the emergency meeting. The academy member Katarina Frostenson, Arnault's wife, claimed in an e-mail that her husband was the victim of a plot, and that the charges against him were outright lies. Another member, and friend of Arnault's, Horace Engdahl, supported Frostenson's account, arguing that there are always rumors surrounding "prominent people," and that a society that wishes to frame those who are accused shows "hysterical traits" (Gustavsson, 2019, p. 62).

The tone in this mail conversation prompted another member, Sara Stridsberg, to react and contact Sara Danius, the Permanent Secretary. Danius subsequently gave her view of the Arnault case in an interview before the emergency meeting. In response to a question about her reaction to the disclosure, she answered that she was "very shaken." She added, "I assume that the information in the article is true, given that there are so many testimonies, and that they are concurrent" (Gustavsson, 2019, p. 63). When asked if she agreed with Horace Engdahl's view of Arnault, she answered that their views in this case were deeply divided (Gustavsson, 2019).

In her account of the Academy's emergency meeting, Gustavsson highlights further details of particular relevance to #MeToo. One of them is the members' personal experiences, one testimony after another revealing incidents involving Arnault. One member said that her daughter had been exposed to sexual harassment "of a criminal nature"; another stated that his wife "no longer wished to accompany him to the dinners hosted by the Academy, because of unpleasant experiences involving Arnault." Female members repeated Arnault's sexual comments and disgraceful suggestions, and so on (Gustavsson, 2019, p. s. 65). Another aspect of relevance to #MeToo was that while most participants in the meeting (there were three absences, including Frostenson) stated that they considered the testimonies in *Dagens Nyheter* quite credible, Horace Engdahl kept a remarkably low profile. Apart from a couple of objections, questioning the relevance of anonymous accusations, and speaking of "Jean-Claude Arnault's seductions," he kept quiet (Gustavsson, 2019, p. 66).

In a press release after the emergency meeting, Danius stated that the Academy would "take measures to ensure that the incidents would not recur."[16] In fact, the implementation of the changes that Danius promised in the press release had already begun. A law firm had been commissioned to carry out an independent investigation of all members' involvement with Arnault. Danius had also informed Frostenson, before the meeting, that she had better leave the room during the discussion of the article in *Dagens Nyheter*. However, Danius' measures, with the intention that the Academy should recognize their role in the Arnault case, faced strong opposition among the members—a group headed by Horace Engdahl. When the legal investigation showed that Frostenson had abused her position in the Academy in various ways, in support of her husband, Danius proposed that Frostenson be expelled from the Academy. The opposition against Danius increased, culminating in a debate article (April 10, 2018), where Horace Engdahl deemed Sara Danius the worst Permanent Secretary in the history of the Swedish Academy's 230 years: "[w]hen we assess the extent of the division we now see in the Swedish Academy, one cannot but draw the conclusion that among all secretaries since 1786, Sara Danius is the one who has been least successful with her task."[17]

This opinion piece was heavily criticized, since Danius enjoyed wide support among the public. Within the Academy, however, the opposition against her gained ground. When Danius on April 12, 2018, proposed some changes to the Academy, including an action plan against sexual harassment, the resistance turned into open conflict. Seven members strongly opposed Danius' proposal, whereas three called for approval. The opponents accused Sara Danius of having caused the Academy's crisis, while her supporters claimed that she was the only one capable of leading the Academy out of the crisis, a crisis caused by the Academy having legitimized Arnault's position for decades, turning a blind eye to his sexual abuse. The meeting concluded with Danius being forced to resign; she was the first woman Permanent Secretary in the history of the Swedish Academy, a position she held for less than three years (Gustavsson, 2019).

The Arnault case closed, in legal terms, in December 2018, when the Court of Appeal convicted Jean-Claude Arnault for two rapes, with a prison sentence of two and a half years. According to the preliminary investigation, most of the crimes he was charged with were time-barred.

Another consequence of the case was that no Nobel Prize in literature was awarded in 2018.[18]

When Sara Danius's resignation was announced, it caused an outrage among the public. Dressed in Sara Danius's signature garment, the neck-tie blouse, women, men, politicians, celebrities, and ordinary people gathered by the thousands, in large manifestations around the country, protesting against the Academy's attempt to cover up their real problem: the sexual abuse and the culture of silence that had allowed this to continue for decades. Or, as one of the protesters, criminologist Nina Rung, put it: "[w]e wants to call attention to a shift. From the stories of sexual abuse by 18 women, the story has been shifted to Sara Danius' ability to lead the Swedish Academy."[19]

Backlash in the Wake of the #MeToo movement

Since #MeToo made its mark in Sweden, harsh or acrimonious comments about feminism have become more common, be it in the manosphere's online communities, in debate articles, books, blogs, or TV talk shows. Comments abound, more or less explicitly claiming that feminism has gone too far, that women have the sexual power, that masculinity in its traditional sense is threatened, and that #MeToo is, in effect, an inquisition. Below examples of resistance from various directions are presented.

According to Susan Faludi, the exact turning point from success to failure occurs when support for the feminist movement is significantly diminished in traditional news media (Faludi, 1991). This applies to the development of the #MeToo movement in Sweden. The movement's first six months may be called a success story, when even those who were in fact staunchly critical against #MeToo were careful to note the movement's merits. For instance, David Eberhard's column in *Göteborgs-Posten,* November 6, 2017, basically critical against #MeToo, is introduced with a tribute to the movement, as a laudable call which, Eberhard hopes, will inspire change. He remarks, however, that the call should target only "the small minority of men who behave like pigs."[20] Approximately six months later, in his book, *The Great Gender Experiment* (*Det stora könsexperimentet*), Eberhard attacks feminism and gender studies in quite a different tone, describing #MeToo not as laudable, but as "a witch hunt on people who were in fact acquitted by the Court" (Eberhard, 2018, p. 159; Lanius, C., 2019).

Even though the resistance against #MeToo grew alongside its success, medial support for the movement was still strong during the spring of 2018, up until May 30, when a TV show transformed the terms of the debate, practically overnight. When Swedish TV's leading investigative journalism show, *Mission: Investigate* (*Uppdrag granskning*) broadcasted the report "#MeToo and Fredrik Virtanen," on May 30, 2018, it had immediate consequences for #MeToo. The program, presented as "a thorough investigation of how media has treated the #MeToo appeal," featured interviews with Fredrik Virtanen and Cissi Wallin. Virtanen was questioned about the allegations against him of sexual abuse. He denied them all, claiming that all were cases of consensual sex by both parties. In response to the allegation that he secretly filmed, and subsequently sent a sex video to a woman with whom he had had sex, he answered:

> I filmed her when she danced naked on a table in front of me./ ... /And this is the thing; if I film her – and we have consensual sex – and I send her the video afterwards, I probably do it for us to meet again. How can this be considered sexual harassment, or some kind of criminal act – these accusations are Kafkaesque ... it is confused with, like, really harsh claims. From totally harmless stuff to this brutal thing with Cissi Wallin.[21]

The questions to Cissi Wallin were fewer and concerned mainly her reasons for accusing Virtanen, whether she had thought of how these accusations may affect his family. She answered that this question is addressed, "almost exclusively, to victims of sexual crimes."[22]

The show was criticized for being biased in Virtanen's favor, causing 2,000 complaints to the Review Board (where it was cleared from bias and convicted only of a minor detail). However, the show contributed to shift the #MeToo debate from women's testimonies to slander and hate campaigns waged against the alleged perpetrators.[23]

With this shift, #MeToo in Sweden entered a backlash period, in the summer of 2018, which was manifested in a different attitude to the men accused of sexual misconduct. When it comes to legal cases, Timell and Virtanen may serve as examples. Timell was acquitted from the rape in a hot pool that he was charged with in March 2018. The reason for the acquittal was that the Court of Appeal classified the offence as sexual harassment, according to the penalty of 2008, which meant that it was time-barred. Fredrik Virtanen in his turn reported Cissi Wallin for aggravated slander, and *she* was sentenced in the District Court in December 2019 (a sentence which is under appeal at the time of writing).

In the public debate, the shift was evident in an increasing number of articles and books that were critical against #MeToo, where the movement was described simply as a campaign against men. Frostenson pleaded a cause for her husband in the book, entitled *K*, with a ruthless attack against Sara Danius' management of the affair, the accusations against Jean-Claude Arnault, the so-called cultural profile.[24]

> I look at my mobile phone. An image appears on the screen: a woman is standing outside Börshuset on Stortorget in the Old Town in Stockholm (*TN*: the seat of the Swedish Academy). She has been Permanent Secretary of the Swedish Academy for little over a year. She stands in the rain, heroic and indignant, under an umbrella, issuing a statement that endorses the witch hunt, the media choir. She expresses her regret and disapproval, dissociating herself and her group from the affair, declaring that she and other ladies in the circle – the stewards of Talent and Taste (*TN*: the Academy's motto)—have been subject to "unwanted intimacy" by "the cultural profile," as you have been rechristened. Huh!
>
> (Frostenson, 2019, p. 11)

In a post on the website 'maskulint.se//rödapillret' (*TN*: the Swedish version of The Red Pill), #MeToo is said to be a phenomenon among the elite, but will soon spread among "real men":

> The widely reported #Metoo-phenomenon is still relatively new, and the majority of those accused appear to be weak, left-leaning beta-men, hypocritical male feminists and sleazy cultural celebrities. I feel no sympathy for these "men" but find the aftermath of these allegations interesting, that is, how they will affect our culture and, not least, legislation. Feminists will not settle for a few victims from the cultural elite; this is only the beginning.[25]

Similar ideas, though phrased more elegantly as aphorisms and maxims, are to be found in a book by a member of the Swedish Academy, Horace Engdahl: *The Indifferent* (*De obekymrade*). The mythical male protagonist, Mahuro, speaks "unabashedly" to the narrator in his dream (Engdahl, 2019, p. 6). Through Mahuro, a world where a "noble" (i.e., gentlemanly) masculinity is described, in figurative terms, a world that is perishing.

> When Mahuro perceives how men around him anxiously learn to pronounce approved phrases about gender and equality, in order to avoid being branded as sexist, he is reminded of the last hour of the Titanic, when people ran around on deck, scrambling for the life boats, or anything to keep them afloat. In our day, masculinity's proud steamer is going down.
>
> (Engdahl, 2019, p. 18)

In another, more argumentative section of the book, #MeToo is compared variously to waterboarding, and to a burlesque low-budget movie from the 1930s (Sw. 'pilsnerfilm'):

> There are elements of old-fashioned sexual disgust in the #MeToo movement; with astonishing success, it has revived the idea that sex is something that women are exposed to. It is like a trip to a Swedish burlesque film from the 1930, where young women were "knocked up." It is amazing to see crafty careerists, knowing full well how to use their attractions, feign helplessness.
>
> #MeToo: Between waterboarding and burlesque! How the movement became a complete success.
>
> (Engdahl, 2019, p. 65)

However, the terms of the debate have changed, given the upsurge of right-wing populism, radical conservatism, and neoliberalism, where anti-feminism is one of the pillars (Kumashiro, 2010). So even in Sweden, where equality is high on the political agenda, it has become legitimate for people to voice their aversion to feminism in public (Sveland, 2013). One example among others is a young male student teacher at a course about democracy and democratic values arguing that:

> #MeToo is a lynch mob, an inquisition of men. Men have become pariah … If a man as much as touches a woman, it is considered rape. There is all this rant about equality, that women should be oppressed. Equality has gone too far. If anyone is oppressed, it is men … Just look at #MeToo; it is clearly oppression of men.

The negative critique of #MeToo is also, as we can see in the quote above, noticeable among Swedish teacher students, even though a more thorough study needs to be done regarding the depth and spread regarding this criticism. Swedish teacher students are often quite anxious to show that they comply with society's and the public school's official policy on gender equality (Hedlin, 2006; Grannäs & Ljungquist, 2015).

The journalist Fredrik Virtanen had just launched his book, *No Mercy* (*Utan Nåd*), with stories about the "mad feminists'" media witch hunt for him, and about his own feelings of inferiority to women "who have the true sexual power" (Lanius, 2019; Virtanen, 2019). The young student, who was informed about Virtanen's case, was upset. He agreed with Virtanen's analysis, adopting his words and his arguments.

Backlash: Not a New Phenomenon

"A BACKLASH AGAINST WOMEN'S RIGHTS is nothing new in American history" (Faludi, 1991, p. 61). Faludi's words, stating that backlashes have been integral to the history of women's emancipation in the United States, are equally relevant to Sweden's history. Feminist advances quite simply give rise to resistance, or backlash, and the feminist movement dates back to the rise of patriarchy, that is, two or three thousand years (Millett, 2000; Lerner, 1987). Let me give a few illustrative examples from this history, primarily from Sweden.

In the biblical myth about the fall of man, a woman rebels against male power, impersonated by Lord God, with a capital L and a capital G. According to the myth, the woman, Eve, is tempted by sin, in the phallic guise of a snake, and eats the forbidden fruit, offering some to the man, Adam. The woman is punished for her rebellion—for introducing knowledge, synonymous with sexuality. Sexuality, a burden of shame, falls on the woman's shoulders alone, as she and Adam are expelled from Eden (Millett, 2000).

Another example of early female rebellion is the saint Bridget of Sweden who, seeing herself as God's envoy on earth, rebelled against patriarchy of her own time, and of times to come. On behalf of her divine mission, she considered herself the most prominent person on earth, and did not shirk from criticizing the world's influential men and their patriarchal authoritarianism. Not surprisingly, her actions were punished, and not just by her contemporaries. The clergy of the Reformation reduced her divine revelations to imbecile dreams, Martin Luther called her crazy: "die Tolle Birgit," and 500 years after her death, the Swedish national writer August Strindberg called her "a domineering and vain woman, who consciously sought sainthood to gain power over 'the other sex'" (Birger Berg, 2003; Witt-Brattström, 2003).

Men's rebellion against patriarchy was punished, too. When Carl Jonas Love Almqvist makes the protagonist in his novel, *Sara Videbeck and the Chapel* (*Det går an*) argue against the statutory power of husbands over their wives, the public indignation knew no bounds. Not only did Sara refuse to obey Albert, in contrast to the biblical Sara's obedience of Abraham, she also refused to be supported by him, she refused to tend to his household, and above all she refused to marry him. This did not mean, however, that she abstained from sexual intimacy with Albert (Almqvist, 2018).

The attacks on Almqvist's confrontation with Romanticism's binary view of women anticipated the late nineteenth-century debate on gender politics and morality. John Stuart Mill's liberal attitude to women as individuals in his *On the Subjection of Women* (1869) posed a threat against the *pater familias*, against the breadwinners' authority. A staunch resistance was mobilized, which meant, in simple terms, the attempt to confine women to their homes. This in turn affected the new suffrage movement, which for fifty years to come would face resistance from all camps of masculinity. The labor movement criticized the suffragettes for sabotaging the class struggle, which to them was of primary importance. Among the bourgeoisie, an aggressive masculinity evolved, and influential men, such as August Strindberg, launched attacks against the suffragettes:

> They [the women] also want the right to vote. Without duties, of course. Without doing military service. That is to say, they are to vote about the lives of men, without risking their own. They want to rule, since they are in the majority. Watch out, men!
> (August Strindberg, Married/Giftas II, 1995, p. 232)

The suffragettes in Sweden were derided and scorned, and so were the men who supported them. The Boulevard Press (*NA*: the Swedish equivalence to "the Yellow Press") included satires and caricatures where women suffragettes were portrayed as unattractive and mannish, and men who supported them as effeminate, dressed in women's clothes. In addition, the resistance reduced the suffragettes through master suppression techniques, particularly that of diminishing. At the outbreak of the First World War, the war served as an excuse for marginalizing "minor issues," such as women's right to vote. In parliament, the conservative member Rudolf Kjellén argued that women must wait, out of loyalty, while the all-important war was still going on. There were no objections to his arguments (Knutsson, 2018, p. 19).

When women finally earned the right to vote, after the war, they expected to be able to remain in the labour market, which had opened up for them during the war, as they replaced men who had been drafted. However, they were again confined to their homes. Unmarried women were allowed to earn a living, in professions considered suitable for them, but to married women large parts of the labour market were closed, thanks to a group of social democrats in parliament who presented motions to restrict married women's right to work. Except for a brief period during the Second World War—when women were once more called in as a labour-force reserve—the labour market did not really open up to married women until the 1970s.

When the feminist movement peaked in the 1970s, many of the reforms that women had fought for since the end of the First World War were finally implemented. The movement also managed to prevent the misogynist report on sexual crimes (1976), one of its proposals being that rape should not be considered a criminal offense, with the exception of severe cases, that pimping should become legal and incest be decriminalized. The struggle against sexual violence in Sweden really began with the publication of Maria-Pia Boëthius' book, *Herself to Blame—A Book about Rape* (Skylla sig själv – en bok om våldtäkt, 1976), about society's view of rape. Despite its progress, however, the feminist vanguard of the 1970s also faced resistance. Representatives of the women's movement were accused of being extremists, who hated men. The men who supported the movement, having organized men's movements during the 1970s, with the purpose to change traditional male roles, were derided as "softies" or "velvet dads" (Hill, 2007).

In the 1980s, essentialist discourse gained ground, a view that had been dominant since Romanticism but had been marginalized during the heyday of political feminism in the 1970s. The difference between the sexes was again seen as biological, causing many pro-feminist men's groups to change direction; they began pushing for a reinstitution of traditional masculinity, often with a conception of an ideal, essential man (Hill, 2007).

The political feminism that evolved during the 1970s soon revived, however. With the slogan "Half of the power, all of the salary," the feminist network from the early 1990s, "Stödstrumporna" (*NA*: literally, "the support stockings"), declared that they considered running for the parliamentary election in 1994, thus putting pressure on the established parties to include gender issue on their agendas (Björk, 1996). A few years later, when the Left Party, with Gudrun Schyman at the helm, announced that they were a feminist party, they surged in the parliamentary election, and feminism made its mark in national politics. Feminism had become acceptable, and even parties who were traditionally indifferent to feminist issues were quick to devise their own version of feminism (Björk, 1996; Sveland, 2013). The currently world-renowned Swedish law that regulates prostitution dates from this period, making it illegal to buy but not to sell sex, apportioning blame primarily to the buyers—the johns.

The backlash following feminism's long golden age this time started with the TV documentary *The Sex War* (*Könskriget*) in 2005. In this show, interviewees were allowed to express their concern about an increasingly fundamentalist feminism, which was reportedly influencing women's shelters and work with domestic violence. A statement by Ireen von Wachenfeldts (head of the National Organisation for Women's Shelters at the time) caused an outcry. She reportedly said, "men are animals," but was quoted out of context; it was a comment on a review of Valerie Solana's *SCUM Manifesto*. But the quote served as proof that feminism was a form of extremism, amounting to hatred of men. The fact that the show was convicted by the Review Board did not help. The damage to feminism was already done.

This time, the decline of feminism did not affect gender equality, however. Not only had equality become a clear political goal, it was also becoming part of the Sweden's self-image. The tenacity of this self-image was evident not least in the anti-feminist movements of the 2010s, with Pär Ström and Pelle Billing at the helm. They coined the term "equalists" to describe their own stance: "for equality, against feminism" (Ström, 2012).

Conclusion

In a statement after the Swedish Academy's demand of Sara Danius' resignation, one of its members, Anders Olsson, defended the action with the argument that it should *not* be interpreted as "patriarchy's victory over a strong woman." As an argument, Olsson states that the conflict underlying the act also "existed between women" and that the Academy is in the process of "electing more women as members."[26] Olsson's statement is interesting, as it brings crucial aspects of patriarchy to light, namely its inability to understand its foundational mechanisms: its variability, and the internalized misogyny when women are allied with men, against other women, because of their subordinate position (Millett, 1970). The inability to see this pattern may also explain the tensions and conflicts that have arisen in connection with the strong impact of #MeToo in Sweden. A country that, at the same time as it is a political democracy, is also a patriarchy disguised in a strong self-image of being a gender equal country. (Björk, 1996).

When #MeToo in political democracy Sweden exposes sexism and sexual violence as a structural problem, the initial success can be explained both by those who understand that men's sexual power over women is an effect of patriarchy and those who deny both patriarchy and such a causation. However, the basis of the welcoming of #MeToo differs. Whereas the first group perceives #MeToo as an expression, a strategy for change, the second group perceives the movement as a laudable "a call to get at the small minority of men who behave like pigs."[27] Nobody in Sweden, a country with political gender equality, wants to be perceived as sexist.

The first reaction of the two media personalities, Timell and Virtanen, after being accused of sexual misconduct and sexism, can be explained in similar terms. Both firmly denied being guilty of a criminal act (rape, in their view), but they did explain themselves and apologized, in relatively humble terms, for their *sexist* behavior. Virtanen's excuse involves his earlier drug and alcohol abuse, which he had overcome. Timell's excuse was that he had not realized that he was sexist, but he still apologized, asserting that he would seek help. At this point, both were thus anxious to rid themselves of the sexist label that had been applied to them. The behavior of the Academy member, Horace Engdahl, may be explained in similar terms, that is, his low profile during the Academy's emergency meeting. An explicit defense of the sex offender, Arnault, would at this time have made him seem sexist, which would not have been consistent with his self-image as part of the cultural establishment in a political democracy where gender equality is crucial.

When Timell, Virtanen, and Engdahl changed their attitudes, at a later phase of #MeToo, it does not need to be seen as a loss of their self-image as reasonably equal men, with a respectful attitude toward women. The same applies to the student who adopted Virtanen's words about #MeToo being a lynch mob against men. All four act to give voice to anti-feminist views, being critical against #MeToo, but it does not mean that they object to equality, or that they see themselves, necessarily, as anti-feminists. On the contrary, both Virtanen and Engdahl have openly dissociated themselves from anti-feminism. Virtanen in several interviews[28] and Engdahl, in a pod interview where he emphasized that he "ha[d] never been an anti-feminist."[29]

Even the anti-feminist statements made by Engdahl after Arnault was convicted of rape: "We (men) live in dangerous times"[30] and Virtanen's as well as the student's parable of #MeToo as lynching mob against men can be understood in terms of the self-image of gender equality, based on these men's inability to see the resilience of patriarchy to its full potential. In the perception that the patriarchal position of domination-subordination was termed to the disadvantage of men, and women's advantage, suddenly emerges to them in its full light the order of power which has hitherto been invisible. However, not in terms of a patriarchy, but well in the name of a matriarchy, run by extreme feminists (Millett, 1970).

When right-wing movements pick up momentum, debate forums open up for increasingly explicit anti-feminist opinions. In this new discourse, influenced by the right wing, essentialist ideas that legitimate sexism and misogyny flourish (Kumashiro, 2010). Anti-feminist views, opinions, and actions multiply, even beyond these ideological fields, and may very well be reconciled with a self-image of being a gender equal and feminist man, as we have seen.

Just like feminist advances in any period have met resistance, #MeToo inspires opposition and conflict (Nylander, 2018,). The teacher student who, in the seminar discussion, attacked feminism and #MeToo received both support and discouragement from his fellow students. One woman and two men supported him, while four women and two men opposed his views. Like the case of the Swedish Academy, the incident in the seminar shows that tensions and conflicts caused by feminist advances (for instance, when #MeToo challenges structures that legitimize men's sexual power over women) are not to be seen in terms of a war between the sexes, but rather as an awareness or, alternatively, a lack of awareness, of the power of patriarchy.

8

Suppression of Teacher's Voices: Agency and Freedom within Neoliberal Masculinist Performativity

Geraldine Mooney Simmie

Introduction

In the pre-Covid-19 world of the last decade, the *Global Educational Reform Movement* (GERM) could be likened to a type of "pandemic" that has worked in overt and covert ways to suppress, constrain, and silence teachers' voice, agency, and academic freedom. GERM has resulted in an international push for neoliberal educational reforms, such as accountability, best practice typologies, standardized testing, and evidence-based research standards (Lingard, Martino, & Rezai-Rashti, 2013). So much so that, various nations and states have adopted hierarchical, data-driven organizational structures resulting in the deskilling and muzzling of teachers by limiting curricular decisions (i.e., scripted curriculum; teaching to the test) and reducing educators to technocratic "workers" and "problem-solvers" (Giroux, 2010; Macrine, 2002, 2020; Rømer, 2019). Neoliberal reforms that work hand-in-glove with neoconservative and nationalistic thinking determined to keep power and privilege in the hands of a new elite at all costs (Sant, 2019; Macrine, 2020). In particular, neoliberal/elite reforms have significantly impacted and exposed with a new intensity how genderized politics affect teachers (mostly women) at all levels of education from early childhood to higher education (Zipin & Brennan, 2003; Osgood, 2016, a,b; Santoro, 2017; Núñez, 2018; Aiston & Kent Fo, 2020; Macer & Chadderton, 2020). While these reforms have been emerging since the late 1980s, the neoliberal turn of late capitalism puts a spotlight on the feminization of teaching with the resultant expectations of working for less and *acquiescing* to oppressions of their intellectual work.

As a result, this chapter explores the impact of the intersections of gender, politics, and neoliberal/elite educational reforms within the global context taking critical feminist and post-colonial theoretical perspectives. The chapter begins with a discussion on the feminization of teaching within neoliberalism. It then takes up the consequential changing roles, and the (re)positioning of teachers as malleable commodities within genderized market-based schemes. The chapter highlights Ireland's educational policies as a backdrop that mirrors global concerns about neoliberal/elite corporate educational reforms. It concludes with a call to educators, through a critical, anti-neoliberal/elite activist resistance, to counter the neoliberal/elite mechanisms of narrow accountability, best practices, typologies, standardized testing, and evidence-based research standards ().

Neoliberalism and Education

Public education, and by extension teaching, is under attack in Europe and across the globe as a result of neoliberal/elite government policies (Ross & Gibson, 2007). The idea is that education has the potential for profit, and therefore has become a key target of the neoliberal project because of its market size (e.g., global spending on education is more than $1 trillion), education's centrality to the economy, and its "potential to challenge corporate globalization if education succeeds in producing critical citizens for a democratic society" (Kuehn, 1999).

As a result, states and governments have introduced curricular reforms that commodify public education by reducing learning to decontexted information, skills, and drills to be taught, tested, and marketized through programs that promote privatization and user fees in place of free, public education (Hursh, 2012, 2017). These neoliberal/elite educational reforms have marketized school as a for-profit venture via international trade and investment agreements, such as GATS and OECD (e.g., establishing working conditions, rates of pay, teacher autonomy). These efforts have resulted in cost-cutting efforts to maximize profit by closing school libraries, reducing the number of special needs teachers, increasing class size, expanding online learning programs to name a few (Ross et al., 2004).[1]

The Organisation for Economic Co-operation and Development's (OECD)[1] *Education at a Glance* (2019), which promotes professionalism, profitability, and accountability, reported that "across OECD's 37 countries, 70% of teachers are women in all levels of education combined" (p. 436). Osgood (2006a) writes that there is "widespread support for the potentially beneficial consequences of heightened professionalism for practitioners, and for the children and families they serve" (p. 5). However, she questions the way this type of professionalism is understood as an apolitical construct and how it "could be used as a means of control and provide increased domination to those in power" (p. 5). Cannella (1997, p. 137) in response to this tyranny of control writes that "discourses and actions associated with professional institutions and practices have generated disciplinary and regulatory powers over teachers (who are mostly women) and children. Standards have been created through which individuals judge and limit themselves, through which they construct a desire to be 'good', 'normal' or both" (Osgood, 2006a, p. 5).

Feminization of Teaching and Masculine Performativity

Women have occupied the teaching profession since the nineteenth century with the shift from male to female teachers in basic schooling. It is considered one of the greatest changes in gender transformation of a single profession in history. The "feminization" of teaching happened because social propaganda surrounding the profession was heavily influenced by prevalent gender stereotypes of the times. So persistent gender-based stereotypes have allowed for poor-pay and the diminishment of teaching as a profession (Drudy, 2008). Yet within our global neoliberal/elite turn, the feminization of teaching has obscured gender inequity and as a result can be useful in the critique of current market-driven education policies. For example, "No single subject is more central to the history of the teaching profession than the changing role of women" (Sedlak & Schlossman, p. 28). Yet being a teacher continues to be considered a low-status profession partially due to its feminization, and the perpetuation of the secondary role of women and teaching in society. Even teachers themselves are seeing the erosion of their status as professionals. This is due to being devalued by policymakers and other officials with little experience in the education field, and it's not improving the education of their students (Bruno, 2018).

Otterstad (2019) argues for a new feminist's materialist ontological turn (p. 641) for examining such phenomenon. Accordingly, the ideological governing apparatuses and superstructures that work in the social world constrain and diminish spaces for teachers' agency, voice, and academic freedom. This compact contributes to new knowledges and meaning-making to open new spaces in relation to how and why teachers' voices matter in schooling and how and why enactment processes of policy reforms need to be understood differently (Mooney Simmie & Lang, 2020). The educational system as a predominant state apparatus is always changing depending on economic crises, and the political legitimation of new needs for workers for a post-industrial state and citizens for a well-functioning society (Arendt, 1961). A recent study in Australia by Macer and Chadderton (2020) examined the patriarchy in education drawing on Althusser's (1971) Marxist analysis of a class-based regimes to explain how state apparatuses function in the education system. For example, a state apparatus is composed of two parts acting separately and more often than not in sync: the repressive state apparatus (government, law, police, prisons, etc.) and a number of ideological state apparatuses (education system, media, religion, culture, politics, etc.). They work together quietly and swiftly to (de)construct teachers' positioning as public intellectuals operating inside a political labyrinth and to (re)construct teachers' positioning in terms of limited "performativity," that is, reduced to that which can be counted and measured (Ball, 2003).

Osgood (2006b) asserts that a "masculinist neoliberal performativity" in education is responsible because it values only what can be counted and measured. It is driven by the rise of neoliberalism's emphasis on performativity that has resulted in a push for an audit-culture with an emphasis on neo-positivism in an era of what Lather and St Pierre have identified as "big data" and "metric mania" (Lather & St Pierre, 2013, p. 629; Lingard, Martino & Rezai-Rashti, 2013). Education's use of epistemological, theoretical, and methodological frameworks which are "masculinist" in nature means that those derived from this masculine norm are constructed through deficit discourses that mark the teacher as "female" along with her devaluation and her misrecognition (Moreau, 2019).

As a social system, education has historically functioned for the patriarchy where "patriarchy is a serviceable term for historically produced situations in gender relations where men's domination is institutionalized" (Connell, 1994, p. 167). This is to say that the overall masculine social supremacy is "embedded in face-to-face settings such as the family and the work-place, generated by the functioning of the economy, reproduced over time by the normal operation of schools, media, and churches" (p. 143). So, it begs the question of whose expertise counts in this masculinist-educational policy space, as well as what other ways of "knowing" and "being" get lost in this genderized translation of teaching as a low status profession.

Teachers' Practices and (Re) Positionings

Such gendered politics in teaching and education reveal the exploitation of teachers, who are positioned as self-sacrificing practitioners performing a (religious) educator's vocation (Butler, 2004; Connell, 1990; Núñez, 2018). In terms of soft skills and feminine values of relational care deemed necessary and important, they are only recognized for their exchange-value and functionality, as commodities which put practitioners' bodies and souls to work primarily for the economy (Mooney Simmie & Moles, 2019). For example, Bourdieu (2001) explained that the education system is a soft-extension of the domestic space that traditionally confined women to the private sphere "all the more powerful because it is for the most part exerted invisibly and insidiously through insensible familiarization with a symbolically structured physical world and early prolonged experience of interactions informed by the structures of domination" (p. 38). Connell (2009) argues that neoliberalism reshapes "the good teacher" and redefines "teacher quality" (Cochran-Smith & Lytle, 2006) in harmful, constricting ways. Scholars suggest that the societal definition of young women as submissive and moral makes them easily manipulated into accepting a standardized education format with curricula designed by male experts (Boyle, 2004).

Teacher's practices and positionings are shaped by this type of universalist pedagogy that appears as new soft modes of accountability, but on closer interrogation reveals a rather debased politics of reflection for a gendered and limited teacher performativity (Brady, 2016, 2019). Nowadays, the ideal "quality" teacher is understood as an "actuarial teacher" constantly doing things in the name of lifelong learning (Ball, 2003; Connell, 2009) and reporting successes in evidence-based practices, such as Visible Pedagogy (Hattie, 2012). Teachers' practices have come under stronger, tighter, and harder political scrutiny than heretofore, underpinned by new matrices of laws and patriarchal procedures, rules, codes, standards, competences, and regulations (Connell, 1990; Mooney Simmie & Moles, 2019).

These neoliberal/elite reforms push for "what works" and the technocratic discourses that underpin teachers' practices, far from improving best practices in classrooms and schools, often leave teachers' bereft of moral purpose and affordances for problem-posing and transformative possibilities (Santoro, 2017). While many teachers may prefer to enact uncritical and expedient approaches that fail to mediate with the wider world, there are nowadays far more dangers. These include symbolic and structural dangers that teachers with diminished agency are reduced to anti-intellectual functionaries, doing "what works" and acting as clones of politicians' anemic ambitions.

The neoliberal state's role in the suppression of teachers' voices and agency is often indirect, insidious, hidden, and institutionalized within an assumed externality of gender-neutrality and a hierarchical system of schooling (Macrine,

2018). It denies the political and the theoretical, and as a result fails to interrupt the reproduction of privilege, to take responsibility for redistribution of resources, and to recognize the non-functional place of feminine care and teaching understood as a practice of freedom (Mooney Simmie, Moles, & O'Grady, 2019). Such oppressions of teachers who are responsible to enact these neoliberal/elite policies, reforms, and curriculum become silenced inside amorphous groupings with no intellectual identity. As a result, human development, the *raison d'etre* for education, takes place amid rhizomatic and inextricable linkages between loss of voice and the challenges of trying to find new emancipatory ways for all to live in a decent society and just global world (Mooney Simmie, 2020b). In addition to class and gender oppression, there are additional intersectionalities that need to be considered here, such as ethnicity, race, and religion.

The problem of teachers' voices, freedom, and agency calls out the institutionalized sexism in education's hierarchical system where the people who "say" what needs to the "done" are for the most part privileged males in powerful positions (e.g., politicians, OECD experts, powerful businessmen, bishops). As a result, for teachers, mostly women, to make "care cheap in the patriarchal capitalist calculus … it had first to be defined as worthless, part of nature rather than society. This was achieved through the equation of care labor with femininity and womanhood. As women were exploitative things, then by default their caring 'nature' was exploitable. Care is not defined as productive work in this calculus" (Lynch & Crean, 2019, p. 2).

Tronto (2013) asserts neoliberal's elitist-ruling class exerts "privileged irresponsibility," stating what needs to be done while requiring someone else to deliver the outcomes, for example, a slave, woman, minority person. Bourdieu (2001) reminds us that the

> strength of the masculine order is seen in the fact that it dispenses with justification: the androcentric vision imposes itself as neutral and has no need to spell out in discourses aimed at legitimating it. The social order functions as an immense symbolic machine tending to ratify the masculine domination on which it is founded: it is the sexual division of labour, a very strict distribution of the activities assigned to each sex, of their place, time and instruments; it is the structure of space, with the opposition between the place of assembly or the market, reserved for men, and the house, reserved for women.
>
> (pp. 10–11)

Santoro (2017) compares the current deficit of (women) teachers' agency and voice in the United States, a felt sense of (de)moralization and suppression in relation to the contemporary reform ensemble, to the moral madness of Cassandra, the female Greek god, who sent warnings in ancient times that were ignored because she was a woman. Male teachers may experience something of this, but are more likely to be regarded as rational if voicing concerns about policy reforms. For this reason, Santoro argues that a feminist analysis is needed to understand moral trouble in a strongly gendered (teaching) environment: "Only by incorporating a feminist perspective that addresses power in the institutional context of teachers' work will we be able to unpack the particular challenges of moral work in a feminized profession" (p. 52).

Juridification and Regulatory Gazes

The scientism in the universal pedagogy discussed above—with its black box of assessment-for-learning tools, for example, structured observations, detailed scientific planning, diagnostics, communal-orientation, peer-feedback, and data analytics—atomizes teachers' practices. It also fails to allow affordances for interrupting, disrupting, and opening possibility in educational practices for academic freedom and for a future grappling with uncertainty. Furthermore, this atomizing structure of teaching informs traditional and neoliberal/elite market-driven notions of pedagogy (Giroux, 2013).

As a result, teachers' workload relies on procedures and power of the laws/reforms, edicts, rules, codes, and standards to police the authoritarian regulatory gazes on teachers' practices under the guise of self-evaluation and a promise of increased teacher autonomy (Bourke, Lidstone, & Ryan, 2015).

This type of overreliance on data and the laws/reforms in education is referred to as "juridification," and demonstrates a hardening of political pressure on teachers' voice, agency, and freedom (Novak, 2019; Edling & Mooney Simmie, 2020). It is a type of asphyxiation from above that prevents any breathing-spaces for educators and such decision-making fails to be understood as a practice of freedom (Freire, 1970/2018; hooks, 1994, 2000; Ball, 2003). This can be clearly seen in policy reforms in the field of teacher evaluation with its over-reliance on new rules, procedures, and modes of public accountability and policy enforcement.

Policy Reform Ensemble in Education in Ireland

Drawing on my emancipatory research and theorizations of teacher learning can help to illustrate how neoliberal/elite educational policy reforms in

Ireland, in the last decade, exemplify the repression of teachers' practices and positionings. Policy reforms in Ireland and the notion of a "good teacher" have particular resonance in a deeply conservative schooling system that is historically grounded in the suppressed truth of gendered and ideological state apparatuses. As a result, it acts as a patriarchal relay, through influential policy actors—a triumvirate consisting of the state, market-based corporations, and the church, where patronage and ownership of nearly all primary and a majority of secondary schools are held by a majority Catholic church. These policymakers and leaders operate an ideological governing apparatus where "father" knows best in education matters (e.g., ministers in the government, state inspectorate, OECD experts, bishops, corporate leaders).

In this system, curricular and teacher education reforms are expertly handled and swiftly moved through the schooling and higher education systems at an unprecedented rate where there are few affordances for critical debate and contrarian views. While there are national public fora for discussion of new policy reforms, these are staged by state agencies and teachers are networked as one among others. Teachers' voices, especially contrarian voices are quickly silenced by calling on "expert voices" for refutation. In this way, a patriarchal hierarchy of differential power relations constantly legitimates proposed reforms as coming from indisputable research evidence and widely understood by all as needed for the twenty-first-century world of work. The ideal citizen is one who "acts" as a competitive individual with Darwinian strength (Edling & Mooney Simmie, 2020) to live an independent life free from burdening the state and/ or society, but all the while releasing social and cultural capital for economic competitiveness.

The (mostly female) good teacher is thought of as a "cailín maith" (the Irish language for a "good girl"), who is obedient, assumes moral responsibility, and does whatever is required of her by policymakers, selflessly picking up the broken pieces in the classroom and in school life, often impossible and under resourced tasks. Irish teachers traditionally work in this patriarchal hierarchical system where there is no great appetite among policymakers for opening public spaces for critical debate, surprises, transgressions, or philosophical co-inquiry (Mooney Simmie, 2020 a,b; Mooney Simmie & Lang, 2020). While a new program for government calls for a National Citizen's Assembly in relation to education, this has already become tightly framed as giving voice to the student.

Educational reform policies in Ireland, in relation to teachers' practices and positionality in the last decade, have proceeded with little or no challenge or critical debate. These reforms circumscribe a universalist pedagogy in the curriculum and teacher learning that rely on narrow modes of public accountability: (a) curriculum reform in lower secondary education, (b) reform of teachers' learning, and (c) changes in teacher evaluation. It is to each of these that I now turn.

Curriculum Reform in Lower Secondary Education

A curriculum policy reform supposed to be a student-centered pedagogy of active learning, tailor-made using classroom-based-assessments for individual student need (Mooney Simmie, 2014, 2015) was introduced in Ireland in 2011 (for ages 12–15 years). The reform aimed to replace a former teacher-centered pedagogy and state examination at the end of a three-year cycle. It required teachers to engage with differentiated planning with a new teacher communal-orientation. This flipped-classroom was legitimated using so-called expert voices of the OECD and was the starting place for the introduction of a big data-driven hierarchical organization (Hattie, 2012; Rømer, 2019). Furthermore, the reform was legitimated by the Minister of Education and Skills as aligning with reforms in other OECD countries. The minister argued that the reform did not require a national debate as changes arose from large-scale evidence based-research (Mooney Simmie, 2014, p. 45).

The claim made was that all students would benefit when this reform was faithfully implemented by quality teachers—with a range of new twenty-first-century life skills aimed at releasing students' entrepreneurial spirit for national economic competitiveness. However, this Junior cycle reform was silent in relation to students' securing a good life with emancipatory possibilities, there was no mention of any need for critical mediation with social justice issues in the wider world, and the new curriculum had little concern for equality of condition or with the notion of a dynamic democracy (Edling & Mooney Simmie, 2020). Schools in deprived areas were officially designated disadvantaged and provided with some additional resources. Moreover, education's social responsibility for public interest values was side-stepped when the state declared it expected some schools as a result of the reform to fare far better than others (Mooney Simmie, 2014).

Needless to say, these reforms encountered difficulties and obstacles with teachers. National teacher strikes were held over a number of years by the secondary teachers' unions, with more than 30,000 members, the *Association for Secondary Teachers of Ireland* (ASTI) and the *Teachers Union of Ireland* (TUI). The public was supportive of teachers' concerns and some reform measures were removed and others delayed. Finally, in 2018 the government quelled dissent using emergency legislation measures, the first time in the history of the trade union movement, through penalizing individual striking teachers by withholding their bonus payments.

By 2020, curriculum reform in junior cycle was legitimated by policy actors in the ideological state apparatuses as a welcome development about to release creativity in all young people and open spaces for teachers' agency and freedom as innovative design thinkers, designing short courses and using formative assessment. Communication, skills, and self-discipline were foregrounded (learning to become a team player and be good and obedient (to the strict father who knows best) and to step up and take personal responsibility and care for emotional wellbeing) while downplaying or eliding any intellectual requirements (subject content and theoretical knowledge) for an academic practice. It is clear that this Junior Cycle framework bears all the hallmarks of a "masculinist" neoliberal/elite ideology for teacher profiling of limited performativity using an evidence-based scientism and a skill-set of obedience and compliance (hooks, 1994; Edling & Mooney Simmie, 2020; Núñez, 2018; Macer & Chadderton, 2020; Macrine, 2020).

Reform of Teachers' Learning

From 2006 onwards, after the Teaching Council became the statutory body with responsibility for annual registration and advocacy of teachers as professionals, the former rhetoric of teachers' professional development changed to a reform ensemble of teacher professional learning and teacher learning (Teaching Council, 2016a, 2016b, 2016c). Teacher learning was reconfigured with the notion that quality teachers work on themselves on a continuous basis (self-evaluation) with teacher identity tied to a new communal-orientation for the production of measurable outcomes—a high-performance learning organization for primacy of the instrumental rather than an educational practice understood as intellectual, relational, and community-building (Ball, 2003; Fielding, 2007).

Ongoing teacher development, across the continuum of teacher education, was portrayed as a career trajectory undertaken in stages, Initial Teacher Education (e.g., four years) followed by a mandatory period of Teacher Induction (e.g., two years) for formal registration and leading to In-career Teacher Learning (Teaching Council, 2011, 2016a, 2016b, 2016c). A spotlight on policy reforms in teacher learning reveals features that strongly align with a masculinist neoliberal/elite policy, such as teacher learning understood as a moral and apolitical endeavor, satisfying a universalist pedagogy for an evidence-based practice and operating within a new regime of legally binding procedures and laws regularly updated by the Teaching Council (Edling & Mooney Simmie, 2018; Mooney Simmie & Edling, 2019).

Such gendered patriarchy, of the ideological and repressive state apparatuses, can be seen first, in the construct of the teacher learner as a disembodied entrepreneur with agency and freedom to constantly engage in a debased politics of self-study; second, doing things to themselves and reporting constant comparison and fidelity to desired policy outcomes as measurable data; and third, showcasing in very public ways these outcomes in an annual marketplace—called Féilte the Irish word for celebration—staged by the Teaching Council (Brady, 2016; Teaching Council, 2018). The positive overtones in this political legitimation conceal the public relations spectacle underway and teachers' neoliberal/elite subjectification and commodification for a limited performativity for a market-led discourse of education.

Teacher Evaluation

The implementation of the flipped classroom created a new teacher workload that required intensive labor according to a universalist pedagogy, fulfilling mandates for tight scientific planning, multiple assessments, and self-evaluation for a limited performativity (Brady, 2016, 2019; Mooney Simmie & Edling, 2019). While these reforms were under way, teachers' salaries and bonus payments were all cut using national emergency legislation in a policy of economic austerity. Despite teacher strikes, new entrants into the profession were awarded lower pay for the same workload and these new teachers found themselves often working for several years in part-time precariat employment and with increased workloads and competition between teachers in the staff room.

This resulted in teachers no longer being registered for life upon completion of post-graduate studies and a one-year diploma in education. Instead they were required to complete a two-year Professional Masters in Education and a further two years of workshops in teacher induction and an annual registration after that if they were to secure employment (Teaching Council, 2018). The new public appraisal system for teachers was legitimated as a soft system of self-evaluation for increased creativity and teacher autonomy. However, this claim was betrayed by the extensive check-lists and externally imposed criteria in this new politics of reflection. Brady (2016, 2019) shows how these new debased modes of self-evaluation rely on an externally imposed panoptical and oppressive gaze rather than the critical reflexivity and intelligent accountability needed for education as a practice of freedom and/or emancipatory possibility (Mooney Simmie, 2012; 2014; 2015; 2020a,b).

Conclusions

This chapter examined the impact of neoliberal/elite reforms on teachers' voice, agency, and freedom in a practice where the GERM policy ensembles, set against a backdrop of austerity economics constrained and suppressed teachers' (mostly women) voices within the confines of a clinical practice and the limited performativity of a big data-driven organization (Ball, 2003; Fielding, 2007; Rømer, 2019). Utilizing critical studies helps us to understand how superstructures and the system of state apparatuses circumscribe the hierarchical and classed functioning of the education system (Freire, 2018/1970; Gunter, 2005; McLaren, 2019; Macer & Chadderton, 2020; Macrine, 2018, 2020). Critical feminist literature gave us insights into the genderized ways the social order functions as an "immense symbolic machine tending to ratify the masculine domination on which it is founded," for a sexual division of labour that (re)positions teachers' practices as an extension of domestic (private) life that is institutionalized and normalized as a gender-neutral and apolitical space (Zipin & Brennan, 2003; Butler, 2004; Connell, 1990, 2009; Osgood, 2016, a, 2016b; Santoro, 2017; Núñez, 2018; Lynch & Crean, 2019).

A critical/feminist interrogation of the political legitimation of global policies (e.g., reforms in curriculum, in teacher professional development, changing status, and working conditions) is needed to unsettle the commonsense apolitical and disembodied view of policy change in education. Moreover, the extent to which reform policies align with a masculinist neoliberal/elite performativity, governance tools for hegemonic closure of teachers' voices and agency, and mediation with the public intellectual role of the teacher as an activist for social justice and public interest values are also in need of major changes (hooks, 1994). The political staging of the competitive individual in teacher education using a masculinist neoliberal/elite unit of analysis facilitated by repressive and ideological state apparatuses uses a soft-centered (communitarian) science of learning and clinical practice stance. A hierarchy of new quality managers brokers no time or space for critical deliberation with a majority of women teachers about practices beyond a disembodied apolitical worldview. Cassandra's moral madness is in evidence as policy is understood as implemented and driven rather than enacted and interpreted and requiring little other than top-down transmission approaches for a careless pedagogy of instrumentalization and the perpetuation of intersectional inequalities (Lynch & Crean, 2019).

The findings and insights of this chapter confirm an institutionalized patriarchal performativity and politics of reflection operating as a GERM pandemic in the contemporary education policy reform ensemble, where reflexivity and critical mediation with the wider world are only noticeable by their absence and silence(ing). This repositions teachers as an apolitical professional class of creative and critical (higher-order) thinkers encased within a hierarchical big data-driven organization. Patriarchal regulation, juridification, and evidence-based procedures act in sync to generate a high-control regime of teachers' bodies and souls as commodities and problem-solvers for primacy of the markets. The chapter shows teachers' voices, agency, and academic freedom as policy actors, while never strong, have become increasingly devalued, disrespected, and suppressed by GERM policies.

Finally, as a counterpoint to the above, an alternative politics of critical principled resistance for teachers' voices and agency acting as problem-posers and transgressors for a practice of academic freedom and emancipation for all is greatly needed. A practice of freedom with new theorizations is required to describe teachers' practices and positionings for an intelligent accountability (Cochran Smith, 2019). We therefore urgently need a new politics of principled resistance that takes back public institutions, schools, and higher education institutes from a patriarchal state apparatus that constrains and suppresses teachers' voices, agency, and academic freedom and offers few practices of existential freedom and critical mediation for teachers within the wider world. The findings in Ireland can be generalized globally to teachers grappling with similar issues of voice, and can have wider implications for education as a practice of freedom. As bell hooks, *Urg(es) all of us to open our minds and hearts so that we can know beyond the boundaries of what is acceptable, so that we can think and rethink, so that we can create new visions, I celebrate teaching that enables transgressions - a movement against and beyond boundaries. It is this movement which makes education the practice of freedom* (1994, p. 12).

9

Marias, Marielles, Malês: Southern Epistemologies, Resistance and Emancipation

Maria Luiza Süssekind and Ines Barbosa de Oliveira

Introduction

The current attacks on democracy, and the rupture with policies developed by popular governments (2003-16) in Brazil, have been producing reverberations all over society, however not without resistance. This chapter addresses the resultant everyday life forms of resistance that point out actions against mainstream ideologies and political policies, bringing the notion of social emancipation as a set of procedural struggles with no defined end, and characterized by the political sense of these struggles' procedures.[1] In the development of our argument, we first situate the 2016 coup d'état[2] and extreme-right-wing President Bolsonaro's first-year mandate and its consequences that we refer to as a "transnational conservative tsunami."[3] The outcomes of which deal and operate with resistances in different dimensions and aspects of social life, and highlight the struggle for solidarity for a just world. This so-called tsunami has shattered social, health, human rights, and educational policies creating policies that menace the stability of democracy.

Second, we draw attention to the plurality of different forms of resistance including a decolonized theoretical approach aimed at recognizing emancipation within invisiblized practices and knowledges. This helps us to displace the centrality of the euro-centrism and to deconstruct the "abyssal" modern thinking, and at the same time, learn from and with the epistemological *South*, as formulated by Boaventura de Sousa Santos (2007). Therefore, we present some of the main and diversified forms of resistance and struggle against colonization, capitalism, and CIS heteropatriarchy (system of power based on the supremacy and dominance of CIS heterosexual men through the exploitation and oppression of all gender identities, including a toxic masculinity). We highlight how black and native feminists' protagonisms both capture and trace those movements in different contexts by drawing on the lyrics of a samba recalling the image of the gay activist, Marielle Franco, and from a narrative of a *cacica*[4] from Amazonas: Marielle Franco, a PSOL councilwoman, black, homosexual, and a favela's resident, defender and militant of the human rights cause, was cowardly murdered in Rio de Janeiro in April 2018. Finally, we demonstrate the importance of political–epistemological action as a means to incorporate everyday life stories into the field of curriculum and teacher education, other possibilities of understanding the complexity that is inherent both to school, everyday life and to the curricula that are created within the tangency of society or the lyrics of a samba.

Marias, Marielles, Malês

The narrative of Marielle's life, as a symbol of the heroes erased from the history books, became the theme of the 2019 carnival of Rio de Janeiro: "Histories for Lulling Adults." It was organized by one of the Rio's oldest and most traditional samba schools, Estação Primeira de Mangueira. It recounts the murder of gay political-activist, Marielle Franco, among other heroes, in the troubled current Brazilian political context. Franco fought for human rights, single mothers like herself, gays, and slum dwellers, and exposed the country's racism, anti-gay violence, and a culture of impunity. Her actions encouraged the Brazilian people to listen to "Marias, Mahins, Marielles, Malês" which stresses the importance of telling the stories that the history books do not.[5] The three names in this song refer to "Maria" most popular female name in Portuguese; "Luiza Mahin," a slave brought to Brazil from Africa at age of six who managed to free herself and return to Africa, where she died rich and successful. Her son, Luiz Gama, a freeman, became one of the first black lawyers in Brazilian history who fought for abolition; and the "Malês," black-Muslim slaves who revolted in 1823 in Bahia, Brazil, but were ultimately defeated.

These three examples help us to recognize our own ongoing fight against the permanent production of social inequality and invisibility, and to value these historical existences and the emancipatory character of their struggles. Knowing that decolonization means the displacement of the hegemonic metaphorical "North," its ideology and narratives of history, the message of this samba allows us to perceive the need to rewrite the current global and metaphorical "South," as well as to rescue other stories from their invisibility. This is a permanent struggle for decolonization, against history's unrelenting commitment to a single ideological narrative of single voice, single story, or single pattern.

This samba also embodies the voice of the black feminists' resistance proposing to decolonize the perception of some Brazilian heroes, who are not seen as such in official history centered in the white and European point of view. Besides Marielle Franco, another woman, the *cacica*, Eronilde Fermin, told us her story and its meaning for the social emancipation and the *ecology of knowledges*. It describes a non-hierarchical relationship between different knowledges, which recognizes the possible circumstantial validity of all of them, as well as the interdependence between them in understanding the world and in the solutions we build to combat the problems we are facing or are facing us.

At a Popular University of Social Movements[6] meeting, in 2019, Eronilde narrated the struggle for her cultural survival and the idea of Asemúyta—an extended and empathic concept of parenthood that includes all mankind and the universe in a whole balance that configures how the people Omagua-Kambeba (Indigenous people from Brazil's Amazon Basin) understand resistance. Navigating the waves of rage brought on by the conservative tsunami, we follow the *marias* as paths to conceive resistance, keeping the struggle alive and the pursuit of emancipation as a continuum.

The counter-hegemonic messages embedded in the 2019 Carnival samba underscore the need for movements based on social emancipation, ecology, feminism, and actions to defend democratic public education. The lessons from the Global South point to improve cognitive and social justice as a condition to replace the low-intensity democracy, based on the privatization of the public good by elites who increase the distances between representatives and represented, through an abstract political inclusion made of social exclusion.[7] On the other hand, high-intensity democracy consists of a set of social relations that are democratized, with shared authority relations of solidarity, where each and every one knows their responsibility to others.

The Political and Epistemological Feminists' Struggles for Democracy and Social Justice

The work of Santos (2000, 2007) indicates that it is not possible to separate, as modernity leads us to believe, the epistemological of political dimensions when we talk about knowledge. Therefore, he argues that every epistemological choice is associated with political convictions and vice versa. Thus, thinking about the current conservative tsunami and its harmful social effects has exposed the hegemony of Northern epistemologies, as well as the patriarchal and capitalist social values that support them. We argue that feminists who struggle against patriarchy and against the coloniality of indigenous peoples are central to our struggles against the conservative tsunami which is fueled by racism and hate, the erasure of differences, and the annihilation of others.[8] The conservative neoliberal educational reforms and policies in Brazil mentioned above legitimate and perpetuate such oppressions that are weaved into everyday life becoming ordinary reflecting Arendt's (1963) banality of evil.

Further, this tsunami's active abyssal lines of capitalism, colonialism, and sexism exist, and continue to flow and grow resulting in erasure and blindness that prevent solidarity from expanding Santos's idea of the future based on the choices of the present time. The exercise, of *unblindness* and *desinvisibilization*, is a political–epistemological framework, a commitment that helps us to create and to recognize the epistemological plurality of the world in the present. Such recognition emerges from digging the present toward an archaeology of existences, as well as through a "sociology of absences."[9] The goal is to make "possible the impossible" objects and to make "present the absent" objects, by looking at the social experience fragments that have not been fully realized within the Eurocentric metonymic reason. This is why it is important to acknowledge and tell the stories of both Marielle and Eronilde as political–epistemological–methodological projects of emancipation, not as an end, but as possible contributions to the struggle; Marielle, a non-white woman, whose body was silenced, brutally assassinated, and emptied of subjectivity.

Cloistered female bodies, governed by the ideals of modesty and the standard of white beauty, are oppressive and violent tools reflected in Davis's (2016) quote, "the ideology of femininity began to forge the wife and mother as ideal models" (p. 45). Clearly, this definition where "woman's place is at home" embeds a strong concept of female inferiority, dependence, and subalternity that has emerged during industrial capitalism which minimizes the importance of domestic work, making its cost invisible and therefore nonexistent, as argued by Federici (2017):

> In fact, the woman's place had always been at home, but during the pre-industrial era the economy itself centered on those in the home and the farmland around it. While men tilled the soil (often with the help of their wives), women were manufacturers, making fabrics, clothes, candles, soap and just about everything that was necessary for the family. The woman's place was right at home—but not just because they gave birth and raised children or met her husband's needs. They were productive workers in the context of the domestic economy, and their work was no less respected than that of their peers. Same historical process, but in differentiated relationships.
>
> (p. 45)

Even though women's bodies are the reproducers and repositories of the workforce, both Davis (2016) and Federici (2017) point to women's subordination arguing that women are invisible within this process and considered passive non-contributors, and removed from economic life. As such, a body that is subordinated economically, socially, and deprived of subjective rights, if considered at all in the reality of some countries, will be considered inferior.

A focus on "global cognitive justice" enables us to better understand the politics of life in the Global South, by moving beyond the Western liberalist understanding of subjects in political practice.[10] Further, according to Santos (2007), "The production of presences happens when we focus on the study and analysis of fragments of social experience not recognized by Eurocentric science" (p. 59). When thinking about a "sociology of absences," he recognizes the production of nonexistence and results in its reconstruction "beyond the relationship of subalternity" (p. 67). Yet, there is no single or univocal way of not existing.

Spivak (2010) writes that "in seeking to learn to speak to (rather than listen to and speak for) the historically muted subject of the subaltern woman, the postcolonial intellectual systematically 'unlearns' female privilege" (p. 295). She argues that intellectuals in Europe and Western countries control the kind of knowledge they assume to be the "truth" through the creation of their colonialist discourses and they prolong control over the subaltern through cultural imperialism by this act. The epistemic violence of imperialist laws and education results in a Western discourse by intellectuals who control the kind of knowledge they assume to be the "truth" through the creation of their colonialist discourse, prolonging the control over the subaltern through cultural imperialism by this act. Spivak (2010) also considers India's perspective where a status of "legally programmed" asymmetry exists in which man and woman live. She adds that this asymmetry "in the long run, cohere(s) with the work of imperialist subject-constitution, mingling epistemic violence with the advancement of learning and civilization. And the subaltern woman will be mute as ever" (Spivak, 2010, p. 295).

Historically, because it is the possession of others (i.e., slave lord, father, and husband) to determine for women what to wear and put on, as well as how to speak and behave at home and outside, in order to be attractive to the man in their life. Away from sports, science, academic, and political activities, where woman live under patriarchy, sexism, and misogyny, they learn to guard their sexual and reproductive decisions.

Feminist bell hooks (2019) goes further, warning that economic equality does not guarantee an end of the sexist male dominance and that men "have the right to command women in any way" (p. 100), including under the threat of physical violence. Sexism, as well as racism, is one of the abyssal lines that draw the construction of modernity. Brazil is one of the most violent places for being black, a woman, or transgender. Classified and hierarchical bodies support this colonial and capitalist project, and it is worth quoting Frederici (2017) at length:

> Much of the violence is directed against women because, in the age of the computer, the conquest of the female body remains a recommendation for the accumulation of work and wealth, as demonstrated by the institutional investment in the development of new reproductive technologies that, more than ever, reduce women to mere wombs. Furthermore, the "feminization of poverty" that accompanied the spread that globalization takes on a new meaning when we remember that it was the first effect of development on women's lives.
>
> (p. 37)

The historical systemic sexism experienced by white women and colonized black women differs; however, both are under the same domination-project of the "white supremacist capitalist patriarchy." As such, we need to consider the intersectionality among race, class, sexuality, and gender[11] as aggravating factors of violence and oppression. For example, when we encounter a poor black female lesbian, we do not have the same approach as for a white male, even if he is poor and homosexual. We assert that Marielle Franco was negotiating these abyssal lines and was unfortunately thrown into the abyss.

Another woman, Eronilde Fermin, the *cacica* of Omagua-Kambeba people, who live in the high Solimões River area, tells how she decides to *speak, although subaltern*, by her own. Eronilde has been menaced by groups that work against the right of land and human rights in indigenous areas causing ecological and human devastation and, controversially, this is happening since one master degree thesis was written about her biography. This academic work that was intended to protect her and her community also exposed and endangered her, putting her in a position of evoking her right to speak. And she does: *I am the hand who's going to write the story of my people and no one's else*. Here, she claims authorship, visibility, and the recognition of her voice.

So, what we look for in the "Global South" is to understand and deconstruct the processes of building and legitimizing the epistemological and political domination of the "North" over the "South." The defense of cognitive justice as a condition of social justice and high-intensity democracy helps us to consider the importance of all social struggles to overcome all kinds of oppression and domination. It means that we believe in the fight for the value of feminists, LGBTQIA+, native people, and all different epistemologies simultaneously, with the anti-capitalist struggle. According to our research, we maintain that the knowledge networks existent within schools and society are composed of all these dimensions of knowledge and social values, and are in conflict or in dialog with each other. This means that, for us, schools, universities, and social movements are social space-times of creation and copresence of multiple epistemes for the study of everyday life which allows us to build an understanding of the all-encompassing epistemological plurality. One that engages our understanding of the university as a *pluriversity* engaged in a contrary logic of weaving and exchanging knowledge, ecologically. The need to destabilize those epistemicidal practices and thinking, and the resultant social oppressions and multiple violences, includes a political and epistemological model to the struggle against such raising fascisms.

The Conservative Tsunami and the Abyssal Cartography

> The former astronaut and retired lieutenant colonel from air force, Marcos Pontes thanked in this Wednesday (31/10/2018) his confirmation ahead to Science and Technology Ministry from the newly elected president Jair Bolsonaro's office (PSL), has affirmed that according to his vow at Air Force Academy—where he graduated as a jet pilot—he would fight "internal and external enemies with the same life's sacrifice."[12]

So, who are these "internal and external enemies" to the minister? Who are these enemies (internal and external) to science and technology? This scenario reflects an atmosphere of hate and violence that seems to be worsened after the electoral season, crowned by memes, threatening music, and public declarations of intolerance. All of which jeopardizes the fraternity principle, and conditions of community, while threatening adversaries with prison sentences and annihilation, considering them as enemies whose ideas must be reported, recorded, banished, or burned. Then, we ask: What kind of hate is this? Who are those enemies? Are there any differences between the hate we feel at the personal level or the transient, situational or relational and these social hates? According to Penna (2015), there is:

> A phenomenon that I call hate to the teachers, I identify visiting some specific pages at social media. I believe that this phenomenon is more perceptible at virtual world due to the sensation of impunity followed by the comments of hate in this space, especially because of the false profiles and anonymity. The

> hate to the teachers is characterized by threats straight to them, with physical violence and even death. These threats are made in absolutely explicit and shocking ways. (…) When contacting with this campaign of hate pointed against teachers, the most pertinent question, in my view, is what is bring forth this hate.[13]
>
> (pp. 295, 296)

Swimming against the current, the teachers are now perceived as "enemies of the nation." Recorded and legally reported throughout governmental websites, teachers are in jeopardy. In addition, leftists, communists, and human rights activists face a growing number of aggressions from President Bolsonaro's cabinet. Beyond an official trend, the volume of violence has grown vastly.

> We assume that we were surprised by something that we weren't expected to live either suffer, we believe today that this tsunami was forming itself in the gap of a very old relief: a colonial-enslaved-heteropatriarchal Brazil.[14]
>
> (p. 6)

The concept of "global conservative neoliberal tsunami"[15] equates the growth and endorsement of the hate among different groups and peoples. We posit that this metaphorical tsunami disseminates the democratizing tendencies of local and the value of difference, with its cascading and tumultuous wave of oppression and sorrow causing victims everywhere. The conservative neoliberal tsunami originates from a paradigmatic displacement of modernity that *glolocalized* its project of narcissistic and abyssal Occidentalism that both oppresses and annihilates millions of peoples (p. 7). This is a resentful modernity that makes unkept promises, and only survives if aims itself at the white northward patriarchal male gaze. This reflects a traditional White, Anglo-Saxon, Protestant (WASP) point of view, as they strive to maintain their privilege. Women, homosexuals, transsexuals, non-white, non-European, non-protestant or catholic people are subsumed by the other side of abyssal line, where non-existent people, beliefs, and epistemologies live. Before, this "positivistic tsunami"[16] that also is represented in the current market-driven curriculum reforms is homogenized. These reforms are inspired by technicists arguments that base success on standardized tests result, such as the Programme for International Student Assessment (PISA), the national literacy assessment (Avaliação Nacional da Alfabetização—ANA, in Portuguese), and the national High School Exam (Exame Nacional do Ensino Médio—Enem, in Portuguese). These approaches "mirror" Santos's (2001) assertion that the educational system (teachers, students, and curriculum) must adapt to these educational reforms.

At the same time, we need to understand how these oppressions "mirror"[17] what's happening globally, and how they are produced by so-called specialists' diagnostics that wrap and produce images of realities more powerful than the real lived realities[18] and offer technocratic educational reforms. The impact of hegemonic globalization on educational reforms, according to Santos (2003), buttresses itself wrapped in the so-called data-driven field of law and science. These so-called experts, producers, and definers of truth make up the triad of economic liberalization, privatization of public assets, and a minor neoliberal state with low-intensity democracy. In this context, the legacy of human rights is denied to the larger population. The technocrats are white men of European and middle-class backgrounds (Santos, p. 37), far from the *marias* or Marielles.[19] These subalternized "different" people are denied their humanity, objectified, and, in some cases, exterminated. We believe that this tsunami feeds off the hate that nurtures itself with disgust, racism, sexism, and intolerance that results in erasure, revulsion, denial, and at times murder[20] to diffuse presumed enemies. For example, during the Covid-19 pandemic crisis that has consumed Brazil a report produced by the Technical Education Committee of the Rui Barbosa Institute[21] found that pre-Covid, schools were sadly involved in distributing baskets of goods for minimum survival of 44 percent of needy families and now that number has gone up to 83 percent. In terms of educational access, the same report indicates that 61 percent of our teachers are not receiving any support to keep up with the educational demands of remote activities for their students.

Thus, as we consider the consequences of the global impact of this "conservative neoliberal tsunami" and its machinery[22] and its institutionalization results in Brazil's educational policies,[23] it seems important to observe how hate has become a social practice of anti-cohesion giving righteous focus on education and teachers as the enemy.

To Arendt (1963), the segregation is an expected behavior in human societies. The practice unites people according to their chosen churches, political parties, professional categories, etc. What we call social practice of anti-cohesion exposes the images, narratives, behaviors, attitudes, and organized actions that characterize the push for the eradication of differences of others. This hatred of the difference is thought to ensure identity. So, it nurtures antisocial, anti-solidarity, and antipathy toward others. And, it is this banality of hate that pushes this conservative tsunami. It's the solidarity of being in a group that drives these hateful attitudes and increases the neo-nationalist movements globally.

This aversion to "differences" within Brazil, specifically and that our society, generally is obsessed by sameness, and has turned "difference" into an enemy. Tragically, when such oppressive racist, sexist, and class behaviors are institutionalized, it gives permission and allows for ongoing dehumanization and destitution of a person and their human rights.

These practices of anti-cohesion are so powerful as cohesion practices that, as Arendt (1963) suggests, even though the decisions apparently strengthen the equality, we force the erasing of differences and feed the hate to them. With Arendt (1963), we understand that the equality of citizenship in the political arena has an enormous power to equalize whatever, by nature and genesis, is different. Thus, as much as the people become equal, in any and all aspect, and how much more equality permeates all the society texture, the more the differences will induce pique, the more evident will become those who are visibly and by nature different from the others (p. 115).

We defend that this Tsunami is fed by hate that Arendt theorized as the banality of evil practices[24] in the everyday life weaving. As pointed out, a conservative wave of hate and violence doesn't appear from nothing. It comes and goes since immemorial times, different societies, rules, and enemies. It is a personal–social hate, historic which enmesh everyday life practices of exploration, annihilation, extermination, that feds the tsunami and nurtures back such a gigantic wave. The "banality of evil" was obvious during the torture practiced in Brazil during the last dictatorial period (1964–85), and was morally relativized, being the product and consequence of the enemy's own acts. Missing is "the most elementary sense of justice" according to Arendt,[25] where one's enemy's judgment succumbs to the acquiescence given to ordinary people (p. 135), and to the annihilation of others as persons, such as the way that Bolsonaro currently defends torture and suggests many times that "Marielle deserved it."

In order to illustrate the debate, the number of complaints for attempted femicide registered at the Call Center for Women in Situations of Violence grew by 425 percent since Bolsonaro was elected and we know underreporting is a pattern in these cases. The information was obtained through the Access to Information Law. Also, during the pandemic crisis, according to Integrated System of Assistance to Women (SIAM) sexual and physical violence increased more than 50 percent.[26]

The radical hate that fed Arendt's analysis over what happened in the Holocaust lives in the conservative neoliberal tsunami and its authorization to antique knowledge in the everyday life in the societies, and today, inspissates the tsunami's waves.[27] The lines that chart the racist's abysms, colonialism, heteropatriarchy, exploration, and destruction of capitalism that feed hate on our everyday life are giving new color to the old social maps.

In terms of education, Brazil is again undergoing intense debates and antagonisms concerning, on the one hand, the constitutionally guaranteed inclusion of religious education in public schools and, on the other, the controversial inclusion of gender and sexual diversity issues in the regulatory framework, standards, policies, and the everyday life of public education.[28] These moral disputes point to the tension between politics and religion.

We highlight how these reform initiatives have created heightened debates and antagonisms in Brazilian education through the imposition of moral guidelines. These disputes about the different views on secularism in a democratic state are most acute, producing panics and mobilizations all over the country. The notion of moral panic, by Moura and Salles (2018),[29] is actuated to define the reaction of a group of people based on the fake or blistered perception that the behavior of another one (teachers in these times), usually a minority or a subculture, is dangerous and represents a threat to society in its entirety. This feeds the mighty conservative tsunami

So it is necessary to admit that long before the coup of 2016 hate resided in our lives. It is evidenced in schools, with the genderist division of toilets, the censorship to male teachers in the care with children, the attribution of affection and motherhood to the female teachers, the euro-white-centric text books, etc. To admit that these violent oppressions have existed for a long time, dating back to the brutal slavery practices on black people still feed racism, being authorized and amplified in the previous dictatorial governments (1937–45 and 1964–85), and now in our present day allows evermore police abuse, the genocide of black young in the urban periphery in Brazilian cities and around the world. Now-colorized hatred scribbled in the toilets and hallways flaunts swastikas exposing the banality of hate in response to race, gender, and social class. The abyssal cartography of hate and violence also can be found in the books, in the speeches, in the jokes, and in the disdain, diminishment, and dehumanization of the "Other."

In everyday schools and universities, we educators swap solidarity in place of the conservative reforms and hierarchy, because we share a belief in life at the schools, in creative intelligence and student's autonomy and that we have something to give. This commitment to democratic education in the classrooms, everyday *thinkedpracticed*[30] demands us to be ever vigilant, astute, and exercise combative resistance, both in curricular creation and in research, in written form and in our collective defiance. As a countering practice we point to epistemologies of the South, which advocates that everyday curricula creation be infused with the promise of cognitive justice,[31] an ecology of knowledge (Santos, 2010), solidarity and thus, opposing the practice of social anti-cohesion.

Marielle and Eronilde: Resistance and Emancipation's Narratives

Certeau (1984) helps us to understand the role and the importance of narratives, sustaining that narrative doesn't intend to express the reality, but aims only to create one space of fiction. In this sense, we can understand that narratives obey a series of rules that prevent the immediate acceptance of their "veracity" while, contradictorily, they put us in front of the fact that this is the only "veracity" possible, considering the impossibility of neutral description of anything. This means that reality, and what we understand of it, cannot be described, only narrated. Thus, narratives can be understood as processes of discourse production throughout which we express what we understand/perceive, what we believe in, and what we believe to exist or can exist, like Santos says, from Ernst Bloch notion of "still-not." That's the way we dialog in this text, looking for possible and credible meanings, more than absolute truth.

From this perspective, the narratives are, to us, a way "to know who we are"[32] and to glimpse the realities beyond what they already are, in what "still-not" are, but that our sociological and democratic action and imagination[33] allow to conceive and fight for. Examples from peripheral everyday life studies of Rio de Janeiro demonstrate the stories that *History does not tell*, as we learned from the samba lyrics of Mangueira in 2019, stories of so many "women, tamoios,[34] mulatos," "marias, mahins, Marielles, Malês," and other subjects that the instituted power insist on not wanting to hear or narrate, seeking to make them invisible. In a counter-hegemonic political epistemological movement of research, we displace those forces from the center to bring to the scene those silenced voices from the inside—out into the open that modernity treats as their own, or their errors and deviations. Where the "light" of the "North" hegemony only sees what its indolent rationality allows and behaves, we seek to perceive the complex networks of un-blindness that make everyday life rich, plural, beautiful, and powerful.

The same is true of the struggle of indigenous Brazilian people for the recognition of their cultures, lands, values, knowledge, and ways of acting.

Although formal legislation protects them from government misdemeanors at all levels, in everyday life their struggle is arduous. In other words, the wars of conquest of plunder and pillage have never ended. Eronilde Fermin's story illustrates this. In the municipality where her people live, during 2012–15, the administration managed to appoint their own representatives to occupy strategic positions as the school coordinator: the Indigenous People position at the City Hall, an office previously held only by Ticuna, the major indigenous nation in that locality. Eronilde shows in her narrative how they used strategies and tactics[35] to remain in the struggle of occupying institutional spaces that is important for the emancipatory struggle:

> I started my work in 2010 teaching. That was when the mayor saw that my work was something very great, that the community liked. I did my very dedicated work. He gave us the opportunity, not because he wanted to, but because of our struggle. He called on ethnic groups to introduce his teachers, to choose a coordinator. He also diagnosed that there were only Ticuna relatives in the coordination.[36]

She also explains how that was possible, even without wanting to the government would have to listen to them and talk to them:

> Our strategy is to never leave the chief alone. We have to go as a group to pressure. If you go alone, the answer is certainly no. Then (we make) a group of people and go. The first (talking) is mine. I already give him (the mayor) an injection before the chief speaks. Then the chief (who needs something) speaks and the mayor cannot run. This is our strategy. They never go alone; we look for a better way to help the community and I have earned this respect from the society.[37]

Eronilde shows, by her tactics, that she realizes the importance of understanding that this represented the violent processes of colonization and *civilization* in Amazonian cities that led to the erasure of the history of her people, its language and its culture. That is why she is dedicated to and continues to engage in the recovery of her native language and the struggle for political representation as an emancipatory tactic.

Similarly, the narratives and understandings found in the lyrics of the Magueira's samba, and the biographical image of Marielle parallels the stories of Eronilde that are unequivocal, show clever ways used by practitioners of everyday life of what was given to them for consumption (Certeau, 1984); small cunning actions in the response to the instituted power tactically circulating in its own field of action. These narratives also show how daily learning can be used to solve problems, as we learned from Southern epistemologies and with the notion of ecology of knowledge.

Thus the idea of recovering the validity of non-scientific knowledge used in solving problems becomes a relevant movement in the fight against these scientific hierarchies. It's important to recognize that the circumstantiality of the knowledge's validity is by no means a "utilitarian" perspective of understanding knowledge. It is the defense of the idea that the validity of knowledge will depend on their capacity for social intervention and not on their degree of scientificity. It depends on the contribution they can make to the solution of the problems that are posed. Thus, we are allied with the emancipatory struggles of subalternized populations of different ethnicities and genders, seeking to demonstrate that this continuum of small everyday struggles is, in itself, emancipatory.

It is also worth mentioning that we understand this alliance goes beyond what would be a formal support for them, but as "relatives" of these interlocutors, in the perspective that we learned from Eronilde herself. She taught us that, in her culture, a relative is not that who has your blood, but the one who fights with you, like you, feeling what you're feeling, suffering what you suffer and fighting your fight. In his language, the word that defines this term is Asemúyta, "my brother who is not of blood, but is my brother who is related to pain and struggle." Solidarizing yourself as a relative, in a new understanding of parenthood, is not just understanding the pain of the other or just supporting the struggle rather, it is to feel the pain and the oppression of the others and to be in his emancipatory struggle with her or him.

Moving toward the Global South: Carnival, Everyday Life, and Feminism

This chapter argued against all forms of epistemic violence such as genderization, racism, the oppression women, and cisgender people in favor of a high-intensity democracy, a politics for difference and for democratic public education.[38] Through an examination of the empirical actions and theoretical research developed within schools, universities, and social movements, we showed how the conversations and narratives share and multiply the knowledge networks to move toward cognitive and social justice. We advocate that everyday life studies are to be based on an epistemological displacement of the Global North and a methodological perspective to research the conceptual demarche (political step) toward building society–knowledge–democracy, through dialogic interactive and decolonial processes. Therefore, a first possible conclusion is that we need to investigate how everyday life constitutes important political–epistemological actions, since it constitutes a means to be incorporated into the field of curriculum and teacher's education, as well as other possibilities for understanding the complexity inherent in both school and everyday life and to create curricula reflecting the lessons embedded with the lyrics of this samba and its linkages to greater society. We also recognize that the study of daily knowledge creation allows us to learn from the South how to weave cognitive and social justice and democratization. Analyzing the narratives and the images of Marielle Franco helps us to focus on cognitive justice in which knowledges of the "South" and the "North" are placed in fair conditions of relationship. Our research demonstrates an effective social contribution to high-intensity democracy, the one that counts on the wide participation of different social groups in the decision-making processes of collective interest. Sexism, as well as racism, is one of the abyssal lines that draw the construction of modernity and their multiple forms are a crescent of violence against women. Thus, the multiple feminist forms of struggle and resistance for democracy achieve an epistemological status of real, original, and unrepeatable production, weaved by practitioners of everyday life within society by solidarity and toward emancipation.

10

The Greek Crisis and the Gender Gap: Reinforcing Connections between Education and Women's Empowerment

Maria Nikolakaki

According to the UN Human Rights Commission, women's human rights are in jeopardy globally.[1] Citing Greece, which has a history of lagging in terms of women's rights, the commission notes that the inequity in women's rights is due to poor implementation, the persistence of discrimination, and the lingering impacts of the crisis and austerity measures. Greece has the lowest rates on the Gender Equality Index for the EU of women's employment which is further exacerbated by marginalized groups, including migrant and Roma-women. Another consequence of the crises is the collapse of social protections and welfare services.[2] While gender inequality is global, this chapter looks specifically at the significant gender-based disparities that have been exploited Greek's national crisis.[3] Greece's gender inequities are further exacerbated with the recent rise of ethnic nationalism that is regaining a foothold in Greek and European politics.[4]

This chapter utilizes feminist intersectionality to explore the current women's inequities in Greece and by exploring the challenges of the current crises, and understanding the possibilities that education can offer in empowering Greek women. Understanding how knowledge is intimately linked to ideologies shaped by power, politics, and education has always been a way to deal with injustice and give power to the oppressed. In response, the chapter examines the historical context of the economic crisis and its intensified gender disparities in terms of women's unpaid care work, unequal pay, access to education, and the elimination of gender-based violence.[5] Then, it looks at the exploitation of the Greek economic crisis as evidence of an emerging post-democracy. In response this chapter emphasizes a feminist understanding of the crisis and the importance of education for women's empowerment in order to accomplish better work-based opportunities, increased financial power, and full participation in civil society. Education can provide women with the knowledge, skills, and self-confidence necessary for better access and opportunities in the workforce, leading to increased income, and less isolation at home or exclusion from financial decisions. Ultimately, the chapter stresses the need for more action, awareness, advocacy, and education (particularly in women studies) for the empowerment of women.

Economic Crisis

For more than a decade, Greece has been mired in severe austerity policies under memorandums imposed by the "Troika" (the decision group formed by the European Commission, the European Central Bank, and the International Monetary Fund [IMF]) which is credited with creating a recession and the highest EU unemployment records. Along with more immediate budgetary cuts and tax increases, the Troika's policies included (i) reductions in wages and prices; (ii) legal and institutional changes aimed at liberalizing labor and other factor markets; and (iii) privatization of public property.[6] The memorandums and the bailout programs created a 25 percent drop in Greece's GDP. This had a critical effect: the debt-to-GDP ratio, the key factor defining the severity of the crisis, through the application of the memorandums would jump from its 2009 level of 127 percent to an unsustainable about 179 percent in 2017.[7]

In 2013, Greece was downgraded from a developed to an emerging economy.[8] The IMF acknowledged in 2013 that it underestimated the damage done to Greece's economy from spending cuts and tax hikes imposed in a bailout, which was accompanied by one of the worst economic collapses ever experienced by a country in peacetime.[9] Erroneously, although they admitted using a false multiplier in their calculations, they continued with the same measures.[10] Needless to say, the hardest hit is Greece's most vulnerable populations of women and children.

In 2009, the debt crisis in Greece was blamed on Greek citizens who were collectively depicted as being "lazy" and "corrupt."[11] Yet, the Organisation for Economic Co-operation and Development (OECD) data show a picture of Greek workers that is far from lazy—declaring, for example, that the Greeks work the longest hours in the EU.[12] In reality, the debt crisis started with a trade deficit crisis within the Eurozone, which included Spain, Italy, Ireland, Portugal, and Greece.[13] Within the Eurozone, trade-costs were reduced between countries, to increase overall trade volume. As a result, labor costs increased in peripheral countries such as Greece relative to core countries (i.e., Germany), without compensating a rise in productivity, and thereby eroding Greece's competitive edge.

On top of that, Germany's wage policies during this phase kept wages low. Subsequently, Greece's current account (trade) deficit rose significantly. By entering the Eurozone, Greece had given up its sovereign monetary tools.[14] Following the 2008 credit crunch, Greece's creditors, consisted of mostly European banks used public bailout monies, to scoop up Greek bonds.[15] Then the Troika stepped in the spring of 2010, in 2012, and again in 2015 to orchestrate bailouts of the Greek government, offering loans in the amount of two hundred and forty billion euros, in exchange for drastic reductions in government spending and other austerity measures to make the Greek economy more competitive.[16] As Kostas Lapavitsays, Professor of Economics at SOAS University (UK),[17] writes:

> The Greek turmoil commenced as a balance of payments, or "sudden stop," crisis-induced by large current account and primary government deficits. It became an economic and social disturbance of historic proportions. Its proximate cause was a loss of competitiveness within the Eurozone due in large part to domestic German wage policies. The bailout policies, imposed by the lenders primarily for reasons of Eurozone stability and adopted by Greece, have had disastrous effects on both the economy and society. The "historical bloc" that dominates Greek society willingly submitted to the bailout strategy, losing sovereignty, for reasons including fear and identity.
>
> (2018, p. 1)

Post-Democracy

The purpose of the Troika was always about crisis management, economic policy oversight, and in-depth analysis on fiscal issues, structural reforms, and macroeconomic imbalances as part of its daily duties, in spite of whatever political party was in power in Greece. As a result of the severe austerity measures, Greece, the historical cradle of democracy, has emerged as a post-democratic state of the EU. A post-democratic state is one where democratic substance is diminished, leveled, and compromised if not irrevocably compromised, but it also challenges nation-states' preconceptions about territory, membership, and power.[18]

According to Crouch (2016), a post-democratic society is one that continues to have and to use all the institutions of democracy, but in a way that they become increasingly a formal shell and into small circles of a politico-economic elite. It is a society marked by pernicious politics that have serious consequence for democracy. Post-democracy's authoritarianism ferments xenophobic movements claiming to represent those suffering from excessive change are indicative of in most authoritarian forms.[19] While he argues that austerity itself is not evidence of post-democracy, it is the way that the crisis is handled that gives evidence of a drift toward post-democracy. He adds:

> First, the Anglo-American financial model that produced the crisis in the first place was designed by a politico-economic elite that corresponds to my concept, as bankers moved in and out of the revolving doors in Washington, designing policies to suit their firms. Then the management of the crisis itself was primarily a rescue operation for banks at the expense of the rest of the population. The most explicit expression of the post-democratic aspects of crisis management was the framing of the Greek austerity package, designed by international authorities in close collaboration with an association of leading bankers. But that was just the clearest case; less formal, similar groupings will be found in most political centres.

Given this situation, Maria Giannacopoulos astutely argues that the paradox of overt and (hyper)visible nature of Greece's sovereign debt crisis has generated a space to broaden understandings of what can constitute or be represented as a sovereign debt crisis.[20] Further, she notes that the current conditions facing the Greek people with the "external and imposed rule[s], a denial of self-determination and austerity designed to produce Greece as an integrated European economy, then what is being experienced by Greek people is effectively imperial rule."[21] This neo-coloniality reflects patterns of hierarchy and domination or resistance[22] and recognizes that "these connections can make it possible to carve out a fresh conceptual space from which to examine the 'global colonial project.'"[23]

It is interesting that there was no mention in any of the 2017 European Gender Equality Index (EIGE) data sets noting the impact of the financial coup d'état creating Greece as a debt-colony by the Troika. This move toward debtor-colonies initiates a transformation of certain nation-states as unequal partners on the lowest chain of asymmetric power relations, in the framework of this governance and conditionality.[24] In fact, in all critical areas, these crises-driven austerity policies sought to promote labor market flexibility and reduce labor costs.

In some countries, such as Greece, the deprivation of basic labor rights (i.e., collective bargaining) raised justified concerns about how the radical changes in the European social model and social protective services weakened women's rights won in previous decades. Under such circumstances, all internal political life and agenda are constantly influenced and co-shaped by powerful actors, such as bureaucracy, financial capital, and key member states, through respective interventions.[25] Hence, the consequences of economic austerity measures forced the government to cut spending and increase taxes. Meanwhile, unemployment has increased in Greece, and precariousness and gig jobs have risen. Needless to say, the debt crisis along with the overwhelming precarity of Greek women's jobs has resulted in dramatically increased unemployment. On top of this, working women are often the breadwinners for families, enclosing extended members, fathers, mothers, sons, and husbands who've lost their jobs.[26] As a fact, a political analysis, based on the data mentioned above, demonstrates the negative consequence of the crisis as it has marginalized the goal of gender equality.

Economic crisis makes—once more in history—the struggle for gender issues to look extravagant. In a number of countries, where austerity policies have been imposed, in addition to the cancellation or reversal of policies promoting gender equality, there has even been observed a decline in state gender equality bodies and institutions. By focusing on the biggest numbers of job losses in the labor market, some miss the indisputable fact that gender inequalities remain a structural and material reality in present societies and women suffer more. In Greece the material reality for women to need to work amid the crisis became an indisputable fact. On the other hand, it is encouraging that, despite the resurgence of conservative and nationalist ideologies in many economically developed countries in recent years, this unfavorable development does not seem to lead at present to a shift in women's attachment to their struggles of independence and autonomy.[27]

The political and economic choices made during the last years of the debt-crisis in Greece have hit the entire society, including environmental degradation, social changes, and the socio-economic environment.[28] The imposition of the neoliberal political–economic remedies and its resultant patriarchal gendered structure of capitalism endangers the society at large, but more specifically women. It is of no coincidence that in November 2019, data released by Greek police show that registered incidents of domestic violence increased by 34.45 percent in the period 2014–18.[29] This discussion has recently become extremely crucial during the Covid-19 health and simultaneous financial crisis as the question has become even more clear as it impacts the most vulnerable populations, women, and children. That said, women in Greece have historically restricted presence (less than 20 percent)[30] from the formal state and its governance even if this year in a symbolic gesture a woman, Katerina Sakellaropolou, was voted by the Greek Parliament as president for the Greek Republic.

Gender and the Debt Crisis

A feminist analysis and formal statistics recognize that neoliberal development and financial crises are closely linked to greater gender inequalities. Irini-Eleni Agathopoulou (2018) reports that within this neoliberal context, wages and jobs are determined by social norms, not productivity per se. But what do these norms reflect? Do they reflect social values and preferences or do they reflect unequal power relations? Social norms are, in fact, gendered because they favor traditional male domains, which are associated with management and money as opposed to (paid or unpaid) labor related to social reproduction.[31] All modern societies share the same model of the middle-class white-male as the dominant human creature. On the other side, as Diana Coole[32] points out, today a woman is expected to coexist and succeed in different roles during her life: "Women occupy a variety of worlds; traditional (as wives and mothers), modern (as workers and citizens) and post-modern (as consumers and shareholders of a modern culture)."

According to the 2017 GEI,[33] Greece was ranked 28th in the EU, last in the ranks of EU gender equality. The GEI of 2019, using figures from 2017, put Greece last once again, after finding that it had the biggest gender gaps measured by six core domains: work, money, knowledge, time, power, and health. On the upside, the country did manage to narrow the gender gap in education, although gender segregation in knowledge domains remained a problematic area. Among young adults (25- to 34-year-olds), women have lower employment rates than men: only 64 percent of young tertiary-educated women were employed in 2018, compared to 79 percent of young men.[34] This is matched by a very low level of labor participation among women in younger (15–24) and older (50–64) age groups, as described in the European Commission's report in 2019. Meanwhile, unemployment has continued to increase in Greece, and the precariousness of gig jobs has risen. On the other side, working women now became the breadwinners for fathers, sons, and husbands who lost their jobs.[35] The consequences of these strict austerity policies on top of the Eurozone crisis have led to further shifts in traditional gender roles.

Employment is considered as a key indicator of measuring gender inequalities, since it significantly affects the behavior and actions of individuals,[36] while it simultaneously carries strong gender characteristics. In Greece, despite noticeable changes in women's participation in paid labor and employment, their work continues to be perceived as "auxiliary" to the work of men who are entrusted with the role of breadwinner and primary income provider.[37] During the last years, the current crisis has literally reversed the trend of an increasing and continuous improvement of women's status in wage labor. Women are historically represented at a greater rate in unemployment, especially in lower status jobs (temporary and precarious forms)[38] In actuality, Greece has one of the lowest rates of women's employment in the EU.[39] This country with the highest unemployment rates recorded in history (youth unemployment hit 60 percent in 2013)[40] has also been compromised by the brain drain of the Greek youth — more than 500,000 have emigrated since 2008—to pursue job opportunities abroad.

Women migrants in Greece experience doubled marginalization. Most of them are undocumented, without social benefits or health insurance and exploited by many of their employers who could hold on to their passports, pay them measly salaries, and not give them days off.[41] The refugee-crisis hit Greece severely. Greece's EU membership, coupled with a shared border with Turkey, means the country witnessed massive inflows of undocumented immigrants looking to enter the EU. Traffickers use Greece not only as a destination but also as a transit stop and as a source country for women and children who are subjected to human trafficking, specifically forced prostitution and conditions of forced labor for men, women, and children.[42]

Women and Social Reproduction

According to the International Labor Organization's (ILO) figures (2017), 32 percent of employed women work part-time, compared with only 9 percent of men.[43] In heterosexual relationships, women are more likely to have lower wages, meaning their jobs are considered a low priority when economic disruptions come along. The extraordinary feminization of the workforce as well as the precarity of women's labor emphasizes the dual role patriarchy and late-capitalism played in social reproduction.[44]

As mentioned above, the gender-gap in part-time employment remains high. Since women are often the ones who take on the responsibilities of caring, as a result, they tend to reduce their working hours. During the early adult years, women tend to sacrifice their employment or delay entry into the labor arena to take care of their children. Parental leave arrangements are scarce, generally unequal in the public vs. private sectors. Childcare rates are among the lowest in the EU and have been decreasing in recent years. In addition, there is an absence of state support for the young mothers, only 8.9 percent (against the EU average of 32.9 percent), and 55.6 percent (EU average: 86.3 percent) of children aged between three and mandatory school. When given the choice of childcare services or leave their jobs, many of women choose the second option, confirming the low value of their work in the market.

Social reproduction is defined as "the individual and collective actions and ideas which every day re-create society, consists the central concept of the current analysis."[45] Progressive feminists have been working to enrich and adapt Marx's reproduction theory to address the following question: What is the role of women in work-force reproduction? Tithi Bhattacharya (2017) astutely asks us what makes neoliberalism prefer to endanger the economic and social reproduction (for women) at such high levels instead of changing policies?

Another consequence of this neoliberal economic crisis is the collapse of social-protections and welfare. As noted above, women are expected to fill the gap in social welfare needs, as public services and local municipal facilities are being eliminated or privatized, including nurseries, day schools, home care assistance, mental health institutions, rehab centers, hospitals, and elder homes. These needs are nowadays mostly covered by the family. This return to the family to cover reproductive needs within this new era of internationalized neoliberalism "creates rudimentary safety nets, executing of certain functions of reproduction outside the commodity sphere so that wage cuts do not fully block the reproduction of labor power, a revival of hierarchies necessary for the reproduction and strengthening of the system of power."[46] At the same time, a new field for capital profitability is created, as previously public services become privatized.[47]

These basic reproductive needs and tasks that have been leveled on women, through a hierarchical system of values based on the sexist, patriarchal, heteronormative ideology, make possible the social reproduction and the acquiesces to the hegemony of capitalism. Social reproduction is fundamentally a class issue, where working-class mothers and schools are expected to prepare their kids for lives as proper "workers" who are obedient, deferential to bosses, and primed to accept "their station" and tolerate exploitation.[48] As Sylvia Federici (2019) says about the capitalism, "Racism and sexism are necessary conditions of existence of the capitalist class. The capitalist class always needs a population without rights, in the colonies, in the kitchen, in plantation, which in fact is determinant on the process of value accumulation. In that way, they represent one of the most important terrains of struggle."

Along with struggles is the preoccupation to fight against fascist ideologies that are overtly aimed at restricting women's rights. For example, the rise of the neo-Nazi party of Golden Dawn gave chills to the country amid the economic crisis. Yet, the Golden Dawn party gained prominence going from fewer than 20,000 votes in 2009's general election to winning more than 7 percent of the vote, and 18 parliamentary seats, in 2012.[49] Incredibly, no other outright fascist party in the EU has made such gains in a general election for years. The Golden Dawn's platform envisaged the key role of women in Golden Dawn's ideological edifice and in the construction of a *nationalist habitus* for women rooted in ideas of anti-feminism, motherhood and family, and the primacy of nation and nationalist sentiment in determining women's lives.[50] According to the neo-Nazi ideology, a woman "is a good national socialist if she stays in the house and has children, because her goal is to breed warriors."[51] While they didn't officially consider the dominant narrative during the years of the Greek crisis, some far-right groups continue to challenge women's rights. However, their disregard for women was on display when Parliament Member Ilias Kassidiaris, the neo-Nazi political leader and later Golden Dawn, attacked two left-wing female politicians on camera—throwing water at the face of one and slapping the other repeatedly. This signaled to the public that women are considered subordinates. It also echoed their refrain that women are meant to be wives and child-bearers dedicated to providing care and raising the members of a nationalist family, while at the same time women's political involvement is considered to be contradictory to their so-called feminine "nature."[52] In 2019 elections and six years after the assassination of Pavlos Fyssas, a left-wing rapper, killed by a Golden Dawn member, the Golden Dawn failed to overcome the threshold to get into the Greek Parliament. That doesn't mean that that Greek Nazism is over, since one of its leading members announced the formulation of another Nazi Party.

During the pre-election period in Athens (May 2012), Greece witnessed an unprecedented attack on a population of poor immigrant women called the "women hunt,"[53] who were referred to as "a hygiene bomb at the basement of Greek family." Many were falsely accused of illegal prostitution and of transmitting HIV in the popular press. One of the women committed suicide unable to continue to live with this shame of the accusations. This one and a half year-long fascist hunt came directly from the Greek government, until many were able to establish their innocence proved they were not prostituting, only being poor living with a serious illness. Nevertheless, their online public humiliation from the media included photos, names, family members, all of which worked to terrorize poor women who might be ill or might be actually working in the sex industry.[54] The trigger of this incident was the ensuing elections precluded with the sensational prosecution of the HIV-positive women. This was unabashedly a pre-electoral political game to entice a kind of "moral panic" within society in order to increase their popularity.[55]

Women Participation in Social Movements and Feminist Awakening

The social movements in Greece created by this new era have been a constant feature in the past few years. As a result, women have exploited the internal contradictions of capitalist patriarchy trying to game the system well as they could, but not in terms of feminist collective struggles. This process has been quite easier for women of the middle classes who case by case might have more chances to access land, capital, and education (Sotiropoulou, 2014). However, all women pro-actively reduced reproductive work by decreasing the number of children and by delaying marriage (Sotiropoulou, 2014).

Nevertheless, many solidarity networks and cooperatives spread throughout Greece. They have turned the thousands of volunteers from passive subjects to active agents of change in food banks, organizing free tuition, helping poor students with homework, to free exchange shops. These women are on the battlefields of social survival of the Greek society. This cooperative model is not unknown to people in this country, it is vibrant and active in a variety of economic sectors. In agriculture, for example, there are around 3,000 cooperatives and 130 women's agricultural and agro-tourism co-ops. The housing co-op movement also has a strong presence, comprising almost 540 co-operatives with 120,000 members. Overall, there are more than 50,600 associations, foundations, and other nonprofit and voluntary organizations with 1.5 million members.[56]

The Academy, Feminist Education, and Women's Empowerment

As a result of the economic crisis, more and more women are turning to education to improve their employability. It is known that women's wages are lower than men's; statistics show that the less education a woman has the greater the wage gap with men. However, wages increase as women become more educated.[57] According to the Greek Constitution, Higher Education is the sole responsibility of the state; private universities are exempted from the Greek Constitution by article 16. This article has been used as a terrain for struggles by the Greek ruling class and the right-wing political parties pushing for privatization while left-wing political parties struggle to keep Higher Education under the public domain. Higher Education, in particular, has been historically considered one of the main forms of upward social mobility in Greece, as in other countries. For the average Greek family, entrance into a university is associated with better employment prospects. Yet, this goal has been jeopardized by the neoliberal economic crises' aggressive budget cuts in public spending, and therefore has prevented Greek families support for their children's educational pursuits.[58] Clearly, Greek society is facing prolonged austerity, new poverty, and reduced expectations, the forces of capital and their representatives as they impose the "Shock Doctrine" (Klien, 2007; Saltman, 2014) to Greek Education. As a result, there have been many forms of protests and struggles in recent years, in the face of the Greek government's attempts to present an image of successful implementation of the reforms.[59]

Within the formal university structure in Greece, there were no women's or gender studies (WGS) until recently. Even today, there are no designated autonomous departments or official studies programs leading to degrees in WGS per se, although certain changes in the direction of the institutionalization of WGS took place last decade. In contrast to what happened in Northern American and Western European universities in earlier years, Greece's establishment of WGS was not the outcome of internal processes or requests from within, let alone the free choice of the state, namely, the Greek Ministry of Education. In fact, "Support of Women" at an academic level was imposed externally by a EU directive in 2000. These measures included a call for postgraduate studies programs on gender and equality in 2002, and resulted in the establishment of four postgraduate programs. A call followed for "cycles of courses" at the undergraduate level, titled "Interdepartmental Study Programs for Topics in Gender and Equality" (ISPs). Eight such (time-limited) programs at different universities were approved. As one can imagine, the ministry's reaction to the EU directive could not be mechanical, given that the ministry had turned a deaf ear to relevant proposals the previous years.[60]

The need for empowering feminist studies cannot be overstressed. As Sara Hlupekile Longwe says:

> Adult education and training for empowerment are concerned with the process of enlightenment, conscientization, and collective organization. This involves a collective effort by adult women to throw off the patriarchal beliefs and

attitudes they imbibed during their years of formal schooling. Gender training may offer such an opportunity; or, alternatively, it may be part of the conservative agenda which perpetuates women's subordination. As a preliminary general definition, gender training may be defined as training to provide the skills and methods for improved gender-orientation of development programs. Such training is provided to development agencies, to enable programs to be designed in a way that recognizes and addresses gender issues that stand in the way of development. Comprehensive training is directed at people at all levels of the development process: from policymakers at one end, to the affected community at the other definitions.

(1998, p. 20)

According to Longwe (1998, p. 20) education for women's empowerment should help women to recognize gender issues in their own personal experience, analyze other gender issues, identify discriminatory practices, identify underlying patriarchal interests/beliefs that legitimate discriminatory practices, recognize opposition to gender-oriented policies, identify specific forms of institutional resistance to policies of gender equality, design strategies to counter political and bureaucratic opposition to policies of gender equality, and suggest a sequence of collective actions as a means of ending discriminatory practices and overcoming patriarchal opposition.

In particular, Pavlina Pavlidou (2011) suggests that the challenges for the Greek academia today involved in the WGS among others are to (a) transform our monologues into collective discourse(s); (b) ground gender issues in the Greek context; (c) connect theoretical thinking inside academia with the actions/activities of women (who have started to form their own collectivities again) outside academia, or, to put it in more general terms, connect the university with society and theory with praxis; (d) inspire and educate a new generation of students who will get involved in gender studies in an essential, rather than casual and utilitarian, way (p. 169). This approach in the academy can bring enlightenment and hope not only for the strengthening of women's right but also for the feminist values of solidarity and collectivity.

Conclusion

Greece ranks as the most patriarchal society in the EU, given its constant last-place Gender Equality scores. Without question, patriarchal societies, and their gender-based divisions, give men a larger share in decision-making, social mobility, and economics, while women as seen above, share a larger work-load. Women, feminists, public intellectual are called on to develop programs to redistribute resources which will undoubtedly run into political resistance. What is needed then is a revolutionary feminism in education[61] one that is "connected to a vision of another society, a society that is not based on the exploitation of human labor …. You cannot change the condition of women without changing the whole of society. It is the whole of society that has to turn the upside-down."[62]

Therefore, learning about women's oppression and paths toward social justice can lead to new ways of understanding the issues, and enacting the learning process itself. Feminist pedagogy draws its strength from engagement with feminism and vice versa.[63] This reflects Paulo Freire's notion of conscientization, suggesting that both men and women are to be educated in gender awareness. This chapter examined feminist responses to the new political forces of authoritarianism and conservativism fueled by the economic crisis. These responses have given rise to feminists' anti-conservative projects that champion changes in family-related policies and wage-inequalities, and to identify critical gender *disparities* caused by austerity-driven poverty, cultural norms and practices, poor infrastructure, violence and fragility. As bell hooks (1994a, p. 207) puts forward, we have the opportunity to labor for freedom, to demand for ourselves and our comrades, an openness of mind and heart that allows us to face reality even as we collectively imagine ways to move beyond accepted boundaries, to transgress. Therefore, feminists seek critical education for all women as a practice toward the promise of freedom.

11

The Emergence of the Anti-gender Agenda in Swedish Higher Education

Guadalupe Francia

The Threat to Gender Studies in Higher Education

After decades of progressive reforms in terms of gender and sexual rights, an anti-gender agenda has emerged that makes gender and sexual rights struggles in different parts of the globe difficult.[1] This anti-gender agenda was already present in the Roman Catholic Church's resistance to the success of gender equality and sexual rights struggles in the mid-1990s.[2] In this anti-gender crusade, the Vatican uses the terms "gender theory" and "gender ideology" as "glue concepts" to refer to a diversity of gender and sexual rights, such as "marriage equality, reproductive rights, gender mainstreaming and sexual education." Considered as a threat to traditional family and society values, this "gender theory/gender ideology" is presented as a form of cultural revolution to be implemented in different educational areas.[3]

No longer limited to the Vatican, this agenda has now been extended to different parts of the world and involves new groups and organizations. It is spread by new types of mobilization and by discourses that are designed to address wider audiences than traditional conservative religious groups.[4] For instance, conservative and radical right-wing parties and movements in Germany, Hungary, Poland, France, and Slovakia have been spreading this anti-gender agenda since 2006.[5]

In Sweden, one of the areas that has been targeted by this anti-gender campaign is gender studies in higher education. Threats and violent acts directed at gender researchers are more common in Sweden today. For example, in 2018 the *Swedish Secretariat for Gender Research* was the victim of a bomb scare.[6] Threatening emails and violent participants at public lectures have led to Swedish universities introducing security measures to protect their gender researchers. In addition, neoliberal conservative debaters, religious groups, and far-right parties have accused gender studies of being based on ideological constructions without scientific evidence. Similar ideas have also been expressed in the press, radio, TV, and on social media.[7]

In order to contribute to a deeper understanding of the advance of this international anti-gender agenda, in this chapter I analyze and discuss the ideological discourses against *gender studies* as a scientific field in higher education published in the Swedish media. I first of all describe gender studies in the Swedish higher education context. This is followed by an introduction to research on the current political context of the global anti-gender agenda. An empirical study of the ideological discourses against gender studies that have appeared in the Swedish media is then presented. Finally, the result of the empirical study is presented and discussed.

Gender Studies in Swedish Higher Education

According to Liinason,[8] gender studies is a large academic field in Swedish higher education that involves the following organizational aspects:

- Gender studies as research activities that are integrated into other subject areas (gender research, research with a gender perspective, and research with a gender aspect)
- Gender studies as a specific subject (departments or central/units with undergraduate and/or PhD training in gender studies)
- Gender studies as transdisciplinary gender research based on a feminist epistemology and methodology that transgresses disciplinary borders and the boundaries between higher education and other sectors in society.[9]

Gender studies research often involves critical studies on the production and reproduction of gender and gender differences. A central issue for this research is the analysis of how gender interacts with other power dimensions, such as material circumstances and age.[10] Initially, gender studies aim to produce scientific knowledge about women's lives in order to make their experiences visible in male-dominated societies. Nowadays, *gender studies* have developed into a wide educational and research topic—in Sweden and internationally—and includes other types of research, such as masculinity studies, queer and sexuality studies, and human–animal studies.[11]

Gender studies as a scientific field is interdisciplinary and involves researchers in the social sciences, humanities, science, technology, and medicine. This interdisciplinary nature results in a diversity of methodologies and theories in gender studies research, which means that "it is difficult to describe gender science as a homogeneous subject."[12] In Sweden the official name of this field is gender studies, but it can also be named as women's/gender/feminist studies (WGFS) in other national contexts.[13] It is also important to note that in order to promote gender research in higher education, the Swedish government created the Swedish Secretariat for Gender Research in 1998. Although the secretariat is housed at the University of Gothenburg and organizationally comes directly under the vice-chancellor and the university's management board, its work applies to all Swedish higher education institutions. Based on research on gender and other critical perspectives, the secretariat organizes activities that are "cross-sectoral, national, Nordic and international; and in collaboration with research councils, government agencies, higher education institutions and other actors." It also provides "expert support through surveys, knowledge reviews and analyses" and includes externally funded and own-funded projects.[14]

According to Rosi Braidotti,[15] since its introduction at the end of the 1980s as an academic subject in European universities, gender studies has been criticized by researchers in other fields for not being scientific. However today, critical arguments against gender studies at higher education are held not only by some actors inside the academy, but even by representatives from conservative and right-wing political groups.[16]

The Role of Academic Capitalism in the Anti-gender Agenda

The rapid increase in economic inequalities as a result of a brutal global capitalism and the breakdown of the traditional political parties has led to the renewal of fascism in national democratic contexts.[17] Furthermore, these inequalities have contributed to the rapid advance of populist radical-right movements that oppose all forms of sexual and diversity rights. Blaming sexual and gender rights struggles for the negative impact of finance capitalism on families' welfare, the far-right collaborates with others to dismantle welfare societies produced by financial capitalism. Given the intimate relationship between capitalism and the far-right, any successful struggle for ethnic and gender diversity also needs to be anti-capitalist.[18]

Based on xenophobia, these radical right-wing movements and parties also propose a return to traditional family values and to fascism and nationalism as a political agenda.[19] In addition, the radical right has openly initiated an almost-religious mission to put an end to gender ideology in all areas of society. At the same time, the political advancement of the radical right has affected other traditional parties, in that they now tend to imitate the restrictive migratory discourse to avoid losing the votes of the right.[20]

According to Ikka Kauppinen,[21] international and national policies aiming to integrate higher education and the knowledge-based economy have been developed around the world in recent decades. This global higher education process, called "academic capitalism," is based on close collaborations between universities and the corporate world. Furthermore, while promoting the reduction of state funding, this academic capitalistic regime also proposes to increase higher education strategies to attract external funding from the market. In this academic capitalism regime, higher education institutions are expected to produce and commodify knowledge in order to finance research and education. By perceiving knowledge as a commodity, teaching, research, and service become integrated with globalizing knowledge capitalism. As a consequence, the social sciences and humanities have been relegated to an underprivileged position in academia. Instead, academic disciplines that are close to and embrace the market have become the winners in the academic capitalism regime.

The advance of the global capitalistic paradigm in education is also present in neoliberal policies in education. Based on a fundamentalist vision of the superiority of the market,[22] this neoliberal paradigm disqualifies gender and identity struggles in education. According to Henrik A. Giroux,[23] the vision of the university as a public sphere fostering citizens in educational culture for democracy, freedom, and justice has been replaced by a neoliberal vision based on the dominance of the market. As a result of the advance of the market ideology in higher education, the humanities and liberal arts have been marginalized and neglected. When the vision of the university as a public good and center for critical education disappeared, students became consumers and academic knowledge became a commodity to be expressed in economic terms.

Gender and Ideological Discourse

By regarding ideological discourses as a way of making gender studies a subject that is eligible for recognition or misrecognition in higher education, I will now point to the need to pay attention to the interaction between ideology and discourse. According to Teum A. van Dijk,[24] ideologies form "the basic social representations of the beliefs shared by a group." Furthermore, ideologies "function as the framework that defines the overall coherence of these beliefs. Thus, ideologies allow new social opinions to be easily inferred, acquired and distributed in a group when the group and its members are confronted with new events and situations."[25] In line with van Dijk,[26] I start out from a large and general conception of ideology that includes positive and negative as well as dominant and non-dominant socially shared basic beliefs. In this context, I argue that the shared and social beliefs of groups are always ideological. Consequently, I start this analysis from the idea that all kinds of arguments for or against gender studies at the higher education are considered as ideological in this analysis.

Ideologies understood as socially shared basic beliefs of groups are associated with the specific and representative properties of these groups.[27] At the same time, ideologies form these groups' social practices. One form of an ideology's influence on social practices is discourse. On the one hand, ideologies are expressed and reproduced by discourses. On the other hand, discourse structures at different levels are influenced by these ideologies, because ideologies "not only may control what we speak or write about, but also how we do so."[28] In addition, "Ideologies typically organize people and society in polarized terms."[29] Based on an "ideological square," the ideological discourse uses strategies to emphasize positive things and de-emphasize negative things about one's own group and other groups, respectively.[30]

In relation to gender studies in higher education, I argue that these ideological discourses recognize some academic approaches to research on gender and misrecognize others. Furthermore, in order to understand the impact of ideological discourses on the anti-gender agenda, it is necessary to pay attention to the performativity of gender. According to Butler,[31] gender is always performative because it is related to the different ways in which a subject becomes eligible for recognition. This performativity establishes modes of intelligibility of the body in space and time that are conditioned and mediated by social norms. This is a process in which some bodies are produced as recognizable and intelligible subjects, while others are not. In the bodies that are evaluated as not being eligible for recognition, Butler includes queers, transgender people, the poor, and the stateless.

Based on Butler,[32] I argue that gender studies as scientific field has a performative function concerning to how different ways produce knowledge on gender and gender differences are recognized or misrecognized as scientific knowledge. In order to illustrate and discuss the role of ideological discourses published in the Swedish media against *gender studies* as a scientific field in higher education, I will present and discuss the results of my research on critical voices against gender studies in Swedish higher education found in the Swedish media. Using the keywords "gender studies" and "ideology," 125 articles were found in the database *Mediearkivet*[33] from 2016 to January 2020. Only articles that included critical voices against gender studies in Swedish higher education were selected, resulting in a total of eighteen analyzed articles.

Voices against Gender Studies in Higher Education

The ideological discourses against gender studies found in the analyzed media articles are advanced by four different groups that tend to de-emphasize the role and position of gender studies in Swedish higher education. The first group consists of journalists, debaters, and press editors in newspapers and journals with a nationwide reach (*Svenska Dagbladet, Dagens samhälle*) as well as the local press (*Sydöstran, Blekinge Läns Tidning, Landskrona Posten, Borås Tidning,* and *Östgösta Correspondenten*). The most prominent voice in this group is Ivan Arpi, the head publisher of the liberal-conservative newspaper *Svenska Dagbladet*. Arpi produced a series of six articles in the newspaper in 2017–18, which were then reproduced by other national and local newspapers, Swedish radio, Swedish TV, and social media. On one of his own websites, Arpi says that the article series is to be published in book form for the think-tank and publishing company Timbro. The book was indeed published in May 2020 with the title *Genusdoktrinen* [The Gender Doctrine]. Arpi also disseminated the content of these articles through Twitter and Facebook.

The second group involves voices from religious groups published in Christian newspapers (*Kyrkans Tidning, Världen idag*). *Världen idag* is a Christian newspaper with a focus on free churches and in particular the Pentecostal movement, but also attracts readers from other denominations. *Kyrkans Tidning* is published by the Church of Sweden and covers a wide range of religious issues. The Church of Sweden is an Evangelical Lutheran Church with 6.1 million members.

The third voice is political representatives of the far-right *Sverigedemokraterna* (SD) (in English, *The Sweden Democrats*, or *The Swedish Democrat*s), published in a debate article in the independent political portal *Altinget*. SD was founded in 1988. Some of SD's founder members had been involved in extreme right-wing parties and organizations, such as the *Framstegspartiet* (*The Progress Party*), *Sverigepartiet* (*The Swedish Party*), and the anti-immigration campaign movement *Bevara Sverige Svenskt* (*Keep Sweden Swedish*). SD has a clear anti-migration agenda and follows the criteria for the populist radical right: nativism, authority, and populism (Widfeldt, 2018). Over the last decade, SD's popularity has increased among the Swedish population. In the 2014 general election it received 12.54 percent of the votes, which increased in 2018 to 17.53 percent.[34]

The fourth voice belongs to representatives from the group *Academic Rights Watch (ARW)*. ARW monitors academic freedom in Sweden by drawing attention to attempts to restrict the fundamental rights of teachers and researchers, such as freedom of expression and opinion, in Swedish higher education.

Gender Studies as a "Glue Concept"

Similar to earlier research,[35] this analysis shows that gender studies are introduced as a "glue concept" that involves different strategies for gender rights. Defining gender studies as a glue concept for different gender mainstreaming activities in higher education has made the field synonymous with non-scientific research activities. By using this kind of generalization as a discursive strategy, the anti-gender discourse suggests that gender studies are not a scientific field because it includes activities that are not considered as academic research':

> It is no longer the subjects or the intellectual development that are at the centre of gender studies, but the emotions. Teachers are sent on a course on "inclusion" and are urged to avoid controversial topics because someone in a group might take offence. The teacher should not comment, either positively or negatively, on a particular group's history or behaviour, or on students' names, provenance or knowledge. Students are encouraged to report teachers or fellow students, for example, for sexism or racism. In this way, a signifier mood is developed, where everyone is afraid of everyone else.[36]

For instance, the article "When Gender Studies Became the Upper Church in Lund" published by Ivar Arpi in *Svenska Dagbladet* equates gender studies with gender mainstreaming activities. He argues that Lund University obliged a teacher to include Judith Butler in a history course on fascism. It is even relevant to pay attention to the use of the word "church" to describe gender studies. By talking about the church instead of science, this article uses the power of gender studies as a metaphor to spread knowledge in the form of religious beliefs to the entire university. This metaphor is even used as a strategy in the anti-gender agenda to oppose gender studies in higher education.

At the same time, by referring to Arpi's critical articles as intertext, the debate article "Gender Policy Is Not the Solution," published in *Kyrkans Tidning*, supports and spreads the description of gender studies as a synonym of gender mainstreams activities. By using intertextuality as a discursive strategy, the authors of this article show that their arguments against gender studies are also supported by other recognized influencers in the media.

These selected examples confirm earlier research[37] showing that these critical voices use gender studies as a glue concept that involves all kind of activities, from gender mainstreams to gender research. By mixing gender research with other kinds of higher education activities, these critical voices tend to misrecognize the role of gender studies as a scientific field.

Gender Studies as the Alien in Higher Education

By talking about gender studies in terms of ideology, religious approach, indoctrination, political activism, a strategy to silence men, or a threat to people's health, the analyzed ideological discourses in the Swedish media intimate that this field has no place in higher education. I argue that these descriptions can be summarized by the metaphor of gender studies as "the alien in the scientific field." The alien metaphor functions as a strategy to de-emphasize the scientific value of gender studies in order to exclude the field from higher education institutions.

The article in *Kyrkans Tidning* relates gender studies to post-Marxism and social constructivism. This article also presents the field as a strategy to silence men. Even in *Världen idag*, gender studies are accused of not being a scientific field, but is instead presented as an "ideologically driven struggle that ignores biological facts" and a tax-funded "religious approach."

> What is called "gender science" is, in fact, not science, but an ideologically driven struggle that ignores biological facts. It has become a kind of new over-ideology that everyone is expected to bow down to, however unscientific it may be. Psychiatrist David Eberhard puts it like this:
>
> "The [gender theories] are problematic because many of these theories ignore biology. Then it is not a scientific approach, but a religious approach. You have decided on a conclusion before exploring what it is." Science and proven experience are replaced by ideology and political thinking.
>
> And this is done in the context of tax-funded research.[38]

This article goes one step further and accuses gender theories of perverting and confusing youth.

> The consequences will be devastating when gender theories and norm criticism search different contexts. Young people are beginning to doubt their own gender identity and the number of gender studies is skyrocketing. The wrestling match

that was previously reserved for a small minority of the population now involves an entire generation. Everyone should question their biological sex and try to define themselves.[39]

Even in the article published by SDs MP, entitled "Stop Gender Indoctrination," gender studies are disqualified as a scientific field by using the term "over ideology," "politicized ideology," and "indoctrination" and the field's scientific value questioned:

> We see a sad development in the academic world, where gender pedagogy and gender research increasingly take the form of an over ideology, which controls and influences other academic activities. Pressures in the form of allocated funds and other things have forced this ideology into more and more secrecy in the higher education world. It is clear to us that this gender ideology, which seems erroneous and misleading under the term "equality", also implies a politicization of academic activities. As such, it also restricts the freedom of educational institutions as well as the freedom of instruction for individual academics.[40]

In the local press, knowledge about gender studies is compared with the "real science" of neurobiology. In the article the author rejects the knowledge contributed by gender studies to science. At the same time, this contribution emphasizes the knowledge about gender that has been produced by other scientific fields, such as neurobiology, which are regarded in this article as "real science." Using polarization as a discursive strategy, the article emphasizes the value of science research based on scientific knowledge, models, and methodologies.

> It is believed that this is about science and claims that gender is a social, self-constructed and self-selected phenomenon. If someone objects to gender having its origins in biological factors, which, on the other hand, are scientific facts, one does not become prolonged in, for example, the university world where this contrived ideology has had a great impact.
>
> ... Annica Dahlström, professor of neurobiology and author of the book "The gender is in the brain," says: "Gender research that claims that gender is a social construct is entirely in the air." She goes on to say that; "the most important difference between women and men has to do with the chromosomes. The female sex hormone is estrogen and the male hormone is testosterone. It's about fundamental physical differences in girls' and boys' brains. Gender identity is in a particular cell nucleus."[41]

To summarize, by describing gender studies as a field with no scientific grounding, these critical voices aim to introduce gender studies as an alien that needs to be eliminated in order to guarantee higher education's mission to produce scientific knowledge.

Gender Studies as an Ideology in Higher Education

The analyzed ideological discourses often describe gender studies as simple ideologies with a connection to academia. In these descriptions the term "ideology" is used as synonym for no scientific knowledge produced by political activists. For instance, the article published by SD's MPs, entitled "Stop Gender Indoctrination" describes the field as one that does not accept critical voices. At the same time, gender studies are characterized by bulky and unscientific theories. Furthermore, science researchers are presented as victims of mainstream strategies who are obliged to read radical feminist gender theories.

The description of gender studies as an ideology with no scientific basis is not only limited to academia and a risk to academic freedom. Gender studies is also described in terms of a threat to be combated because it involves children and young people and is a malicious ideology that can be spread to other public institutions.

> It is not only universities that are affected. My sources in the government offices, the Swedish armed forces and various authorities tell similar stories. Gender mainstreaming and gender certifications are also spreading there.[42]

The saddest thing is its influence in preschools and schools.[43]

> That these perspectives [gender and diversity] should not only be forced into syllabuses that deal with completely different things, but that the staff should also be retrained in the right gender and diversity ideology is a development that should not go unnoticed. It is difficult to reconcile with academic freedom that political ideology is made the upper church for all research.[44]

In addition, in the debate article "Gender Studies Contributes to Mental Illness" the field is introduced as an ideology that threatens the health of young people. It is relevant to note that this debate article was published in February 2018 by *Sydöstran* and on March 9 in *Blekinge Läns Tidning*. As a consequence, it is thought that scientific researchers need to start a war to protect science from gender studies' ideological attacks: "Science must take back power from ideology."[45]

Even the article published by SD's MPs entitled "Stop Gender Indoctrination" accuses gender studies of "scientific bias." Using the term "politicized ideology" to refer to gender studies as a research field, the authors propose that all public funding for gender studies should be stopped and position themselves as opponents to gender studies' argumentation of gender difference. Using generalization as a discursive strategy, they argue that gender difference is always biological:

> What we are strongly opposed to is the gender science that has no scientific basis and that has also adopted a form of politicized ideology. All science from the Middle Ages onwards shows with all desirable clarity that there are biological differences between the sexes, which is exactly why we say gender in the plural. We oppose the underlying idea in gender science that these differences would be negative. The key for us is that everyone should be given the same opportunities, regardless of gender.[46]

In order to combat gender studies, these politicians recommend withdrawing the state grant to the Swedish Secretariat for Gender Studies Research at Gothenburg University:

> As a clear indication of the increasingly influential gender ideology in the academic world, we are withdrawing the grant to the Secretariat for Gender Studies. The sum may be modest, but someone must still put their foot down on this issue.[47]

In an article published in the conservative newspaper *Expressen*, the authors accuse women of threatening academic freedom because they "show a greater tendency towards depressive reactions and feelings such as stress and anxiety." The authors of the article—three men and one woman—introduce themselves as "Theology doctor in ethics, author, bourgeois opinion maker," professor of psychology, professor of theoretical philosophy, and lecturer in New Testament exegetics. One of the authors is also the president of ARW.

Using intertextuality as a discursive strategy, the authors of this article argue that the increasing number of women in Sweden's higher education endangers universities' scientific work. Referring to psychological research on personal characteristics (five-factor theory) and a report from the Swedish National Audit Office about gender differences in sick leave statistics, they argue that biological differences are the reason why men are more predisposed to defend academic freedom. It is relevant to note that the article was published as a response to a protest letter signed by 150 academics, students, and cultural workers against a lecture given by Richard Jomshof MP, from SD. The article also points out that the majority of protests against academic freedom come from academics from scientific fields with a considerable over-representation of women. As examples of these "feminine" academic fields, the authors place gender studies in first place, followed by sociology, social anthropology, art sciences, cultural sciences, and global studies. In order to combat the female academic culture that threatens universities, the authors propose to act proactively to prevent this culture taking over higher education:

> The universities and their partners should now act proactively before the situation worsens and closes up around freedom of expression, without which the intellectual life of our colleges will disappear and society in the end will stagnate.[48]

To summarize, by describing gender studies as a dangerous ideology related to political activism, these critical voices aim to problematize the dissemination of scientific knowledge produced by gender studies research to academia and society at large.

Conclusion

In order to contribute to a deeper understanding of the advancement of this international anti-gender agenda in the global society, this chapter has analyzed and discussed the ideological discourses against *gender studies* as scientific field in higher education published in the Swedish media. Even though this research is only based on eighteen articles found during the selected period, the analyzed data represents groups that are important influencers in Swedish society, such as journalists and debaters in the local and national press, and in particular the liberal conservative media, religious groups, politicians from far-right parties, and representatives of Academic Rights Watch. Even though this research cannot confirm the ideological similarities between these four groups, it can confirm that these groups share similar ideological discourses against gender studies.

Based on the conception of ideological discourses as a way of making gender studies as a subject eligible for recognition or misrecognition, this research points to the need to pay attention to the connection between ideology and discourse.

The discourse that describes gender studies as an alien that will take over higher education and society as a whole disqualifies this field as a producer of scientific knowledge. Instead, the field is introduced as a dominant political ideology that risks jeopardizing the quality of Swedish higher education.

In these selected texts, gender studies are described in terms of ideology, activism, and Marxism as a way of arguing for its expulsion from academia.

By using polarization as a discursive strategy, these groups make a distinction between the "scientific knowledge" that is represented in science and "the political ideology" of gender studies. At the same time, they argue for the existence of biological gender differences with the support of research in biology and neuroscience. As a result of this kind of polarization, these groups establish norms in terms of which scientific knowledge is eligible for recognition and which is not.

The fact that gender studies is introduced as a glue concept can be interpreted as a strategy to simply hide the complexity of higher education institutions, in which administrative, teaching and research activities, and activities intended to disseminate scientific knowledge to society at large coexist. By remaining silent about the scientific value of gender research, these voices also aim to misrecognize the dissemination of this research to society and the possibility of using this scientific knowledge for gender and other kinds of social reforms.

Consequently, these ideological discourses against gender studies cannot be interpreted as isolated attacks in the Swedish media on an academic field. Rather, these discourses need to be interpreted in the context of a wider political arena that questions social, gender, and sexual rights struggles all around the world. The advancement of a brutal capitalism in all areas of the global society has even been present in higher education policies and practices and has transformed the vision of universities. The idea of a public sphere participant in justice struggles has been replaced by a university model based on a neoliberal ideology that prioritizes knowledge that is expressed in economic terms.[49] In this neoliberal model, scientific fields, as for instance gender studies, that do not follow the knowledge norm of the market risk being conceived as pure ideology. Consequently, this type of scientific field risks becoming an alien against which different conservative groups have started a war in order to expel it from higher education and from the larger global society.

Conclusion

Silvia Edling and Sheila L. Macrine

The scholars and emerging researchers in this volume discuss the various intersections and bifurcations among neoliberalism, conservatism, and nationalism viewed through a transnational feminist lens, by considering the consequences of late-capitalism and globalization on women—cutting across nations, genders, races, sexualities, and class.

Globally, there is a great deal of evidence confirming coalitions among the radical-right aimed at building broad-spectrum conservative alliances toward a certain kind of global solidarity.[1] Their prime objective is to harness their collective powers capable of exchanging the dominance of (neo)liberal regimes with more conservative ones (Korolczuk & Graff, 2018; Rydgren, 2018a). This is all in the name of Conservatism, which is emerging as a common-value-system meshing a wide-range of movements such as: religious fundamentalism, far-right politics, right-wing extremism, neo-nationalists and neo-fascist movements, protectionism, fathers' rights groups, among other conservative parties/groups in general (Kumashiro, 2010a). In this text, we referred to this collective as the Far-Right consisting of assemblages of conservative groups (Rydgren, 2018a) that are both political reactions against, and at times in collaboration with neoliberal politics.

That said, this concluding chapter discusses some general patterns and themes that emerged throughout the volume, as well as adding some forward-thinking insights. Accordingly, we reflect on (a) current and emerging conservative trends in gender-perception and oppression within the various chapters; (b) examine some past motivations to women's oppressions to better understand the human condition; and (c) exposes how right-wing politics—narrows educational spaces for interpretation and critique, divisions along educational lines, and shows the necessity of open and broad educational spaces—in light of (gender) equality and social justice. Indeed, "the corrosion of women's human rights is a litmus test for the human rights standards of the whole society" (United Nations Human Rights Council, 2018).[2]

The book opens with a *Foreword*, written by Distinguished Professor Antonia Darder who elegantly describes the importance of this volume. She writes that the transnational liberation of women can only be accomplished through an "embodied politics" and transnational feminist struggles committed to unfettering our bodies, minds, and hearts by unapologetically embracing our liberation as sensual, thinking, knowing, feeling, and loving subjects. This is followed by a chapter by noted Feminist scholar Professor Chandra Talpade Mohanty who provides a master class on global feminist politics as she unpacks the notion of "Transnational Feminist" theory and politics—challenging globalization and neoliberalism's power, dominance and oppressions against women and children. This critical look at the glocalization of women's oppressions is a significant contribution of this volume and to the Transnational Feminist literature. These opening chapters set the stage for our contributing women-scholars, and public-intellectuals from across the globe as they contextualize women's oppressions and suppressions in their countries locally to demonstrate unifying themes globally.

Current Trends—The Rise of Conservative Movements and White Male Supremacy

Current trends indicate that various far-right conservative movements and many religious organizations support social structures that are male-centered, male-identified, male-dominated, and hostile to gender while valorizing qualities narrowly defined as masculine.[3] The common thread among these movements is their commitment to the revival of traditional gender roles and values, which makes it harder to advance and advocate for gender justice. In other words, while women and LGBTQ persons are encouraged to take part in organized efforts and resistance movements, they are silenced and marginalized compared to straight men (Kitschelt, 2007; Muddle, 2014; Kinnvall, 2015; Blee, 2016). Contributing author, Melchor Hall reminds that such hidden gender-biases go hand-in-hand with racism and are often overlooked in the oppression of women of color—not the least through the system of "technological surveillance." Similarly, Süssekind and Oliveira's chapter highlights the dimensions of coloniality to uncover how race, ethnicity, and gender intersect to produce various forms of oppression, compounded by ideals of colonialism, where some nations are seen as more superior and dominant. They argue for emancipation from such "invisibilized practices" and knowledges by advocating for resistance to and struggles against colonization, heteropatriarchy, and capitalism, as black and native feminists.

The women in this volume, from different countries, languages and disciplines, come together to critique traditional heteronormative ways of life and give us hope by pointing to where we go from here. In their own contexts, these women-scholars explain how various conservative groups sustain oppressive notions of gender roles and biological reproduction based on traditional and fixed ideas of gender (Goodwin, 2011; Kinnvall, 2015; Grzebalska, 2016; Korolczuk & Graff, 2018). They argue that feminists' views are seen as inconsistent with patriarchal-values and conservative religious-views. In fact, many conservative parties and the anti-feminist ideologies have strong ties to religious organizations. Take for example, the Catholic Church's stance on gender. It is so prevalent that even the Pope, in 2015, reinforced traditional gender roles when he asserted that teaching about gender identity in schools is tantamount to "Ideological Colonization" by stating that:

> [i]n Europe, America, Latin America, Africa, and in some countries of Asia, there are genuine forms of ideological colonization taking place, [a]nd one of these—I will call it clearly by its name—is [the ideology of] "gender." Today children—children!—are taught in school that everyone can choose his or her sex.
> (Quinlan, 2016, p. 1)

In addition, these ideas on anti-genderism put feminist scholars, researchers, and actors at risk for retribution, severe attacks, and silencing from various conservative entities (Kováts, 2016, pp. 175–6; see also Hankivsky & Skoryk, 2014; Francia, in this volume). Pointing to the growing hypermasculinity in society, Mooney-Simmies' chapter demonstrates how neoliberalism's masculinist-performativity intersects within ever-present nationalistic far-right movements, also taken up by other authors in this volume.

This rapid rise of conservative movements can be best understood as reactions to the economic crises, regression, and the instability of 2008 (Köttig & Blum, 2016). Fueled by the market-driven reform policies, the neoliberal turn (Harvey, 2007; Grzebalska, 2015; Korolczuk & Graff, 2018) has weakened welfare states, ravaged social-safety nets, increased unemployment, hollowed education (Macrine, 2016, 2020), and significantly exacerbated marginalization, racism, and gender-based biases. In addition, right-wing justifications for these measures result in blatant increases in discrimination and anti-immigration policies and protections, coupled with a distrust for established political parties, as well as generating fear of identity loss and insecurity over employment.

Other extreme forms of right-wing populism like ethno-nationalism, Euro-centrism, Nativism, and Protectionism have propagated hegemonic messages claiming that national identity, cultural heritage, and genetic purity are threatened. These forces have resulted in knee-jerk oppositions and even revulsions to any kind of multiculturalism or immigration. Growing anxiety over this presumed weakening of a nation's cultural and moral fabric along with threats to gene-pools has garnered even stronger negative sentiments than economic setbacks alone (Kinnvall, 2015, p. 519). This sense of insecurity, moral panic, and fear was intensified, not only by waves of immigration starting in 2015, but also with the tragic terrorist attacks in cities like Istanbul, Stockholm, Brussels, and Paris. Needless to say, these concerns need to be taken seriously especially in light of the upsurge of conservative movements, like the far-right ideology that stresses cultural rather than social belonging (Vieten, 2016, pp. 622–3).

Reactions to globalization, and its corresponding openness, also generate feelings of moral decline, increase relativism, divorce freedom from responsibility, and create a false sense of morality (Korolczuk & Graff, 2018, p. 806; Ofsted 2012). While reactions to global neoliberalism and its unpredictability contribute to the rise of conservative movements, there is also variability in how these groups tap into, enhance, and manipulate their own ideals and structures. For example, Mulinari & Neergaard (2016) show how the disassembling of welfare-state institutions that began in Sweden in the 1980s, by the social-democratic political party, was resurrected in 2006 as a far-right-wing racist political party called the *New Democracy*. Similarly, Grabowska (2015) points to the *Law and Justice* party, Poland's ultra-conservative and hard-right political party's alliances with neoliberalism. In similar fashion, Hungary's right-wing political party, the *Fidesz* party, elected a Prime Minister Viktor Orbán, whose vision for Hungary is an *"illiberal democracy,"* reminiscent of the strong-arm tactics of nation-states such as Russia and Turkey.

Countries that are moving toward authoritarian states are not the exception. As neo-nationalist, anti-immigration, and Islamophobic movements rise, we witness a significant upsurge in ultra-conservative political parties globally, not seen since the fascist Nazi party in Germany. Take for example the right-wing *Golden Dawn* party in Greece (see Nikolakaki, this volume), the so-called thuggish *English Defense League* (EDL), along with the *United Kingdom Independence Party* (UKIP) claiming responsibility for the Brexit victory, the

National Front in France, the advent of *Alternative für Deutschland* (AfD) Germany's far-right political *party,* Netherlands' right-wing *Party for Freedom* (PVV), the far-right-wing populist *Austrian Freedom Party*, and not to mention Trump's authoritarian successes celebrating the alt-white and religious fundamentalist in the United States.

Hegemonically, conservative messages espouse traditional-gender norms while at the same time hijack and appropriate feminist language to further right-wing ideologies attacking democracy (see Goodman this volume; Krizsan & Roggeband, 2018). As such de-democratization moves forward, opposition to gender-equality and previous gains in gender equity policies are being erased. It is noted that gender equality is seriously losing ground in countries, that is, Croatia, Hungary, Poland, and Romania, where authoritarianism and neo-nationalism have taken root.

Far from a new phenomenon, tensions among various worldviews such as conservative, social, and liberal stances have existed for the millennia. Yet the zeitgeist of today's global far-right politics and the intensification of conservative forces have created "dangerous times" for democracy, as well as gender and racial equity. These imaginings remind us of the cyclical nature history repeating itself, at the same time they mask the inexorable presence of human struggles, oppressions, inconsistencies, complexities, and constant change (Kinnvall, 2015, p. 518; Edling et al. 2020a, b). For this reason, it is important to be mindful of the oscillating patterns that exist transnationally between and among conservative groups to better grasp the contexts and particularity of certain groups that occur simultaneously (See for instance Vieten, 2016, p. 623; Blee, 2016, pp. 191–2).

Formations of new conservative movements, attributed to the universal broadening of group ideologies and their umbrella agendas, are considered unique. At the moment, smaller conservative enclaves join forces with other conservative groups thus develop larger bodies of power such as neo-nationalism, neo-fascism, and protectionism (See Macrine & Edling, this volume). These movements are reminiscent of strong sentiments of Nazi Germany. Drawing on a strongly dualistic and essentialistic worldviews of Hitler's *Mein Kampf*— Jews, democrats, disabled, gay/lesbian persons, and pacifists, among others, were viewed as pure evil, genetically inferior, violent, and abominations that threatened the livelihoods of Germans. While the Germans citizens were presented as divine, genetically pure, and utterly good. At the same time, it was (some) of these very German citizens (among others) whose duty it was to exterminate and torture millions of persons deemed as weak and genetically inferior (Ofstad, 2012). While it is still hard to fathom such horrors, the threat and growth of right-wing conservatism echo Hannah Arendt's (1968) prescient notion of "dark times."

While conservative groups are gaining momentum, there are inconsistences that shift arguments and rhetoric depending on location, and what serves their cause best in a particular moment. Given these context specific mixed agendas among various far-right groups, one claims to support free speech and democracy arguing that these principles have been hijacked by the "left" and liberals (Peeters, 2007). At the same time, they reject the ethical dimensions of democracy that stress the importance of social justice, basic human rights, and pluralism in everyday life (Rydgren, 2018). Other groups purport to uphold liberal values like gender equality, individualism, and human rights, yet undemocratically position themselves against certain immigrant cultures pictured as patriarchal, authoritarian, and gender oppressing (Kinnvall, 2015; also, Macrine & Edling-this volume). The idea of *appropriating* certain concepts like democracy, feminism, and gender equality in the pursuit of specific aims is exemplified in Goodman's chapter. She demonstrates how feminism is being taken over by neoliberalism to veil the consequences of neoliberal practice. The ambition of this type of appropriation is to use concepts generally deemed as "good" and twist their content to suit one's own agenda regardless of the consequences of action, creating logical inconsistencies between words and action.

Strong Anti-genderism—and the Dismantling the "Public Good"

Globally, we are witnessing a "serious backlash against women's rights" catalyzed by the rise of authoritarianism that has rolled back gender-violence protections and support systems.[4] For instance, one common agenda embraces a broader critique of liberal democracies and its ideologies by narrowing focus on anti-feminism/anti-genderism. In this way, gender and racial equality have been weaponized by conservative groups who have discredited women's organizations as foreign agents' that threaten national identity (Krizsan & Roggeband, 2018) and use anti-immigration, anti-gender, and racist rhetoric to enflame. Their claim is to protect democracy by opposing certain immigrants, along with radically strong aversions to gender equity and ideology (Kováts, 2016). These rising trends toward de-democratization across Europe and the Americas threaten previous gender equity gains. Woefully, Krizisan and Roggeband argue that de-democratization has been barely analyzed through the lens of gender equality, and so far, efforts to systematically analyze the implications for an inclusive democracy and the representation of gender interests are lacking and under attack (Krizsan & Roggeband, 2018).

Internationally, there is a growing the hostility toward gender studies and gender education by conservative forces outside the academy who seek to disparage and delegitimize gender equity.[5] Anti-genderism is particularly prominent in Francia's and Ljungquist's chapter, where they show the significant increases in rhetoric against gender-research in the public debates and in reaction against the Me-Too movements in Sweden. The ideology of anti-genderism is characterized by three interconnecting factors:

1. Ideas about the essence of man, human dignity in relation to Christianity, and the belief in the pure objectivity present in science grounded on positivism (especially manifested in brain research and neuroscience). Essence of man and cultural identity is *de facto* gender conservative, hierarchical in relation to various groups, and heteronormative (Korolczuk 2014; Korolczuk & Graff, 2018).
2. A support of a dark and negative image of cultural, intellectual, and social history, where all the evils (cultural and moral destructions) in the present are caused by Friedrich Engels, Sigmund Freud, Karl Marx, feminism, the Frankfurt school, postmodernism, among others (ibid.).

Speaking to this, Inny Accioly's chapter calls attention to how Brazil's "School without Party" actively works to criminalize teachers, as well as to erase perceived ideological indoctrination such as gender studies, social justice education, and anything to do with Marxism. Likewise, Gundula Ludwig's chapter highlights how Germany's right-wing-party AfD systematically attacks feminists and queer ideas and politics.

3. A conviction that people and groups representing an evil force financed by transnational companies like Google and Amazon (regarded as part in neoliberal exploitations) have colonized power in a sinister way by their stress on human rights, everyone's equal value, and human health. Those adhering to anti-genderism are thus fighting against colonization where the majority is deemed as being suppressed by a minority (ibid.).

Movements adhering to anti-genderism have also been fruitful in engaging people at a grassroots level arguing that the nation-states interfere in the free-upbringing of their children (Fábián & Korolczuk, 2017; Höjdestrand, 2017;

Strelnik, 2017). At a general level, conservatives counteract gender-equity in several related ways, namely (a) they claim gender theory is simply an expression of gender ideology and should be erased/eliminated, (b) gender theory should not be allowed to infuse social practice, and (c) that gender issues should not be a political enterprise but a private matter (see Francia in this volume; Korolczuk & Graff, 2018). Here, we see a rigorous split between "public good" and private interests implying that the flow of everyday life is not within the public-domain but the private-matter rather than dependent upon state intervention (Francia & Edling, 2016). This attitude reflects the systematic destruction of welfare state interventions particularly in matters related to vulnerable people, such as the plight of refugee women discussed in Macrine and Edling's chapter. They examine how women refuges and LGBTQ people are oppressed or harmed in numerous ways and subsequently, rendering space and acceptance of violence in general.

Perceptions of Gender Roles and Their Consequences for People's Life Conditions

As mentioned earlier, while there are many differences within conservative far-right groups, there is a shared desire to create a hierarchical social systems for men and women's responsibilities, based on fixed ideas of privilege, femininity, and masculinity, which several of the chapters address (Horton & Rydström, 2011). Based on heterosexual norms, women are traditionally viewed as mothers, nurturers, and caregivers—strongly linked to the home and core family values. It follows that women's bodies and unborn children are considered as sacred making abortion an abomination (Akkerman, 2015; Kinnvall, 2015; Köttig & Blum, 2016). Conservative perceptions position white women as primarily mothers, reproducers, and caregivers for the future of a strong national population and concurringly pictured as a counterbalance to the Muslim-threat of high nativity (Goodwin, 2011).

Aside from revering women's role as biological reproducers and caregivers, such conservative gender roles involve cherishing strength and loathing weakness in an organized hierarchy. In this view, women and femininity are considered as weak, while men and masculinity are regarded as symbols of dominance and strength (Jewkes, et. al., 2016). An extreme example can be seen in the studies on how the Nazi S.S. soldiers were socialized and trained to idealize hypermasculinity. Hypermasculinity is based on an idea that men are radically different from women and that feminine traits are repulsive. In this view, femininity is seen as representing soft values like weakness (Messerschmidt, 1993; Sudda, 2012; Edling, 2016), tolerance, democracy, and kindness, whereas masculinity symbolizes strength, aggressiveness, toughness, control, dominance, and so forth (Dillon, 2013a). Cultural reproductions of such severe hypermasculine-based gender roles can be found in some athletic programs, military schools (Larsson, 2005), elite boarding schools, radical religious organizations, which play crucial roles in establishing and maintaining violent and oppressive cultures (Poynting & Donaldson, 2005; Francia & Edling, 2016). Moreover, there appear to be correlations between a country's high degree of authoritarianism and the greater the rate of gender inequality (Brandt & Henry, 2012).

Today's increases in toxic hypermasculinity parallel the upsurge of far-right movements. The concept of hypermasculinity or the "macho personality" has been defined in various ways, for example: Mosher and Sirkin (1984) have operationally defined it as the inflation of stereotypic masculine attitudes and behaviors involving callous attitudes toward women, and the belief that violence is manly and danger is exciting. Burk, Burkhart, and Sikorski (2004) describe it as magnified valuation of status, self-reliance, aggressive activities, dominance over others, and devaluation of emotion and cooperation. These attributes are linked to aggression toward women, aggression to men who violate gender-norms, and linked to increased risk-taking behavior (drugs, alcohol, larger numbers of sexual partners, depression, poor coping skills (Corprew & Mitchell, 2014). Furthermore, hypermasculinity also points to men's sense of being threatened and overpowered by multiculturalism and feminism in ways that generate feelings of loss of control, order, and power (Kinnvall, 2015). Similarly, Coleman & Bassi (2011) speak about this privileged masculine identity as patriarchal and authoritarian. They describe how privileged masculine performances work within spaces of (anti-)globalization politics in ways that bolster, as much as contest, the order that these movements seek to subvert or overthrow. In her chapter, Chandra Talpade Mohanty demonstrates how this tendency to a militant-masculinity results in building walls across the world creating borders between "us and them" in ways that makes the relational ability of building bridges appear as something feminine and even dangerous in that it threatens control and domination. A return to an image of an ideal and pure manhood cleaned from the pollution of femininity becomes a solution and a salvation. Similar feelings of loss among men create a commonality, as well as a drive to solve the problem socially (Kinnvall, 2015).

Emancipation, Education and the Scientific Tradition of Interpretation

Iris Marion Young (1997) maintains that researchers, and people in general, have a tendency to get bored of concepts by constantly searching for new solutions without first acknowledging whether old problems are solved and whether long applied concepts are still useful to handle current challenges. With this in mind, we turn to past explanations to understand the growth of conservative groups and their demands for putting an end to woman's emancipation from essentialism and determinism. As history has shown the past relentlessly creeps into the present and gives all people the possibility learn from it to reshape the future (Ammert, 2009).

Several of our chapters examine the importance of emancipation and resisting oppressive structures (see Susskind & Oliviera; Accioly; & Mohanty, this volume). The process of emancipating women from the dominance of patriarchal systems based on ideas of dichotomy and essentialism has a long history (Schwabenland, et.al., 2017). Indeed, the desire for emancipation, that is, liberation, is not a new phenomenon but has continuously flared up at points in history where a group of people struggled to break free from a dominating power order, and control (Edling & Mooney Simmies, 2017). During the eighteenth to nineteenth centuries, the will for emancipation was reborn in the Age of the Enlightenment as an answer to the dominance of the church's and the monarchy's strong hold on people's minds (Kant & Abbott, 1898). Subsequently, ideas of emancipation became a rallying cry for oppressed groups of people at various places in the world, including French Revolution in 1889, the industrial workers struggle to be freed from the oppression of unequal wealth distribution, the Emancipation Proclamation in 1863 that marked the end of slavery and the suffragettes fighting for women's rights and the vote as well as freedom from patriarchy at the end of the nineteenth century. Accordingly, it is important to bear in mind that the notion of emancipation is not an exclusive concept for a particular group of people in society but is a force or power of a collective striving for eliminating oppression. At the moment the radical-right together with other conservative groups aim to emancipate themselves from the so-called oppression of, for instance, liberal democracy, neoliberalism, sexual freedom, and gender ideologies felt as suffocating, and for them, socially dangerous (Korolczuk & Graff, 2018). As such, the very phenomenon of emancipation is always positioned in the clash between various value systems, and hence worldviews rendering it inevitably dilemmatic to its nature (Honig, 1994).

Currently, there is a tendency among conservatives, like far-right groups, to argue that the logic positivism provides truth, while the gender theory research is gibberish (Korolczuk & Graff, 2018). These attitudes provide a challenge for the claims favoring dualism, essentialism, and determinism. However, the arguments to locate women's and men's essence (and hence places in society), to keep gender roles separated in hierarchical relationships, and to stress empiricism over the power of interpretation are all supporting the same ideology of many conservative movements. This is paradoxically unsubstantiated by scientific evidence, and at the same time they claim to be more scientific than gender scholars and researchers.

Genetic Determinism: Scientific Racism and Genderism

Epistemological violence, a legacy of positivism's interpretation, that uses science to portray minorities, women, gays and lesbians, subaltern groups, lower classes, people with disabilities, etc., as inferior (Spivak, 1995). This type of interpretation of social-scientific data on the "Other" is produced when empirical data shows the inferiority of or problematizes the "Other," even when data allow for equally viable alternative interpretations (Teo, 2011). This kind of biological determinism claims to rely on "objectivity" of testable hypotheses, and the systematic collection and analysis of data (Graves, 2015). While strict versions of biological determinism were thought to have been abandoned, today, much of what we learned in the nineteenth century still informs the far-right and conservatists' arguments that justify neo-nationalism, protectionism, ethnic purity, anti-gender, and racist oppressions and policies. Many extreme right-wing movements and neo-nationalist validate their ideas and justifications for movements like protectionism based on the legacy of scientific/positivistic justifications. However, their rhetoric is reminiscent of eugenetics and the genetic determinism justified by the Nazis.

Based on Charles Darwin's the notion of "survival of the fittest," Francis Galton, coined the term "eugenics" in 1883. Early eugenic ideas were discussed in Ancient Greece and Rome, and the actual word is derived from the Greek word "well-born." Galton's nineteenth century scientific theory of superiority of certain human genetics confirmed social thinking, rendering colonization, the class system, and the subservience of women as a scientific necessity.[6] This concept was considered the scientific confirmation of the biological inferiority of races, women and social classes. Historically, empirical psychology's methods and commitments to "objectivity" produced research that is considered as racist, classist, and sexist, etc. This throwback "scientific research" is used today by conservative groups to portrayed minorities, women, gays and lesbians, subaltern groups, lower classes, people with disabilities, and so on as inferior. The consequences of some of these early theories in psychology have led to the detrimental interpretations of racialized and genderized groups that are being resurrected today. As a result, an epistemological violence is recreated bringing harm to certain racialized groups (Teo, 2011) and here education plays an imperative role to provide with tools for interpretation.

The Narrowing of Educational Spaces—and the Importance of Keeping Them Open

Historically, education has played a key role in forming future citizens and has therefore been of high interest to governments. Accordingly, education has always been seen in relation to what the power in a society finds desirable and as such is intertwined with ideology of the reigning value system(s) (Mooney-Simmies & Edling, 2016). After the horrors of the Second World War many countries signed the Human Rights Declaration, and the Convention of Children's Right (later in the 1980s), based on a desire to advance and cherish a broad definition of democracy in which plurality and everyone's equal value have a core position. These agreements have in various ways impacted education and teacher education in many countries and have been viewed as oppressive by conservative movements, like the far-right. Within the critic of liberal ideals, a wide range of conservative groups have hegemonically altered worldviews indicating that the radical right also has educational goal (Idriss-Miller & Pilkington, 2017, p. 135). This is of special interest consider when considering our youth, because they appear to be more susceptible and keener to support far-right groups and subcultures stimulating violent behavior (ibid., 137–8).

While the purposes of education have been adapted and altered over the years and helpful in understanding what today's society finds as desirable, or where the focus of education is headed, and also how various competing ideologies influence the possibilities of these purposes. Certainly, education has always been subjected to various ideological battles that influence the conditions of education. Some of these ideologies give space to broad democracy, that is, including aspects such as democracy, critical thinking (taking into account the need for systematic interpretation), plurality and gender equality others move in an opposite direction (Cochran-Smith & Fries, 2001, p. 3; Mooney Simmies & Edling, 2016, 2020;). At the moment approaches to broad education are under attack from both conservative movements and neoliberalism, placing education in the power of numbers and competition, a narrow positivism, and religious fundamentalism.

As stated in volume's opening, education in various countries tends to oscillate between broad and narrow ways of grasping both the scope of educational purposes and teacher professionalism. In a general sense, education has three different purposes: to provide with knowledge, to socialize, and promote equal treatment (Edling, 2016). Put differently, it has the possibility to enhance various forms of qualifications, socialization, and/or subjectification (Biesta, 2010). Traditional views of education/knowledge were seen as needing to be impartial and separated from values and social relations (Englund, 1986). Yet there is growing support that education needs to take place within a broader environment where learning about issues of equity and social justice is taught, intertwined and mutually co-dependent (Allodi, 2010, p. 93; Håkansson & Sundberg, 2012). This is because knowledge is neither absolutely neutral nor objective, and therefore teaching is never neutral (Giroux, 2006). Thus, *"[k]nowledge must be linked to the issue of power, which suggests that educators and others must raise questions about its truth claims as well as the interests that such knowledge serves"* (Giroux, 1988, pp. 7–8). Like Giroux, Freire defines educational practice as not, "an all-embracing neutral category of social science" but it is essentially a political function. Bourdieu (1989) argues that symbolic power that is not translated into political power simply ends up reinforcing dominant social relationships.

So, the notion of "broad education" is relevant today given the global anti-racism protests like *Black Lives Matter* and anti-genderism movements. Accordingly, research suggest that teaching social (educational) issues is much needed, as well as more complex, dynamic, and relational ideas, rather than the current neutral, essentialist, and deterministic ones. In response, educators and professionals will need to *critically interpret* such curriculum and their assignments (e.g., Giroux, 2015; Macrine, 2016; Edling, 2020). In other words, students need to understand privilege, rethink power, and to be able to analyze and reframe what it means to be historically disenfranchised and to see the values and stories from other cultures. This means that schools and teachers must also interrogate their practices and how they gained institutional privilege as well.

Education today is seen as market-driven (Chomsky & Pollin, 2017) and exacerbated by global financial recessions creating panic for not being able to attain national economic competitiveness. This sense of anxiety and fear has led to major neoliberal educational reforms strengthening evaluations and high stakes-testing (Hursh, 2013; Macrine, 2016; McLaren, 2016; Giroux, 2020). This is done while at the expense of intellectuals capable of critical thinking involving an ability to interpret purpose(s), content, and relationships between entities expressed through language (Giroux, 2015), as well as an awareness of their consequences for human condition (Edling et al., 2020). These neoliberal educational reforms are mainly fueled by mega corporations, multi millionaires (i.e., Betsy Devos in the United States), and hedge-fund managers who approach education as market-driven without connections to education as a "public good" (Giroux, 2015). Accordingly, the neoliberal paradigm driving these attacks on public and higher education disdains democracy and views public and higher education as a toxic public sphere that poses a threat to corporate values, ideology, and power to (Giroux, 2013).

While, there have been generations of conservatives who see scholars and educators as responsible for corrupting the young and teaching them to hate their countries, one stands out.[7] The University of Toronto's right-wing guru, Jordan Peterson, who writes that, it is no secret that the right sees institutions of higher education as ground zero for political conflict with professors and educators and dangerous people (ibid.). The strong movement toward a revival of positivism in education touts research supporting disembodied learning that is disconnected from interpretative skills. For instance, skills to understand the context and conditions of education, what people should learn (content), why content is significant to learning (purpose), who benefits from the content, and who decides how people learn. Yet the very complexities of education are often overlooked and omitted in current educational reform policies and procedures (e.g., Biesta, 2012). Much of the educational reforms are technocratic in nature and based on test outcomes drawing on positivistic scientism rather than being interested in understanding reality; that is, closely interlaced with the dynamics and multi-layered features of human life (Mooney Simmies, this volume).

Besides the radical increases of *Human Capital Theory* (where education is seen as an investment that produces future benefits) linked to the logic of positivism, there is a tendency in several countries to interconnect education with religion, where women's values are regarded as inferior to masculine ones. Take, for example, the United States and Poland, where many religious fundamentalists have been intensely working to eliminate sex education and view sex education on gender and power relations as problematic for boys (Haste, 2013). This sense of "masculinity in crisis" is one reason for the growth of moral panic and anti-genderism, which feeds on the instability and anxieties created by neoliberalism (Korolczuk & Graff, 2018, p. 803). For example, in Poland the "Third point in 'Declaration of Faith for teachers' stress that teachers need to place God's law superior to human law in order to oppose 'totalitarian genocide.'" Recommendations by EU regarding the need to oppose such discriminatory views are considered ideological, totalitarian, and oppressive (Grabowska, 2015, p. 58). Similar tendencies point to growing restrictive legislations that target activists defending the rights of black and brown persons, refugees, migrants, and asylum-seekers remained in place, exerting a chilling effect on civil society can be found in the United States and Hungary (Rakar, 2005; Lugosi, 2018; Jahn, 2019) along with many other countries.[8]

Today, we are reminded of the ongoing fight for women's rights celebrating the Centennial of women's right to vote, unfortunately women are still fighting for human the rights over their own bodies. It must be noted the continued systemic violence against people of color, particularly, the police brutality that has emerged is an issue of social justice—marked by protests around the globe-where black and brown people of both genders are being murdered and brutalized by police with near impunity.

In response, the contributors to this volume collectively challenge the existing fixed, hegemonic, and toxic masculine performativity, and the racism inherent in society today. They argue that the spaces for critical thinking and deliberation within the public sector and within the field of education that stress the importance of democracy are under attack globally. Therefore, we need to aware and work for change to actively change the social conditions for equity, rather than merely foster an obedient and active workforce to preserve status quo. In reaction, this volume unmasks the dangers of how masculinity continues to be valued, produced, performed, and consumed, while stressing the need for all of us to challenge such fixed hegemonic masculine performativities (Hickey-Moody, 2019), and to combat anti-racial and anti-gender rhetoric and actions.

As we prepare to submit this volume, we mourn the passing of feminist icon and champion for justice, women's equality and LGBTQ rights, Supreme Court Justice Ruth Bader Ginsberg. Affectionately referred to as *"Notorious RBG,"* we cannot think of a more relevant warrior for justice marked by an unwavering faith in democracy. In a recent documentary, RGB (2018), she recalls the sentiments, Sarah Grimké's (1838): *"I ask no favors for my sex. I surrender not our claim to equality. All I ask of our brethren is that they will take their feet from off our necks and permit us to stand upright."*

Notes

Introduction

1. Edling & Mooney Simmies (2020); Fraser (2019); Giroux (2014); Goodman (2010); Harvey (2005); Keskinen (2012); Macrine (2016/2020); Mohanty (2003); Saltman (2014).
2. Elomäki & Kantola (2018).
3. Welch (2013).
4. McCoy & Somer (2018).
5. Ibid.
6. Edling & Simmie (2018); Fraser (2017); Giroux (2019).
7. Ibid.
8. Freire (1985).
9. Iris Marion Young (1988, p. 278).
10. CRC 1977/1981/1983.
11. Guldmann, Rony (2017).
12. Elomäki & Kantola (2018); Macrine (2016).
13. Goodman (2013).
14. Nagar & Swarr (2010, p. 2).
15. Parekh & Wilcox (2018).
16. Mohanty (2013).
17. Keskinen (2012); Macrine (2016).
18. Monbiot (2017).
19. Davidson (2008).
20. Monbiot (2017, p. 3).
21. Parekh & Wilcox (2018).
22. Bergeron (2001).
23. Chomsky (2011).
24. Simme & Edling (2016, p. 4).
25. Smith (2012).
26. Harvey (2005).
27. Macrine (2016); Mentan (2015).
28. McCafferty (2010, p. 543).
29. Macrine (2016, p. 309).
30. Brown (2003).

31 Brenner & Theodore (2002, p. 28).
32 Fischer (2019).
33 Castles (2000); Delanty, Wodak, & Jones (2008); Guibernau (2007); Kumashiro (2010); Milanovic (2016); Rydberg (2018).
34 The Economist (2014).
35 Rydberg (2018, p. 3).
36 Flyvbjerg (1998, p. 5).
37 Johnson (2014).
38 https://freedomhouse.org/report/freedom-world/2019/democracy-retreat
39 Brown (2003).
40 Gellner (1981); Harris (2009); O'Leary (1997).
41 Harmes (2012).
42 Ibid.
43 Gray, O'Regan, & Wallace (2018).
44 Castles (2000); Delanty, Wodak, & Jones (2008); Kumashiro (2010); Milanovic (2016); Rydberg (2018).
45 Giroux (2019).
46 Bedie (1996); Jorgensen (2001); Spruce (2012).
47 Freire (1978); Mooney Simmies & Edling (2017).
48 Giroux (2006).
49 Giroux (2019, p. 1).
50 Giroux (2010).
51 Edling (2012/2018).
52 Biesta (2010).
53 Giroux (1981).
54 Edling (2012/2018).
55 Ibid.
56 Cf. Biesta (2010).
57 Roberts (2016).
58 Christensen & Jensen (2012).
59 Blackwell, Briggs & Chiu (2015, p. 1).
60 Nancy Fraser (2019).
61 Swarr & Nagar (2010, p. 2).
62 Grewal & Kaplan (1994).
63 Disch & Hawkesworth (2016).
64 Desai (2005).
65 Grewal & Kaplan (1994); Alexander & Mohanty (1997).
66 Conway (2018).
67 Grewal & Kaplan (1994); Mohanty (2003); Swarr & Nagar (2010).
68 Giroux (2006, 2009); Macrine (2016).

69 Ibid.
70 Keskinen (2012).
71 Gunewardena & Kingsolver (2007, p. 1).
72 Fraser (2019).
73 Monbiot (2016).

Chapter 1

1   For a discussion of neoliberalism and feminist critique, see my essay "Feminism across Borders: On Neoliberalism and Radical Critique," 2013.
2   The 1991 book *Third World Women and Feminist Perspectives* co-edited with Ann Russo and Lourdes Torres emerges from this conference.
3   This essay draws on an earlier essay, "Imperial Democracies, Militarized Zones, Feminist Engagements," *The Economic and Political Weekly*, Vol. XLVI, No. 13, March/April 2011, Special Issue on *Reflections on Empire*, pp. 76–84.
4   For an excellent analysis of the historical and current interweaving of US labor, immigration, and racial regimes, see A Naomi Paik, *Bans, Walls, Raids, Sanctuary: Understanding Immigration for the Twenty-First Century*, University of California Press, 2020.
5   See Azza Basarudin and Khanum Sheikh, "The Contours of Speaking Out: Gender, State Security, and Muslim Women's Empowerment," *Meridians, Feminism, Race, Transnationalism* Vol. 19, No. 1, April 2020, pp. 107–35. Under the Trump administration, CVE has been revamped to reflect Trump's rhetoric of getting tougher on "Islamic Terrorism." Thus, while revamping the funding structure and priorities for CVE, the Trump administration also floated the idea of changing CVE to "Countering Jihadist Terrorism," of "Countering Radical Islamic Extremism."
6   See discussion of "constitution free zones" at http://lipanapachecommunitydefense.blogspot.com/Lipan *Apache Women Defense* (accessed January 30, 2010).
7   See also Yael Berda's (2013) analysis of the role of documentation and data management as technologies of civilian population management in the occupied West Bank.
8   This analysis was developed collaboratively with my colleague Jacqui Alexander, and first presented at the National Women's Studies Association conference in Denver, November 2010.
9   See the organizing work of the O'odham Solidarity across Borders Collective at:http://oodhamsolidarity.blogspot.com/2010/04/movement-demands-autonomy-oodham.html (accessed January 30, 2010).
10 See www.grassrootsleadership.org.
11 Border Patrol agents increased from 3,600 in 1986 to 20,000 in 2018.

12. Information about these coalitions and the cross-border organizing is based on personal communication with scholar/organizer Alan Gomez, who has been involved in this struggle for a number of years.

Chapter 2

1. https://www.theguardian.com/global-development/2016/oct/18/70-of-migrants-to-europe-from-north-africa-trafficked-or-exploited-un-united-nations-survey
2. https://www.refugeesinternational.org/https://www.refugeesinternational.org/
3. https://refintl.squarespace.com/reports?category=Report&offset=148958630746
4. U.S. Immigration Crisis as Tens of Thousands of Children Flee Central American Violence without Parents, *EURONEWS* (February 7, 2014, 5:27 PM), http://www.euronews.com/2014/07/02/us-immigration-crisis-as-tens-of-thousands-of-children-flee-central-american-/
5. https://www.odi.org/sites/odi.org.uk/files/resource-documents/201911_gender_in_displacement_hpg_working_paper_web.pdf
6. http://www.thesavorytort.com/search/label/Privileges%20and%20Immunities
7. https://sfgov.org/dosw/sites/default/files/How%20to%20do%20a%20Gender%20Analysis%20081114.pdf
8. https://apps.unizg.hr/rektorova-nagrada/javno/stari-radovi/3748/preuzmi
9. https://www.unhcr.org/1951-refugee-convention.html [20–07-20]
10. https://www.iom.int/who-is-a-migrant
11. https://sverigeforunhcr.se/blogg/flykting-eller-migrant-enligt-unhcr
12. https://www.worldvision.org/refugees-news-stories/syrian-refugee-crisis-facts
13. https://journals.iium.edu.my/intdiscourse/index.php/islam/article/download/1250/818/
14. https://reliefweb.int/report/australia/analysis-unhcr-s-2018-global-refugee-statistics-how-generous-australia-s-refugee
15. https://www.refugeecouncil.org.au/2018-global-trends/[180720]
16. https://www.worldvision.org/refugees-news-stories/syrian-refugee-crisis-facts
17. https://www.cfr.org/backgrounder/rohingya-crisis
18. https://www.refugeecouncil.org.au/2018-global-trends/[180720]
19. https://www.unhcr.org/globaltrends2018/
20. https://www.unhcr.org/women.html [21-07-20]
21. https://www.unhcr.org/figures-at-a-glance.html [21-07-20]
22. https://www.un.org/sexualviolenceinconflict/wp-content/uploads/2020/06/2019-REPORT-OF-THE-SECRETARY-GENERAL-ON-CRSV-ENGLISH.pdf
23. United Nation as Security Council meeting of September 28, 2017, https://www.un.org/press/en/2017/sc13012.doc.htm

24 https://www.rescue.org/article/different-battle-same-fight-meet-women-crises-working-toward-equality
25 https://www.ncbi.nlm.nih.gov/pmc/articles/PMC5834240/
26 https://www.unwomen.org/en/news/in-focus/end-violence-against-women/2014/rights [21-07-20]
27 https://www.theguardian.com/global-development/2020/feb/21/a-step-away-from-hell-the-young-male-refugees-selling-sex-to-survive-berlin-tiergarten
28 https://nawo.org.uk/the-refugee-crisis-is-a-feminist-issue/
29 https://populismobserver.com/2018/04/30/populism-or-neo-nationalism/
30 https://www.un.org/press/en/2017/sc13012.doc.htm
31 https://www.erudit.org/fr/revues/refuge/2018-v34-n1-refuge03925/1050857ar.pdf?embed=
32 https://www.nytimes.com/2019/06/19/world/refugees-record-un.html
33 https://www.unhcr.org/neu/government-donors/swedish-government/sweden-empowers-refugee-women-and-girls
34 https://www.nbcnews.com/think/opinion/trump-s-wall-mexico-follows-footsteps-authoritarian-leaders-throughout-history-ncna956411
35 https://www.politifact.com/factchecks/2019/jan/25/donald-trump/trump-said-1-3-migrant-women-sexually-assaulted-jo/
36 https://id.erudit.org/iderudit/1050857ar
37 https://www.tandfonline.com/doi/full/10.1080/15564886.2019.1671283
38 https://www.e-ir.info/2017/09/18/securitization-of-refugees-in-europe/
39 https://www.justsecurity.org/65018/trump-builds-support-for-border-wall-on-the-backs-of-women/
40 https://www.unhcr.org/5630f24c6.html
41 https://www.atlanticcouncil.org/blogs/new-atlanticist/violence-against-women-driving-migration-from-the-northern-triangle/
42 https://www.scb.se/hitta-statistik/sverige-i-siffror/manniskorna-i-sverige/asylsokande-i-sverige/[21-07-20]
43 https://www.migrationsverket.se/download/18.4cb46070161462db1132033/1557926648591/Sveriges%20flyktingkvot%202019.pdf [21-07-20]
44 https://www.scb.se/hitta-statistik/sverige-i-siffror/manniskorna-i-sverige/asylsokande-i-sverige/[21-07-20]
45 https://www.migrationpolicy.org/article/search-safety-growing-numbers-women-flee-central-america

Chapter 3

1 Accioly (2018).
2 Svampa (2019).

3   Ibid.
4   Ibid.
5   Accioly (2020).
6   Gomes (2020).
7   Fontes (2010).
8   Global Witness (2017/2019).
9   Chesnais (2016, p. 14).
10 Federici (2004).
11 Davis (2016).
12 Accioly, Gawryszewski, & Nascimento (2016).
13 Chesnais (2016, p. 8).
14 Chesnais (2016).
15 Friends of Earth (2019).
16 Accioly (2018).
17 *Marcha das Margaridas* [The Daisies' March] is a march that since 2000 joins peasant women in Brazil's Capital to struggle in defense of working women's rights. In 2019, the march brought together around 100,000 women.
18 Marcha das Margaridas (2019, p. 33, our transl.).
19 Castro and Pinto (2014).
20 Ibid.
21 Fondo de Acción Urgente de América Latina (2016).
22 Ibid.
23 Federici (2004).
24 Fondo de Acción Urgente de América Latina (2016).
25 Damasceno (2019).
26 Accioly (2020).
27 Ibid.
28 Portal G1 (2019).
29 Instituto de Pesquisa Econômica Aplicada and Fórum Brasileiro de Segurança Pública (2019).
30 Meneghel and Portella (2017, p. 30, our transl.).
31 Ibid.
32 Lima (2020).
33 Gimenes (2020).
34 Lobato (2019).
35 Ministry of Education (2020, our transl.).
36 Freitas (2018).
37 Carta Capital (2020).
38 Basilio (2019).
39 Mies (2014, p. 303).
40 Federici (2019).

41 Federici (2004/2019).
42 Galeano (1991, p. 135).
43 Federici (2019).
44 Mies (2014).
45 Ibid (p. 297).
46 Ibid.
47 Ibid.
48 Federici (2019).
49 Federici (2004).
50 Federici (2019, p. 139).
51 Svampa (2015).
52 Federici (2019).
53 CPT Nacional (2020).
54 Amada (2019).
55 Indigenous Women's March (2019, our transl.).
56 Marcha das Margaridas (2019, p. 3, our transl.).
57 Indigenous Women's March (2019).

Chapter 4

1   Lang & Peters (2018, p. 15).
2   Salzborn (2017, p. 35).
3   Lang (2017a).
4   Kemper (2016).
5   Dietze (2019); Leidinger & Radvan (2018).
6   Hark & Villa (2015); Lang (2017b).
7   Sauer (2020, p. 34).
8   Schutzbach (2019).
9   Ibid. (author's transl.).
10 Ibid.
11 Glynos & Howarth (2007, p. 150).
12 Laclau (1996/2007, p. 36).
13 Laclau & Mouffe (1985); Laclau (1996/2007).
14 Laclau (1996/2007).
15 Laclau (1990, p. 21).
16 Laclau (1996/2007, p. 44).
17 Laclau (2000, p. 142).
18 Glynos and Howarth (2007, p. 15).
19 Glynos (2011, p 70).

20 AfD (2016, p. 47, author's transl.).
21 Sauer (2020, p. 25).
22 Irigaray (1977, p. 24).
23 To make visible that the definition of an "Other" is already an effect of power relations, I use the term "other-ed" Other.
24 Quijano (2000).
25 Ibid. (p. 542).
26 Ibid.
27 Ibid.
28 Ahmed (2000, p. 22).
29 Ibid. (p. 21).
30 Ibid.
31 AfD (2017, p. 40, author's transl.); see also AfD (2016, p. 54).
32 AfD (2017, p. 40, author's transl.); see also AfD (2016, p. 55).
33 Storch (2013).
34 Ibid.
35 Lefort (1999, p. 296).
36 Laclau (1990, p. 21).
37 Ibid.
38 Ibid.
39 Ibid. (p. 61).
40 Ibid.
41 Ibid. (p. 34).
42 Ibid.
43 Butler (1990).
44 Butler (2000a, p. 29).
45 Lefort (1990, p. 296).
46 Butler (1999, p. xx).
47 Butler (1990, p. 139).
48 Butler (2000b, p. 272).
49 Lugones (2007, p. 202).
50 Ibid. (p. 206).
51 AfD (2016, p. 55); AfD (2017, p. 41).
52 AfD (2017, p. 41, author's transl.).
53 Hark & Villa (2015, p. 22).
54 Weed (2011, p. 295).
55 Hark & Villa (2015, p. 33, author's transl.).
56 Ibid.
57 Laclau (2005).
58 Nocun (2016, p. 33).
59 AfD (2016, p. 67, author's transl.).

60 AfD Landesverband Hamburg (2015, p. 11, author's transl.).
61 Nocun (2016, pp. 11–12).
62 Ibid. (p. 19).
63 Kemper (2016).
64 AfD (2016, p. 56, author's transl.).
65 Keil (2019).
66 Gauland (2019).
67 Butler (2004).
68 Butler (2010, p. 14).
69 Ibid. (p. 25).
70 Ibid. (p. 13).
71 Ibid.
72 Butler (2004, p. 26).
73 Rancière (1999, p. 102).
74 Ibid.
75 Ludwig (2019).

Chapter 6

1 Much of this filmography information is cited from Danny Leigh's interview with Amirpour: "The Skateboarding Iranian Vampire Diaries," *The Guardian*, May 7, 2015, https://www.theguardian.com/film/2015/may/07/skateboarding-iranian-vampire-ana-lily-amirpour-feminism-porn-girl-walks-home-alone-at-night
2 For example, referring to "the process of feminism's evolution in the dramatically changed social context of rising neoliberalism," Fraser writes, "I propose to chart not only the movement's extraordinary successes but also the disturbing convergence of some of its ideals with the demands of an emerging new form of capitalism—post-Fordist, 'disorganized,' transnational. Conceptualizing this phase, I shall ask whether second-wave feminism has unwittingly supplied a key ingredient of … 'the new spirit of capitalism'" (210).
3 Sophie Lewis sees this as offering a possibility for resistance: "the challenge to which we must rise involves affirming a politics that has a place for the killing of subjects – a politics of abortion that resists 'preemptive compromise' on the question of what it is exactly gestators sometimes kill" (140). Her primary example here is in resistance to oppressive and even deadly forms of immigration control.
4 Mary Ann Johanson, "A Girl Walks Home Alone at Night Movie Review: Blood Pressure," *Flick Filosopher* (March 31, 2015): https://www.flickfilosopher.com/2015/03/a-girl-walks-home-alone-at-night-movie-review-blood-pressure.html

5 O'Malley.
6 Edelman explains, "In its coercive universalization ..., the image of the Child, not to be confused with the lived experiences of any historical children, serves to regulate political discourse—to prescribe what will *count* as political discourse—by compelling such discourse to accede in advance to the reality of a collective future whose figurative status we are never permitted to acknowledge ... That figural Child alone embodies the citizen as an ideal, entitled to claim full rights to its future share in the nation's good ... Hence, whatever refuses this mandate by which our political institutions compel the collective reproduction of the Child must appear as a threat not only to the organization of a given social order but also, and far more ominously, to social order as such, insofar as it threatens the logic of futurism on which meaning always depends" (11).
7 So Mayer, "Film of the Week: A Girl Walks Home Alone at Night," *Sight & Sound* 25, 6 (June 2015): https://www.bfi.org.uk/news-opinion/sight-sound-magazine/reviews-recommendations/film-week-girl-walks-home-alone-night

Chapter 7

1 https://www.cbsnews.com/news/#Metoo-more-than-12-million-facebook-posts-comments-reactions-24-hours/
2 https://www.cbsnews.com/news/#Metoo-more-than-12-million-facebook-posts-comments-reactions-24-hours/
3 https://www.cafe.se/tarana-burke-#Metoo/
4 https://edition.cnn.com/2017/11/09/world/#Metoo-hashtag-global-movement/index.html
5 https://edition.cnn.com/2017/11/09/world/#Metoo-hashtag-global-movement/index.html
6 https://www.businessinsider.com
7 https://www.svt.se/nyheter/lokalt/norrbotten/hon-skickade-forsta-metoo-tweeten-i-sverige
8 https://reliefweb.int/report/world/global-gender-gap-report-2020
9 https://www.aftonbladet.se/nyheter/a/79WJ4/grafik-sa-blev-#Metoo-ett-globalt-vral
10 https://www.expressen.se/nyheter/har-ar-samtliga-#Metoo-upprop/
11 https://www.expressen.se/nyheter/har-ar-samtliga-#Metoo-upprop/
12 https://www.svd.se/12-kvinnor-anklagar-aftonbladetprofil-for-sextrakasserier-och-overgrepp
13 https://www.expressen.se/noje/martin-timell-bryter-tystnaden-och-erkanner-/

14 https://www.expressen.se/nyheter/virtanen-betett-mig-javligt-risigt/https://www.aftonbladet.se/nyheter/a/GvO8m/virtanen-jag-har-betett-mig-tolpigt-och-skitstovligt
15 https://www.dn.se/kultur-noje/18-kvinnor-kulturprofil-har-utsatt-oss-for-overgrepp/
16 https://www.dn.se/kultur-noje/akademien-i-krismote-bryter-med-kulturprofilen/
17 https://www.expressen.se/kultur/ide/jag-forfaras-over-raheten-i-akademiens-maktkamp/
18 https://www.bbc.com/news/world-europe-43999240
19 https://www.expressen.se/nyheter/hundratals-samlades-i-knytblusmanifestation/
20 https://www.gp.se/ledare/jamstslldhet-handlar-inte-om-att-kvinno- ar-offer-1.4795432
21 https://www.svt.se/nyheter/granskning/ug/#Metoo-och-fredrik-virtanen
22 https://www.svt.se/nyheter/granskning/ug/#Metoo-och-fredrik-virtanen
23 https://feministisktperspektiv.se/2018/08/07/backlash-mot-#Metoo-rorelsen/
24 Frostenson's book is addressed to her husband
25 https://maskulint.se/roda-pillret/#Metoo/
26 https://www.sydsvenskan.se/2019-02-26/sara-danius-lamnar-akademien-for-gott
27 https://www.gp.se/ledare/jamstslldhet-handlar-inte-om-att-kvinno- ar-offer-1.4795432
28 https://www.aftonbladet.se/nyheter/a/GvO8m/virtanen-jag-har-betett-mig-tolpigt-och-skitstovligt
29 https://www.expressen.se/kultur/jag-har-aldrig-varit-nagon-antifeminist/
30 https://www.expressen.se/nyheter/horace-kritik-mot-arnault-domen-vi-lever-i-en-farlig-tid/

Chapter 8

1 OECD is an intergovernmental economic organization with thirty-seven member countries, founded in 1961 to stimulate economic progress and world trade.

Chapter 9

1 Santos (1995/2007); Oliveira & Süssekind (2018).
2 Souza (2016).
3 Oliveira & Süssekind (2018).
4 Female gender for *cacique*, the title of the chief or political leader of South American native people.
5 https://www.letras.mus.br/sambas/mangueira-2019/

6 The Popular University of Social Movements (UPMS) was created within the World Social Forum (WSF) in 2003, with the aim of promoting shared knowledge and extending, linking, and strengthening forms of resistance to neoliberal globalization, capitalism, colonialism, sexism, and other relations based on domination and oppression. The UPMS concept of co-learning seeks to bridge the divide among various knowledges.
7 Santos (2007); Paraskeva (2016/2011).
8 Süssekind, Porto, Reis (2018); Oliveira & Süssekind (2018).
9 Santos (2014).
10 Ibid.
11 Lugones (2014).
12 https://noticias.uol.com.br/politica/ultimas-noticias/2018/10/31/ex-astronauta-diz-que-combatera-inimigos-internos-e-externos-como-ministro.htm?cmpid=copiaecola
13 Personal translation from the authors.
14 Oliveira & Sussekind (2018).
15 Süssekind, Porto, Reis (2018).
16 Süssekind (2014).
17 Ibid. (2014).
18 Santos (2001).
19 Oliveira & Sussekind (2018, p. 6).
20 Ibid. (2018, p. 7).
21 CTE-IRB (2020).
22 Certeau (1984, p. 147).
23 Oliveira & Sussekind (2018, p. 6).
24 Arendt (1963).
25 Arendt (1963).
26 https://fiquemsabendo.com.br
27 Oliveira & Sussekind (2018).
28 Carvalho & Sívori (2017, p. 1).
29 Cohen (1972), Moura & Salles (2018, p. 137).
30 Oliveira (2012); Sussekind (2012).
31 "As a postabyssal epistemology, the ecology of knowledges, while forging credibility for nonscientific knowledge, does not imply discrediting scientific knowledge" (Santos, 2007, p. 26).
32 Manguel (2018).
33 Santos (2000).
34 Native Brazilian people.
35 CERTEAU (1984).
36 Eronilde Fermin's, omagua-kambeba cacica, narratives at UPMS-ANPEd, 2019. The National Association of postgraduation and educational research/ANPEd organizes workshops in cooperation with UPMS since the Niteroi 39th annual meeting in

Niteroi, Rio de Janeiro, Brazil. https://anped.org.br/news/39a-anped-debate-educacao-publica-de-20-24-de-outubro-na-uff-em-niteroi-rj
37 Ibid.
38 Paraskeva (2016).

Chapter 10

1   https://www.ohchr.org/en/issues/women/wrgs/pages/wrgsindex.aspx
2   Matsaganis (2011, pp. 501–12).
3   "*OHCHR,* April 12, 2019, https://www.ohchr.org/EN/NewsEvents/Pages/DisplayNews.aspx?NewsID=24480&LangID=E
4   https://www.theguardian.com/news/2020/mar/03/golden-dawn-the-rise-and-fall-of-greece-neo-nazi-trial
5   Dighe (2018).
6   Skaperdas, S. (2015).
7   FT June 26, 2013.
8   https://www.globalcapital.com/special-reports?issueid=yw0d4m2xby4z&article=yvxr1lhxstny
9   "For hard-hit Greeks, IMF mea culpa comes too late (Reuters)," June 6, 2013. Retrieved May 2020.
10 "*Marianne: The Incredible Errors by IMF Experts & the Wrong Multiplier.*" *KeepTalkingGreece.com.* January 22, 2013. Retrieved May 29, 2020.
11 Skaperdas, S. (2015).
12 https://www.bbc.com/news/world-europe-31803814
13 Gaitanou E. (n.d.).
14 Hale, Galina, January 14, 2013.
15 http://www.cadtm.org/Banks-are-responsible-for-the
16 Gopal (2015).
17 Lapavitsas (2018).
18 Hocking & Lewis (2007).
19 Crouch (2016).
20 Giannacopoulos (2015).
21 Ibid.
22 Chowdhry & Nair (2002).
23 Watson (2014, p. 5, cited in Giannacopoulos).
24 Mikelis, K. (2019).
25 Ibid.
26 Gender Equality Index: Greece (2019).
27 Economic Crisis and the Future of Gender Equality (2018).

28 Sotiropoulou (2014).
29 https://edition.cnn.com/2020/01/22/europe/greece-president-katerina-sakellaropoulou-intl/index.html
30 http://www.isotita.gr/en/gender-disaggregated-data-women-power-decision-making-greece-november-2017/
31 Ibid.
32 Diana Coole (1993, p. 222).
33 GEI—a composite indicator that measures the complex concept of gender equality and, based on the EU policy framework.
34 OECD (2019).
35 Gender Equality Index (2019).
36 Jahoda (1982); Davou (2015).
37 Papageorgiou (2006); Stratigaki (2013); Karamessini (2014).
38 Kosyfologou (2017); Pandelidou-Malouta (2014).
39 https://www.europarl.europa.eu/meetdocs/2014_2019/documents/femm/dv/national-parliaments_state-of-play_/national-parliaments_state-of-play_en.pdf
40 https://www.reuters.com/article/us-greece-unemployment/greek-youth-unemployment-over-60-percent-in-february-idUSBRE9480EZ20130509
41 https://sistersofeurope.com/being-a-migrant-and-a-woman-is-like-double-marginalisation/
42 Papanicolaou (2008-10-16).
43 Ministry of Interior, General Secretariat for Gender Equality (2019, p. 4).
44 Eller (2018).
45 Sotiropoulou (2014).
46 Federici (2010).
47 Portaliou (2016).
48 Aruzza, Battacharya and Fraser (2019, p. 24).
49 https://www.theguardian.com/news/2020/mar/03/golden-dawn-the-rise-and-fall-of-greece-neo-nazi-trial
50 Koronaiou & Sakellariou (2017).
51 Trilling (2020).
52 Koronaiou & Sakellariou (2017).
53 Sioula-Georgoulea (2015).
54 EnetEnglish (2014).
55 Sioula-Georgoulea (2015).
56 Nasioulas (2012).
57 Sotiropoulou (2014).
58 Sotiris (2013).
59 Vatikiotis & Nikolakaki (2012).
60 Pavlidou (2011, p. 168).
61 Longwe (1998).

Chapter 11

1 Gunnarsson Payne (2019).
2 Garbagnoli (2016).
3 Kuhar & Zobec (2017, p. 4).
4 Ibid.
5 Kováts & Põim (2015); Kováts (2018).
6 Göteborg Universitet (2018).
7 Feminetik.se (2004); Hedengren (2013); Bard (2017); Enqvist (2018); Publikt (2018); Andersson & Olsson (2019); Arpi (2019); Aftonbladet (2020), Sveriges Radio (2020).
8 Liinason (2011).
9 Ibid.
10 Centre for Gender Research (2020).
11 Ibid.
12 Ibid.
13 Liinason (2011).
14 The Swedish Secretariat for Gender Research (2020).
15 Göteborgs universitet (2019).
16 Ibid.
17 Badiou (2016).
18 Arruza, Bhattacharya, & Fraser (2019); Fraser & Jaeggis (2019).
19 Akkerman (2012); Rydgren (2018a/2018b); Rydgren & van der Meidenv (2016), Copsey (2018).
20 Kováts & Põim (2015).
21 Kauppinen (2015).
22 Macrine (2016); Bottrell & Manathunga (2019).
23 Giroux (2011).
24 van Dijk (2000, pp. 14–15).
25 Ibid.
26 van Dijk (2000).
27 van Dijk (1996/2000/2009).
28 van Dijk (2000, p. 28).
29 van Dijk (2000, p. 44).
30 van Dijk (2000).
31 Butler (2009).

32 Ibid.
33 Mediearkivet is the largest digital news archive in the Nordic countries and includes news and articles from printed and digital editorial media as well as radio and TV.
34 Valmyndigheten (2018).
35 Kuhar & Zobec (2017, p. 4).
36 Enqvist (2018) [my translation].
37 Kuhar & Zobec (2017, p. 4).
38 Berggren (2019) [my translation].
39 Ibid. [my translation].
40 Reslow, P., Stenkvist, R., Rubbestad, M. & Grubb, J. (2019) [my translation].
41 Nilison (2018) [my translation].
42 Arpi (2020) [my translation].
43 Karlsson-Bernfalk (2018) [my translation].
44 Arpi (2017) [my translation].
45 Arpi (2020) [my translation].
46 Reslow, Stenkvist, Rubbestad, & Grubb (2019)[my translation].
47 Ibid.
48 Heberlein, Madison, Olsson, & Zetterholm (2020) [my translation].
49 See Giroux, (2011).

Conclusion

1 https://crws.berkeley.edu/research
2 United Nations, "Report of the Working Group on the Issue of Discrimination against Women in Law and in Practice," A/HRC/38/46, United Nations, New York, May 14, 2018, p. 5.
3 https://oxfamblogs.org/fp2p/understanding-the-far-rights-framing-of-masculinities-and-hostility-to-gender/
4 https://www.nytimes.com/2019/12/04/us/domestic-violence-international.html
5 https://www.insidehighered.com/news/2018/12/05/gender-studies-scholars-say-field-coming-under-attack-many-countries-around-globe
6 http://dangerouswomenproject.org/2017/02/28/eugenics-and-feminism/
7 https://www.chronicle.com/article/how-the-right-learned-to-loathe-higher-education/?bc_nonce=vq1ot38trx8hhaxdcfypc8&cid=reg_wall_signup
8 https://www.amnesty.org/en/countries/europe-and-central-asia/hungary/report-hungary/

References

Foreword

Brown, W. (2015). *Undoing the Demos: Neoliberalism's Stealth Revolution*. New York, NY: Zone Books.

Coulter, K. (2009). Women, poverty policy, and the production of neoliberal politics in Ontario, Canada. *Journal of Women, Politics, and Policy, 30*(1), 23–45.

Dana, S. (2018). Interview with Simphiwe Dana in *New African Women* (May).

Dalla Costa, G. F. (2008). *The Work of Love: Unpaid Housework and Sexual Violence at the Dawn of the 21st Century*. Brooklyn, NY: Autonomedia.

Dalla Costa, M. & James, S. (1975). *The Power of Women and the Subversion of the Community*. Bristol: Falling Wall Press.

Darder, A. (2015). *Freire and Education*. New York: Routledge.

Equal Justice Initiative (2018). *Incarceration of Women Is Growing Twice as Fast as That of Men*. Retrieved from: https://eji.org/news/female-incarceration-growing-twice-as-fast-as-male-incarceration/

Federici, S. (2004). *Caliban and the Witch*. Brooklyn, NY: Autonomedia.

Fox, J. (2015). *Marx, The Body, and Human Nature*. Reston, VA: AIAA.

Foucault, M. (1995). *Discipline and Punish*. New York, NY: Vintage.

Giroux, H. (2011). The disappearing intellectual in the age of economic Darwinism. *Policy Futures in Education, 9*, 163–71.

Giroux, H. (2012). Higher education, critical pedagogy, and the challenge of neoliberalism: Rethinking the role of academics as public intellectuals. *Revista Aula de Encuentro*. Numero Especial (15–27).

Gore, A. (2017). What happened when I tried to put a breastfeeding mom on my magazine's cover in *Huffpost*.

hooks, b. (2000). *Feminism Is for Everybody*. New York: Pluto Press.

hooks, b. (2004). *The Will to Change: Men, Masculinity, and Love*. New York, NY: Washington Square Press.

Kraidy, M. M. (2013). The body as medium in the digital age: Challenges and opportunities. *Communication and Critical/Cultural Studies, 10*(2–3), 285–90.

Lorde, A. (1982). "Learning from the 60s" address was delivered as part of the celebration of the Malcolm X weekend at Harvard University (February). Retrieved from https://www.blackpast.org/african-american-history/1982-audre-lorde-learning-60s/

Marx, K. (1844). *Estranged Labour*. Economic and Philosophical Manuscripts of 1844. London, UK. https://www.marxists.org/archive/marx/works/1844/manuscripts/labour.htm

Moraga, C. (1981). Theory in the flesh. In Moraga, C. & G. Anzaldua (Eds.), *This Bridge Called My Back: Writings by Radical Women of Color*. San Francisco, CA: Aunt Lute Press.

Moraga, C. (2009). The politics of LGBT life: Interview with Cherrie Moraga on *Liberacion: The Nexus of Politics, Art, & Struggle*. WEFT 99.1 FM.

Phillip, A. (2015). *Confronting Gender Inequality: Despite Major Changes, Progress Has Been Slow and Uncertain*. London, UK: London School of Economics. Retrieved from https://blogs.lse.ac.uk/politicsandpolicy/confronting-gender-inequality-since-the-suffragettes-key-institutions-remain-profoundly-gendered/

Shapiro, S. (1998). *Pedagogy and the Politics of the Body*. New York, NY: Routledge.

Introduction

Alexander, M. Jacqui & Mohanty, C. T. (Eds.) (1997). *Feminist genealogies, colonial legacies, democratic futures*. New York: Routledge, p. xviii.

Allen, A. (2016). Feminist Perspectives on Power, *The Stanford Encyclopedia of Philosophy* (Fall 2016 Edition), (Ed.) Edward N. Zalta https://plato.stanford.edu/archives/fall2016/entries/feminist-power/

Allodi, M. (2010). The meaning of the social climate of learning environments: Some reasons why we do not care enough about it. *Learning Environments Research*, *13*(2), 89–104.

Bauman, Z. (1995). Dream of Purity. In *Theoria: A Journal of Social and Political Theory*. No. *86*, Dimensions of Democracy, pp. 49–60.

Bergeron, S. (2001). Political economy discourses of globalization and feminist politics. *Signs*, *26*(4), 983–1006. www.jstor.org/stable/3175354

Biesta, G. (2010). *What Is Education For? Good Education in an Age of Measurement: Ethics, Politics, Democracy*. Boulder, IL: Paradigm Publishers.

Blackwell, M., Briggs, L., & Chiu, M. (2015). Transnational feminisms roundtable. *Frontiers: A Journal of Women Studies*, *36*(3), 1–24. https://frontiers.osu.edu/current-issue/previous-issues/volume-36-no.-1-special-issue-transnational-feminisms-summer-institute

Bellamy, R. & Palumbo, A. (Eds.) (2010). *From Government to Governance*. London: Ashgate.

Brown, W. (2003). Neo-liberalism and the end of liberal democracy. *Theory and Event* *7*(1), 1–43.

Byrne, C. (2017). Neoliberalism as an object of political analysis: An ideology, a mode of regulation or a governmentality? *Policy and Politics*, *45*(3), 343–60.

Christensen, A.-D. & Jensen, S. Q. (2012). Doing intersectional analysis: Methodological implications for qualitative research. *NORA—Nordic Journal of Feminist and Gender Research*, *20*(2), 109–25. https://doi.org/10.1080/08038740.2012.673505

Cochran-Smith, M. & Fries, M. K. (2001). Sticks, stones, and ideology: The discourse of reform in teacher education. *Educational Researcher, 30*(8), 3–15.

Collins, P. H. (2002). *Black Feminist Thought: Knowledge, Consciousness, and the Politics of Empowerment* (2nd ed.). London: Routledge.

Collins, P. H. (2011). Piecing together a genealogical puzzle. *European Journal of Pragmatism and American Philosophy* [Online], III-2 2011, http://journals.openedition.org/ejpap/823. doi:10.4000/ejpap.823

Collective, Combahee River. (1977/1981/1983). A black feminist statement. In: G. Anzaldúa & C. Moraga (Eds.), *This Bridge Called My Back: Writings by Radical Women of Color* (pp. 210–18). (2nd ed.). Latham: Kitchen Table/Women of Color Press.

Conway, J. (2018). Troubling transnational feminism(s): Theorising activist praxis. *Feminist Theory, 18*(2): 205–27. doi:10.1177/1464700117700536.

Crenshaw, K. (1989). "Demarginalizing the intersection of race and sex: A black feminist critique of antidiscrimination doctrine, feminist theory and antiracist politics," University of Chicago Legal Forum: Vol. 1989.: Issue 1, Article 8. http://chicagounbound.uchicago.edu/uclf/vol1989/iss1/8

Davidson, N. (2008). Nationalism and neoliberalism. *The Variant, 32*(3), 36–8. Retrieved from https://strathprints.strath.ac.uk/27178/1/Nations_and_Neoliberalism.pdf

Davies, B. & Bansel, P. (2007). Neoliberalism and education. *International Journal of Qualitative Studies in Education, 20*(3), 247–59. Retrieved from https://www.researchgate.net/publication/233226041_Neoliberalism_and_Education/citations

Desai, M. (2005). Transnationalism: The face of feminist politics post-Beijing. *International Social Science Journal, 57*, 319–30. doi:10.1111/j.1468-2451.2005.553.x

Dillon, C. (2013). Tolerance means weakness': The Dachau concentration camp S.S., militarism and masculinity. In *Historical Research, 86*(232), pp. 373–417.

Disch, L. & Hawkesworth, M. (2016). *The Oxford Handbook of Feminist Theory*. Oxford, New York: Oxford University Press. doi:10.1093/oxfordhb/9780199328581.001.0001.

Droit, P. & Ferenczi, T. (2008). The left hand and the right hand of the state. *The Variant, 32*(3), 1.

Edling, S. (2012/2018). *Vilja andra väl är inte alltid smärtfritt. Att motverka kränkning och diskriminring i förskola och skola.* [Wanting others' well-being is not always painless. To oppose violence and discrimination in preschool and school]. Lund: Studentlitteratur.

Edling, S. & Mooney Simmie, G. (2018). Democracy and emancipation in teacher education: A summative content analysis of teacher educators' democratic assignment expressed in policies for teacher education in Sweden and Ireland between 2000–2010. *Citizenship, Social and Economic Education* (CSEE), *17*(1), 20–34.

Edling, S. & Simmie, G. M. (2020). *Democracy and Teacher Education: Dilemmas, Challenges, and Possibilities*. London, NY: Routledge.

Elomäki, A. & Kantola, J. (2018). Theorizing feminist struggles in the triangle of neoliberalism, conservatism, and nationalism. *Social Politics: International Studies in Gender, State & Society, 25*(3), 337-60. https://doi.org/10.1093/sp/jxy013

Englund, T. (1986). Curriculum as a political problem: Changing educational conceptions, with special reference to citizenship education. Diss. Uppsala, Lund: Studentlitteratur.

Englund, T. (2005). *Läroplanens och skolkunskapens politiska dimension*. Stockholm: Daidalos.

Fischer, K. (2019). Neoliberal think tank networks. Global dialogue, international sociological association, *Austria, 8*(2). http://globaldialogue.isa-sociology.org/neoliberal-think-tank-networks/

Flyvbjerg, B. (1998). *Rationality and Power: Democracy in Practice*. Chicago and London: University of Chicago Press.

Francia, G. & Edling, S. (2016). Children's rights and violence: A case analysis at a Swedish boarding school. *Childhood, 24* (1), 1-17.

Fraser, N. (2017). From progressive neoliberalism to Trump—and beyond. *American Affairs Journal, 1*(4), https://americanaffairsjournal.org/2017/11/progressiveneoliberalism-trump-beyond/.

Freire, P. (1985). *The Politics of Education*. South Hadley, MA: Bergin & Garvey.

Freire, P. (2019). *The Old Is Dying and the New Cannot Be Born: From Progressive Neoliberalism to Trump and Beyond*. London: Verso Books.

Fuchs, C. (2018). The rise of authoritarian capitalism. *GLOBAL Dialogue, 8*(3), 11-12.

Gellner, E. (1981). Nationalism. *Theory and Society, 10*(6), 753-76.

Giroux, H. A. (2006). Higher education under siege: Implications for public intellectuals. *Thought and Action, 63-78*.

Giroux, H. A. (2009). The attack on higher education and the necessity of critical pedagogy. In S. L. Macrine (Ed.), *Critical Pedagogy in Uncertain Times: Hope and Possibilities* (pp. 11-26). New York: Palgrave Macmillan US. https://doi.org/10.1057/9780230100893_2

Giroux, H. A. (2010). Rethinking education as the practice of freedom: Paulo Freire and the promise of critical pedagogy. *Policy Futures in Education, 8*, 715-21.

Giroux, H. A. (2014). Austerity and the poison of neoliberal miseducation. *symploke, 22*, 9-21. Project MUSE muse.jhu.edu/article/566830.

Goodman, R. T. (2010). *Feminist Theory in Pursuit of the Public: Women and the "Re-Privatization" of Labor (Education, Politics and Public Life)*. New York, NY: Palgrave Macmillan.

Goodman, R. T. (2013). *Gender Work: Feminism after Neoliberalism*. New York: Palgrave Macmillan.

Grewal, I. & Kaplaneds, C. (1994). *Scattered Hegemonies: Postmodernity and Transnational Feminist Practices.* Minneapolis: University of Minnesota Press.

Guldmann, R. (2017). Conservative claims of cultural oppression: The nature and origins of conservaphobia (January 29, 2017). http://dx.doi.org/10.2139/ssrn.2907830

Gunewardena, N. & Kingsolver, A. (Eds.) (2009). *The Gender of Globalization: Women Navigating Cultural and Economic Marginalities.* Santa Fe, N.M.: School for Advanced Research Press; Oxford: James Currey.

Harmes, A. (2012a). The rise of neoliberal nationalism: The rise of neoliberal nationalism. *Review of International Political Economy, 19*(1), 59–86. https://doi.org/dx.doi.org/10.1080/09692290.2010.507132

Harmes, A. (2012b). The rise of neoliberal nationalism. *Review of International Political Economy, 19*(1), 59–86.

Harris, E. (2009). *Nationalism: Theories and Cases.* Edinburgh: Edinburgh University Press.

Harvey, D. (2005). *A Brief History of Neoliberalism.* Oxford: Oxford University Press, p. 84.

Hooghe, L. & Marks, G. (2008). A postfunctionalist theory of European integration: From permissive consensus to constraining dissensus. *British Journal of Political Science, 39*(October 2008), 1–23. https://doi.org/10.1017/S0007123408000409

Johnson, P. M. (2005). "Right-wing, rightist." A Political Glossary. Auburn University website: http://webhome.auburn.edu/~johnspm/gloss/right-wing.phtml.

Macrine, S. L. (2016). Pedagogies of neoliberalism. In: S. Springer, K. Birch & J. MacLeavy (Eds.), *Handbook of Neoliberalism* (pp. 294–305). New York: Routledge.

Macrine, S. L. (2020). Critical pedagogies of neoliberalism. In S.L. Macrine (Ed.), *Critical Pedagogy in Uncertain Times: Hope and Possibilities*, 2nd ed. New York, NY: Palgrave Macmillan. https://link.springer.com/book/10.1007/978-3-030-39808-8

McCoy, J. & Somer, M. (2019). Toward a theory of Pernicious polarization and how it harms democracies: Comparative evidence and possible remedies. *The ANNALS of the American Academy of Political and Social Science, 681* (1), 234–71. doi:10.1177/0002716218818782.

McLaughlin, L. (2004). Feminism and the political economy of transnational public space. *Sociological Review, 52*(1), 157–75.

Mentan, T. (2015). *Unmasking Social Science Imperialism: Globalization Theory as a Phase of Academic Colonialism.* Mankon, Bamenda: Langaa RPCIG. www.jstor.org/stable/j.ctvh9vxhh

Moghadam, V. (1998). Gender and the global economy. In: Revisioning Gender (Ed.), *Myra Feree, Judith Lorber, and Beth Hess* (pp. 128–60). London: Sage.

Moghadam, V. (1999). Gender and globalization: Female labor and women's mobilization. *Journal of World-Systems Research, 5*(2), 366–89. https://doi.org/10.5195/jwsr.1999.139.

Moghadam, V. (2005). *Globalizing Women: Transnational Feminist Networks*. Baltimore: Johns Hopkins Press.

Mohanty, C. T. (1991). *Under Western Eyes. In Third World Women and the Politics of Feminism*, (Ed.) C. T. Mohanty, A. Russo & L. Torres. Bloomington: Indiana University Press.

Mohanty, C. T. (2003a). Under western eyes. Revisited: Feminist solidarity through anticapitalist struggles. *signs, 28*(2), 499–535. https://www.jstor.org/stable/10.1086/342914

Mohanty, C. T. (2003b). *Feminism without Borders: Decolonizing Theory, Practicing Solidarity*. Durham, NC: Duke University Press.

Mohanty, C. T. (2005). *Feminism without Borders: Decolonizing Theory, Practicing Solidarity*. H-Women, H-Net Reviews. July, 2005, http://www.h-net.org/reviews/showrev.php?id=10752

Monbiot, G. (2016a). Neoliberalism: The ideology at the root of all of our problems. *Guardian*, April 15, 2016, https://www.theguardian.com/books/2016/apr/15/neoliberalism-ideology-problem-george-monbiot

Monbiot, G. (2016b). *How Did We Get into This Mess?: Politics, Equality, Nature*. London: Verso Books.

Mooney Simmie, G. & Edling, S. (2016). Ideological governing forms in education and teacher education: A comparative study between highly secular Sweden and highly non-secular Republic of Ireland. *Nordic Journal of Studies in Educational Policy, 2*, 32041, 1–12. doi:10.3402/nstep.v2.32041

Nagar, R. & Swarr, A. L. (2010). Introduction: Theorizing transnational feminist praxis. In: A. Swarr & R. Nagar (Eds.), *Critical Transnational Feminist Praxis*. Albany: State University of New York Press.

O'Leary, B. (1997). On the nature of nationalism: An appraisal of Ernest Gellner's writings on nationalism. *British Journal of Political Science, 27*(2), 191–22.

Olssen, M. (2016). Neoliberal competition in higher education today: Research, Accountability and Impact. *British Journal of Sociology of Education, 37*(1), 129–48, doi:10.1080/01425692.2015.1100530

Parekh, S. & Wilcox, S. (2018). Feminist perspectives on globalization. In Edward N. Zalta (Ed.), *The Stanford Encyclopedia of Philosophy* (Spring 2018 Edition). Palo Alto, CA: Stanford University Press. https://plato.stanford.edu/archives/spr2018/entries/feminism-globalization/.

Pitre, N. Y. & Kushner, K. E. (2015). Theoretical triangulation as an extension of feminist intersectionality in qualitative family research. *Journal of Family Theory and Review, 7*, 284–98. doi:10.1111/jftr.12084

Poynting, S. & Donaldson, M. (2005). Snakes and leaders: Hegemonic masculinity in ruling-class boys' boarding schools. *Men and Masculinities, 7*(4), 325–46.

Reilly, N. (2007). Cosmopolitan feminism and human rights. *Hypatia: A Journal of Feminist Philosophy, 22*(4), 180–98. doi.org/10.1111/j.1527-2001.2007.tb01327.x

Roberts, S. A. (2016). *Neoliberal Education Reform: Gendered Notions in Global and Local Contexts*. New York, NY: Routledge.

Roosevelt, F. D. (1938). Message for American education week. September 27, 1938, http://www.presidency.ucsb.edu/ws/?pid=15545.http://www.presidency.ucsb.edu/ws/?pid=15545.

Saltman, K. J. (2014). The austerity school: Grit, character, and the privatization of public education. *Symploke, 22*, 41–57. Project MUSE muse.jhu.edu/article/566832.

Simmie, G. M. & Edling, S. (2016). Ideological governing forms in education and teacher education: A comparative study between highly secular Sweden and highly non-secular Republic of Ireland. *Nordic Journal of Studies in Educational Policy, 1*, doi: 10.3402/nstep.v2.32041

Smith, C. (2012). A brief examination of neoliberalism and its consequences. *The Society Pages, Sociology Lens*, 2 October 2012. https://thesocietypages.org/sociologylens/2012/10/02/a-brief-examination-of-neoliberalism-and-its-consequences/

Swarr, A. L. & Nagar, R. (2010). *Critical Transnational Feminist Praxis*. Albany: State University of New York Press.

Welch, S. (2013). Introduction: Hyperdemocracy, the cognitive dimension of democracy, and democratic theory. In *Hyperdemocracy* (pp. 1–13). New York: Palgrave Macmillan US. https://doi.org/10.1057/9781137099174_1

What's gone wrong with democracy (2014, February). *The Economist*. Retrieved from https://www.economist.com/essay/2014/02/27/whats-gone-wrong-with-democracy

Young, I. M. (1988). Five faces of oppression. *The Philosophical Forum, xix*(4), 270–90.

Zinn, M. B. & Dill, B. T. (1996). Theorizing difference from multiracial feminism. *Feminist Studies, 22*(2), 321–31.

Chapter 1

Abdo, N. (2010). Imperialism, the state, and NGOs: Middle eastern contexts and contestations. *Comparative Studies of South Asia, Africa and The Middle East, 30*(2), 238–49.

Abu-Lughod, L. (2002). Do Muslim women really need saving? Anthropological reflections on cultural relativism and its other. *American Anthropologist, 104*, 784–90.

Agamben, G. (2005). *State of Exception*. Chicago: University of Chicago Press.

Arditti, R. (1999). *Searching for Life: The Grandmothers of the Plaza de Mayo and the Disappeared Children of Argentina*. Berkeley, CA: University of California Press.

"AWS Open Letter to Home Minister and Press Statement following the police harassment at National Conference, Wardha, 21-4 January, 2011." Sanhati http://sanhati.com/articles/3190/(Accessed January 30, 2011).

Barker, I. (2009). (Re)Producing American soldiers in an age of empire. *Politics and Gender, 5*, 211–35.

Bannerji, H., Mojab, S. & Whitehead, J. (2010). Of property and propriety: The role of gender and class in imperialism and nationalism: A decade later. *Comparative Studies of South Asia, Africa and the Middle East, 30*(2), 262–71.

Basu, A. (Eds.) (2010). *Women's Movements in the Global Era, the Power of Local Feminisms.* Boulder, CO: Westview Press.

Berda, Y. (2013). Managing dangerous populations: Colonial legacies of security and surveillance. *Sociological Forum, 28*(3), 627–30.

Bhan, M & Duchinski, H. (2020). "Introduction: Occupation in context, The cultural logics of occupation, settler violence, and resistance. In *Critique of Anthropology*, 28(1) 1–14.

Bhatt, S. (2003). State terrorism vs. Jihad in Kashmir. *Journal of Contemporary Asia, 33*(2), 215–44.

Brennan, T. (2003). *Globalization and Its Terrors.* New York: Routledge.

Butalia, U. (Eds.) (2002). *Speaking Peace, Women's Voices from Kashmir.* London: Zed Books.

Chisti, M. (2010). Gender and the development battlefield in Afghanistan: Nation builders versus nation betrayers. *Comparative Studies of South Asia, Africa and the Middle East, 30*(2), 250–61.

Chomsky, N. "U.S. Savage Imperialism." Talk given June 2010, published in Z Magazine, December 2010. www.zcommunications.org/zspace/noamchomsky

Comfort, S. (Eds.) (2011a). Works and days, special issue on *invisible battlegrounds, Feminist resistance* In: *The Global Age of War and Imperialism,* 29.

Comfort, S. (2011b). Introduction, invisible battlegrounds. *Works and Days, 29,* 7–39.

Dankelman, I. (2008). Gender and Climate Change: local security in an era of global environmental change. Security Disarmed, 70–72. University, Nijmegen.

Das, R. (2007). Broadening the security paradigm: Indian women, anti-nuclear activism, and visions of a sustainable future. *Women's Studies International Forum, 30,* 1–15.

Dingo, R. (2004). Securing the nation: Neoliberalism's U.S. family values in a transnational gendered economy. *Journal of Women's History, 16*(3), 173–86.

Duschinski, Hayley. (2010). Reproducing regimes of impunity, fake encounters and the informalization of everyday violence in Kashmir valley. *Cultural Studies, 24*(1), 110–32.

Duschinski, H.(2009). Destiny effects: Militarization and the institutionalization of punitive punishment in Kashmir Valley. *Anthropological Quarterly, 82*(3), 691–718.

Eley, G. (2007). Historicizing the global, politicizing capital: Giving the present a name. *History Workshop Journal, 63,* 154–88.

Eisenstein, Z. (2007). *Sexual Decoys, Gender, Race and War in Imperial Democracy.* London: Zed Books.

Enloe, C. (2007). *Globalization and Militarism: Feminists Make the Link.* Lanham, MD: Rowan and Littlefield.

Federici, S. "War, Globalization and Reproduction" http://www.nadir.org/nadir/initiativ/agp/free/9-11/federici.htm#a2 (accessed 2010).

Golash-Boza, T. (2016). The parallels between mass incarceration and mass deportation: An intersectional analysis of state repression. *Journal of World-Systems Research,* Supplement Special Issue: *Coloniality of Power and Hegemonic Shifts, 22*(2), 484–509.

Gordon, A.(2006). Abu ghraib: Imprisonment and the war on terror. *Race and Class*, *48*(1), 42–59.

Greenberg, J. (2005). Generations of memory: Remembering partition in India/ Pakistan and Israel/ Palestine. *Comparative Studies of South Asia, Africa and the Middle East*, *25*(1), 89–110.

Hennessy, R. (2011). Gender adjustments in forgotten places: The north-south encuentros in Mexico. *Works and Days*, *29*, 181–202.

Hudson, Natalie Florea (2010). "Gender, Human Security and the United Nations: Security Language as a Political Framework for Women". Political Science Faculty Publications. Paper 53. http://ecommons.udayton.edu/pol_fac_pub/53

Jad, I. The demobilization of a Palestinian women's movement: From empowered active militants to powerless and stateless "citizens." In Basu (Eds.), *Women's Movements in the Global Era*, 2010, pp 343–74.

Johnson, P. (2010). Displacing Palestine: Palestinian householding in an era of asymmetrical war. *Politics and Gender*, *62*(2), 295–304.

Kaul, N. (2018). India's obsession with Kashmir: Democracy, gender, (anti-) nationalism. *Feminist Review*, *119*, 126–43.

Kelly, T. (2006). Documented lives: Fear and uncertainties of law during the second Palestinian *Intifada. Journal of the Royal Anthropological Institute*, *12*(1), 89–107.

Khan, N. (2009). *Islam, Women and Violence in Kashmir, between India and Pakistan*. New York: Palgrave Macmillan.

Kotef, H. (2010). Objects of security: Gendered violence and securitized humanitarianism in occupied Gaza. *Comparative Studies of South Asia, Africa and the Middle East*, *30*(2), 179–91.

Kotef, H. & Merav, A. (2007). (En)Gendering checkpoints: Checkpoint watch and the repercussions of intervention. *Signs*, *32*, 973–96.

Lipan Apache Women Defense http://lipanapachecommunitydefense.blogspot.com/ (accessed January 30, 2010).

Lutz, C. (2002). Making war at Home in the United States: Militarization and the current crisis. *American Anthropologist*, *104*(3), 723–35.

Mahmood, S. (2008). Feminism, democracy and empire: Islam and the war of terror. In J. Scott (Ed.), *Women's Studies on the Edge* (pp. 81–114). Durham, NC: Duke University Press.

Malik, I. (2018). Gendered politics of funerary processions: Contesting Indian sovereignty in Kashmir. *Economic and Political Weekly*, *53*(47), 973–96.

Martinez, E. (2008). Vilified and prohibited memories: The making of a gendered and racialized national-transnational enemy. *Canadian Women's Studies*, *27*(1), 23–8.

Mojab, S. (2010). Introduction: Gender and empire. *Comparative Studies of South Asia, Africa and the Middle East*, *30*(2), 220–3.

National Network for Immigrant and Refugee Rights. Injustice for all: The rise of the U.S. immigration policing regime. produced by HURRICANE, December 2010, www.nnir.org

Nordstrom, C. (2004). *Shadows of War: Violence, Power and International Profiteering in the Twenty-first Century*. Berkeley, CA: University of California Press.

Nguyen, M. T. (2011). The biopower of beauty: Humanitarian imperialisms and global feminisms in the age of terror. *Signs, 36*(2), 359–83.

O'odham Solidarity Across Borders Collective, http://oodhamsolidarity.blogspot.com/(accessed January 30, 2010).

Oza, R. (2007). Contrapuntal geographies of threat and security: The United States, India, and Israel. *Environment and Planning D: Society and Space, 25*, 9–32.

Paik, A. (2020). *Naomi, Bans, Walls, Raids, Sanctuary: Understanding Immigration for the Twenty-Frist Century*. Oakland, CA: University of California Press.

Platt, K. (2011). Women on wars and walls: Cultural poetics from Palestine to South Texas. *Works and Days, 29*, 329–60.

Qassoum, M. (2003). Imperial agendas: "Civil society" and global manipulation intifada. *Between the Lines, 3*(19), 6–26.

Riley, R., Mohanty, C. T. & Pratt, M. B. (Eds.) (2008). *Feminism and War: Confronting U.S. Imperialism*. London: Zed Press.

Roy, A. (2004). *An Ordinary Person's Guide to Empire*. Cambridge, MA: South End Press.

Saliba, N. (2008). International women's day statement, *La Voz de Esperanza, 4*.

Saliba, N. (2006). Resistance through remembering and speaking out. *La Voz de Esperanza, 29*, 7–10.

Sidhwa, B. & Butalia, U. (2000). Discussion on the partition of India. *History Workshop Journal, 50*, 230–328.

"Stand With the People of Egypt," *Avaaz*, https://secure.avaaz.org/en/democracy_for_egypt/?cl=926146401 (accessed January 30, 2011).

Sutton, B, Morgen, S. & Novkov, J. (Eds.) (2007). *Security Disarmed, Critical Perspectives on Gender, Race, and Militarization*. New Brunswick, NJ: Rutgers University Press.

Tambe, A. (2010). Coda. *Comparative Studies of South Asia, Africa and the Middle East, 30*(2), 218–19.

Tamez, M.G. (2011).Our way of life is our resistance: Indigenous women and anti-imperialist challenges to militarization along the U.S.-Mexico border. *Works and Days, 29*, 281–318.

Wilson, K., Ung, J., & Purewal, N. (2018). Gender, violence and the neoliberal state in India. *Feminist Review, 119*, 1–6.

Chapter 2

Aguirre, M. Z. & Hökfelt, E. (2009). Riktlinjer för utredning och bedömning av kvinnorsskyddsbehov: ett fungerande verktyg? In F. Bjorn & L. Anna (Eds.), Asylsökande i *Sverige: ett rättssäkert och värdigt mottagande för barn och vuxna?*

(pp. 119–45). Malmö: Department of International Migration and Ethnic Relations (IMER).

Akram, M. S. (2013). Millennium development goals and the protection of displaced and refugee women and girls. *Laws*, 2, 283–313.

Altman, M. & Pannell, K. (2012). Policy gaps and theory gaps: Women and migrant domestic labor. *Feminist Economics*, 18(2), 291–315. https://doi.org/10.1080/135457 01.2012.704149.

Arzheimer, K. (2018). Explaining electoral support for the radical Right. In J. Rydgren (Ed.), *The Oxford Handbook of the Radical Right* (pp. 143–65). Oxford: Oxford University Press.

Bauman, Z. (2016). *Strangers at Our Door*. Malden, MA: Polity.

Beck, M. (2017). Securitization of the Recent influx of refugees from the Middle East to Europe. E- international relations. *News Analysis of SDU's Resource Center on Middle East Studies*, 1–9.

Benhabib, S. (2004). *The Rights of the Other. Aliens, Residents, and Citizens*. Cambridge: Cambridge University Press.

Berry, M., Garcia-Blanco, I., & Moore, K. (2015). Press coverage of the refugee and migrant crisis in the EU: A content analysis of five European countries. www.unhcr.org/56bb369c9.html (accessed January 31, 2017).

Bexelius, M. (2001). *Kvinnor på flykt. En analys av svensk asylpolitik ur ett genusperspektiv*, 1997–2000, Rådgivningsbyrån för asylsökande och flyktingar: Stockholm.

Bexelius, M. (2008). *Asylrätt, kön och politik. En handbok för jämställdhet och kvinnors rättigheter*. Rådgivningsbyrån för asylsökande och flyktingar: Visby.

Brosius, H. B. & Eps, P. (1995). Prototyping through key events: News selection in the case of violence against aliens and asylum seekers in Germany. *European Journal of Communication*, 10(3), 391.

Budgeting for Women's Rights: Monitoring Government Budgets for Compliance with CEDAW(2008) Created by UNIFEM, this document summarizes how to monitor government budgets for compliance with CEDAW. www.unwomen.org/~/media/Headquarters/Media/Publications/UNIFEM/BudgetingForWomensRights SummaryGuideen.pdf

Carastathis, A., Kouri-towe, N., Mahrouse, G., & Whitley, L. (2018). Introduction in Intersectional feminist interventions in the refugee crisis. *REFUGEE*, 34(1), 3–15. https://doi.org/10.7202/1050850.

Chouliaraki, L. & Zaborowski, R. (2017). Voice and community in the 2015 refugee crisis: A content analysis of news coverage in eight European countries. *International Communication Gazette*, 79(6–7), 613–35. ISSN 1748-0485.

Cohen, S. (2006). *Deportation Is Freedom! The Orwellian World of Immigration Controls*. London: Jessica Kingsley Publishers.

Cohen, S., Humphries, B., & Mynott, E. (Eds.) (2002). *From Immigration Controls to Welfare Controls*. London & New York: Routledge.

Crawley, H. & Skleparis, D. (2018). Refugees, migrants, neither, both: Categorical fetishism and the politics of bounding in Europe's "migration crisis." *Journal of Ethnic and Migration Studies, 44*(1), 48–64. https://doi.org/10.1080/136918 3X.2017.1348224

Crouch, Crouch (2004). *Post-democracy*. Cambridge: Polity Press.

De Genova, N. (2013). Spectacles of migrant "illegality": The scene of exclusion, the obscene of inclusion. *Ethnic and Racial Studies 36*(7), 1180–98.

Dembour, M. B. & Martin, M. (2011). The French calaisis: Transit zone or dead end? In M.-B. Dembour & T. Kelly (Eds.), *Are Human Rights for Migrants? Critical Reflections on the Status of Irregular Migrants in Europe and the United States* (pp. 124). New York: Routledge.

Edwards, A. (2016). Global forced displacement hits record high. UNHCR, June 20, 2016, http://www.unhcr.org/enus/news/latest/2016/6/5763b65a4/global-forced-displacement-hits-record-high.html.

Elgenius, G. & Rydgren, J. (2019). Frames of nostalgia and belonging: The resurgence of ethno- nationalism in Sweden. *European Societies, 21*(4), 583–602.

Fassin, D. (2013). The precarious truth of asylum. *Public Culture, 25*(1), 39–63.

Filippi, A. (2018). The politics of immigration controversies, [by Hannah Jones, Yasmin Gunaratnam, Gargi Bhattacharyya, William Davies, Sukhwant Dhaliwal, Kirsten Forkert, Emma Jackson and Roiyah Saltus]. *Refuge, 34*(1), https://doi.org/10.7202/1050857ar

Freire, P. (1970). *Pedagogy of the Oppressed*, New York: Herder and Herder.

Freire, P. (1978). *Pedagogy in Process: The Letters to Guinea Bissau*, New York: Continuum.

Gasslander, T. (2015). Uniformerade nazister deltog i SD-demonstration mot flyktingar, *EXPO,* October 19. http://expo.se/2015/uniformerade-nazister-deltog-i-sddemonstration-mot-flyktingar_6952.htm

Gender Analysis, Assessment and Audit: Manual and Toolkit (2012). Drafted by ACDI/VOCA for international gender consultations. The manual offers great insight into an effective but sensitive approach to interviewing impacted populations. www.acdivoca.org/site/Lookup/ACDI-VOCA-Gender-Analysis-Manual/$file/ACDI-VOCA-Gender-Analysis-Manual.pdf

Hameed, S., Sadiq, A., & Din, A. U. (2018). The increased vulnerability of refugee population to mental health disorders. *Kansas Journal of Medicine, 11*(1), 1–12.

Holloway, K., Stavropoulou, M., & Daigle, M. (2019). *Gender in Displacement: The State of Play*. Humanitarian Policy Group Working Paper, available at: https://odi.org/en/publications/gender-in-displacement-the-state-of-play/

Horn, D. & Parekh, S. (2018). Introduction to "displacement." *Signs: Journal of Women in Culture and Society, 43*(3).

Human Rights Watch (1993). *Human Rights Watch World Report 1993—South Africa*, January 1, available at: https://www.refworld.org/docid/467fca61c.html (accessed July 28, 2020).

Jungar, A.-C. & Jupkas A. R. (2014). Populist Radical Right Parties in the Nordic Region: A New and Distinct Party Family? *Scandinavian Political Studies, 37*(3), 215–38.

Kaye, R. (1998). Redefining the refugee: The UK media portrayal of asylum seekers. In, K. Koser & H. Lutz (Eds.), *The New Migration in Europe* (p. 167). London: Palgrave Macmillan.

Kinnvall, C. (2016) The Postcolonial has Moved into Europe: Bordering, Security and Ethno-Cultural Belonging. *JCMS: Journal of Common Market Studies*, 54: 152–168. doi:10.1111/jcms.12326.

Korolczuk, E. & Gragfg, A. (2018). Gender as "Ebola from Brussels": The Anticolonial Frame and the Rise of Illiberal Populism. *Signs Journal of Women in Culture and Society, 43*(4), 797–821.

Kuby, G. (2015). *The Global Sexual Revolution: Destruction of Freedom in the Name of Freedom*. Kettering: LifeSite/Angelico Press.

Lubbers, M, Gijsberts, M., & Scheepers, P. (2002). Extreme right-wing voting in Western Europe. *European Journal of Political Resistance, 41*(3), 345–78.

Ludwig, G. (2018). Post-democracy and gender: New paradoxes and old tensions. *Distinction: Journal of Social Theory, 19*(1), 28–46.

Mathema, S. (2018). *They Are (Still) Refugees: People Continue to Flee Violence in Latin American Countries*. Center for American Progress. Retrieved from https://cdn.americanprogress.org/content/uploads/2018/05/31133207/They-Are-Still-Refugees-brief1.pdf

Millbank, A. (2016). Moral confusion and the 1951 Refugee Convention in Europe and Australia, Research Report (Victoria: Australian Population Research Institute, March 2016),http://tapri.org.au/wp-content/uploads/2016/02/1951-Convention.pdf.

Mudde, C. (2007). *Populist Radical Right Parties in Europe*. New York: Cambridge University Press, 13.

Mudde, C. (2017). Why nativism, not populism, should be declared word of the year. *The Guardian*, December 7, 2017. https://www.theguardian.com/commentisfree/2017/dec/07/cambridge-dictionary-nativism-populism-word-year

Mudde, C. (2019). *The Far Right Today*. Polity: Cambridge.

Norocel, C. (2013). *Our People a Tight-knit Family under the Same Protective Roof: A Critical Study of Gendered Conceptual Metaphors at Work in Radical Right Populism*. Helsinki: Helsinki University [thesis]. https://helda.helsinki.fi/bitstream/handle/10138/42162/ourpeopl.pdf?sequence=1&isAllowed=

Otterbeck, J. (2004) "Vad kan man egentligen begära? Läromedelstexter om islam" ["What can we really expect? Textbooks on Islam"]. *Didaktikens forum, 1*(1), 56–74.

Pérez Arguello, M. F. & Couch, B. (2018), Violence against women driving migration from the Northern Triangle. *New Atlanticist*, Thursday, November 8, 2018. https://www.atlanticcouncil.org/blogs/new-atlanticist/violence-against-women-driving-migration-from-the-northern-triangle/

Pittaway, E. & Bartolomei, L. (2018). *From Rhetoric to Reality: Achieving Gender Equality for Refugee Women and Girls*. Waterloo, Canada: Centre for International Governance Innovation.

Pittaway, E. & Pittaway, E. (2004). Refugee woman: A dangerous label: Opening a discussion the role of identity and intersectional oppression in the failure of the international refugee protection regime for refugee women. *Australian Journal of Human Rights, 20; 10* (1). DOI: 10.1080/1323238X.2004.11910773.

Pocock, N. S. and Chan, C. WK (2018). Refugees, Racism and Xenophobia: What Works to Reduce Discrimination?. *Our World*, 2018-06-20. https://ourworld.unu.edu/en/refugees-racism-and-xenophobia-what-works-to-reduce-discrimination

Russel, D. (2008). "Femicide: Politicizing the killing of females." Paper presented at the Interagency Gender Working Group Meeting on Strengthening Understanding of Femicide, Washington, DC. May. http://www.igwg.org/Events/femicide.aspx

Rydgren, J. (2007). The sociology of the radical right. *Annual Review of Sociology, 33*, 241–62.

Rydgren, J. (2017). Divided by memories? Beliefs about the past, ethnic boundaries, and trust in northern Iraq. *Geopolitics, History, and International Relations, 9*(1), 128–75.

Rydgren, J. (2018). *The Oxford Handbook of the Radical Right* (Oxford Handbooks). Cambridge: Oxford University Press.

Sajjad, T. (2018). What's in a name? 'Refugees', 'Migrants' and the politics of labelling. *Race & Class, 60*(2), 40–62. doi:10.1177/0306396818793582

Segenstedt, A. (2015). *Tortyrskador i asylprocessen under lupp. Hur värderas tortyrskador i den svenska asylprocessen och vad krävs för att få skydd?* [Röda Korset]. Solna: Williamssons Offsettryck AB.

Shinn, C. (2017). Protracted refugee situations: A feminist perspective on refugee depiction by UNHCR. *ProQuest Dissertations and Theses*. https://search.proquest.com/docview/1964667060?accountid=9645

SOU (2004:31). *Flyktingskap och könsrelaterad förföljelse. Betänkande av Utredningen om förföljelse på grund av kön eller sexuell läggning.*

Sullivan, J. D. (1994). Women's human rights and the 1993 world conference on human rights. *American Journal of International Law, 88*(1), 152–67.

Thimm, V. (2018). Muslim mobilities and gender: An introduction. *Social Sciences 7*(1), 2.

United Nations High Commission for Refugees (2001). San remo expert roundtable summary conclusions—gender-related persecution. In *Refugee Protection in International Refugee Law*. Geneva: Author.

United Nations High Commission for Refugees (2018). Syria Emergency. UNHCR, http://www.unhcr.org/syria-emergency.html.

United Nations Security Council. (2017). *Security council meetings coverage: resolution 2286.*

Van D. B., Fennema, M., & Tillie, J. (2005). Why some anti-immigrant parties fail and others succeed? *Competition Political Studies, 38*(5), 537–73.

Chapter 3

Accioly, I. (2018). *Educação e Capital Imperialismo: As influências Político-Pedagógicas do Banco Mundial nas relações entre Brasil e Moçambique*. PhD diss., Universidade Federal do Rio de Janeiro.

Accioly, I. (2020). The attacks on the legacy of Paulo Freire in Brazil: Why is he still disturbing so many? In Sheila L. Macrine (Eds.), *Critical Pedagogy in Uncertain Times*, London: Palgrave, pp. 117–38.

Accioly, I., Gawryszewski, B., & Nascimento, L. (2016). The commodification of education in the context of a dependent capitalist economy. In Roberto Leher & Inny Accioly (Eds.), *Commodifying Education: Theoretical and Methodological Aspects of Financialization of Education Policies in Brazil*, 21–36. Boston: Sense/Brill.

Amada, C. (2019). "Words from the Zapatista Women at the Opening of the Second International Gathering of Women Who Struggle," December 27, 2019. Accessed June 3, 2020. http://enlacezapatista.ezln.org.mx/2019/12/30/words-from-the-zapatista-women-at-the-opening-of-the-second-international-gathering-of-women-who-struggle/.

Basilio, A. L. (2019). "Mães e professoras denunciam assédio em colégio militar do Amazonas." *Carta Capital*. Accessed June 3, 2020. https://www.cartacapital.com.br/educacao/maes-e-professoras-denunciam-assedio-em-colegio-militar-do-amazonas/.

Capital, C. (2020). Escola cívico-militar em Rondônia afasta professores por interesse em sindicato. Accessed June 3, 2020. https://www.cartacapital.com.br/educacao/escola-civico-militar-em-rondonia-afasta-professores-por-interesse-em-sindicato/.

Castro, A. L. & Pinto, R. P. (2014). The body of Brazilian women in the construction of national identity. *Ciências Sociais Unisinos 50*(1), 34–40.

Chesnais, F. (2016). *Finance Capital Today Corporations and Banks in the Lasting Global Slump*. Boston: Brill.

CPT Nacional (2020). *Confitos no Campo Brasil 2019*. Goiania: CPT.

Damasceno, V. (2019). "Weintraub repete acusações contra universidades com base em reportagens" *Exame*. Accessed Jun 3, 2020. https://exame.abril.com.br/brasil/ministro-da-educacao-repete-que-ha-plantacoes-de-maconha-nas-universidades/

Davis, A. (2016). *Mulheres, Raça e Classe*. São Paulo: Boitempo.

Federici, S. (2004). *Caliban and the Witch: Women, the Body and Primitive Accumulation*. New York: Autonomedia.

Federici, S. (2019). *Re-enchanting the World: Feminism and the Politics of the Commons*. Oakland: PM Press.

Figueiredo, P. (2019). "Número de mortes de lideranças indígenas em 2019 é o maior em pelo menos 11 anos, diz Pastoral da Terra." *G1*.

Fondo de Acción Urgente de América Latina (2016). *Extractivismo en América Latina: Impacto en la vida de las mujeres y propuestras de defensa del territorio*. Bogotá: FAU América Latina.

Fontes, V. (2010). *O Brasil e o capital-imperialismo: teoria e história [Brazil and the capital-imperialism: theory and history]*. Rio de Janeiro: EPSJV/Editora UFRJ.

Freitas, L. C. (2018). *A Reforma Empresarial da Educação: Nova Direita, Velhas Ideias*. São Paulo: Expressão Popular.

Friends of Earth (2019). Harvard and TIAA's farmland grab in Brazil goes up in smoke. *Medium.Com*. Accessed Jun 3, 2020. @foe_us/harvard-and-tiaas-farmland-grab-in-brazil-goes-up-in-smoke-52dbfe57debf

Galeano, E. (1991). *The Book of Embraces*. New York: W. W. Norton.

Gimenes, E. (2020). Fechamento de vagas e escolas em zonas rurais preocupam famílias. *Brasil de Fato*. Accessed June 3, 2020. https://www.redebrasilatual.com.br/sem-categoria/2020/01/fechamento-escolas-zonas-rurais-preocupam/

Global Witness (2017). *At What Cost? Irresponsible Business and the Murder of Land and Environmental Defenders*. Global Witness.

Global Witness (2019). *Enemies of the State? How Governments and Business Silence Land and Environmental Defenders*. Global Witness.

Gomes, R. (2020). Bolsonaro se cerca de ministros militares prevendo ano difícil. *Rede Brasil Atual*.

Indigenous Women's March. (2019). *Final Report of the Indigenous Women's March: Territory: Our Body, Our Spirit*. Brasília: Cimi. Accessed June 3, 2020. https://cimi.org.br/2019/08/marcha-mulheres-indigenas-documento-final-lutar-pelos-nossos-territorios-lutar-pelo-nosso-direito-vida/

Instituto de Pesquisa Econômica Aplicada and Fórum Brasileiro de Segurança Pública (2019). *Atlas da Violência 2019*. Brasília: IPEA; FBSP.

Lima, J. D. (2020). Como o governo Bolsonaro trata a questão do HIV. *Nexo Jornal*, 2–3. Accessed June 3, 2020. https://www.nexojornal.com.br/expresso/2020/02/06/Como-o-governo-Bolsonaro-trata-a-quest%C3%A3o-do-HIV.

Lobato, S. (2019). *A cidade dos trabalhadores: insegurança estrutural e táticas de sobrevivência em Macapá*. Belém: Editora Paka-Tatu.

Marcha das Margaridas (2019). *Marcha das Margaridas' Report 2019*. CONTAG, FETAG, STTR and Movimento de Mulheres Camponesas.

Meneghel, S. N. & Portella, A. P. (2017). Femicides: Concepts, types and scenarios. *Ciência & Saúde Coletiva*. 22(9), 3077–86.

Mies, M. (2014). The need for a new vision: The subsistence perspective. In Maria Mies & Vandana Shiva (Eds.), *Ecofeminism* (pp. 297–324). New York: Zed Books.

Ministry of Education. Ministério da Educação (MEC). Accessed February 25, 2020. http://escolacivicomilitar.mec.gov.br/.

Palhares, I. (2020). Código de conduta para escola cívico-militar do MEC inclui corte de cabelo e veto a bermuda. *Estadão*. Accessed June 3, 2020. https://educacao.

estadao.com.br/noticias/geral,governo-cria-codigo-de-conduta-para-escolas-civico-militares-com-regras-de-vestuario-e-comportamento,70003183824.

Portal G1 (2019). "Em vídeo, Damares diz que 'nova era'começou: 'meninos vestem azul e meninas vestem rosa.'" *G1*.

Rede Brasil Atual (2019). Ações do governo Bolsonaro deixam indígenas em total insegurança. *RBA*.

Svampa, M. (2015). Feminismos del Sur y ecofeminismo. *Nueva Sociedad 4* (March), 127–31.

Svampa, M. (2019). What the new right wing brings to Latin America between the political and the social: New areas of dispute. *Rosa Luxemburg Stiftung 22* (August), 01–20.

Chapter 4

AfD (2016). Programm für Deutschland. Das Grundsatzprogramm der Alternative für Deutschland. https://www.afd.de/wp-content/uploads/sites/111/2017/01/2016-06-27_afd-grundsatzprogramm_web-version.pdf

AfD (2017). Programm für Deutschland. Wahlprogramm der Alternative für Deutschland für die Wahl zum Deutschen Bundestag am 24. September 2017. Beschlossen auf dem Bundesparteitag in Köln am 22./23. April 2017. https://www.afd.de/wp-content/uploads/sites/111/2017/06/2017-06-01_AfD-Bundestagswahlprogramm_Onlinefassung.pdf

AfD Landesverband Hamburg (2015). Wahlprogramm zur Bürgerschaftswahl 2015, S.11: https://alternative-hamburg.de/wp-content/uploads/2014/12/B%C3%BCrgerschaftswahl-Programm-D.pdf

Ahmed, S. (2000). *Strange Encounters. Embodied Others in Post-Coloniality*. London/New York: Routledge.

Butler, J. (1990). *Gender Trouble. Feminism and the Subversion of Identity*. New York/London: Routledge.

Butler, J. (1999). *Gender Trouble. Feminism and the Subversion of Identity*. Tenth Anniversary edition. New York/London: Routledge.

Butler, J. (2000a). Restaging the universal: Hegemony and the limits of formalism. In J. Butler, E. Laclau & S. Žižek (Eds.), *Contingency, Hegemony, Universality: Contemporary Dialogues on the Left* (pp. 11–43). London: Verso.

Butler, J. (2000b). Dynamic conclusions. In J. Butler, E. Laclau & S. Žižek (Eds.), *Contingency, Hegemony, Universality. Contemporary Dialogues on the Left* (pp. 263–80). London: Verso.

Butler, J. (2004). *Precarious Life. The powers of mourning and violence*. London: Verso.

Butler, J. (2010). *Frames of War*. When life is grievable. London: Verso.

Dietze, G. (2019). *Sexueller Exzeptionalismus. Überlegenheitsnarrative in Migrationsabwehr und Rechtspopulismus*. Bielefeld: transcript.

Gauland, A. (2019). Die Schleuserei unter Missbrauch der „Seenotrettung" generell unterbinden. https://afdkompakt.de/2019/07/11/die-schleuserei-unter-missbrauch-der-seenotrettung-generell-unterbinden/

Glynos, J. (2011). Fantasy and identity in critical political theory. *Filozofski vestnik*, 32(2), 65–88.

Glynos, J. & Howarth, D. (2007). *Logics of Critical Explanation in Social and Political Theory*. London: Routledge.

Hark, S. & Villa, P-I. (2015). Eine Frage an und für unsere Zeit. Verstörende Gender Studies und symptomatische Missverständnisse. In S. Hark & P-I. Villa (Eds.), *Anti-Genderismus. Sexualität und Geschlecht als Schauplätze aktueller politischer Auseinandersetzungen* (pp. 15–39). Bielefeld: transcript.

Irigaray, L. (1977). *The Sex Which Is Not One*. Ithaca: Cornel University Press.

Keil, W. (2019). 95 Prozent der im September aus Seenot Geretteten sind Wirtschaftsflüchtlinge. https://afdkompakt.de/2019/11/04/95-prozent-der-im-september-aus-seenot-geretteten-sind-wirtschaftsfluechtlinge/

Kemper, A. (2016). Geschlechter- und familienpolitische Positionen der AfD. In H. Kellershohn & W. Kastrup (Eds.), *Kulturkampf von rechts. AfD, pegida und die Neue Rechte* (pp. 147–61). Münster: Unrast.

Laclau, E. (1990). *New Reflections on the Revolution of Our Time*. London: Verso.

Laclau, E. (1996/2007). *Emancipation(s)*. London: Verso.

Laclau, E. (2000). Identity and hegemony: The role of universality in the constitution of political logics. In J. Butler, E. Laclau & S. Žižek (Eds.), *Contingency, Hegemony, Universality* (pp. 44–89). London and New York.

Laclau, E. (2005). *On Populist Reasons*. London and New York: Verso.

Laclau, E. & Mouffe, C. (1985). *Hegemony and Socialist Strategy. Towards a Radical Democratic Politics*. London: Verso.

Lang, J. (2017a). "Gender" und "Gender-Wahn" – neue Feindbilder der extremen Rechten https://www.bpb.de/politik/extremismus/rechtsextremismus/259953/gender-und-genderwahn#footnode18–19

Lang, J. (2017b). Feindbild Feminismus. Familien- und Geschlechterpolitik in der AfD. In S. Grigat (Ed.), *AfD & FPÖ. Antisemitismus, völkischer Nationalismus und Geschlechterbilder* (pp. 61–78), Baden-Baden: Nomos.

Lang, J. & Peters, U. (2018). Antifeminismus in Deutschland. Einführung und Einordnung des Problems, In J. Lang & U. Peters (Eds.), *Antifeminismus in Bewegung. Aktuelle Debatten um Geschlecht und sexuelle Vielfalt*. (pp. 13–28). Hamburg: Marta Press.

Lefort, C. (1999). *Democracy and Political Theory*. Oxford: Polity Press.

Leidinger, C. & Radvan, H. (2018). Antifeminismus und Familismus von rechts., In A. Häusler (Ed.), *Völkisch-autoritärer Populismus. Der Rechtsruck in Deutschland und die AfD* (pp. 93–100). Hamburg: VSA.

Ludwig, G. (2019). The Aporia of promises of liberal democracy and the rise of authoritarian politics, Distinktion. *Journal of Social Theory*. https://doi.org/10.1080/1600910X.2019.1669688

Lugones, M. (2007). Heterosexualism and the colonial/modern gender system. *Hypatia*, 22(1), 186–209.

Nocun, K. (2016). Wie sozial ist die AfD wirklich? Eine Expertise zu Positionen in der AfD bei der Sozial- und Steuerpolitik. https://www.boell.de/sites/default/files/2016-6-wie-sozial-ist-die-afd.pdf

Quijano, A. (2000). Coloniality of power, eurocentrism and latin America. *Nepantla: Views from the South, 1*(3), 533–80.

Rancière, J. (1999). *Disagreement. Politics and Philosophy*. Minneapolis: University of Minnesota Press.

Salzborn, S. (2017). Von der offenen zur geschlossenen Gesellschaft. Die AfD und die Rennaissance des deutschen Opfermythos im rechten Diskurs. In S. Grigat (Ed.), *AfD und FPÖ. Antisemitsmus, völkischer Nationalismus und Geschlechterbilder* (pp. 29–40), Baden-Baden: Nomos.

Sauer, B. (2020). Authoritarian right-wing populism as masculinist identity politics. The role of affects. In G. Dietze & J. Roth (Eds.), *Right-Wing Populism and Gender. European perspectives* (pp. 22–39). Bielefeld: transcript.

Schutzbach, F. (2019). Anti-Feminismus macht rechte Positionen gesellschaftsfähig. https://www.gwi-boell.de/de/2019/05/03/antifeminismus-macht-rechte-positionen-gesellschaftsfaehig

Storch, von B. (2013). Zu Familie, Bildung und Gender Mainstreaming. https://www.youtube.com/watch?v=5pqdUVDlpS4

Weed, E. (2011). From the 'Useful' to the 'Impossible' in the Work of Joan W. Scott. In J. Butler & E. Weed (Eds.), *The Question of Gender Joan W. Scott's Critical Feminism*. (pp. 287–311). Bloomington, Indiana University Press.

Chapter 5

Alexander, M. (2012). *The New Jim Crow: Mass Incarceration in the Age of Colorblindness*. New York: The New Press.

Anthias, F. & Yuval-Davis, N.(1992). *Racialized Boundaries: Race, Nation, Gender, Colour and Class and the Anti-Racist Struggle*. London: Routledge.

Benjamin, R. (2019). Introduction: discriminatory design, liberating imagination. In R. Benjamin (Ed.), *Captivating Technology: Race, Carceral Technoscience, and Liberatory Imagination in Everyday Life* (pp. 1–22). Durham, NC: Duke University Press.

Brock, A. (2020). *Distributed Blackness: African American Cybercultures*. New York: New York University Press.

Brown, W. (2006). American nightmare: Neoliberalism, neoconservatism, and de-Democratization. *Political Theory, 34*(6), 690–714.

Browne, S. (2015). *Dark Matters: On the Surveillance of Blackness*. Durham, NC: Duke University Press.

Buolamwini, J. (2018). The hidden dangers of facial analysis. *The New York Times* (June 22), A25.

Carruthers, C. A. (2018). *Unapologetic: A Black, Queer, and Feminist Mandate for Radical Movements*. Boston, MA: Beacon Press.

Chowdhry, G. & Nair, S. (2002). Introduction: Power in a postcolonial world: Race, gender, and class in International Relations. In G. Chowdhry & S. Nair (Eds.), *Power Postcolonialism and International Relations: Reading Race, Gender and Class* (pp. 1–32). London: Routledge.

Duster, T. (2019). Foreword. In R. Benjamin (Ed.), *Captivating Technology: Race, Carceral Technoscience, and Liberatory Imagination in Everyday Life* (pp. xi–xiii). Durham, NC: Duke University Press.

Eubanks, V. (2017). *Automating Inequality: How High-Tech Tools Profile, Police, and Punish the Poor*. New York: St. Martin's Press.

Fanon, F. (1963). *The Wretched of the Earth*. New York: Grove Press.

Hall, Kia M. Q. (2016). A transnational black feminist framework: Rooting in feminist scholarship, Framing contemporary black activism. *Meridians*, 15(1), 86–104.

Hall, K. Melchor Quick Hall (2019). Technology in black feminist world. *Froniers: A Journal of Women Studies*, 40(2), 243–57.

Hall, K. Melchor Quick Hall (2020). *Naming a Transnational Black Feminist Framework: Writing in Darkness*. New York: Routledge.

Kelley, R. D. G. (2002). *Freedom Dreams: The Black Radical Imagination*. Boston: Beacon Press.

Khan-Cullors, P. & Bandele, A. (2017). *When They Call You a Terrorist: A Black Lives Matter Memoir*. New York: St. Martin's Griffin.

Manchanda, N. & Leah, de H. (2018). Gender, nation, and nationalism. In R. B. Persaud & A. Sajed (Eds.), *Race, Gender and Culture in International Relations: Postcolonial perspectives* (pp. 80–98). London: Routledge.

McIlwain, C. D. (2020). *Black Software: The Internet and Racial Justice, from the AfroNet to Black Lives Matter*. New York: Oxford University Press.

Miller, A. (2019). Shadows of war, traces of policing: The weaponization of space and the sensible in preemption. In R. Benjamin(Ed.), *Captivating Technology: Race, Carceral Technoscience, and Liberatory Imagination in Everyday Life* (pp. 85–106). Durham, NC: Duke University Press.

Nakamura, L. (2002). *Cybertypes: Race, Ethnicity, and Identity on the Internet*. New York: Routledge.

Nakamura, L. (2008). *Digitizing Race: Visual Cultures of the Internet*. Minneapolis: University of Minnesota Press.

Noble, S. U. (2018). *Algorithms of Oppression: How Search Engines Reinforce Racism*. New York: New York University Press.

O'Neill, C. (2016). *Weapons of Math Destruction: How Big Data Increases Inequality and Threatens Democracy*. New York: Crown.

Poster, W. R. (2019). Racialized surveillance in the digital service economy. In R. Benjamin (Ed.), *Captivating Technology: Race, Carceral Technoscience, and*

Liberatory Imagination in Everyday Life (pp. 133–69). Durham, NC: Duke University Press.

Raji, D., Gebru, T., Mitchell, M., Buolamwini, J., Lee, J., & Denton, E. (2020). Saving face: Investigating the ethical concerns of facial recognition. *Proceedings of the 2020 AAAI/ACM Conference of AI, Ethics, and Society (AIES '20), 7*(8).

Roberts, D. (2011). *Fatal Invention: How Science, Politics, and Big Business Re-Create Race in the Twenty-First Century*. New York: The New Press.

Scannell, R. J. (2019). This is not minority report: Predictive policing and population racism. In R. Benjamin (Eds.), *Captivating Technology: Race, Carceral Technoscience, and Liberatory Imagination in Everyday Life* (pp. 107–29). Durham, NC: Duke University Press.

Zuboff, S. (2019). *The Age of Surveillance Capitalism: The Fight for a Human Future at the New Frontier of Power*. New York: PublicAffairs.

Chapter 6

Arendt, H. (1963). *Eichmann in Jerusalem: A Report on the Banality of Evil*. New York: Penguin Books.

Arruzza, C., Bhattacharya, T., & Fraser, N. (2019). *Feminism for the 99%: A Manifesto*. London and New York: Verso.

Chu, A. L. (2019). *Females*. London and New York: Verso.

Deutscher, P. (2017). *Foucault's Futures: A Critique of Reproductive Reason*. New York: Columbia University Press.

Edelman, L. (2004). *No Future: Queer Theory and the Death Drive*. Durham, NC, and London: Duke University Press.

Fortunati, L. (1995). *The Arcane of Reproduction: Housework, Prostitution, Labor and Capital*. (Ed.) J. Fleming & H. Creek. Brooklyn, NY: Autonomedia.

Fraser, N. (2013). *Fortunes of Feminism: From State-Managed Capitalism to Neoliberal Crisis*. London and New York: Verso.

Haraway, Donna (2016). *Staying with the Trouble: Making Kin in the Chthulucene*. Durham, NC, and London: Duke University Press.

Johanson, M. A. (2015). A girl walks home alone at night movie review: Blood pressure. *Flick Filosopher* (31 March): https://www.flickfilosopher.com/2015/03/a-girl-walks-home-alone-at-night-movie-review-blood-pressure.html. (accessed March 1, 2020).

Leigh, D. (2015). Interview with Amirpour: The Skateboarding Iranian Vampire Diaries. *The Guardian* (May 7): https://www.theguardian.com/film/2015/may/07/skateboarding-iranian-vampire-ana-lily-amirpour-feminism-porn-girl-walks-home-alone-at-night.

Lewis, S. (2019). *Full Surrogacy Now: Feminism against the Family*. London and New York: Verso.

Mayer, S. (2015). Film of the Week: A girl walks home alone at night. *Sight & Sound*, 25(6), https://www.bfi.org.uk/news-opinion/sight-sound-magazine/reviews-recommendations/film-week-girl-walks-home-alone-night. (accessed March 1, 2020).

McRobbie, A. (2013). Feminism, the family and the new 'Mediated' maternalism. *New Formations*, 80(81), 119–37.

Mottahedeh, N. (2008). *Displaced Allegories: Post-Revolutionary Iranian Cinema*. Durham, NC and London: Duke University Press.

O'Malley, S. (2014). "A girl walks home alone at night (2014)." *Rogerebert.com* (November 21, 2014): https://www.rogerebert.com/reviews/a-girl-walks-home-alone-at-night-2014. (accessed March 1, 2020).

Ong, A. (2009). A Bio-Cartography: Maids, Neo-Slavery, and NGOs. In S. Benhabib & R. Judith (Eds.), *Migrations and Mobilities: Citizenship, Borders, and Gender*. New York University Press.

Rich, A. (1995). *Of Woman Born: Motherhood as Experience and Institution*. New York and London: W. W. Norton & Company.

Rose, J. (2018). *Mothers: An Essay on Love and Cruelty*. New York: Farrar, Straus and Giroux.

Rottenberg, C. (2018). *The Rise of Neoliberal Feminism*. Oxford, UK and New York: Oxford University Press.

Watkins, S. (2018). Which feminisms? *New Left Review*, 109, 5–76.

Yee, V. (2020). Saudi law granted women new freedoms. Their families don't always agree. *The New York Times* (March 14, 2020): https://www.nytimes.com/2020/03/14/world/middleeast/saudi-women-rights.html?action=click&module=News&pgtype=Homepage. (accessed 14 March 2020).

Chapter 7

Aftonbladet (2017a). 'Virtanen: Jag har betett mig tölpigt och skitstövligt'. Retrieved June 10, 2020 from https://www.aftonbladet.se/nyheter/a/GvO8m/virtanen-jag-har-betett-mig-tolpigt-och-skitstovligt

Aftonbladet (2017b). "Så blev ##Metoo ett globalt vrål." Retrieved June 10, 2020 from https://www.aftonbladet.se/nyheter/a/79WJ4/grafik-sa-blev-#Metoo-ett-globalt-vral

Almqvist, C. & Love, J. (2018). *Det går an*. **1838**. Reprinted. Stockholm: Modernista.

Askanius, T. & Møller Hartley, J. (2019). Framing gender justice: A comparative analysis of the media coverage of #metoo in Denmark and Sweden. *Nordicom Review*, 40(2), 19 36. doi:10.2478/nor-2019-0022.

BBC (2018). Nobel Prize for Literature delayed amid Swedish Academy ´sex assault 'scandal. Retrieved June 10, 2020 from https://www.bbc.com/news/world-europe-43999240

Beauvoir, S. (1995). *Le deuxieme sexe 1*. **1949**. Reprinted. Paris: Gallimard.
Bergh, B. (2003). *Heliga Birgitta. Åttabarnsmor och profet*. Lund: Historiska media.
Björk, N. (1996). *Under det rosa täcket*. Stockholm: Wahlström & Widstrand.
Bloomfield, E.F. (2019). Rhetorical constellations and the inventional/intersectional possibilites of #MeToo. *Journal of Communication Inquiry, 43*(4), 394–414. Doi: 10.1177/01968559919866444
Boëthius, Maria Pia (1976). *Skylla sig själv: en bok om våldtäkt*. Stockholm: Liber.
Business Insider (2018). 'It's a very scary time for young men in America'. *Business Insider*. Retrieved June 10, 2020 from https://www.businessinsider.com
Café (2017). "Bråk om vem som faktiskt startade rörelsen Me Too." Retrieved June 10, 2020 from https://www.cafe.se/tarana-burke-#Metoo/
Clayhills, H. (1991). *Kvinnohistorisk uppslagsbok*. Stockholm: Rabén & Sjögren.
CNN (2017). "#Metoo-hashtag-global-movement". Retrieved June 10, 2020 from https://edition.cnn.com/2017/11/09/world/#Metoo-hashtag-global-movement/index.html
De Benedictis, S., Orgad, S., & Rottenberg, C. (2019). #MeToo, popular feminism and the news : A content analysis of UK newspaper coverage. *European Journal of Cultural Studies, 22*(5–6), 718–38. Doi:10.1177/1367549419856831
Eberhard, D. (2018). *Det stora könsexperimentet*. Stockholm: Bladh by Bladh AB.
Eduards, M. (2002). *Förbjuden handling: om kvinnors organisering och feministisk teori*. Malmö: Liber ekonomi.
Ekonomifakta.se (2020). 'Kvinnor på arbetsmarknaden'. Retrieved June 24, 2020 from https://www.ekonomifakta.se/Fakta/Arbetsmarknad/Jamstalldhet/Kvinnor-pa-arbetsmarknaden—internationellt/
Engdahl, H. (2019). *De obekymrade*. Stockholm: Albert Bonniers förlag.
Expressen (2017a). 'Här är samtliga ##Metoo-upprop'. Retrieved June 10, 2020 from https://www.expressen.se/nyheter/har-ar-samtliga-#Metoo-upprop/
Expressen (2017b). 'Martin Timell bryter tystnaden – och erkänner'. Retrieved 10 June from https://www.expressen.se/noje/martin-timell-bryter-tystnaden-och-erkanner
Expressen (2018a). 'Jag förfäras över råheten i Akademiens maktkamp'. Retrieved June 10, 2020 from https://www.expressen.se/kultur/ide/jag-forfaras-over-raheten-i-akademiens-maktkamp/
Expressen (2018b). 'Hundratals samlades I knytblusmanifestation'. Retrieved June 10, 2020 from https://www.expressen.se/nyheter/hundratals-samlades-i-knytblusmanifestation/
Expressen (2018c). 'Vi lever i en farlig tid'. Retrieved June 10, 2020 from https://www.expressen.se/nyheter/horace-kritik-mot-arnault-domen-vi-lever-i-en-farlig-tid/
Faludi, S. (1991). *Backlash. The Undeclared War against American Women*. New York: Free Rivers Press.
Feministisktperspektiv.se (2018). 'Backlash mot #Metoo-rörelsen'. Retrieved 10 June from https://feministisktperspektiv.se/2018/08/07/backlash-mot-#Metoo-rorelsen/
Frostenson, K. (2019). *K*. Stockholm: Bokförlaget Polaris.

Gemzöe, L. (2006). *Feminismer*. Stockholm: Bilda förlag.
Göteborgs-Posten (2017). 'Jämställdhet handlar inte om att kvinnor är offer'. Retrieved June 10, 2020 from https://www.gp.se/ledare/jamstalldhet-handlar-inte-om-att-kvinnor-ar-offer-1.4795432
Grannäs & Ljungquist (2015). Berättelsen som forum för kontroversiella frågor. In C. Ljunggren, I. U. Ost & T. Englund (Eds.), *Kontroversiella frågor: Om kunskap och politik i samhällsundervisningen*. Malmö: Gleerups.
Gustavsson, K. (2019). Stockholm: Albert Bonniers förlag.
Gustavsson, M. (2017). '18 kvinnor: Kulturprofilen har utsatt oss för övergrepp', *Dagens nyheter*, 24 November, 18.
Hedlin, M. (2006). *Jämställdhet, en del av skolans värdegrund*. Stockholm: Liber.
Hill, H. (2007). *Befria mannen!* Umeå: Bokförlaget H: ström.
Knutsson, U. (2018). 'Elin Wägner: Tro på ljuset är kvinnoplikt'. In A. Håkan (Ed.), *Demokratins genombrott. Människor som formade 1900-talet*, Bengtsson och Lars Ilshammar (p. 19). Lund: Historiska media.
Kumashiro, K. (2010), 'Seeing the bigger picture: Troubling movements to end teacher education'. *Journal of Teacher Education*, 61(1–2), 56–65.
Lanius, C. (2019). Torment porn and feminist witch hunt: Apprehensions about the# Metoo Movement on/r/AskReddit. *Journal of Communication Inquiry*, 43(4), 415, 436. Doi:10.1177/0196859919865250
Lerner, G. (1987). *The Creation of Patriarchy*. Oxford: Oxford University Press.
Maskulint.se (2019). "Vad ##Metoo egentligen handlar om och vad det innebär för svenska män" Retrieved June 10, 2020 from https://maskulint.se/rodapillret/#Metoo/
Mendes, K., Ringrose, J., & Keller, J. (2018). #MeToo and the promise and pitfalls of challenging rape culture through digital feminist activism. *European Journal of Women's Studies*, 25(2), 236–46. doi:10.1177/1350506818765318
Mill, J. S. (1988). *The Subjection of Women*. **1869**. Indianapolis: Hackett Publishing Co.
Millett, K. (2000). *Sexual Politics*. **1970**. Reprindet. Chicago: University of Illinois Press.
Mohanty, C. (1988). 'Under western eyes: Feminist scholarship and colonial discourses'. *Feminist Review*, 30, 49–74.
Nylander, L. (2018, januari). Ingen väg tillbaka efter #metoo. Hämtad 15 december från https://www.forskning.se/2018/01/10/ingen-vag-tillbaka-efter-metoo/
OmVärlden (2019). '##Metoo två år – så går det i världen'. Retrieved June 10, 2020 from https://www.omvarlden.se/Branschnytt/nyheter-2019/#Metoo-i-varlden/
Report (2020). Retrieved June 10, 2020 from https://reliefweb.int/report/world/global-gender-gap-report-2020
Strindberg, A. (1955). *Giftas II*. **1884**. Reprinted. Stockholm: Albert Bonniers förlag.
Ström, P. (2012). *Mansförbjudet. Könsdiskriminering av män och pojkar*. Stockholm: BoD.

Sveland, M. (2013). *Hatet. En bok om antifeminism.* Stockholm: Leopard förlag.
SVT.se (2018). 'Granskning.UG. #Metoo och Fredrik Virtanen'. Retrieved June 10, 2020 from https://www.svt.se/nyheter/granskning/ug/#Metoo-och-fredrik-virtanen
Sydsvenskan.se (2019). 'Sara-Danius lämnar Akademien för gott'. Retrieved June 10, 2020 from https://www.sydsvenskan.se/2019-02-26/sara-danius-lamnar-akademien-for-gott
Virtanen, F. (2019). *Utan nåd – en rannsakning.* Oslo: Gloria forlag AS.
Witt-Brattström, E. (2003). *Heliga Birgitta. I dig blev den stora Guden en liten pilt.* Stockholm: Norstedt.

Chapter 8

Aiston, S. J. & Kent Fo, C. (2020). The silence/ing of academic women. *Gender and Education.* DOI: 10.1080/09540253.1716955
Apple, M. W. (2012). *Education and Power* (2nd ed.). New York: Routledge.
Apple, M. W. (2013). *Can Schooling Change Society? Can Society Change Schooling?.* New York: Routledge.
Arendt, H. (1961). The crisis in education, in *Between past and future: six exercises in political thought* (pp. 173–96). New York: Viking Press.
Ball, S. J. (2003). The teacher's soul and the terrors of performativity. *Journal of Education Policy, 18*(2), 215–28. DOI: 10.1080/0268093022000043065
Black, P. & William, D. (1998). Inside the black box: Raising standards through classroom assessment. *Phi Delta Kappan, 80*(2), 139–44, 146–8.
Bourdieu, P. (2001). *Masculine Domination.* Stanford, CA: Stanford University Press.
Bourke, T., Lidstone, J., & Ryan, M. (2015). Schooling teachers: Professionalism or disciplinary power?. *Educational Philosophy and Theory, 47*(1), 84–100.
Boyle, E. (2004). *The Feminization of Teaching in America.* MIT Womens's and Gender Studies Louis Kamph Prize Essay. https://stuff.mit.edu/afs/athena.mit.edu/org/w/wgs/prize/eb04.html
Brady, A. M. (2016). The regime of self-evaluation: Self-conception for teachers and schools. *British Journal of Educational Studies, 64*(4), 523–41. DOI:10.1080/00071005.2016.1164829
Brady, A. M. (2019). Anxiety of performativity and anxiety of performance: Self-evaluation as bad faith. *Oxford Review of Education.* DOI:10.1080/03054985.2018.1556626
Bruno, R. (2018). When did the U.S. stop seeing teachers as professionals? *Harvard Business Review.* https://hbr.org/2018/06/when-did-the-u-s-stop-seeing-teachers-as-professionals
Butler, J. (2004). *Undoing Gender.* New York: Routledge.
Cannella, G. (1997). *Deconstructing early childhood education: Social justice and revolution.* New York: Peter Lang.

Cochran-Smith, M. (2019). *Marilyn Cochran-Smith—Rethinking Accountability*. U-tube pod-cast. https://www.youtube.com/watch?v=q2-MvmUvevg

Cochran-Smith, M. & Lytle, S. L. (2006). Troubling images of teaching in no child left behind. *Harvard Educational Review, 76*(4), 668–97.

Connell, R. (1990). The state, gender and sexual politics. Theory and appraisal. *Theory and Society, 19*, 507–44.

Connell, R.W. (1994). The state, gender and sexual politics: Theory and appraisal. In L. Radtke & H. J. Stam (Eds.), *Power/Gender: Social Relations in Theory and Practice* (pp. 141–67). London: Sage Publications.

Connell, R. (2009). Good teachers on dangerous ground: Towards a new view of teacher quality and professionalism. *Critical Studies in Education, 50*(3), 213–29.

Conway, P., Murphy, R., Rath, A., & Hall, K. (2009). *Learning to Teach and Its Implications for the Continuum of Teacher Education: A Nine Country Cross-national Study*. Maynooth: The Teaching Council.

Drudy, S. (2008). Gender balance/gender bias: The teaching profession and the impact of feminization. *Gender and Education, 20*(4), 309–23. DOI: 10.1080/09540250802190156

Edling, S. & Mooney Simmie, G. (2020). *Democracy and Teacher Education: Dilemmas, Challenges and Possibilities*. 1st Edition. London and New York: Routledge.

Fielding, M. (2007). The human cost and intellectual poverty of high performance schooling: Radical philosophy, John Macmurray and the remaking of person-centred education. *Journal of Education Policy, 22*(4), 383–409.

Freire, P. (2018/1970). *Pedagogy of the Oppressed with a New Introduction by Donaldo Macedo and an Afterword by Ira Shor*. New York: Bloomsbury.

Giroux, H. A. (2010). In defense of public school teachers in a time of crisis. *Policy Futures in Education, 8*(6), 709–14.

Giroux, H. (2013). Neoliberalism's war against teachers in dark times. *Cultural Studies Critical Methodologies, 13*, 458–68. https://doi.org/10.1177/1532708613503769

Griffiths, M. (2006). The feminization of teaching and the practice of teaching: Threat of opportunity? *Educational Theory, 56*, 387–405. Doi:10.1111/j.1741-5446.2006.00234.x

Gunter, H. M. (2005). Conceptualizing research in educational leadership. *Educational Management Administration & Leadership, 33*(2), 165–80.

Hattie, J. (2012). *Visible Learning for Teachers Maximizing Impact on Learning*. Oxon, Abingdon: Routledge.

Hederman, M. P. (2019). *Living the Mystery What Lies between Science and Religion*. Dublin: Columba Books.

hooks, b. (1994). *Teaching to Transgress Education as the Practice of Freedom*. New York and London: Routledge.

hooks, b. (2000). *Feminism Is for Everybody. Passionate Politics*. Cambridge, MA: Sound End Press.

Hursh, D. (2012). Rethinking schools and society/combating neoliberal globalization. In *Education and the Reproduction of Capital* (pp. 101–12). New York: Palgrave Macmillan US.

Hursh, D. (2017). The end of public schools? The corporate reform agenda to privatize education. *Policy Futures in Education, 15*(3), 389–99. https://doi.org/10.1177/1478210317715799

Hyslop Margison, E. J. & Naseem, M. A. (2010). *Scientism and Education Empirical Research as Neo-Liberal Ideology.* Springer.

Kuehn, L. (1999). Responding to globalization of education in the Americas: Strategies to support public education. Paper presented at the IDEA conference in Quito, Ecuador.

Lather, P. & St. Pierre, E. A. (2013). Post-qualitative research. *International Journal of Qualitative Studies in Education, 26*(6), 629–33. https://doi.org/10.1080/09518398.2013.788752

Lingard, B., Martino, W., & Rezai-Rashti, G. (2013). Testing regimes, accountabilities and education policy: Commensurate global and national developments. *Journal of Education Policy, 28*(5), 539–56. https://doi.org/10.1080/02680939.2013.820042

Lynch, K. & Crean, M. (2019). On the question of cheap care: Regarding a history of the world in seven cheap things by Raj Patel and Jason W. Moore. *Irish Journal of Sociology*, 1–8. DOI: 10.1177/0791603519835432

Macer, M. & Chadderton, C. (2020). The reproduction of the gender regime: The military and education as state apparatuses constraining the military wife student. *Gender and Education*, 10.1080/09540253.2020.1765994

Macrine, S. L. (2002). *Pedagogical Bondage: Body Bound and Gagged in a Technorational World.* In S. & S. Shapiro (Eds.), *Body Movements: Pedagogy, Politics, and Social Change* (pp. 133–45). Cresskill, NJ: Author.

Macrine, S. L. (2018). Chapter 26. Pedagogies of neoliberalism. In S. Spinnger, K. Birch & J. MacLeary (Eds.), *The Handbook of Neoliberalism* (pp. 294–305). New York: Routledge International Handbook.

Macrine, S. L. (2020). *Critical Pedagogy in Uncertain Times: Hope and Possibilities.* New York: Palgrave Macmillan. https://link.springer.com/book/10.1007/978-3-030-39808-8

McLaren, P. (2019). Resisting fascist mobilization: Some reflections on critical pedagogy, liberation theology and the need for revolutionary socialist change. *Educational Philosophy and Theory.* DOI: 10.1080/00131857.2020.1716450

Mooney Simmie, G. (2007). Teacher Design Teams (TDTs)—Building capacity for innovation, learning and curriculum implementation in the continuing professional development of in-career teachers. *Irish Educational Studies, 26*(2), 163–76. DOI: http://dx.doi.org/10.1080/03323310701295914

Mooney Simmie, G. (2009). *The Policy Implementation Process in the Upper Secondary Education System (Senior Cycle) and videregående skolen in Science and Mathematics in the Republic of Ireland and the Kingdom of Norway from 1960–2005.* PhD thesis. Dublin: Trinity College Dublin.

Mooney Simmie, G. (2012). The pied piper of neo liberalism calls the tune in the republic of Ireland: An analysis of education policy text from 2000–2012. *Journal for*

Critical Educational Policy Studies, *10*(2), 485–514. DOI: http://www.jceps.com/wp-content/uploads/PDFs/10-2-18.pdf

Mooney Simmie, G. (2014). The neo-liberal turn in understanding teachers' and school leaders' work practices in curriculum innovation and change: A critical discourse analysis of a newly proposed reform policy in lower secondary education in the Republic of Ireland. *Citizenship, Social and Economics Education*, *13*(3), 185–98. DOI: http://dx.doi.org/10.2304/csee.2014.13.3.185

Mooney Simmie, G. (2015). McLaren's pedagogy of insurrection and the global murder machine in education in "Austerity Ireland." Book Review: Pedagogy of Insurrection, by Peter McLaren. *Journal for Critical Educational Policy Studies*, *13*(3), 221–9. http://www.jceps.com/archives/2782

Mooney Simmie, G. (2020a). Chapter 28. The power, politics, and future of mentoring. In B. J. Irby, J. N. Linda Searby, F. K. Boswell & R. Garza (Eds.), *The Wiley International Handbook of Mentoring: Paradigms, Practices, Programs, and Possibilities*. First Edition (pp. 453–69). Hoboken, NY: John Wiley & Sons, Inc.

Mooney Simmie, G. (2020b). Chapter: Remaining a student of teaching forever: Critical reflexive insights from a lifetime of multiple teacher identities in the Republic of Ireland. In C. A. Karaman & S. Edling (Eds.), *International Perspectives on Professional Learning and Identities in Teaching: Narratives of Successful Teachers* (Editors). Routledge: Research in Teacher Education Series.

Mooney Simmie, G. & Edling, S. (2019). Teachers' democratic assignment: A critical discourse analysis of teacher education policies in Ireland and Sweden. *Discourse: Studies in the Cultural Politics of Education*, *40*(6), 832–46.

Mooney Simmie, G. & Lang, M. (2020). *School-Based Deliberative Partnership as a Platform for Teacher Professionalization and Curriculum Innovation*. Routledge Research Teacher Education Series. London and New York: Routledge.

Mooney Simmie, G. & Moles, J. (2019). Teachers' changing subjectivities: Putting the soul to work for the principle of the market or for facilitating risk? *Studies in Philosophy and Education*, 1–16. First Online: 19 October. DOI: 10.10007/s11217-019-09686-9

Mooney Simmie, G., Moles, J., & O'Grady, E. (2019). Good teaching as a messy narrative of change within a policy ensemble of networks, superstructures and flows. *Critical Studies in Education*, *60*(1), 55–72. DOI: 10.1080/17508487.2016.1219960

Moreau, M. P. (2019). *Teachers, Gender and the Feminisation Debate*. London: Routledge.

Ng, J. C., Stull, D. D., & Martinez, R. S. (2019). What if only what can be counted will count? A critical examination of making educational practice "scientific." *Teachers College Record*, *121*(1–26), 121.121308

Novak, J. (2019). Juridification of educational spheres: The case of Sweden. *Educational Philosophy and Theory*, *51*(12), 1262–72.

Núñez, X. P. (2018). Performing the (religious) educator's vocation. Becoming the "good" early childhood practitioner in Chile. *Gender and Education*. DOI: 10.1080/09540253.2018.1554180

OECD (2019). *Education at a Glance*, OECD Indicators. Paris: Author. DOI:https://doi.org/10.1787/f8d7880d-en

Osgood, J. (2006a). Deconstructing professionalism in early childhood education: Resisting the regulatory gaze. *Contemporary Issues in Early Childhood*, 7(1), 5–14.

Osgood, J. (2006b). Professionalism and performativity: The feminist challenge facing early years practitioners. *Early Years*, 26(2), 187–99.

Otterstad, A. M. (2019). What might a feminist relational new materialist and affirmative critique generate in/with early childhood education? *Qualitative Inquiry*, 25(7), 641–51.

Paolantonio, M. D. (2019). The malaise of the soul at work: The drive for creativity, self-actualisation, and curiosity in education. *Studies in Philosophy and Education*, http://doi.org/10.1007/s11217-019-09653-4

Rømer, T. A. (2019). A critique of John Hattie's theory of visible learning. *Educational Philosophy and Theory*, 51(5), 587–98.

Ross, E. W. & Gibson, R. (Eds.) (2007). *Neoliberalism and Education Reform*. Cresskill, NJ: Hampton Press.

Ross, E. W., Gabbard, D., Kesson, K., Mathison, S., & Vinson, K. D. (Eds.) (2004). *Defending Public Schools* (Vols 1–4). Westport, CT: Praeger.

Sant, E. (2019). Democratic education: A theoretical review (2006-2017). *Review of Educational Research*, 89(5), 655–96.

Santoro, D. A. (2017). Cassandra in the classroom: Teaching and moral madness. *Studies in Philosophy of Education*, 36, 49–60.

Tan, E. (2014). Human capital theory: A holistic criticism. *Review of Educational Research*, 84(3), 411–45.

Teaching Council Act (2001). Dublin: Government of Ireland, http://www.irishstatutebook.ie/eli/2001/act/8/enacted/en/html

Teaching Council (2011). *Policy on the Continuum of Teacher Education*. Maynooth: Author.

Teaching Council (2016a). *Cosán Framework for Teachers' Learning*. March 2016. Maynooth: Author.

Teaching Council (2016b). *Codes of Professional Conduct for Teachers. Updated 2nd Edition. July 2016*. Maynooth, Co. Kildare: The Teaching Council.

Teaching Council (2016c). *Droichead an Integrated Induction Framework for Newly Qualified Teachers. March 2016*. Maynooth, Co. Kildare: Author.

Teaching Council (2018). *Féilte Sharing Teaching, Connecting Learning. Féilte 2018 Innovation Report*. 5–6 October 2018. Mary Immaculate College, Limerick. Maynooth, Co. Kildare: Author.

Thomas, M. A. M. & Vavrus, F. K. (2019). The pluto problem: Reflexivities of discomfort in teacher professional development. *Critical Studies in Education*. DOI: 10.1080/17508487.2019.1587782

Tronto, J. C. (2013). *Caring Democracy Markets, Equality, and Justice*. New York & London: New York University Press.

Vincent-Lancrin, S., et al. (2019). *Fostering Students' Creativity and Critical Thinking: What It Means in School*. Paris: Educational Research and Innovation, OECD Publishing. https://doi.org/10.1787/62212c37-en

Watson, C. (2014). Effective professional learning communities? The possibilities for teachers as agents of change in schools. *British Educational Research Journal*, 40(1), 18–29.

Zipin, L. & Brennan, M. (2003). The suppression of ethical dispositions through managerial governmentality: A habitus crisis in Australian higher education. *Int. J. Leadership in Education*, 6(4), 351–70. DOI: 10.1080/1360312032000150742

Chapter 9

Arendt, H. (1963). *Eichmann in Jerusalem: A Report on the Banality of Evil*. New York: The Viking Press.

Carvalho, M. C. & Sívori, H. F. (2017). Gender, sexuality and religious instruction in Brazilian educational policy. Cadernos Pagu (50). https://doi.org/10.1590/18094449 201700500017

Casanova, J. (1994). *Public Religions in the Modern World*. Chicago: Chicago University Press.

Casanova, J. (2007). O mal-estar do ensino religioso nas escolas públicas. *Cadernos de Pesquisa*, 37(131), maio/ ago, 303–32.

Certeau, M. (1984). A Invenção do Cotidiano 1: as artes do fazer. The invention of everyday life: 1. The arts of making. Petropolis. Vozes.

Certeau, M. (1984). *The Invention of Everyday Life: 1. The Arts of Making*. Oakland: University of California Press.

Certeau, M. (1988). *The Writing of History*. New York: Columbia University Press.

Cohen, S. (1972). *Folk Devils and Moral Panics: The Creation of the Mods and the Rockers*. Oxford: Basil Blackwell.

Comitê Técnico de Educação do Instituto Rui Barbosa/Technical Education Committee of the Rui Barbosa Institute (CTE-IRB). A educação não pode esperar. [Education can't wait]. Brazil, 2020.

Federicci, S. (2017). *Calibã e a Bruxa: Mulheres, Corpo e Acumulação Primitiva. [Caliban and the Witch]*. São Paulo: Elefante.

hooks, b. (2019). *O Feminismo É Para Todo Mundo: Políticas Arrebatadoras. [Feminism Is for Everyone]*. Rio de Janeiro: Rosa dos Tempos.

Lugones, M. (2014). Rumo a um feminismo descolonial. [Towards a decolonial feminism]. *Revista de Estudos Feministas*, 22(3), 935–52. https://doi.org/10.1590/%25x

Manguel, A. (2018). *A Cidade das Palavras: As histórias que contamos para saber quem somos. [The City of Words]*. São Paulo: Cia das Letras.

Moura, F. P. & Salles, D. D. C. (2018). O Escola Sem Partido e o ódio aos professores que formam crianças (des)viadas. *Revista Periódicus, 1*(9), 136. https://doi.org/10.9771/peri.v1i9.25742

Oliveira, I. B. & Sussekind, M. L. (2018). Dimensões político-epistemológicas do equívoco conservador na educação: A base curricular brasileira no contexto dos currículos nacionais. *Revista Portuguesa De Educação, 31* Especial, 55–74. https://doi.org/10.21814/rpe.14806

Paraskeva, J. (2011). Conflicts in curriculum theory. In *Challenging Hegemonic Espistemologies*. New York: Palgrave.

Paraskeva, J. (2016). Curriculum epistemicides. In *Towards an Itinerant Curriculum Theory*. New York: Routledge.

Penna, F. (2015). Sobre o ódio ao professor: entrevista com Fernando Penna [About hating teachers: interview]. Movimento-revista de educação, Niterói, ano 2, n. 3, pp. 294–301.

Santos, B. de S. (1995). *Pela Mão de Alice: o Social e o Político na Pós-modernidade. [By the Hand of Alice]*. São Paulo: Cortez.

Santos, B. de S. (2001). *A Crítica da Razão Indolente: Contra o Desperdício da Experiência. [The Critique of Indolent Reason]*. São Paulo: Cortez.

Santos, B. de S. (Eds.) (2003). *Democratizar a democracia – Os Caminhos da Democracia Participativa. [Democratize democracy]*. Porto: Afrontamento.

Santos, B. de S. (2007). *Para além do pensamento abissal: das linhas globais a uma ecologia de saberes. [Beyond abyssal thinking]*. Novos estudos CEBRAP, 79, 71–94. https://doi.org/10.1590/S0101-33002007000300004

Santos, B. de S. (2010). Para além do pensamento abissal: das linhas globais a uma ecologia de saberes. [Beyond abyssal thinking: global lines and the ecology of knowledges]. In SANTOS, B. de S.; MENESES, M. P. (org.). *Epistemologias do sul*. São Paulo: Cortez.

Souza, J. (2016). *Radiografia do Golpe: Entenda Como e Porque Você Foi Enganado*. Rio de Janeiro: LeYa.

Spivak, G. C. (2010). *Pode o subalterno falar? [Can the subaltern speak?]*. Belo Horizonte: Editora UFMG.

Süssekind, M. L. (2014). Taking advantage of the paradigmatic crisis: Brazilian everyday life studies as a new epistemological approach to the understanding of teachers' work. *Citizenship, Social and Economics Education, 13*(3), 199–210. https://doi.org/10.2304/csee.2014.13.3.199

Sussekind, M. L., Porto, M. M., & Do A. R., Matheus, S. (2018). The (im) possibilities of the common: An opinion on the erasing of differences in Brazilian curriculum reform. *Sociology International Journal, 2*(1), 4–7. https://doi.org/10.15406/sij.2018.02.00027

Chapter 10

Agathopoulou, E. (2018,03 12). Φεμινιστικές προκλήσεις στα χρόνια της καπιταλιστικής κρίσης, *avgi.gr* Retrieved April 4, 2020 from http://www.avgi.gr/article/10811/8763376/pheministikes-prokleseis-sta-chronia-tes-kapitalistikes-krises

Aruzza, C., Battacharya, T., & Fraser, N. (2019). *Feminism for the 99%: A Manife*sto. Verso. London, New York.

Bhandar, B. (2011). Plasticity and post-colonial recognition: "Owning, knowing and being." *Law Critique, 22*, 227–49.

Bhattacharya, T. (Eds.) (2017). *Social Reproduction Theory Remapping Class, Recentering Oppression*. London: Pluto Press.

Coole, D. (1993). *Women in Political Theory: From Ancient Misogyny to Contemporary Feminism*. Brighton: Harvester Wheatsheaf.

COVID-19 sex-disaggregated data tracker (2020). Global Health 5050, GH5050, https://globalhealth5050.org/covid19/

Crouch, C. (2016). The march towards post-democracy, ten years on. *The Political Quarterly, 87*(1), 71–5.

Dalla Costa, M. & James, S. (1975). *Women and the Subversion of the Community, Falling Wall Press & Individuals from the Women's Movement in England and Italy*. Bristol, UK: Wiley Blackwell.

Davaki, K. (2013). *Policy on Gender Equality in Greece, European Parliament*. Retrieved from https://www.europarl.europa.eu/RegData/etudes/note/join/2013/493028/IPOL-FEMM_NT(2013)493028_EN.pdf

Davou, B. (2015). "Investigating the psychological effects of the Greek financial crisis", Retrieved April 5, 2020 from http://blogs.lse.ac.uk/greeceatlse/2015/10/22/psychological-effects-of-the-greek-financial-crisis/

Delphy, C. & Chaperon, S. (Eds.) (2002). *Le cinquantenaire du "Deuxième sexe"*. Paris: Syllepse.

Driscoll, B. (2020,03 14). "Higher risk" of domestic abuse during coronavirus self-isolation, warn campaigners, *huffingtonpost.co.uk*. Retrieved April 4, 2020 from https://www.huffingtonpost.co.uk/entry/domestic-violence-coronavirus_uk_5e6b9c9ec5b6bd8156f63d01

Eller, J. D. (2018). Producing and reproducing bodies. *Cultural Anthropology 101*, 58–75. https://doi.org/10.4324/9781315731025-5

ELSTAT—Hellenic Statistical Authority (2017). Retrieved April 4, 2020 from http://www.statistics.gr/el/statistics/-/publication/SJO02/2017-M10

EnetEnglish (2014, 04 7). Court awards HIV-positive women compensation for unjust imprisonment. Retrieved April 4, 2020 from http://www.enetenglish.gr/?i=news.en.article&id=1844

English, L. M. & Irving, C. J. (2015). Critical feminist pedagogy. In *Feminism in Community*. Rotterdam: International Issues in Adult Education. SensePublishers.

Europa, Factsheet on Undeclared Work – GREECE (2017). Retrieved April 9, 2020 from: http://www.google.com/search?q=Undeclared+and+irregular+labor+greece&rlz=1C1GCEA_enGR786GR786&oq=Undeclared+and+irregular+labor+greece&aqs=chrome.

Eurostat (2020). Unemployment by sex and age—annual average (Last update: 01-04-2020). Retrieved April 4, 2020 from: http://appsso.eurostat.ec.europa.eu/nui/show.do?dataset=une_rt_a&lang=en

Federici, S. (2013). Revolucion en punto cero: Trabajo domestico, reproduccion y luchas feminists. *Revolution at point zero: Domestic labour, reproduction and feminist struggles*, Traficantes de Suenos-Mapas, traduccion: Scriptorium (Fernandez-Cuervos, C. & Martin-Ponz, P.).

Federici, S. (2019a). 8 Minutes with Silvia Federici (video). Retrieved April 4, 2020 from https://www.youtube.com/watch?v=CDf0NDNfWEQ

Federici, S. (2019b). «Marx imagined a totally asexual worker» (video). Retrieved April 4, 2020 from https://www.youtube.com/watch?v=HWrJQI4R-9E&t=3s

Fraser, N. (2013). *Fortunes of Feminism—From State-managed Capitalism to Neoliberal Crisis*. London & New York: Verso.

Gender Equality Index (2019). Greece (2019), European Institute for Gender Equality. Retrieved April 4, 2020 from https://eige.europa.eu/publications/gender-equality-index-2019-greece

General Secretariat for Gender Equality (2017,07 26). Gender-disaggregated data on the status of girls and education in Greece. Retrieved April 6, 2020 from http://www.isotita.gr/en/gender-disaggregated-data-status-girls-education-greece/

Giannacopoulos, M. (2015). *Sovereign Debts: Global Colonialism, Austerity and Neo-Liberal Assimilation*, Law Text Culture, 19, 2015, 166–93. http://ro.uow.edu.au/ltc/vol19/iss1/9, (accessed 18 May 2020).

Gopal, A. (2015). What austerity looks like inside Greece, *The New Yorker*, 1/4/2020 https://www.newyorker.com/business/currency/what-austerity-looks-like-inside-greece

GSGE—General Secretarial of Gender Equality, Gender Equality Observatory. Retrieved April 5, 2020 from http://paratiritirio.isotita.gr/genqua_portal/

Guillaume, M. (2017,03 08). En Argentine, «le movement féministe ne peut pas se permettre d'être patient», *Libération*. Retrieved April 9, 2020 from https://www.liberation.fr/planete/2017/03/08/en-argentine-le-mouvement-feministe-ne-peut-pas-se-permettre-d-etre-patient_1554029

Hale, G. (14 January 2013). "Balance of payments in the european periphery." Federal Reserve Bank of San Francisco. Retrieved June 15, 2020.

Hocking, J. J. & Lewis, C. H. (2007). *Counter-Terrorism and the Post-Democratic State*. 1st ed. Cheltenham, UK: Monash University, Edward Elgar Publishing.

hooks, b. (1994). *Teaching to Transgress. Education as the Practice of Freedom*. London: Routledge.

Jahoda, M. (1982). *Employment and Unemployment: A Social-Psychological Analysis*. Cambridge: Cambridge University Press.

Karamesini, M. & Rubery, J. (2014). *Women and Austerity: The Economic Crisis and the Future for Gender Equality*. London: Routledge.

Klein, N. (2007). *The Shock Doctrine: The Rise of Disaster Capitalism*. New York: Henry Holt and Company.

Koronaiou, A. & Sakelariou, A. (2017). Women and golden dawn: Reproducing the nationalist habitus. *Gender and Education, 29*(2), 258–75. DOI: 10.1080/09540253.2016.1274382

Kosyfologou, A. (2017). Greece, austerity, gender inequality and feminism after the crisis. The gendered aspects of the austerity regime in Greece: 2010–2017, Rosa Luxemburg Stiftung: Athens. Retrieved April 5, 2020 from https://www.academia.edu/36983039/The_gendered_aspects_of_the_austerity_regime_in_Greece_2010_2017

Lapavitsas, C. (2018). Political economy of the Greek crisis. *Review of Radical Political Economics, 51*(1), 31–51.

Longwe, S. H. (1998). Education for women's empowerment or schooling for women's subordination? Gender and development. *Education and Training, 6*(2) (July, 1998), 19–26.

Lowe, L. (1998). "Work, immigration, gender: New subjects of cultural politics." *Social Justice, 25*(3 (73)), 31–49. JSTOR, www.jstor.org/stable/29767084. (accessed 18 May, 2021).

"Marianne: The incredible errors by IMF experts & the wrong multiplier." KeepTalkingGreece.com. January 22, 2013. Retrieved April 15, 2020 from

Matsaganis, M. (2011). The welfare state and the crisis: The case of Greece. *Journal of European Social Policy - J EUR SOC POLICY, 21*, 501–12. doi:10.1177/0958928711418858

Mayes, E. (2005). Private property, the private subject and women—Can women truly be owners of capital? In M. A. Fineman & T. Dougherty (Eds.), *Feminism Confronts Homo Economicus—Gender, Law and Society* (pp. 117–28). Ithaca, NY and London: Cornell University Press.

Ministry of Interior, General Secretariat for Gender Equality (March 2019). Women's Unemployment. Retrieved April 4, 2020 from http://www.isotita.gr/wp-content/uploads/2019/04/Observatory-19th-e-bulletin-Womens-Unemployment.pdf

Nasioulas, I. (2012). Social cooperatives in greece. Introducing new forms of social economy and entrepreneurship. *International Review of Social Research, 2*(2), 151–71.

Nikolakaki, M. (2019). Greece's struggle over academic asylum. https://newpol.org/greeces-struggle-over-academic-asylum/

OECD Economics Department Working Papers No. 1106. (2014). Fairly sharing the social impact of the crisis in Greece. (www.oecd.org/eco/etudes/Grèce). © *OECD*.

OECD (2013). *OECD Economic Surveys GREECE Summary Main Findings*.

Panagiotis, S. (2013). Neoliberalism and higher education in Greece (Presentation made at the EĞITIM-SEN Conference on Higher Education, 22 February 2013, in Ankara). Retrieved April, 4, 2020 from http://egitimsen.org.tr/wp-content/uploads/2015/07/032b6c37a05cd6c_ek.pdf

Pantelidou-Malouta, M. (2002). *Το φύλο της δημοκρατίας. Ιδιότητα του πολίτη και έμφυλα υποκείμενα.* Αθήνα: Σαββάλας.

Pantelidou-Malouta, M. (2014). *Φύλο – Κοινωνία – Πολιτική.* ΚΕΤΗΙ-Κέντρο Ερευνών για Θέματα Ισότητας: Athens.

Papageorgiou, Y. (2006). *Hegemony and Feminism.* Athens: Typothito [in Greek].

Papageorgiou, Y. & Petousi, V. (2018). Gender resilience in times of economic crisis. Findings from greece. *PArtecipazione e COnflitto The Open Journal of Sociopolitical Studies,* Issue *11*(1), 145–74. Retrieved April, 4, 2020 from https://www.academia.edu/36754948/GENDER_RESILIENCE_IN_TIMES_OF_ECONOMIC_CRISIS_Findings_from_Greece

Papanicolaou, Georgios (2008-10-16). *The Sex Industry, Human Trafficking and the Global Prohibition Regime: A Cautionary Tale from Greece. Trends in Organized Crime.* 11(4), 379–409. doi:10.1007/s12117-008-9048-7. ISSN 1936-4830.

Pateman, C. (1988). *The Sexual Contract.* Stanford, California: Stanford University Press.

Pateman, C. (1989). *The Disorder of Women: Democracy, Feminism and Political Theory.* Stanford: Stanford University Press. και Cambridge: Polity.

Pateman, C. (1988). *The Sexual Contract.* Stanford, Calif.: Stanford University Press.

Pavlidou, T. S. (2011). Gender studies at Greek universities. *Aspasia.*

Peters, M. A. (2016). Biopolitical economies of debt. *Analysis and Metaphysics 15,* 7–19.

Portaliou, E. (2016). Greece: A country for sale. *Jacobin, 09*(12). https://www.jacobinmag.com/author/eleni-portaliou

Richardson, J. (2010). Feminism, property in the person and concepts of self. *British Journal of Politics and International Relations, 12,* 56–71.

Scott, J. W. (1997). Deconstructing equality-versus-difference: Or the uses of poststructuralist theory for feminism, στο D. T. Meyers (Ed.), *Feminist Social Thought: A Reader* (pp. 759–70). London: Routledge.

Sioula-Georgoulea, I. (2015). Approaching Twitter sociologically: a case study of the public humiliation of HIV-positive women. *Επιθεώρηση Κοινωνικών Ερευνών, 144*(144), 103–28. Doi:https://doi.org/10.12681/grsr.8625

Skaperdas, S. (2015). Myths and self-deceptions about the greek debt-crisis. *Revue d'économie politique, 125*(6), 755–85. Doi:10.3917/redp.256.0755

Sledziewski, É. (2002). Révolution Française. στο G. Fraisse & M. Perrot (Eds.), Histoire des femmes en Occident. Le XIXe siècle, 45–62.

Sotiris, P. (2013a). Neoliberalism and higher education in Greece (Presentation made at the EĞITIM-SEN Conference on Higher Education, 22 February 2013, in Ankara). Retrieved April, 4, 2020 from http://egitimsen.org.tr/wp-content/uploads/2015/07/032b6c37a05cd6c_ek.pdf

Sotiris, P. (2013b). Reading revolt as deviance interface. *A Journal for and about Social Movements Article*, 5(2), 47–77.

Sotiropoulou, I. (2014). Greek economy as a failure of capitalist patriarchy and the choice of dystopia in "Greece and Austerity Policies: Where Next for its Economy and Society?" Conference organised by World Economic Association. Available at: http://greececonference2014.weaconferences.net/

Technological Institute of Athens-Department of Social Work (ΤΕΙ Αθήνας-Τμήμα Κοινωνικής Εργασίας). Γεννήσεις στην Ελλάδα [Birth giving in Greece] 1931–2008. Retrieved April, 4, 2020 from http://users.teiath.gr/angtsal/Birth.htm

Trilling, D. (2020). The rise and fall of Greece's neo-Nazis. *The Guardian*. https://www.theguardian.com/news/2020/mar/03/golden-dawn-the-rise-and-fall-of-greece-neo-nazi-trial

Tsomou, M. (2020). *Gender Politics in Greece What has changed for Greek women since the crisis?* Athens Goethe-Institut. https://www.goethe.de/en/kul/ges/eu2/fem/21269245.html

Varika, E. (1999). Le paria ou la difficile reconnaissance de la pluralité humaine. *Revue des deux mondes*, 11/12.

Varika, E. (2000). Égalité. στο H. Hirata, F. Laborie, H. Le Doaré et al. (Eds.), *Dictionnaire critique du féminisme* (pp. 54–60). Paris: PUF.

Vatikiotis, L. & Nikolakaki, M. (2012). Resistance in Greece, *academia.eu*. Retrieved April 9, 2020 from https://www.academia.edu/5222767/Resistance_in_Greece-Vatikiotis_and_Nikolakaki

Watson, I. (2009). "Sovereign spaces, caring for country, and the homeless position of aboriginal peoples" *South Atlantic Quarterly* 108/1, Winter, 28–51.

Zambarloukou, S. (2015). Greece after the crisis: Still a South European welfare model?, *European Societies*, 17, 653–73.

Chapter 11

Aftonbladet (2020). Hot mot genusforskare skadligt för democratic [Threats to gender researchers harmful to democracy] Retrieved February 9, 2020 from https://www.aftonbladet.se/ledare/a/OpBgOV/hot-mot-genusforskare-skadligt-for-demokratin

Akkerman, T. (2012). Comparing radical right parties in government: Immigration and integration policies in nine countries (1996–2010), *West European Politics*, 35(3), 511–29. DOI: https://doi.org/10.1080/01402382.2012.665738

Andersson, C. & Olsson, E. J. (2019). Genusvetare illustrerar oavsiktligt kritiken [Gender scientists inadvertently illustrate the criticism]. *Universitetsläraren* 10 June 2019. Retrieved February 9 from https://universitetslararen.se/2019/06/10/genusvetare-illustrerar-oavsiktligt-kritiken/

Arpi, I. (2017). Så blev genusvetenskap överkyrka i Lund. [So, gender science became the upper church in Lund] *Svenska Dagbladet*. November 4, 2017.

Arpi, I. (2019). "Utomlands ser de mig som feminist." Bokmässa *Svenska Dagblade*t. Bokmässa 2019-09-29 Retrieved May 11, 2021 from https://www.svd.se/ivar-arpi-utomlands-ser-de-mig-som-feminist

Arpi, I. (2020). Så *tar genusideologin över svenska universitet*. [This is how the gender ideology takes over Swedish universities] Retrieved May 6, 2020 from https://www.kickstarter.com/projects/1506708889/sa-tar-genusideologin-over-svenska-universitet

Arruza, C., Bhattacharya, T., & Fraser, N. (2019). *Feminism for the 99%: A Manifesto*. London: Verso.

Badiou, A. (2016). *Ocurrió durante el horror de una profunda noche. Conferenica de Alain Badiou sobre lo que significa Donald Trump*. Universidad de California Los Angeles (UCLA) 9/11/2016.

Bard, A. (2017). Den nya mansrollen, del 2: Alexander Bard: "Genusäktenskap är rena helvetet " [The New Man Role, Part 2: Alexander Bard: "Gender marriage is pure hell"]. *Katerina Magasin*. NOVEMBER 16, 2017 10: 48. Retrieved February 9, 2020 from https://katerinamagasin.se/den-nya-mansrollen-del-2-alexander-bard-genusaktenskap-ar-rena-helvetet/

Berggren, L. (2019). Vågar man hoppas på verklig jämställdhet? *Världen idag*. Ledare 25th February 2019. Retrieved May 11, 2021 from https://www.varldenidag.se/ledare/vagar-man-hoppas-pa-verkligjamstalldhet/repsbv!W9U4Sd12Z7EQG64KZxK9Aw/

Bottrel, D. & Manathunga, C. (2019). *Resisting Neoliberalism in Higher Education. Volume 1. Seeing Through the Cracks*. New York: Palgrave Critical University Studies.

Butler, J. (2009). Performativity, precarity and sexual politics AIBR. *Revista de Antropología Iberoamericana*, www.aibr.org Volumen 4, Número 3. Septiembre-Diciembre 2009, pp. i–xiii. Madrid: Antropólogos Iberoamericanos en Red. ISSN: 1695-9752.

Centre for Gender Research (2020). *Genusvetenskap som ämne*. Uppsala Universitet. Retrieved February 20, 2020 from https://www.gender.uu.se/about-us/vad-ar-genusvetenskap-/

Copsey N. (2018). The radical right and fascism. In J. Rydgren (Ed.), *The Oxford Handbook of the Radical Right*. New York: Oxford University Press.

Dijk, Teun Adrianus van (1996). *Análisis del discurso ideológico*.VERSION 6.UAM-X. MEXICO, 15–43.

Dijk, Teun Adrianus van (2000). Ideology and Discourse. A Multidisciplinary Introduction. Pompeu Fabra University, Barcelona. Retrieved February 16 from http://www.discourses.org/OldBooks/Teun%20A%20van%20Dijk%20-%20Ideology%20and%20Discourse.pdf

Dijk, Teun Adrianus van (2009). *Society and Discourse: How Social Contexts Influence Text and Talk*. Cambridge: Cambridge University Press.

Enqvist, I. (2018). Politiska agendor hindrar högskolans verkliga uppdrag [Political agendas hinder the university's real mission] *Göteborgs Posten*. Retrieved February 9, 2020 from https://www.gp.se/debatt/politiska-agendor-hindrar-högskolans-verkliga-uppdrag-1.8868638

Feminetik.se (2004). Genusvetenskap - ideologi eller vetenskap? [Gender science – ideology or science?]. 2004- 04-30. Retrieved February 9 from http://www.feminetik.se/diskutera/index.php?sub=3&mid=9073

Frazer, N. (1997). Heterosexism, Misrecognition, and Capitalism: A Response to Judith Butler. Social Text, No. 52/53, Queer Transexions of Race, Nation, and Gender (Autumn–Winter, 1997), pp. 279–89. Durham, North Carolina: Duke University Press. Stable URL: https://www.jstor.org/stable/466745 Accessed: 07-02-202012:22 UTC

Fraser, N. (2014). In Stein Lubrano Sara & Lenhard Johannes. *Crises and Experimental Capitalism: An Interview with Nancy Fraser*. Kings' Review— April 11, 2014 Retrieved from http://kingsreview.co.uk/articles/crises-and-experimental-capitalism-an-interview-with-nancy-fraser/[2019-10-29]

Fraser, N. & Jaeggi, R. (2019). *Capitalism. A Conversation in Critical Theory*. Cambridge and Medford: Polity Press.

Garbagnoli, S. (2016). Against the heresy of immanence: Vatican's "Gender" as a new rhetorical device against the denaturalization of the sexual order. *RELIGION & GENDER, 6*(2), 187–204. DOI: 10.18352/rg.10156

Giroux, H. A. (2011). Beyond the swindle of the corporate university: Higher education in the service of democracy. *Truthout*, January 18, 2011. Retrieved February 22, 2020 from https://truthout.org/articles/beyond-the-swindle-of-the-corporate-university-higher-education-in-the-service-of-democracy/

Gunnarsson Payne, P. (2019). Därför attackeras genusvetenskap. Dagensarena 28 juli 2019. Hämtad: från https://www.dagensarena.se/essa/darfor-attackeras-genusvetenskapen/

Göteborg Universitet (2018). Misstänkt bomb var attrapp. [Suspected bomb was a dummy] Nyhet 2018- 12-18 Retrieved February 9, 2020 from https://www.gu.se/omuniversitetet/aktuellt/nyheter/detalj//misstankt-bomb-var-attrapp.cid1603091

Göteborgs universitet (2019). *Genusforskning behövs nu mer än någonsin*. Nyhet 2019-10-01. https://www.gu.se/omuniversitetet/vision/likabehandling/Nyheter/Nyheter_detalj//genusforskning-behovs-nu-mer-an-nagonsin.cid1646100

Heberlein, A., Madison, G., Olsson, E. J., & Zetterholm, M. (2020). Kvinnor hotar det fria ordet vid högskolorna [Women threaten the free speech at Higher Education institutions], *Expressen*, January 8, 2020. Retrieved June 14, 2020 from https://www.expressen.se/debatt/sa-hotas-hogskolornas-yttrandefrihet-av-kvinnor/

Hedengren, O. G. (2013). När genusideologi går före vetenskap. [When gender ideology takes precedence over science]. *Realtid.se. 2013-11-25*. Retrieved January 9 from https://www.realtid.se/nar-genusideologi-gar-fore-vetenskap

Karlsson-Bernfalk, M. (2018). Genusvetenskap bidrar till psykisk ohälsa. [Gender science contributes to mental illness] *Blekinge Läns Tidning* March 9, 2018.

Kauppinen, I. (2015). Towards a theory of transnational academic capitalism. *British Journal of Sociology of Education*, 36(2), 336–53. DOI: 10.1080/01425692.2013.823833

Kováts, E. (2018). Questioning consensuses: Right-wing populism, anti-populism, and the threat of gender ideology. *Sociological Research Online*, 23(2), 528–38.

Kováts, E. & Põim, M. (eds.) (2015). *Gender as a Symbolic Glue. The Position and Role of Conservative and Fair Right Parties in the Anti-gender Mobilization in Europe.* FEPS—Foundation for European Progressive Studies, with the financial support of the European Parliament and by Friedrich-Ebert-Stiftung Budapest.

Kuhar, R. & Zobec, A. (2017). The anti-gender movement in Europe and the educational process in public schools. *Center for Educational Policy Studies Journal*, 7(2), 29–46.

Liinason, M. (2011). *Feminism and the Academy. Exploring the Politics of Institutionalization in Gender Studies in Sweden.* Doctoral Thesis. Centre for Gender Studies, Lund University. Retrieved February 12 from https://lup.lub.lu.se/search/ws/files/6315937/1776392.pdf

Macrine, S. (2016). Pedagogies of neoliberalism. In S. Springer, K. Birch & J. MacLeavy. (Eds.) *Handbook of Neoliberalism*. Publisher: Routledge New York, London.

Nilsson, I. (2018). Genusvetenskap bidrar till psykisk ohälsa. Debatt.[Gender studies contribute to mental illness]*Blekingen läns Tidning*. Debatt. 2018-03-9. Retrieved May 11, 2021 from https://www.blt.se/debatt/genusvetenskap-bidrar-till-psykisk-ohalsa/

Publikt (2018). *Oro och sorg på genussekretariatet* [Concern and sorrow at the Gender Secretariat] Retrieved February 9, 2020 from https://www.publikt.se/artikel/oro-och-sorg-pa-genussekretariatet-22085

Radio, Sveriges (2020). Kvinnorna och yttrandefriheten. *Filosofiska rummet* Radioprogram 23rd February 2020. Retrieved February 23 from https://sverigesradio.se/avsnitt/1445915

Reslow, P., Stenkvist, R., Rubbestad, M. & Grubb, J.S.D. (2021) Stoppa genusindoktrinering [SD: Stop gender indoctrination] Journalist Axel Berggren. *Altinget.* Debatt. Retrieved May 11, 2021 from https://www.altinget.se/artikel/sd-stoppa-genusindoktrinering

Rydgren, J. (2018a). *The Oxford Handbook of the Radical Right.* Oxford: Oxford University Press.

Rydgren, J. (2018b). The radical right: An introduction. In J. Rydgren (Ed.), *The Oxford Handbook of the Radical Right* (OXFORD HANDBOOKS ONLINE © Oxford University Press).

Rydgren, J. & Van Der Meiden, S. (2016). *Sweden, Now a Country Like All the Others? The Radical Right and the End of Swedish Exceptionalism.* Working Paper Series Nr 25 June 2016. (Stockholm: Department of Sociology, Stockholm University, 2016).

The Swedish Secretariat for Gender Research (2020). Retrieved February 22, 2020 from https://genus.gu.se/english/?languageId=100001&disableRedirect=true&returnUrl= http%3A%2F%2Fgenus.gu.se%2F

Valmyndigheten (2018). Val till riksdagen- Röster. Retrieved from https://data.val.se/val/val2018/slutresultat/R/rike/index.html

Widfeldt, A. (2018). *The Growth of the Radical Right in the Nordic Countries. Observations from the Past 20 years.* Washington, DC: Migration Policy Institute. Retrieved May 9, 2021 from https://www.migrationpolicy.org/sites/default/files/publications/TCM-RadicalRightNordicCountries-Final.pdf

Conclusion

Akkerman, T. (2015). Gender and the radical right in western Europe: A comparative analysis of policy agendas. *Patterns of Prejudice, Special Issue on Gender and Populist Radical Right Politics, 49*, 1–2.

Allodi, M. (2010). The meaning of the social climate of learning environments: Some reasons why we do not care enough about it. *Learning Environments Research, 13*(2), 89–104.

Ammert, N. (2009). *Det osamtidigas samtidigt: Historiemedvetande i svenska historieläroböcker under hundra år.* Lund & Uppsala: Sisyfos förlag.

Arendt, H. (1968). *Men in Dark Times.* New York: Harcourt Brace & World, Inc.

Belkhir, J. A. & Duyme, M. (1998). Intelligence and race, gender, class: The fallacy of genetic determinism: Rethinking intelligence from the position of the oppressed. *Race, Gender & Class (Towson, Md.), 5*(3), 136–76.

Biesta, G. J. (2007). Why "What works" won't work: Evidence-based practice and the democratic deficit in educational research. *Educational Theory, 57*(1), 1–22. Doi: doi:10.1111/j.1741-5446.2006.00241.x

Biesta, G. J. (2010). *What Is Education For? Good Education in an Age of Measurement: Ethics, Politics, Democracy.* Boulder, IL: Paradigm Publishers.

Biesta, G. J. (2012). Giving teaching back to education: Responding to the disappearance of the teacher. *Phenomenology & Practice, 6*(2), 35–49.

Blee, K. (2016). Similarities/differences in gender and far-right politics in Europe and the USA. In M. Köttig, R. Bitzan & A. Petö (Eds.), *Gender and Far Right Politics in Europe* (pp. 191–203). Palgrave MacMillan, Retrieved from http://ebookcentral.proquest.com. Created from linne-ebooks on [2020-03-16 09:10:19].

Bourdieu, P. (1989). Social space and symbolic power. *Sociological Theory, 7*(1), 14–25. Doi:10.2307/202060

Brandt, M. J. & Henry, P. J. (2012). Gender inequality and gender differences in authoritarianism. *Personality and Social Psychology Bulletin, 38*(10), 1301–15.

Burk, L.R., Burkhart, B.R., & Sikorski, J.F. (2004). Construction and preliminary validation of the auburn differential masculinity inventory. *Psychology of Men and Masculinity*, 5(1), 4–17. doi:10.1037/1524-9220.5.1.4

Chomsky, N. & Pollin, R. (2017). Breaking through the political barriers to free education. *Truthout*, October 31, 2017, https://chomsky.info/20171031/

Cochran-Smith, M. & Fries, K. M. (2001). Sticks, Stones, and Ideology: The discourse of reform in teacher education. *Educational Researcher*, 30(8), 3–15.

Cochran-Smith, M., Keefe, S., Carney, E., & Cummings, M. (2018). Teacher educators as reformers. Competing agendas. *European Journal of Teacher education*, 41(5), 572–90.

Coleman, L. M. & Bassi, S. A. (2011). Deconstructing militant manhood. *International Feminist Journal of Politics*, 13(2), 204–24. https://doi.org/10.1080/14616742.2011.560039

Corprew, C. S. III & Mitchell, A. D. (2014). Keeping it frat: Exploring the interaction among fraternity membership, disinhibition, and hypermasculinity on sexually aggressive attitudes in college-aged males. *Journal of College Student Development*, 55(6), 548–62. https://doi.org/10.1353/csd.2014.0062

Dillon, C. (2013). Tolerance means weakness': The Dachau concentration camp S.S., militarism and masculinity. *Historical Research*, 86(232), 373–417.

Edling, S. (2016). *Demokrati Dilemman i läraruppdraget. Att arbeta för lika villkor [Democracy dilemmas in the teacher assignment. To work for equal conditions]*. Stockholm: Liber.

Edling, S. (2020). Läraryrket och det etiska behovet av att existera i utrymmet mellan det säkra och det osäkra [Teacher profession and the ethical need to exist in the space between the certain and uncertain]. *Utbildning & Demokrati*, 9(2), 101–30.

Edling, S. & Mooney Simmie, G. (2017). Democracy and emancipation in teacher education: A summative content analysis of teachers' democratic assignment expressed in policies for Teacher Education in Sweden and Ireland between 2000–2010. *Citizenship, Social & Economic Education, 1–15*. DOI: 10.1177/2047173417743760 LINK: http://journals.sagepub.com/eprint/jFcYzHFHvbI2DYyFIAs2/full

Edling, S. & Mooney Simmie, G. (2020). *Democracy and Teacher Education: Dilemmas, Challenges and Possibilities*. New York, London: Routledge, Taylor and Francis Group.

Edling, S., Sharp, H, Löfström, J., & Ammert, N. (2020a). The good citizen: Revisiting moral motivations for introducing historical consciousness in history education drawing on the writings of Gadamer. *Citizenship, Social and Economic Education*, 19(2), 133–50.

Edling, S., Sharp, H., Ammert, N., & Löfström, J. (2020b). Why is ethics important in history education?: A dialogue between the various ways of understanding the relationship between ethics and historical consciousness. *Ethics and Education*, 15(3), 336–54.

Englund, T. (1986). *Curriculum as a Political Problem: Changing Educational Conceptions, with Special Reference to Citizenship Education*. Dissertation. Uppsala, Lund, Sweden: Studentlitteratur.

Fábián, K. & Korolczuk, E. (2017). *Rebellious Parents: Parental Movements in Central-Eastern Europe and Russia*. Bloomington: Indiana University Press.

Francia, G. & Edling, S. (2016). Children's rights and violence: A case analysis at a Swedish boarding school. *Childhood*, 24(1), 5–67.

Fugate, J. M. B., Macrine, S. L., & Cipriano, C. (2018). The role of embodied cognition for transforming learning. *International Journal of School and Educational Psychology*, 1–15. https://doi.org/10.1080/21683603.2018.1443856

Galasso, N. (2020). Why is the far-right so hostile to gender? How does it understand masculinity? https://oxfamblogs.org/fp2p/understanding-the-far-rights-framing-of-masculinities-and-hostility-to-gender/

Giroux, H. A. (1988). Border pedagogy in the age of postmodernism. *Journal of Education*, 170(3), 162–81. doi:10.1177/002205748817000310

Giroux, H. A. (2006). *Henry giroux on critical pedagogy and the responsibilities of the public intellectual*. In America on the Edge. New York: Palgrave Macmillan. https://doi.org/10.1057/9781403984364_1

Giroux, H. (2013). Neoliberalism's war against teachers in dark times. *Cultural Studies Critical Methodologies, 13*, 458–68. https://doi.org/10.1177/1532708613503769

Giroux, H. A. (2014). *Neoliberalism's War on Higher Education*. Chicago: Haymarket Books.

Giroux, H. A. (2015). *Dangerous Thinking in the Age of the New Authoritarianism*. Boulder, CO: Paradigm Publishers.

Giroux, H. A. (2020). *On Critical Pedagogy*. London: Bloomsbury Academic.

Goodwin, M. J. (2011). *New British Fascism: Rise of the British National Party*. Abingdon: Routledge.

Goodwin, M. (2013). The roots of extremism: The English defense league and the counter-Jihad challenge. Chatham House. http://www.openbriefing.org/docs/rootsofextremism.pdf

Grabowska, M. (2015). Cultural war or "business as usual"? Recent instances, and the historical origins of a "backlash" against women's and sexual rights in Poland. In *Anti-Gender Movements on the Rise? Strategising for Gender Equality in Central and Eastern Europe*, 54–64. Heinrich-Böll-Stiftung, https://www.boell.de/sites/default/files/2015-04-anti-gender-movements-on-the-rise.pdf?dimension1=division_demo

Graves, J. L. (2015). Great is their sin: Biological determinism in the age of genomics. *The ANNALS of the American Academy of Political and Social Science, 661*(1), 24–50. Doi:10.1177/0002716215586558

Grimké, S. M. (1838). *Letters on the Equality of the Sexes, and the Condition of Woman*. Addressed to Mary S. Parker. Boston, MA: I. Knapp. https://search.library.wisc.edu/catalog/999474581002121

Grzebalska, W. (2015). Poland. In E. Kováts, & M. Põim (Eds.), *Gender as Symbolic Glue. The Position and Role of Conservative and Far Right Parties in the Anti-gender Mobilizations in Europe* (pp. 83–103). Budapest: FEPS – FES.

Grzebalska, W. (2016). Why the war on 'Gender Ideology' matters–And not just to feminists. Anti-genderism and the crisis of neoliberal democracy, 7 March. Available at: http://visegradinsight.eu/why-the-war-on-gender-ideology-matters-and-not-just-to-feminists/

Gupta, A.H. (2019). Across the globe, a "serious backlash against women's rights." In her words, December, 4, 2019. *New York Times*. https://www.nytimes.com/2019/12/04/us/domestic-violence-international.html

Håkansson, J & Sundberg, D. (2012). *Utmärkt undervisning. Framgångsfaktorer i svensk och internationell belysning (Excellent education. Success factors from a Swedish and International perspective)*. Stockholm: Natur och Kultur.

Hankivsky, O. & Marfa, S. (2014). The current situation and potential responses to movements against gender equality in Ukraine. *East/West*, *1*(1), 19–43.

Harvey, D. (2007). *A Brief History of Neoliberalism*. Oxford, UK: Oxford University Press.

Haste, P. (2013). Sex education and masculinity: the "problem" of boys. *Gender and Education*, *25*(4), 515–27. https://doi.org/10.1080/09540253.2013.789830

Hickey-Moody, A. (2019). *Deleuze and Masculinity*. 1st Edition. Palgrave Macmillan. pp. 210.

Höjdestrand, T. (2017). "Nationalism and civicness in Russia: Grassroots mobilization in defense of 'family values.'" In Fábián and Korolczuk, *Rebellious Parents: Parental Movements in Central-Eastern Europe and Russia*, pp. 31–60.

Honig, B. (1994). Difference, dilemmas, and the politics of home. *Social Research*, *61*(3), 563–97.

Horton, P. & Rydström, H. (2011). Heterosexual masculinity in contemporary Vietnam: Privileges, pleasures, and protests. *Men and Masculinities*, *14*(5), 542–64.

Hursh, D. (2013). Raising the stakes: High-stakes testing and the attack on. *Public Education in New York. Journal of Education Policy*, *28*(5). Doi: 10.1080/02680939. 2012.758829

Idriss-Miller, C. & Pilkington, H. (2017). In search of the missing link: Gender, education and the radical right. *Gender and Education*, *29*(2), 133–46.

Jahn, B. (2019). The sorcerer's apprentice: Liberalism, ideology, and religion in world politics. *International Relations*, *33*(2), 322–37.

Jewkes, R., Morrell, R., Hearn, J., Lundqvist, E., Blackbeard, D., Lindegger, G. et al. (2015). Hegemonic masculinity: combining theory and practice in gender interventions. *Culture, health & sexuality*, *17 Suppl 2*(sup2), S112–S127. https://doi.org/10.1080/13691058.2015.1085094

Kinnvall, C. (2015). Borders and fear: Insecurity, gender and the far right in Europe. *Journal of Contemporary European Studies*, *23*(4), 514–29.

Kitschelt, H. (2007). Growth and persistence of the radical right in postindustrial democracies: Advances and challenges in comparative research. *West European Politics*, *30*(5), 1176–206.

Kolb, B. & Och Wishaw, I. Q. (2006). *An Introduction to the Brain and Behaviour*. New York: Worth, Retrieved from https://www.tandfonline.com/doi/full/10.1080/13691058.2015.1085094

Kottig, M. & Blum, A. (2016). Introduction. In M. Kottig, R. Bitzan & A. Peto (Eds.), *Gender and Far Right Politics in Europe*. Palgrave MacMillan, Retrieved from http://ebookcentral.proquest.com Created from linne-ebooks on [2020-03-16 09:10:19].

Korolczuk, E. (2014). The war on gender' from a transnational perspective—lessons for feminist strategising. In Heinrich Böll Foundation (Ed.), *Anti-gender Movements on the Rise? Strategising for Gender Equality in Central and Eastern Europe* (pp. 43–53), Publication Series on Democracy, vol. *38*. Berlin, Germany: Heinrich Böll Foundation.

Korolczuk, E. & Graff, A. (2018). Gender as "Ebola from Brussels": The anti-colonial frame and the rise of illiberal populism. *Signs, Journal of Women in Culture and Society (Chicago, Ill.)*, *43*(3), 797–821.

Korolczuk, E. & Renata, E. H. (2017). In the name of the family and nation: Framing fathers' activism in contemporary Poland. In F. Katalin & E. Korolczuk (Eds.), *Rebellious Parents: Parental Movements in Central-Eastern Europe and Russia* (pp. 113–44). Bloomington: Indiana University Press.

Kováts, E. (2016). The emergence of powerful anti-gender movements in Europe and the crisis of liberal democracy. In M. Köttig, R. Bitzan & A. Petö (Eds.), *Gender and Far Right Politics in Europe* (pp. 175–88). New York, NY: Palgrave MacMillan, Retrieved from http://ebookcentral.proquest.com. Created from linne-ebooks on [2020-03-16 09:10:19].

Krieger, N. (2019). Measures of racism, sexism, heterosexism, and gender binarism for health equity research: From structural injustice to embodied harm-an ecosocial analysis. *Annual Review of Public Health*, *41*, 37–62. https://doi.org/10.1146/annurev-publhealth-040119-094017

Krizsan, A. & Roggeband, C. (2018). Towards a conceptual framework for struggles over democracy in backsliding states: Gender equality policy in Central Eastern Europe. *Politics and Governance*, *6*(3), 90–100. https://doi.org/10.17645/pag.v6i3.1414

Kuby, G. (2013). Europe's Cassandra: German sociologist Gabriele Kuby discusses conversion, the global sexual revolution, freedom, family, and faith. Interview by Alvino-Mario Fantini. *Catholic World Report*, August 14. http://www.catholicworldreport.com/Item/2501/europes_cassandra.aspx.

Kumashiro, K. K. (2010). Seeing the bigger picture. Troubling movements to end teacher education. *Journal of Teacher Education*, *61*(1–2), 56–65.

Larsson, E. (2005). *Från adlig uppfostran till borgerlig utbildning Kungl. Krigsakademien mellan åren 1792 och 1866 [From Nobel upbringing to Bourgeois education]*. Uppsala: Acta Universitatis Upsaliensis.

Lugosi, N. (2018). Radical right framing of social policy in Hungary: Between nationalism and populism. *Journal of International and Comparative Social Policy*, *34*(3), 210–33.

Lynch, K. (2010). Carelessness: A hidden doxa of higher education. *Arts & Humanities in Higher Education*, *9*(1), 54–67.

Lynch, K. (2015). Control by numbers: New managerialism and ranking in higher education. *Critical Studies in Education, 56*(2).

Mackinnon, C. A. (1987). *Feminism Unmodified: Discourses on Life and Law 38–39.* Cambridge, MA: Harvard University Press.

Macrine, S. L. (2016a). *Critical Pedagogy in Uncertain Times: Hopes and Possibilities* (2nd edition). New York: Palgrave Macmillan.

Macrine, S. L. (2016b). Pedagogies of neoliberalism. In S. Springer, K. Birch & J. MacLeavy (Eds.), *Handbook of Neoliberalism* (pp. 294–305). New York: Routledge.

McLaren, P. (2016). *Pedagogy of Insurrection.* New York: Peter Lang.

Messerschmidt, J. (1993). *Masculinities and Crime: Critique and Reconceptualization of Theory.* Lanham, MD: Rowman and Littlefield.

Messerschmidt, J. W. (2004). *Flesh and Blood. Adolescent Gender Diversity and Violence.* Lanham: Rowman & Littlefield Publishers.

Mooney Simmie, G. & Edling, S. (2016). Ideological governing forms in education and teacher education: a comparative study between highly secular Sweden and highly non-secular Republic of Ireland. *Nordic Journal of Studies in Educational Policy, NordSTEP, 2*(32041), 1–12.

Mosher, D. L. & Sirkin, M. (1984). Measuring a macho personality constellation. *Journal of Research in Personality, 18*, 150–63.

Mudde, C. (2014). Introduction: Youth and the extreme right: Explanations, issues, and solutions. In C. Muddle (Ed.), *Youth and the Extreme Right* (pp. 1–18). New York: IDebate Press.

Mulinari, D. & Neergaard, A. (2016). Doing racism, performing femininity: Women in the Sweden democrats. In M. Köttig, R. Bitzan & A. Pető (Eds.), *Gender and Far Right Politics in Europe* (pp. 13–26). Palgrave MacMillan, Retrieved from http://ebookcentral.proquest.com. Created from linne-ebooks on [2020-03-16 09:10:19].

Ofstad, H. (2012). *Vårt förakt för svaghet [Our disgust for weakness].* Stockholm: Karneval förlag.

Peeters, M. A. (2007). The new global ethic: Challenges for the church. The Institute for Intercultural Dialogue Dynamics. http://www.laici.va/content/dam/laici/documenti/donna/filosofia/english/new-global-ethic-challenges-for-the-church.pdf

Poynting, S. & Donaldsson, S. (2005). Snakes and leaders: Hegemonic masculinity in ruling-class boys' boarding schools. *Men and Masculinities, 7*(325), 325–46.

Quinlan, C. (2016). Pope calls teaching about gender identity 'ideological colonization'. ThinkProgress, August 4. https://thinkprogress.org/pope-calls-teaching-about-gender-identity-ideological-colonization-e2207eaf5784#.k32ic4r5l

Rydgren, J. (2018). The radical right. An introduction. In J. Rydgren (Ed.), *The Oxford Handbook of the Radical Right.* Oxford: Oxford University Press.

Schwabenland, C., Lange, C., Onyx, J. & Nakagawa, S. (Eds.) (2017). *Women's Emancipation and Civil Society Organisations: Challenging or Maintaining the Status Quo?* Bristol: Policy Press.

Spivak, G. C. (1995). Can the subaltern speak? In B. Ashcroft, G. Griffiths & H. Tiffin (Eds.), *The Post-colonial Studies Reader* (pp. 24–8). London: Routledge.

Strelnik, O. (2017). Conservative parents' mobilization in Ukraine. In Fábián Katalin & Elżbieta Korolczuk (Eds.), *Rebellious Parents: Parental Movements in Central-Eastern Europe and Russia* (pp. 61–90). Bloomington: Indiana University Press.

Sudda, M. S. (2012). Gender, fascism and the right-wing in France between the wars: The catholic matrix. *Politics, Religion & Ideology, 13*(2), 179–95.

Takar, T. (2005). The role of the Roman Catholic Church in the service provision of education in Slovenia and Hungary. *Social Compass, 52*(1), 83–101.

Teo, T. (2011). Empirical race psychology and the hermeneutics of epistemological violence. *Hum Stud 34*, 237–55. https://doi.org/10.1007/s10746-011-9179-8

Vieten, M. U. (2016). Far right populism and women: The normalisation of gendered anti-Muslim racism and gendered culturalism in the Netherlands. *Journal of Intercultural Studies, 37*(6), 621–36.

West, B. & Cohen, J. (2018). *RBG*: A Documentary. (DVD). Magnolia Home Entertainment (Firm). RBG. Co-produced by Storyville Films and CNN Films.

Young, I. M. (1990). *Justice and the Politics of Difference*. Princeton, NJ: Princeton University Press.

Young, I. M. (1997). *Intersecting Voices: Dilemmas of Gender, Political Philosophy, and Policy*. Princeton, New Jersey: Princeton University Press. ISBN 9780691012001

Index

African Americans
  enslavement 62, 91
  mistreatment in the U.S. 90
  transparent positionality 102
Aftonbladet 126–7
airport security
  marginalized communities and 99, 105
  racial surveillance 89–90, 97
Almqvist, Carl Jonas Love, *Sara Videbeck and the Chapel (Det går an)* 134
Alves, D. 66
American Muslim Women's Empowerment Council (AMWEC) 27
Amirpour, A. L. 108, 116
anti-feminism 1, 12–15
  feminism versus 123
  nationalist sentiment 179
  right-wing populism 76, 133
anti-genderism. *See also* refugee women
  academic capitalism's role 187–8
  interconnecting factors 205
  LGBTQ people 206
anti-imperialism 23–4, 38
anti-racist feminism 13, 23–5, 37, 39, 72, 211
Arbery, A. 23
Arendt, H. 111
Armed Forces Special Powers Act (AFSPA, India) 32
Association of Parents of Disappeared Persons (APDP, India) 33
asylum seekers 25–6, 36, 41–3, 45–8, 51–4, 56–7
  from Africa to Europe 84
  restrictive legislations 213
  as the world of Others 86
Atwood, M. 108
authoritarianism
  anti-genderism 204
  capitalism links with 59
  contemporary neo-nationalism 42

democratic ideology 49
emancipatory dimensions 11–13, 17–18
feminist responses 183
gender politics 28, 207
geopolitical processes 39
global far-right politics 203
ideological impetus 3
Islamic fundamentalism 115
masculinist era 14–15
neoliberal ideology 107–8, 119–20
patriarchal 134
post-democracy 174
radical movements 5–7
refugee women and 51
right wing 4
autonomy
  fantasmatic promise 84–7
  sexual 108, 117
  teacher 142, 147, 151
  student 165
  women's 175

Bandung 31
biological sex
  feminists' views 201, 206
  gender studies 192–3, 195, 197
  phallic economy 79
  scientific racism and genderism 92, 209–10
  in tech economy 110
  traditional masculinity and 136
BLM (Black Lives Matter) 39
Boethius, M-P. *Herself to Blame—A Book about Rape* 136
Bolsonaro, J. 24, 60–1, 65–8, 71, 155, 161–2, 164
borders and bridges. *See also* migrants
  gendered violence 30–1
  impunity culture 30
  militarized regimes 31–4
  neoliberal regimes 25–9

solidarity issues 38–40
surveillance technologies 101–2
transnational necessity 23–5
US imperial policy 34–8
Brazil. *See also* Bolsonaro, J.; emancipation
    Call Center for Women in Situations of Violence 164
    CIS heteropatriarchy 155–6
    civic-military schools 67–8
    colonialism 63
    conservative reforms, problems of 65–7
    conservative tsunami 155, 157–8, 161–5
    Constitutional Amendment 95 64
    current education policies 67
    cycle of Dictatorial Right 60
    educational debates 65–7, 165–6
    Escola Sem Partido ("School without Party") 66
    exploitation of labor 59
    extractivism 61–2, 64, 69–70, 73
    Fermin, Eronilde's narrative 160
    forms of resistance and struggle 155–6
    gender and sexuality, negative impacts of neoliberalism 64–8
    hate and violence (race, gender, and social class) 157–66
    HIV/AIDS prevalence 67
    indigenous women's struggle 68–72
    latest stage of neoliberalism 60–4
    Marcha das Margaridas 63, 71
    Marielle's life narratives 156–7
    peasant women's struggles 68–72
    popular governments (2003–16) 155
    rural-school closures 67
    violence against women 71
    Workers Party (*Partido dos Trabalhadores* - PT) 60
Burke, T. 124–5
Butler, J. 81–2, 85, 145, 182, 189, 191

Carter, L. 126
children. *See also* women
    Casa Padre shelter 25
    far right nationalism, negative impact 3–4
    Gaza deaths 33
    gender-based violence 41, 53
    oppression against 11, 42
    parents separation 36
    refugee crisis 43, 45–8, 52, 56
    sexual exploitation 48
Chomsky, N. 5
Cixous, H. 78
climate destruction 23, 85
colonialism 6, 13, 25, 32, 79, 82, 158, 164, 201
    African slave women 62
conservatism
    anti-Blackness 91
    anti-immigration policies 41
    capitalism links with 59
    conceptions of power 4–7, 19
    gendered politics 12–15, 206–7
    illiberal political climate 2–3
    radical 133
    right-wing 199, 204
    rise of 2–3
    transnational Black feminist (TBF) analysis 90, 92
    triangulation 1, 17
    white women, perception of 206
    women refugees in Sweden 53–5
Covid-19 pandemic 23, 42, 141, 163, 175

Dalit feminists 39
Danius, S. 127–32
Death (Joy Division's band) 115
decolonial feminism 24, 38, 168
Down by Law (film) 115

Eberhard, D., *Great Gender Experiment, The (Det stora konsexperimentet)* 130
education 2, 4, 10–15. *See also* higher education, Sweden
    current focus 210–14
    international students 38
    migrants 44
    neoliberalism and 142–3
    schooling and 7–9
    teaching profession and 15–19
emancipation
    anti-capitalist struggle 161
    black and native feminists' protagonisms 156, 160, 165
    concept of parenthood 157
    conservative tsunami 155, 157–8, 161–5

for democracy and social justice 157–66
domination of the "North" over the "South" 160–1
educational debates 162–3
epistemological of political dimensions 157–66
Fermin, Eronilde's narrative 166–8
forms of epistemic violence 155
forms of resistance 155–6
importance of narratives 166–8
Marielle's life narrative 156–7
popular governments (2003–16) 155
Popular University of Social Movements (UPMS) 157
power of interpretation 208–9
sexual and physical violence 164–5
violence and oppression 160–6
Engdahl, H. 128–9, 133, 138
Indifferent (De obekymrade), The 132
Erdovan, T. 23

feminism
 anti-feminism versus 123
 anti-racist 13, 23–5, 37, 39, 72, 211
 decolonial 24, 38, 168
 everyday life 168–9
 film theory 108, 114–18
 and Islamism 117–18
 neoliberal version of 109–10
 second wave 110
feminist struggle 23, 37, 200
 for democracy and social justice 157–66
First World War 135
Floyd, G.'s violent death 23, 28, 39
Frostenson, Katarina 128

gender. *See also* gender gap; gender studies
 debt-crisis 176–7
 gap 176–7
 ideological discourse 189–90
 role perceptions 206–7
 and sexuality 64–8
gender studies
 as alien in higher education 192–4
 as a "glue concept" 191–2
 in higher education 190–1
 ideological discourse 188–90
 as ideology in higher education 194–6

Germany. *See also* right-wing populism
 Alternative fur Deutschland (AfD) 75–6, 78, 80–5, 203, 205
 fascist Nazi party 202–3
 gender and sexual politics 75–6, 80–1, 185
 phallic economy 78–80
 Sachsen and Thuringen election 75
 wage policies 173
Girl Walks Home Alone at Night, A (Amirpour's film) 108, 113–15, 118–19
Global Educational Reform Movement (GERM) 141, 152
Global North 13, 24–5, 85, 168
 epistemological displacement of 168
Global South 14, 24, 43, 85, 157, 159–60
Greece
 cooperative model 180
 COVID-19 175
 economic crisis 171–3, 175
 gendered social norms 176–7
 Gender Equality Index 171, 174, 176
 human trafficking 177
 patriarchal gendered structure of capitalism 175
 post-democracy 173–6
 Sakellaropolou, K. 176
 social reproduction and women 177–80
 sovereign debt-crisis 174
 Troika's austerity policies 172–4
 women empowerment 180–2
 women's employment 176–7
 women's rights 171, 175
Gustavsson, M. 127
 Club, The 128

Hanna, A. 164
Haraway, D. 111
health care systems 42, 45, 48, 67, 99, 112
hegemony
 democratic and anti-democratic struggles 76–7
 fantasmatic promises 76–7
Hello Hello (Richie's song) 115
higher education, Sweden
 Academic Rights Watch 196
 anti-gender agenda 187–8

securitized regimes 25-8
  fantasmatic promises 30, 80-3
  impunity culture 30
September 11, 2001, attacks 89
sexual abuse 42, 48, 62, 67, 123, 125, 129-31
sexuality 9-10, 24, 72, 75, 80, 82, 86, 111, 113-14, 118, 134, 160, 186
  neoliberal and the conservative agendas 64-8
Sight and Sound (British Film Institute's film) 115
social justice 2-3, 6, 10-11, 13, 16-17, 43, 92, 149, 152, 157
Solana, V. 136
Spain, debt-crisis 172
Storch, von B. 81
surveillance technologies. *See also* technological tools
  border and boundaries 101-2
  racism and anti-blackness 102-4
Sweden. *See also* higher education; #MeToo movement
  anti-gender agenda in higher education 185-97
  Arnault Case 127-30
  backlash against women's rights 133-7
  Bridget, saint 134
  gender equality 123
  gender studies in higher education 186-7
  media reporting 126-130
  migration policies and legislation 53-5
  Mission:Investigate (Uppdrag granskning) 131
  #quietontheset (#tystnadtagning) 126
  Sex War, The (Konskriget, TV show) 136
  #withoutprofessionalsecrecy (#utantystnadsplikt) 126
  #withwhatright (#medvilkenrätt) 126

Tamez, E. G. 35
Tamez, M. 35
Taylor, B. 23
teachers
  evaluation 151-2
  learning reforms 150-1
  soft skills and feminine voice 144-7
  symbolic and structural dangers 145
teaching
  feminization 143-4
  genderized politics 141-4
  hierarchical system of schooling 145-6
  institutionalized sexism 146
  "masculinist neoliberal performativity" 143-4
technological tools
  Black resistance 102-4
  conventional boundaries 101-2
  ethical implications 102
  white supremacy 103
Thriller (film) 115
Timell, M. 126-7, 137-8
transnational Black feminism (TBF) 90
  guiding principles 98
  intersectionality 98-9
  scholar-activist orientation 99-100
  solidarity 100-1
  surveillance technologies 89-104
transnational feminism 10-12. *See also* transnational Black feminism (TBF)
  definition 13
  place-based resistance 23-40
  refugee crisis 41-57
Trump, D. 24, 26, 36, 38, 51, 90, 107, 125

UNHCR 44, 46, 48, 51, 54, 56
UN Human Rights Commission 171
United States. *See also* Trump, D.
  academic curricula 38
  backlash against women's rights 133-7
  Biden Administration 107
  dark—and Black—truth 89-104
  Iran policy 107
  longest government shutdown 35
  neoconservatism 91-4
  #MeToo movement 124-5
  Obama administration 107
  question of nationalism 91-4
  rape culture 109
  refugee women 51-3
  sexual violence in 124
  teachers' agency 107-8

TIAA 63
white supremacy 90–1, 96
"women's empowerment" policies 111
Women's Liberation Movement (WLM) 124
universalist pedagogy 145, 148–9, 151. *See also* public education
   overreliance on data and the laws/reforms 147
UN Security Council 46, 50
   Iran's membership 107
US-Mexico border 26, 31, 35, 37, 51
US Secure Fence Act 34

violence
   culture of impunity 30
   gender-based 4, 17, 41, 53
   hate, race and gender 10, 157–66
   incarceration 27–8
   militarized 26, 29, 31–2
   normalized 26, 30, 33, 37
   oppression and 2, 14, 160–6
   sexual and physical 3, 124, 164–5
Virtanen, F. 126–7, 131, 133, 137–8, 126
   No Mercy (Utan Nad) 133
Volcker plan 111
Vonnegut, K. 114

Wallin, C. 126, 131
Wallstrom, M. 126

Washington Consensus 60
Weinstein, H. 123–5
white male supremacy 103
   far-right conservative movements 200–4
women. *See also* children; refugee women
   Brazilian 59–60, 63–73
   of color 11, 24, 37
   cross-border solidarities 39
   to deny reproduction 115
   empowerment 29, 180–2
   as entrepreneurial mother 112
   exploitation 3–4
   involuntary prostitution 47–8
   Kashmiri 37
   Muslim 27, 33, 48
   oppressions of 1–3, 42–3, 56
   Palestinian 33, 36
   place-based resistance 24–9
   religious fundamentalism 120
   sexual abuse 123
   social movements 180
   social reproduction 177–80
   subordination 3–4
   Third World 11, 24
   victims of sexual violence 33
World Bank 111

xenophobia 3–4, 13, 29, 38, 49, 56, 76, 174, 187